# Roses and Thorns

# ROSES and THORNS

The Second Blooming
of the Hundred Flowers
in Chinese Fiction
1979 – 1980

PERRY LINK

Editor

University of California Press ▼ Berkeley, Los Angeles, London

University of California Press
Berkeley and Los Angeles, California
University of California Press, Ltd.
London, England
© 1984 by
The Regents of the University of California

**Library of Congress Cataloging in Publication Data**
Main entry under title:
Roses and thorns.
1. Chinese fiction — 20th century — Translations into English.
2. English fiction — Translations from Chinese.
I. Link, E. Perry (Eugene Perry), 1944–
PL2658.E8R6    1984      895.1′35      83-9147
ISBN 0-520-04979-9
ISBN 0-520-04980-2 (pbk.)
Printed in the United States of America

1   2   3   4   5   6   7   8   9

# ROSES AND THORNS
## Ai Qing

### 1
God and the Devil
Are both human images

### 2
Those who crucified Jesus were Romans
Those who prayed to Jesus were also Romans

### 3
I have never seen crocodile tears
But I have heard lies from smiling faces

### 4
Roses have thorns to guard their fragrance
Honeybees have stings to guard their honey

### 5
Only an idiot
Argues with an idiot

### 6
Rage cannot rhyme
Squabbling has no meter

### 7
Time flows downstream
Life struggles upstream

### 8
I walked quite a distance in my dreams
And woke up still in bed

### 9
When silkworms spit out their strands
They do not envision the Great Silk Road

10

There are so many stars
But I've never seen them collide

11

When you're walking toward the light
Don't forget there's a shadow behind you

12

Petroleum like water, and gunpowder like mud
Silently await only a spark

13

If you are ugly
Don't blame the mirror

14

Wherever you find vultures
You will find rotten flesh

Originally published in *Renmin ribao*, 10 July, 1980. Translated by Perry Link.

# CONTENTS

# PREFACE

Such a large number of interesting stories were published in China during 1979 and early 1980 that the process of selecting from them has inevitably been somewhat arbitrary. I am indebted to many suggestions from friends in China, as well as to W. J. F. Jenner and Howard Goldblatt, who selected the stories they have translated here. Six of the stories, those by Wang Meng, Dai Qing, Kong Jiesheng, Jin He, Zhang Jie, and Chen Rong were widely discussed in China during 1979–80; since I first noticed them because of their impact among readers, they can be viewed in part as indirect selections by the Chinese readership itself. I have relied more on my own judgment in choosing the other stories. In such a short anthology, it is impossible, of course, to represent every important author. That many of the better-known ones are omitted is not necessarily a judgment on their quality.

In matters of translation, the editor and translators have emphasized both naturalness in English and fidelity to the Chinese. In the translation of literary works, both of these standards are, in an important sense, ultimately the same question of fidelity. Perhaps the most common source of distortion in translation between languages as different as Chinese and English is an awkward literalness that can completely change the tone of language. Especially in literary translation, we feel such a change of tone is just as seriously "unfaithful" as the mistranslation of a denotative sense. The effort to bring a reasonable uniformity of translation style to this volume involved a protracted editing process that was, I know, a burden to some of the translators. My warmest thanks go to all the translators, both those who bore the brunt of the oppressive editing and those who were quite free from it, for their fine work and remarkable patience and good will over a preparation period that was too long.

A glossary is provided for readers who may be unfamiliar with certain Chinese names or special terms. For the convenience of the American reader, all references to amounts of money have been converted to U.S. dollars at the 1979 exchange rate of approximately 1.5 *yuan* to $1.00. Other references to weights and measures in the metric system or in traditional Chinese units have been converted to pounds, feet, acres, and so on, but metric units have been retained in a few scientific and technical contexts. The short introductions to the stories, except for the three by Donald A. Gibbs, were done by the editor.

This project was conceived and begun in China in 1980 under a fellowship from the Committee on Scholarly Communication with the People's Republic of China. My sincere thanks go to the CSCPRC, as well as to my Chinese host organizations, the Chinese Academy of Social Sciences and Zhongshan University. My grateful thanks also go to the Center for Chinese Studies of the University of California at Berkeley for support during the final stages of preparation of the manuscript in 1981 – 82.

P. L.

*Los Angeles*
*February 1983*

# INTRODUCTION

Following Stalin's death in 1953, a new leadership gradually braked the great Soviet machine, shifted its gears, and altered its course. A similar shift occurred in China following the death of Mao Zedong in 1976. In each case, there was a temporary disengagement of the controls on expression, following which some small human voices began to emerge. Gradually these voices increased in boldness, until their volume and authenticity exceeded anything that had been heard for decades. (That in each case the crescendo of voices reached its peak just three years after the death of the Great Leader—1956 and 1979 respectively—is a coincidence of timing from which social scientists might perhaps derive a law.) When three years were over, the gears of control began to reengage, and the machines began trundling in their new directions. A young Chinese poet described his "wrinkles" as "ruts left on my body/ By the wheels of history reversing."[1]

In both countries the fiction writer has had a duly prescribed role — that of "engineer of human souls," in Stalin's famous formulation. Yet during the relaxations after the deaths of Stalin and Mao, many of the better writers were able to set aside their wrenches and look more sensitively at their societies. They found formidably large and complex problems, but, in most cases, were moved not to reject society but to feel even deeper concern for it. What really is the truth? What has been happening to our country and people? In asking these questions, Chinese writers were following in a modern tradition that arose in the early 1900s, after the humiliating military defeat of China by Japan and a period during which China feared dismemberment by the imperialist

1. Cai Kun, "Zhouwen," *Qishi niandai* (Hong Kong), no. 142 (November 1981), p. 39. The most obvious sense of this line is an indictment of the ten years of rule (1966–76) by the ultra-leftist "Gang of Four." The more abstract interpretation—referring to reversals generally—is my own responsibility, not the poet's.

powers.[2] The trend became especially pronounced in the 1920s and early 1930s, in the wake of another shock to national dignity at the Paris Peace Conference in 1919, leading to the famous "May Fourth Movement" in China.[3] With the publication around the same time of some trenchant stories by the great modern writer Lu Xun (1881–1936), China's literary elite tended increasingly to assume that something was profoundly wrong with her society and national character. It became the calling of the responsible writer to investigate society and to expose its illnesses, so that China could eventually become strong and unified, and more humane as well. Telling the bitter truth became a patriotic duty and a literary virtue.

## A "Path" Emerges

In the early twentieth century, almost all Chinese writers — including the socially engaged writers of whom we have just been speaking and writers of the burgeoning popular fiction of the time[4] — basically accepted the premise that writers should express their personal visions of life. To be sure, there were fads among writers, as well as literary associations that subscribed to lists of principles; but these, at least as writers viewed it, resulted from coincidence of feelings rather than acceptance of an external authority. But in the 1930s, with the founding of the influential League of Left-Wing Writers, a major new assumption gained acceptance. Inspired by the Russian revolution, many took the view that there must be an objectively true "path" for China's progress and that there were "correct" ways in which literature should help to lead the way. A writer's personal vision, no matter how carefully considered or sincerely expressed, was no longer necessarily its own justification. It could be "incorrect" — not merely *thought* to be incorrect by others, but "objectively" incorrect as determined by immutable Marxist laws. Chinese writers embraced these new assumptions partly because of their overriding concern for the fate of China. As the Japanese invaded in the

2. Literature of the late Qing period (1895–1911) is introduced in Milena Dolezelova-Velingerova, ed., *The Chinese Novel at the Turn of the Century* (Toronto: University of Toronto Press, 1980).

3. On the May Fourth Movement, which was a major political, intellectual, and literary series of events in the late 1910s and early 1920s, see Tse-tsung Chow, *The May Fourth Movement: Intellectual Revolution in Modern China* (Stanford, Calif.: Stanford University Press, 1967). On May Fourth Literature, see C. T. Hsia, *History of Modern Chinese Fiction* (New Haven, Conn.: Yale University Press, 1961), and Merle Goldman, ed., *Modern Chinese Literature in the May Fourth Era* (Cambridge, Mass.: Harvard University Press, 1977).

4. See Perry Link, *Mandarin Ducks and Butterflies: Popular Fiction in Early Twentieth Century Chinese Cities* (Berkeley and Los Angeles: University of California Press, 1981).

1930s, and as the Nationalist government grew increasingly corrupt in the 1940s, a majority of China's writers eventually turned leftward for answers. Would that there *were* a "path"! The West was strong, and its strength came from science; if Marxism — a "science" from the West — knew a path, so much the better.

In original Marxism, history determines which ideas are ultimately correct; after Lenin's revisions, history was replaced by a proletarian party that determined correctness on its own. But in Chinese literary circles in the 1930s, neither history nor a party was firmly in control. There were heated public debates on the correct path for Chinese literature. Each faction proffered its own arbiter of objective truth. Eventually, over the decade from 1942 to about 1952, this confusing situation was brought to an end, and the leadership of the Communist Party of China emerged as the final arbiter of correctness in literature. In May 1942, Party Chairman Mao Zedong delivered his famous "Talks at the Conference on Literature and Art" at Yan'an, the communists' remote wartime base in Shaanxi Province.[5] Mao distinguished "political criteria" from "artistic criteria" in the evaluation of literary work, and stressed that political criteria must take precedence. In practice, this came to mean that political leaders, rather than writers or literary critics, had the crucial say in determining a work's "correctness." Since the authority structure in the Party was hierarchical, it also naturally followed that higher-level political authorities could overrule lower-level ones, regardless of who had more expertise in literary matters. Later events have produced many examples of the exercise of the Party's non-literary authority over literature in China. The "correct path" for writers has twisted often and abruptly, and for reasons entirely extraneous to literature itself. Yet the control system that determines the correct path has remained basically intact, adjusting to sharp political turns by altering its goals, but not its basic structure. Mao's "Talks" have emerged as the most important turning point in Chinese literature in the twentieth century.

## The Articulation of a Control System

Literary control, which had been well established in the communist base areas before 1949, was extended to all writers on the Chinese mainland after 1949. The approach was gradual, lest rebellion by intellectu-

5. The best translation of Mao's "Talks" in English is in Bonnie S. McDougall, *Mao Zedong's Talks at the Yan'an Conference on Literature and Art* (Ann Arbor: University of Michigan Center for Chinese Studies, 1980).

als needlessly disrupt the transfer of power.[6] Although writers were admonished almost immediately to learn from the Soviet Union and to "remold incorrect ideological outlooks," no guidelines about what actually to write or to avoid writing appeared until the spring of 1951. At that time, a film called *The Story of Wu Xun* was widely criticized in the Party press. Wu Xun was a nineteenth-century educator who, according to the film, had begun with nothing and worked hard for thirty years to strengthen China by establishing new schools.[7] The film was criticized for suggesting that education and reform, rather than revolution, constituted the right path for China. The purpose of this criticism, without doubt, was not just to weed out a faulty work, but to draw an ideological line for all writers and artists by giving a specific example of what should be avoided. This has become a standard method in the political control of literature in the People's Republic.

A related method, also using negative examples, has involved criticizing not ideas but selected individual writers. Soon after the criticism of *The Story of Wu Xun* came a literary rectification campaign directed at major literary figures such as Mao Dun, China's most famous living novelist at the time, and Ai Qing, a prominent poet.[8] These and subsequent criticisms of leading figures have often been related to factional struggles in literary politics, as well as in the larger realm of politics generally. Their aim, accordingly, has been to discredit certain people and their followers in toto, not merely particular literary ideas. An interesting anomaly has resulted—namely, that writers who are in political favor can often freely make statements that, if they were to come from someone in disfavor, would be grounds for punishment.[9]

An important function of *ad hominem* literary campaigns, other than discrediting individuals for political reasons, has been to bring pressure on many others whose ideas might be said to resemble those of the targeted person. The question of which individuals can be attacked by association is left, especially in big campaigns, to local Party leaderships. Local leaders have had considerable discretionary power, and

6. Merle Goldman, *Literary Dissent in Communist China* (New York: Atheneum, 1971). Goldman's book is a fine introduction to literary politics in communist China from the early 1940s through 1959.

7. For an account of Chinese films, see Jay Leyda, *Dianying: Electric Shadows* (Cambridge, Mass.: M.I.T. Press, 1972). *The Story of Wu Xun* is discussed on pp. 197–98.

8. Ai Qing's poem "Roses and Thorns" (1980) is the epigraph to this volume.

9. For example in 1973, when literary controls in China were tight, Li Xifan, literary editor at *People's Daily* and a close associate of Jiang Qing, felt free to speak of Lao She, Xu Zhimo, Zhang Henshui, and many other writers who then were unmentionable *bêtes noires* for nearly everyone else in China. See Perry Link, "Li Hsi-fan on Modern Chinese Literature," *China Quarterly*, no. 58 (April–June 1974), pp. 349–56.

practices have by no means been uniform. In the clampdown of 1951, for example, a story called "Between Husband and Wife" by a little-known writer named Xiao Yemu was criticized for its "petit bourgeois" menta.ity. The purpose clearly was not to deprive Xiao of political power, since he possessed little, but to warn by example. After this campaign, "petit bourgeois thought," as identified by one's local leadership, could be held against one. The campaign against Bai Hua in 1981 was similar in this regard, except that it was more extensive and that Bai Hua was somewhat more famous at the outset than Xiao Yemu had been.[10] In the Bai Hua campaign, the key error was "bourgeois liberalism." But it is important to note that during both campaigns (and many in between), there was no clear definition of terms such as "petit bourgeois" or "bourgeois liberal." To some extent such vagueness has surely been deliberate, for its advantages in controlling writers are clear. First, it allows flexibility in local Party decisions about whom to criticize. Second, it has the effect of inducing many writers to keep an extra distance from the announced errors, just to ensure safety.

After a respite in 1953, the pressure on writers with incorrect literary ideas was reapplied with greater force in 1954 and 1955. The new pressure took the form primarily of a campaign against the writer Hu Feng, who had argued in fall 1954 that the "crude sociology" of political critics that "uses Marxism and political-policy phrases to judge works of art . . . can stifle the real feelings of creativity and art."[11] The role and attitude of political critics of literature were also wrong, Hu asserted: they acted like "judges who set down the deciding word," and had "an extremely cold attitude toward the creative process."[12] Hu argued that creative inspiration depends essentially on the subjective impressions of individual writers.

For several months, there was debate in Chinese newspapers about Hu Feng's ideas, but increasingly the conclusions were steered toward a repudiation of them. The Party answered that "subjectivism" led people away from the scientific truth of Marxism-Leninism, and that creative writers could not train themselves in this objective truth, but needed Party guidance. Other charges against Hu Feng were that he worshipped bourgeois culture; that his mistakes were not just artistic but —

10. One indication of the arbitrary selection of negative examples for use in nationwide campaigns is that Xiao Yemu's story was published and even praised in the Party press before it was suddenly discovered, six months later, to be severely flawed. Similarly Bai Hua's filmscript *Unrequited Love* had been out for two years — and had gone largely unnoticed — until it was abruptly attacked for being fraught with bourgeois liberalism.

11. Goldman, *Literary Dissent*, p. 145.

12. Goldman, *Literary Dissent*, p. 146.

much more serious—political ones; that in fact they were not mistakes at all, but sly attempts to usurp the Party's and Mao's leadership of literature and art; and that he had conspired with Nationalist agents and hence was "counterrevolutionary."[13] That these charges were largely arbitrary and groundless was essentially beside the point, as most writers came to realize. The apparent point—in any case, the effect—was to escalate the stakes involved in disobedience to the Party. Simple fear became a clearer factor in literary control than it had been previously. Hu Feng himself spent nearly all of his next twenty years either in prison or confined to his room. (He was released, but still only partly exonerated, in 1979.)

## Socialist Realism and a New Establishment

In place of "bourgeois" approaches to literature, the Party sought in the early 1950s to promote socialist realism. This theory, borrowed from the Soviet Union, asked that works be "good at combining the reality of today with the ideals of tomorrow," as an authoritative Chinese critic put it in 1952.[14] Later, especially in the two unusually free years 1956 and 1979, there were to be lively debates over whether "the reality of today" could include the dark side of life; but for the most part, writers in the first decade of the People's Republic took "reality" to mean primarily the war against Japan (1937–45), the war against the Nationalists (1945–49), land reform campaigns (1947–51), state-planned industrialization and agricultural collectivization (beginning in 1952 or 1953), and other major campaigns in which the Party played a leading role.[15] The admixture of "ideals" meant, in practice, that clear distinction be made between the right path and the wrong path, between heroes and villains. Heroes were larger than life and overcame great adversity. Leading examples of socialist realist full-length novels were Yang Mo's *The Song of Youth*, about the anti-Japanese and anti-Nationalist student movement between 1931 and 1935; Qu Bo's *Tracks in the Snowy Forest*, about communist counterinsurgency against remnants of Nationalist armies in the late 1940s; Liu Qing's *The Builders*, about agricultural

13. Goldman, *Literary Dissent*, pp. 151–54.
14. Zhou Yang, "Shehuizhuyi xianshizhuyi: Zhongguo wenxue qianjin de daolu" (Socialist realism: Chinese literature's path to progress), *Xinhua yuebao*, 1953, no. 2. Reprinted in *Zhongguo xiandai wenxueshi cankao ziliao*, ed. Department of Chinese, Beijing Normal University (Beijing: Gaodeng jiaoyu chubanshe, 1959), vol. 3, pp. 203–11; quotation from p. 203.
15. For a review of the novels of the 1950s organized according to these basic topics, see Joe C. Huang, *Heroes and Villains in Communist China: The Contemporary Chinese Novel as a Reflection of Life* (London: C. Hurst and Co., 1973).

collectivization in the mid-1950s; and Luo Guangbin and Yang Yiyan's *Red Crag*,[16] about communist martyrs in Nationalist prisons just before Liberation. The idealism in these books is unquestionably sincere. They were written by revolutionaries who were emerging from the turmoil and suffering of the 1930s and 1940s, and who had high hopes for the new regime; and they were read primarily by young people, whose natural idealism was reinforced by the new revolutionary rhetoric of the early 1950s. The behest of socialist realism to "combine the ideals of tomorrow with the reality of today" seemed natural and correct. In the thaw of the post-Mao period, many of this 1950s generation, writers and readers alike, reemerged from the brave new world of the Cultural Revolution to call the early and mid-1950s "the golden age" of the Revolution, when ideals were authentic. By that time, several things seemed clearer in hindsight: that revolutionary ideals are harder to achieve than they first appear; that restraints on expression in campaigns such as the one against Hu Feng could not, ultimately, be separated from curbs on everyone's freedom of expression; and that, in retrospect, literary life in the 1950s had been rather narrow. Not only did the socialist realist works of those years resemble one another in important ways, but there were, in fact, not very many of them. Compared to the years before 1949, the print runs of new novels increased sharply, but the number of new titles fell just as sharply. Before 1949, a new novel was usually printed in only a few thousand copies, whereas in the fifties, printings of tens or hundreds of thousands were standard. Yet the number of new titles published, which had averaged at least 150 per year before 1949,[17] declined to less than 8 per year for the period of 1949–66.[18]

16. The four examples I give here are listed, for lack of a more interesting order, in their order of popularity according to a survey I made among seventy-four students of literature at Zhongshan University, Guangzhou, in April 1980. Yang Mo's *Qingchun zhi ge* was published in 1958 by Renmin wenxue chubanshe in Beijing; it has been translated by Nan Ying as *The Song of Youth* and published by the Foreign Languages Press (Beijing, 1964). Qu Bo's *Linhai xueyuan* (2d ed., Beijing: Renmin wenxue chubanshe, 1959) has been translated by Sidney Shapiro as *Tracks in the Snowy Forest* (Beijing: Foreign Languages Press, 1962). Liu Qing's *Chuangyeshi* (Beijing: Zhongguo qingnian chubanshe, 1960) has been translated by Sidney Shapiro as *The Builders* (Beijing: Foreign Languages Press, 1964). Luo Guangbin and Yang Yiyan's *Hongyan* (Beijing: Zhongguo qingnian chubanshe, 1962) has been translated as *Red Crag* Beijing: Foreign Languages Press, 1978, no translator cited).

17. Between 1912 and 1949 there were, on the average, probably more than 135 novels published in the popular "Butterfly" tradition alone, to say nothing of the more elite and political literature of the period. See Perry Link, *Mandarin Ducks and Butterflies*, pp. 15–16.

18. The figure of 120 novels for 1949–66 is from Joe C. Huang, *Heroes and Villains*, p. xii. The average number of novels published per year dropped even lower during 1966–76.

As the publishing of fiction came increasingly to be channeled and managed from above during the 1950s, so did the organization, pay, and living conditions of writers. Borrowing from the Soviet Union, China's leaders created an All-China Federation of Literary and Art Workers, and under it a Chinese Writers' Association. Through the association, the Party leadership organized the editorial boards of China's literary magazines, sponsored meetings on literary controversies, ran seminars and training sessions for young writers, assigned subcommittees to write or edit certain kinds of collective works, and handled liaison with other "units" in the Chinese bureaucracy, as well as with foreign countries. The association served the complementary functions of providing the Party with a means of monitoring and controlling creative writing and of establishing a clear-cut ladder of success for writers within the new order. In every province, as well as the "autonomous" cities of Beijing, Tianjin, and Shanghai,[19] a provincial (or municipal) branch was established. Shanghai's branch, one of the larger ones, grew to about a thousand members by the early 1960s.[20] In addition, for writers of national stature, a national level of the association was established in Beijing, where there were about 1,550 members as of early 1982.[21]

For writers, a main incentive for trying to join the Writers' Association was prestige, but there were a number of practical advantages as well. An association member could attend lectures and seminars, join trips to the countryside or elsewhere to "experience life" (*tiyan shenghuo*, widely considered in China to be highly beneficial for writers), and, at the highest levels, even join delegations traveling abroad. Other benefits included occasional work leaves, which in some instances were financed by the association.[22] Finally, the association was the only route to the prestige and advantages of a "professional writer," whose state-assigned work was to write and whose work unit became the Writers' Association itself.[23] Competition to join the association was keen. Each branch established its own criteria for membership, normally requiring at least one

19. Beijing, Tianjin, and Shanghai, though cities, are parallel to provinces in the Chinese governmental administration.

20. Interview with representatives of the Shanghai Writers' Association, 17 June 1980.

21. Feng Mu, "Guqijinlai, zhengqu wenxue chuangzuo de geng da fanrong" (Get things moving and make literary creation flourish even more), *Wenyibao*, 1982, no. 2:12.

22. Some branches had "creative writing funds" (*chuangzuo jijin*) on which members could draw during approved leaves from work. If a writer earned manuscript fees or royalties as a result of his leave, he was required to use these to repay the fund up to the amount originally drawn.

23. The number of professional writers per branch, as of the early 1980s, varied from three (Guangxi Province) to thirty-two (Guangdong Province).

published book and a number of recommendations by current members, and had its own complex procedures for processing applications.

## Shifting Policy and Fluctuating "Scope"

After the first six years of the People's Republic, there was reason to expect a period of stability in China's literary politics. Literary dissent of the Hu Feng variety had been squelched; the doctrine of socialist realism was clearly established as "correct"; several literary examples of socialist realism were widely read and appreciated; and the Writers' Association had extended a massive bureaucracy across the whole Chinese literary scene. But when literature is tied to politics, as it is in China, and when political directions change abruptly, which has also been the case in the People's Republic, stability is elusive. Since 1955 China's writers have had to adapt to constant shifts in literary politics. With each shift, it has been stated or implied that *now* the right policy is here once and for all. It has always been taboo (and even punishable) to suggest openly that the "correct" policy might change in a year or two, yet nearly all writers have learned to reckon this obvious possibility into their private plans. The more astute have come to realize, for example, that it is risky to invest time in full-length novels. Who can say what the political climate will be like when the novel is finished? Wang Meng, whose story "Eye of the Night" is included here, wrote his first full-length novel in the mid-1950s. Titled *Long Live Youth,* it was about idealistic high-school graduates in the years right after the Revolution. It was serialized in the Shanghai newspaper *Wenhuibao* in 1957. But shortly after the serialization had begun, Wang Meng was severely criticized for an entirely different story and was sent to do twelve years of labor reform, first outside Beijing and later in remote Xinjiang province. The result was that *Long Live Youth* was not published in book form until 1979, by which time the author found it embarrassingly "naive and immature."[24] Meanwhile, beginning in 1973 in Xinjiang, Wang Meng tentatively attempted a full-length novel about life in a Uighur village that of necessity included favorable references to the policies of the Cultural Revolution. After 1976, when most of these policies were one by one reversed and even denounced, Wang Meng's manuscript became increasingly unpublishable — unless, of course, he were to invest considerable time in reworking the political references and implications.[25] As of 1983, Wang Meng has yet to find time for this reworking.

24. Wang Meng, "Postscript" to *Qingchun wansui* (Beijing: Renmin wenxue chuanshe, 1979), p. 346.
25. Interview with Wang Meng, 3 August 1980, Beijing.

It is not only political issues that writers in China have been obliged to treat with care; to some extent, every issue in their writing has been subject to political review. Literary policy, despite its variations, has been consistent in assuming literature to have a tremendous influence on all aspects of the ideas of youth. Virtually all China's writers, from the mid-1950s on, have inevitably become aware of a certain "scope" allowed them. If they stay within its bounds,[26] they can say just about what they like. But, unfortunately, the scope can expand and contract with political changes, and in years of extremism, such as 1966–69, can close almost completely. The causes of this expansion and contraction have been several. The crudest factor has been that opposing groups in the leadership have at different times managed to get the upper hand. The leadership of literature by Mao Zedong and Jiang Qing (Chiang Ch'ing) before 1976 differed markedly from that of Deng Xiaoping after 1978, and the crucial reason for this shift was simply that Mao Zedong died and power changed hands. A second and related reason for shifts in literary policy has been that Party policy toward scientific and technological modernization has shifted several times, and the Party's view of the importance of intellectuals has shifted accordingly. When intellectuals are considered important, writers are given more scope. It is true that at times (for example, during the Cultural Revolution) a sharp distinction has been made between the bulk of intellectuals, who were treated very badly, and a select few, such as the scientists who developed China's hydrogen bomb, doctors who performed medical operations on top leaders, and so forth. But these exceptions aside, intellectuals have generally seen their fortunes rise and fall as a group.

A third reason for the shifting scope for writers has involved changes in the willingness of the top leadership to trust intellectuals. In 1956 Mao Zedong apparently felt that, after six and a half years of the People's Republic, China's writers had become sufficiently loyal to the Party that, if given leeway, they could be trusted to voice criticisms aimed only at *improving* the Party rather than opposing it.[27] In his famous "Hundred Flowers"[28] Campaign of 1956 and early 1957, Mao

26. "Within bounds," as noted above, can mean different things for people in different stations. And for most writers, the borderlines of the scope are intentionally kept somewhat vague.

27. For details of this interpretation of Mao's reasoning, see Richard Solomon, *Mao's Revolution and the Chinese Political Culture* (Berkeley and Los Angeles: University of California Press, 1971), pp. 268–329.

28. The phrase "hundred flowers" stands for the slogan "Let a hundred flowers bloom, and a hundred schools of thought contend" that was announced by Mao Zedong in a speech on 2 May 1956. The phrase originated in the Warring States period (475–221 B.C.) to describe contention among philosophical schools.

encouraged writers to speak out, and the criticism of the Party that resulted went well beyond mere suggestions for improvement. A severe crackdown on intellectuals, termed the Anti-Rightist Campaign, followed in 1957. Many Chinese intellectuals have put a more cynical interpretation on this sequence of events. They feel that the Party leadership in 1956 deliberately "went fishing" in order to catch potential critics, and that this motive may have been involved during the relaxation of 1979 as well. Ultimately there is no way to verify the "fishing trip" interpretation, since it turns on the private motivations of a very small and secretive group of people. But there is no doubt that the theory is widely believed.

## The Shock of the Anti-Rightist Campaign and the Bifurcation of Language

The Anti-Rightist Campaign of 1957 wounded Chinese writers more deeply than many people inside and outside China realized for many years. After 1978, when writers were encouraged to denounce the Gang of Four and the "ten years of waste" (the last ten under Mao), many insisted on beginning their tales of woe with 1957. This emphasis was somewhat inconvenient for the post-Mao leadership, many of whom had been supporters of the crackdown in 1957. Yet the continuities between 1957 and 1966–76 were too obvious to deny, and leaders who had backed the earlier campaign, once they had been on the receiving end of the persecution during 1966–76, obviously felt regrets about 1957. The number of people formally designated as "rightists" in 1957 has never been published, and given the confusion of the campaign, it is doubtful whether the government's classified figures would be entirely accurate even if they were available. Estimates of the number, from a variety of sources, average around a half a million.[29] The usual punishment for a "rightist" was to be ordered out of one's work unit and sent to be reformed through labor in either the countryside or urban factories. Other punishments varied widely: people were criticized, had to write confessions, lost Party membership and other privileges, became subject to blackmail by people threatening to "expose" them further, saw their children publicly denounce them, and so on. An indeterminable number opted for suicide.

29. Chinese intellectuals both inside China and outside make estimates that range from the low to the high hundreds of thousands; see, for example, Li Yi, "Liu Binyan he tade shidai" (Liu Binyan and his times), *Qishiniandai* (The Seventies) (Hong Kong), no. 12 (1982), p. 70. In April 1958 Mao Zedong cited a figure of 300,000, and during the Cultural Revolution, Chen Yi spoke of 400,000 rightists seized in 1957; see Roderick Mac-Farquhar, *The Origins of the Cultural Revolution*, vol. 1 (London: Oxford University Press, 1974), pp. 314, 405.

The targets of the Anti-Rightist Campaign were, in most cases, precisely those who had spoken out a year earlier in the Hundred Flowers campaign. Yet how much speaking out qualified one as a rightist was necessarily uncertain because of a system of quotas. In the early stages of the campaign, a top leader, widely believed to have been Mao Zedong himself, apparently made the casual estimate that 5 percent of Chinese were still "rightists." This figure of 5 percent then became institutionalized as a guideline that was handed down mechanically from Beijing to the provinces and from the provinces to the counties. Below the county level, quotas for individual work units could be as high as 10 percent or as low as 1 percent, depending on how many outspoken intellectuals a unit was perceived as having. When the buck could be passed no further, the people at the bottom had to decide which of them would fill their quota as rightists. This naturally led to bitter dissension, especially in work units such as schools and universities, where many intellectuals had spoken out in harmony during the Hundred Flowers period, and now had to decide who would take the rap. A somewhat different problem developed in work units that had few intellectuals: even though no one had spoken out during the Hundred Flowers phase, someone still had to plead guilty to having done so. To say that no one in a given unit was a rightist was unacceptable, and could itself be viewed as a "rightist mistake," since it contradicted the received wisdom implicit in the quota.

Most of the writers represented in this book were too young to be hit directly by the Anti-Rightist Campaign, although many have family members who were. Of those directly affected, Wang Meng ("Eye of the Night") was the most famous as a rightist. His case was propagandized at the national level and was more important than any other in exemplifying the aims of the campaign.[30] Ai Qing ("Roses and Thorns") was also declared a rightist and sent to "the great northern wasteland" in Heilongjiang Province. Huang Qingyun ("Annals of a Fossil") was not stigmatized, but her husband was. The stories by Wang Zhecheng and Wen Xiaoyu, Dai Qing, and Chen Rong all reveal painful memories of the Anti-Rightist Campaign.

This campaign had important consequences for the use of language, both written and oral, by China's intellectuals. The distinction between formal official language and ordinary speech, which in various forms is centuries old in China, had continued to be part of life in the People's Republic. Official language, which was used for formal political purposes, was grammatically and lexically limited, stylistically stand-

---

30. See Goldman, *Literary Dissent*, pp. 182–86.

ardized, somewhat Westernized, and quite uniform across China. It carried the air of official "correctness"—whether or not it was used in knowing independence of facts. By contrast, informal language, which was used for the great majority of everyday purposes (including *informal* political ones), was natural Chinese in all its dialectical and other variations—not limited or stylized, not Westernized, and without claim to the transcendent "correctness" of formal language. What the shock of the Anti-Rightist Campaign accomplished, especially among intellectuals, was a sudden charging of this distinction with a political sensitivity that made it much sharper and more pervasive than it had been before. Of necessity, the use of formal political language became more and more common in daily life. As it spread, it developed a complex relationship with ordinary speech, where talk about everything from public affairs to fish in the market proceeded in very different ways. Not only do the messages differ at the two levels, but grammar and diction also shift in ways that signal clearly whether one is speaking "for the record."

Differing usages at the two linguistic levels have led to many ironies, not the least of which is the word "rightist" itself. Ever since the Anti-Rightist Campaign, the word "rightist" in ordinary discourse has come to mean "people who were labeled 'rightists' in 1957." These people, although they represent a range of opinion, generally have favored more freedom for literature and art, more compassion for the poor, more openness to foreign countries, less militarism in society, and other views that in the West (and even, generally speaking, in China before 1957) would count as moderately leftist, or "liberal." But in China they are "rightist," while the opposing views—favoring controls on literature and art, favoring militarism, and opposing foreign cultural influences— are often associated with the orthodox "left." The impact of the official use of "right" and "left" has been so great that ordinary language has entirely adopted them as labels for, if not descriptions of, certain categories of people. (The question of how often implicit quotation marks are retained around the terms in the minds of speakers and listeners is a crucial one but impossible to answer.)

In some social situations, the bifurcation of language has facilitated an almost mandatory hypocrisy. For example, in required political discussion meetings, when people are obliged to represent their support for official policies, official language naturally becomes their medium for doing so; meanwhile among trusted friends outside such meetings, ordinary speech remains the medium for one's true views, which may or may not be the same. In general, Chinese intellectuals have done as well as can be expected in resisting this hypocrisy, although the Anti-Rightist

Campaign obliged almost everyone to accept it to some extent. In times of political relaxation, such as 1979–80, writers have been able to object to the intrusiveness and insensitivity of official language. Every story in this volume contains at least some evidence of this objection.

## The Respite of the Late 1950s and Early 1960s

During the eight years between the Anti-Rightist Campaign of 1957–58 and the earthshaking Cultural Revolution that began in 1966, China's writers were — by the standards in the People's Republic — relatively free from trouble. But even during this lull, a few writers were sent for labor reform, and no writer could afford to forget the question of the permissible "scope." The vagaries of literary politics caused the borderlines of that scope to seem rather constantly in flux — as if fidgeting deliberately to keep writers nervous. In 1958–59 the Great Leap Forward, a quixotic plan conceived by Mao to produce everything "more, faster, better, and cheaper," led to great dislocations in the Chinese economy, primarily because each of the four stated goals was reached except the third — better — where rapid retrogression occurred. Though essentially an economic movement, the application of the principles of the Great Leap Forward was so pervasive that, in many localities, production quotas were set for poems as well as for steel. Factory workers and peasants were encouraged to bring original poems to work each day. If one defines "poetry" uncritically, it seems certain that far more Chinese poems were written in 1958–59 than in all of history before then. Unfortunately, their quality was generally as low as that of the homemade iron[31] they praised, and their overwhelming numbers were accompanied by no advance in the flexibility allowed serious poets and writers. On the contrary, the scope permitted writers continued to narrow during the Great Leap Forward as part of an effort to drive home the message that the relatively free speech of the Hundred Flowers period had been a mistake. The literary doctrine of socialist realism was forcefully reasserted in Mao Zedong's slogan "Literature should be the combination of revolutionary realism and revolutionary romanticism," which was proclaimed to be not only an advance over regular Soviet-style socialist realism but "a scientific summation of all of

31. Part of the Great Leap Forward was a campaign to make homemade iron in every back yard.

literary history."[32] In fact, Mao's idea was basically the same as socialist realism except that it put somewhat more emphasis on the "romantic" projection of ideals in ordinary life (meaning, essentially, that heroes were to be more nearly perfect). Lest writers miss the point, another anti-rightist movement was launched in the fall of 1959. It was not as vigorous as the 1957 campaign, but neither did it have to be.

The years 1960 and 1961 saw a qualified relaxation in literary controls. It was clear that poor harvests in 1959–61, which had created hardship and even, in certain cases, starvation, had resulted primarily from the disastrous policies of the Great Leap Forward. The leadership was obliged to revert to more standard strategies for economic development, and this retrenchment required an increased reliance on China's scientists and technicians. The need for their cooperation was redoubled when China's rift with the Soviet Union caused the abrupt departure of Soviet advisers in the summer of 1960.

To a certain extent, the wooing of scientists made things better for writers and artists as well. Many of the "rightist" labels of 1957 were removed in 1961;[33] a relatively large number of interesting books were published from 1961 to 1963; some good films were made; and a powerful literary official named Shao Quanlin sponsored an emphasis on "middle characters" in literature. Middle characters were ordinary people who were neither heroes nor villains, whose idealism might be flawed by selfishness, and who — like most people in China — subscribed superficially to political campaigns while inwardly experiencing doubts or apathy. The "middle characters" theory obviously made significant literary art more possible. But the response from writers was more subdued than during the Hundred Flowers days of 1956. Burned once, writers were hesitant to take a second risk so quickly. Although the call to portray middle characters included the promise that literary freethinking would not be confused with, or punished as, political freethinking, most writers were skeptical that such an elusive distinction could be maintained in the hurly-burly of actual political life. Besides, the official justification for allowing middle characters was not

32. Zhou Yang, "Xin min'ge kaituole shige de xin daolu" (New poems have blazed the way to a new poetry), *Hongqi* (Red Flag), 1958, no. 1. Reprinted in *Zhonguo xiandai wenxue cankao ziliao*, vol. 3, pp. 697–703; quotation from p. 697.

33. The rightist labels that remained after 1961 stayed affixed until November 1978, when a blanket pardon was declared (but even then, not completely implemented).

to provide more artistic latitude for writers, but to make literary propaganda more effective by giving readers some characters with whom they could more easily identify, thereby making it easier to lead them toward socialist goals. Some writers were simply unwilling to write propaganda, subtle or otherwise. Others, though willing, had to wonder how the political "correctness" of their efforts might be judged. Even a speech by Zhou Enlai calling for literary democracy, in June 1961, was insufficient to reassure most writers.[34]

## The Cultural Revolution

In retrospect, this skepticism was justified. Beginning in September 1962, at the Tenth Plenum of the Party's Eighth Congress, Mao Zedong again focused criticism on intellectuals by admonishing everyone "never to forget the class struggle." Traditional operas were denounced as "ghost stories," and banned six months later. Two months after that, in May 1963, Mao announced a "Socialist Education Campaign," calling it the most important since Land Reform and, among other things, vital to the reform of all genres of literature. In the autumn of 1964, Shao Quanlin was attacked for his "middle characters" theory, and the famous writer Ouyang Shan was criticized for his novel *Three Family Lane* and sent to the countryside for labor reform. Shao and Ouyang had both apparently been named by Mao himself as targets.

But these events were only a prelude to the Cultural Revolution, which burst forth in summer of 1966. First wall posters at Beijing University, and then editorials in *People's Daily*, called for the overthrow of China's "capitalist roaders." Young Red Guards organized in major cities and soon split into opposing factions. The chaos that resulted turned violent after September 1967, when Jiang Qing issued a call to "attack with words but defend with weapons." Since all sides could easily conceive themselves as on the defensive, weapons appeared nearly everywhere and led to what the leadership soon approvingly called "all-out civil war." But when the established institutions collapsed they were

34. A famous chapter in Chinese literary dissidence began in 1961 when the journalist Deng Tuo began publishing essays in the *Beijing Evening News* that were veiled, but penetrating, attacks on Mao Zedong and some of his policies. See Merle Goldman, *China's Intellectuals: Advise and Dissent* (Cambridge, Mass.: Harvard University Press, 1981), pp. 25–38. Though admired in the intellectual community, Deng Tuo did not represent a trend that included many other writers. He had patronage in very high places, well beyond the reach of the average writer.

replaced not, as Maoist theory had predicted, by a new socialist order sprung naturally from the progressive consciousness of the laboring masses, but by a confusion of competing power centers at all levels, held together by personal loyalties to strongmen who traded protection for support in the centuries-old pattern that Chinese Marxists call "feudalism." (In retrospect, this result was hardly surprising.) The neo-"feudalistic" patterns that emerged in the Cultural Revolution included the playing of favorites, the use of the "back door" (private connections), and the exchange of bribes on a scale that far exceeded what went on in the earlier years of the People's Republic. Ironically, the Cultural Revolution, one of whose slogans was to "smash the 'four olds'"—old thought, old culture, old customs, and old habits—exacerbated some of the very problems it was intended to solve.

Another irony is that the Cultural Revolution, although a literary wasteland, had literary policy at its heart. Literary debates heralded its arrival;[35] Jiang Qing, one of its principal movers, took literary policy as her special domain; Yao Wenyuan, another of the Gang of Four, moved to the apex of power through literary criticism. The ancient Chinese assumption of the fundamental affinity of literature, morality, and politics, now sharpened by an extremist interpretation of Stalin's notion that writers should be the engineers of souls, left literary policy, if not literature, in a very important position.

A major literary guideline of the Cultural Revolution was "the three prominences," which meant that positive characters should stand out from the crowd, that heroes should stand out among the positive characters, and that superheroes should stand out among the heroes. To exemplify these principles, Jiang Qing promoted "eight model plays" that were to be emulated throughout China and—at least in theory—"adapted" to suit local interests, dialects, and so forth. In fact, however, the authoritarianism of Jiang and her colleagues was so fearsome that no one dared alter the model plays in the slightest. Widths of doorsteps were copied to the centimeter.

In fiction, where there was only slightly more leeway than in drama,

35. These debates concerned a play by Wu Han called *Hai Rui Dismissed from Office* in addition to the criticisms, mentioned above, of Deng Tuo, Ouyang Shan, and "ghost stories." See Goldman, *China's Intellectuals*, pp. 25–38 and 105–7, and James R. Pusey, *Wu Han: Attacking the Present through the Past* (Cambridge, Mass.: East Asian Research Center, Harvard University, 1969).

the required adherence to "the three prominences" yielded stereotyped stories that were distinguishable only in harmless detail. To be published, stories were supposed to be written by workers, peasants, soldiers, or committees drawn from those groups. Some officials and a few intellectuals did find ways to count themselves and their families as "workers," but only one contemporary novelist, Hao Ran, became well known during the Cultural Revolution. His lengthy novel *The Golden Road* (1972) recounts thirty years of Party organizational efforts in a north China village. Although its lively and colorful descriptions do represent the only noteworthy passages of published fiction in China during ten years, the novel is seriously flawed by its mandatory portrayal of political ideals as reality. Other than Hao Ran, the only Chinese writer whose works were readily available in bookstores during the Cultural Revolution was the famous Lu Xun (1881–1936). The reason Lu Xun's stories were made available was not the obvious one — that they are the best in modern China — but that Mao Zedong and Jiang Qing had decided to invoke Lu Xun's moral authority in their efforts to purge Zhou Yang, Xia Yan, and others whom Lu Xun had opposed in the 1930s for wholly different reasons.[36] Traditional Chinese works of fiction, such as *Dream of the Red Chamber* and *Water Margin*, were occasionally published in the early and middle 1970s, but never in nearly sufficient quantity to supply the potential demand. Western fiction was not available publicly, although Jiang Qing did announce a short list of books of "recommended reading" that included *Jane Eyre, A Tale of Two Cities, The Scarlet Letter, The Red and the Black, The Count of Monte Cristo,* and *Gone with the Wind.* These books were available only to those with privileged access to "internal circulation" (classified) materials.

Hence fiction and drama did exist during the Cultural Revolution, and were slightly more substantial — but only slightly — than the clichés of the post-Mao period have admitted. The more momentous fact of the Cultural Revolution years is that most of China's known writers were treated harshly, even brutally. Banishment and forced labor were common fates; murder and suicide occurred, but to what extent is not determinable. Individual circumstances varied widely — whether owing to the severity of one's "crimes," to protection by someone in high position,

36. For more on these questions, see Merle Goldman, "The Political Use of Lu Xun in the Cultural Revolution," a paper presented at a conference on "Lu Xun and His Legacy," Assilomar, Calif., 22–28 August 1981.

or to sheer luck. When writers were allowed to speak out about these things in the late 1970s, many avoided the horrible details, finding it too painful to relive them in words. It was easier to take refuge in formulas such as "the ten years of waste" or "the times when Lin Biao and the Gang of Four were running rampant," while speaking in detail only of events before 1966 or after 1976.

## After Mao: The Second Blooming of the Hundred Flowers

When the Gang of Four was arrested in October 1976, creative writers were not the first to denounce them, although no group could have despised these architects of the Cultural Revolution more. Having been severely attacked twice, writers well knew the value of prudence. The first denunciations of the Gang in the arts were by cartoonists, whose large, multicolored posters, sometimes lurid or even shockingly gross in a manner designed to mirror the shockingly gross methods of the Gang, appeared along avenues in Beijing, Shanghai, and other major cities. Simultaneously comedians' dialogues (*xiangsheng*) that cracked jokes at the expense of Jiang Qing and others appeared as if from nowhere. Actually they were based on a stock of oral satire that had long been circulating underground. It is likely that one reason cartoonists and comedians were among the first to risk audacity in the years after Mao was that their barbs, involving humor as they do, could be viewed as "lighter" problems in case anything were incorrect.

The first published short story to attract national attention during the post-Mao literary thaw was "The Homeroom Teacher" by Liu Xinwu.[37] The author dares to describe both a juvenile delinquent (thereby mentioning in print an obvious social problem that everyone had been supposed to ignore until then), and a young woman whose intelligence had been wasted by her extremely rigid indoctrination in political dogma. She believes nothing unless it appears in a Party newspaper. Both she and the juvenile delinquent, the author suggests, represent ways in which the Gang of Four distorted the lives and minds of youth. The publication of this bold story cannot be attributed entirely to the audacity of the author. Certainly some of the risk was his, but the story could not have appeared in the prestigious *People's Literature* with-

37. "Ban Zhuren," *Renmin wenxue*, November 1977; translated as "Class Counselor" in Bennett Lee and Geremie Barme, eds., *The Wounded: New Stories of the Cultural Revolution 77–78* (Hong Kong: Joint Publishing Co., 1979).

out approval from high-ranking Party leaders. In large part, then, the story's publication signaled a deliberate and approved widening of the scope for creative writers. This scope was expanded further in August 1978, when another pathbreaking story, "Scar" by Lu Xinhua, appeared in a Shanghai newspaper.[38] It tells how a young woman is pressured into abandoning her "counterrevolutionary" parents during the Cultural Revolution, and then, because even that is not enough to rid her of their political taint, sees her romance with a young man destroyed when he is driven to break his association with her. Thus both her family of birth and her potential family by marriage are ruined by politics. Despite the Cultural Revolution, the family has remained the most cherished social unit in China, and for innumerable readers the publication of "Scar" created an opportunity to spill forth with tales of their own family trage- dies. Many of these real-life stories found their way into print as fiction, and for more than a year Chinese literature was dominated by what was called "scar literature."

The scope of scar literature gradually widened to include themes not only of broken families but of oppressive officials, dirty prisons, mindless dogmatism, corruption, abuse of privilege, extremes of pov- erty, and anything else that could be charged against the Gang of Four and their rule. In this collection, "The Transcript" by Lin Jinlan, "Three Professors" by Cao Guanlong, and "The Gap" by Lao Hong are good examples of scar literature in the larger sense. The political leadership had various reactions to scar literature, but for most of the twelve months following the Third Plenum of the Eleventh Party Congress in December 1978, when writers and other intellectuals were urged to "lib- erate thought," the predominant official opinion was to tolerate scar lit- erature and even occasionally to encourage it. So long as popular anger was directed at the Gang of Four, "scar literature" served the interests of the new leadership by discrediting the people they had overthrown. The new political program was, moreover, "modernization," and it again became obvious that the cooperation of intellectuals would be necessary to reach Party goals. Because all intellectuals, writers and sci- entists alike, had so recently been tarred with the same heavy brush, it would be hard to expect scientists to work in peace if writers were still being harassed. The scope allowed writers thus expanded until, in

38. "Shanghen," *Wenhuibao* 11 August 1978; translated as "The Wounded" in Lee and Barme, *The Wounded*.

autumn 1979, it was wider than it had been at any time under the People's Republic.

In their exuberance, writers began in 1979 to explore social problems that could not neatly be attributed to the Gang of Four alone. With this development, the political leadership naturally became uneasy. Where would the probing stop? Might it undermine their own rule? Writers, aware of the danger of a backlash, were generally careful to cover their more penetrating observations with pro forma denunciations of the Gang of Four. The point of these covers was not to deceive officialdom, who in any case would not have been easily hoodwinked, but to satisfy the hierarchy that writers were continuing to point young readers in basically the right direction.

In China politically acceptable literary works have often been called "flowers"; when they carry criticisms they are said to bear "thorns." In early 1980, the political leadership gradually made it clear that the thorns had grown too numerous. On 16 January 1980 Deng Xiaoping made it clear in a major speech that writers must not question the "four unmoveables": socialism, Party leadership, the dictatorship of the proletariat, and Marxism-Leninism-Mao-Zedong-Thought. In February a "Conference on Playwriting" in Beijing drew the line more concretely by criticizing a play and two filmscripts whose thorns had been a bit too sharp. Beginning in March, newspapers and authoritative journals exhorted writers "to consider the social effects" of their writing—i.e., not to encourage what the leadership regarded as political or moral misbehavior. The result of the clampdown was, for several months, an awkward stand-off between many writers and the leadership. Several aspects of this stand-off are suggested in the poem "Roses and Thorns" by Ai Qing that prefaces this book. In 1981, with successive campaigns against the writer Bai Hua and "bourgeois liberalism," all the outstanding questions were resolved in favor of the political leadership.

The stories collected here are all, in varying degrees, "thorny" works from 1979 and early 1980. (Most works published in early 1980 were written in 1979, before the tightening up.) However we judge them as literary works, they have an irreducible dignity, as well as a place in the tradition of socially engaged Chinese letters, because of the constituency they speak for—a quarter of the world's population, whose sufferings in recent years have only begun to be understood. Dai Qing's "Anticipation," for example, caused a great stir when it was published because it "spoke for the people" in the straightforward sense of saying publicly what many readers clearly had in mind but could not, or dared not, express themselves. The story tells of the sufferings of married couples who are required to live widely apart for years because of work assignments in different localities. Resentment over such circumstances, as massive as it was mute, had been festering in China for years; Dai Qing's contribution, simple and yet magnificent, was to place a story in the public press for all to see and applaud. Similarly, Jin He, in "Reencounter," brings up the problem of the two-faced official — certainly a familiar figure to many in China — although here the young author remains sensitive enough to let the reader understand some of the official's own dilemmas. Zhang Jie, in "Love Must Not Be Forgotten," pleads on behalf of countless young people for the freedom to marry for love rather than in conformity to social expectations — a freedom the communist revolution has not, alas, succeeded in establishing. The outcries in these stories are clearly representative of millions.

But some writers "spoke for the people" in a more refracted, and ultimately larger, sense. Moving beyond the expression of what was already in their readers' minds, these writers attempted to interpret the shocking violence and buzzing confusion of recent Chinese history. Why do we Chinese do such things to one another? What went wrong? In 1979–80 most people, including most writers, were still emotionally too close to their experiences to attempt a well-balanced, complete interpretation. Besides, ironically, many who sought to interpret the whole experience had little to go on. (Many intellectuals in China told me, during my stay in 1979–80, that they could not interpret the Cultural Revolution because they essentially knew only what happened to themselves.) Yet a few writers did attempt to crawl from beneath the rubble, take a look around, and place the troubled scene in broader perspective. Chen Rong's "At Middle Age," included here, represents the best of these tentative efforts. The author seems endowed with a spiritual gyroscope and steadiness of eye that lets her see more deeply, if still not broadly, into recent events. Huang Qingyun's "Annals of a Fossil," though much shorter, also achieves some distance from the madness it describes by insulating itself with a layer of sprightly whimsy. But no literary work of recent years comes close to the epic account that waits to be told.

If the most exciting theme of Chinese fiction in 1979–80 was documentation and protest of problems in society, another important emphasis was certainly exploration of the West. Almost entirely isolated from the West for three decades, and even from the Soviet Union for two, many Chinese writers, especially among the younger generation, intuitively felt that a gap needed to be closed. There was intense curiosity about what people in China had been "missing." Expectations were often exaggerated, since they arose partly in relation to perceived advances in Western technology. What, as it were, were the counterparts in fiction of computers and stereo tape recorders? The answers, as they circulated rather faddishly in late 1979 and early 1980, were flashbacks, black humor, and stream of consciousness. When writers tried these methods for themselves, flashbacks were the easiest to achieve (partly because they were hardly new to Chinese literature) and were therefore most common. Flashbacks within flashbacks also appeared, as did other, more complex, but usually rather silly, manipulations of time. Black humor was known only by reputation and by a few translations of stories by Kurt Vonnegut. No Chinese imitations, to my knowledge, were ever published.[39]

Stream of consciousness was the most interesting of the "Western" influences. Although writers like Virginia Woolf and James Joyce were not widely known or read, a few Chinese writers experimented with stream of consciousness and published their results. By summer of 1980, the name of Wang Meng had become most closely associated with these experiments. "Eye of the Night" (1979), included here, shows only the beginnings of Wang's tendency in this direction; "The Sound of Spring" (1980) and "Dream of the Sea" (1980) are more representative. Although Wang Meng denied a conscious effort to imitate Western stream of consciousness (arguing that Chinese literature had many adequate precedents) he was nonetheless widely championed among the young precisely for his exploration of Western technique. For several months in 1980, the political leadership seemed to be encouraging experiments with literary form (Wang Meng's "The Sound of Spring" won a short story prize), perhaps because formal experiments were seen as a relatively innocuous way for youth to spend its energies. But stream of consciousness certainly also had its enemies among conservatives. How

---

39. Wang Meng's adaptations of Uighur popular humor called "Anecdotes of Section Chief Maimaiti" (*Maimaiti chuzhang yishi*) resemble black humor, but are explicitly attributed by Wang Meng to Xinjiang, not the West.

could fiction lack a story? Why should it be needlessly hard to understand? "If I can't understand it," said Liu Baiyu, a powerful figure
in literature and art in the People's Liberation Army, "then neither can
the masses; and if the masses can't understand it, how can it be socialist art?"[40]

Besides exposure of social problems and experiment with technique, a third component of the thaw of 1979–80, and actually the largest in numbers of examples, was the reversion to popular themes that
had been banned during the Cultural Revolution.[41] Romantic love, for
example, could be suggested during the Cultural Revolution only subtly
and in the most politically sanitized ways, as when a couple marries out
of intense shared hatred of the class enemy. In the late 1970s, when
romance again became an acceptable theme, examples gushed forth in
a flood whose startling proportions surely must be attributed to the ten
dry years that had gone before.[42] Even in stories whose main themes
were exposure of corruption or war with Vietnam, romantic subthemes
were frequently added as if they were obligatory ornaments.

Detective stories and spy stories also made a comeback, especially
among the popular readership in cities.[43] The Guangdong People's Publishing House reprinted *The Adventures of Sherlock Holmes* in order to
make money to subsidize its more "serious" literary publications. Spy
stories from the Soviet Union that had been translated during the 1950s
again became popular items in libraries. Although knight-errant (*wu-
xia*) stories, which are so popular in Chinese communities outside the
People's Republic, were still not deemed fit for publication, there were
obvious signs of strong reader interest in them. Examples brought in
from Hong Kong were highly coveted. And when the French-Italian
film *Zorro* (a surrogate for the Chinese knight-errant if ever there was
one) was shown in major cities, tickets on the black market reached ten
times their face value.

40. Interview with Liu Baiyu, Beijing, 11 August 1980.
41. Themes that were banned during the Cultural Revolution survived among many
readers in hand-copied volumes (*shouchaoben*) that circulated underground.
42. For the developmental stages of the romantic love theme in the late 1970s see
Kam Louie, "The Politics and Morality of Love in Post-Gang of Four Short Stories," a
paper presented at a conference on "Contemporary Chinese Literature: New Forms of
Realism?" St. John's University, New York, 28–31 May 1982.
43. See Jeffrey C. Kinkley, "Crime Fiction," a paper presented at the conference on
"Contemporary Chinese Literature: New Forms of Realism?" (see note 42).

## Writers' Livelihood

A professional writing career has never been easy in China (which is not to say it is easy anywhere else). Between 1900 and 1920, when modern printing presses made mass-produced fiction possible in China, a few former journalists found it possible to make a living as writers of popular fiction.[44] Royalty agreements, and sometimes contracted salaries, became established in commercial publishing. While a small number of writers could make handsome livings from best sellers, their glamorous example was out of reach for the great majority, who normally earned livings in roles such as schoolteacher, journalist, or copyist, while writing in their spare time. This basic pattern has persisted in new socialist rubrics in the People's Republic, where the great majority of writers are "amateurs" who, if they do have salaries, draw them from "work units" such as factories or schools.[45] Two differences from the pre–1949 years are that the whole system of rewarding writers (and, as we have seen, punishing them) has become institutionalized as never before, and that it has become less possible to live handsomely from writing, even for authors who earn considerable sums from it.

The salaries that amateur writers in China draw from their work units are the same as those of other workers in the same units, i.e., 40 to 80 *yuan* per month for factory workers and up to 200 or 300 *yuan* per month for high-level intellectuals in universities or research institutes. The salaries of professional writers attached to branches of the Writers' Association are not much different from other salaries, ranging from about 70 *yuan* per month to, in rare cases, 300 or more. The salary is paid whether one writes or not, and the salary level is fixed much more according to seniority than to productivity. Thus even the most prominent and active of the relatively young professional writers, such as Wang Meng and Zhang Jie, were drawing salaries under 100 *yuan* in the early 1980s, while older writers, though they had essentially retired, were receiving more.[46] The determination of professional salaries is

44. See Perry Link, *Mandarin Ducks and Butterflies*, pp. 149–55.
45. During the Cultural Revolution, amateur status was exalted as the *only* one that could provide the proper outlook for writing "correct" works.
46. Once conferred, professional status cannot be revoked even if a writer ceases to write altogether. And salaries, while they can go up, cannot go down. Since the central and provincial governments fix limits on the number of professional writers, it often happens that older writers hold down professional positions that could be better used by younger writers.

made according to a complex hierarchical ranking system in which a writer (like all professional "literature and art workers") is assigned to one of eight grades. Sometimes a writer is placed on the ladder for cadres (officials), where there are twenty-four grades. But in either case, a writer who moves into professional status cannot expect an immediate salary hike of significant size. Beginning professional salaries normally match what a writer had been making in his original work unit. The main incentives for transfer to professional status are not money but prestige and more free time for writing.

In addition to salaries, writers in the People's Republic earn "manuscript payments" (*gaochou*) according to formulas that have changed several times since 1949. Most of the time (specifically 1958–66 and 1978 to now), there have been both "basic manuscript payments" (*jiben gaochou*), based on the number of characters in a text, and supplemental "print-run payments" (*yinshua gaochou*), based on the number of copies printed. The "basic" payment is calculated, as it was in pre-communist China, as a certain amount per thousand characters. In 1979–80, the state permitted editorial boards to offer from two to seven *yuan* per thousand characters (U.S. $1.30 to $4.70), depending on their opinion of a manuscript's quality.[47] In practice, the lower end of this range was seldom used; most payments were at the five, six, or seven *yuan* rates. Poetry was paid by the number of lines, with twenty lines, regardless of length, counting the same as one thousand characters in other genres.[48] When a piece is contributed to a literary magazine or a newspaper, the basic payment is the only one. But when a book is published, the author gets both a basic payment and a "print-run" payment calculated as a percentage of the basic payment as shown in table 1. It is worth noting that, unlike in Western royalty systems, the author's share goes down, rather than up, as printings continue, reflecting the difference between the socialist assumption that the rich need not get richer and the capitalist's need to cover costs before distributing profits. A less obvious, but very important, difference is that the author's share is calculated not on the basis of the number of copies sold but by the number printed. Since the

47. In July 1980 the rates were raised to range from three to ten *yuan* per thousand characters, with thirteen for "special manuscripts" (*tegao*) (interview at Wenyi chubanshe, Shanghai, 16 June 1980).

48. An exception to this rule allowed somewhat higher payments for poetry in traditional Chinese forms.

Table 1

Print-Run Payments as Percentage of Basic Payment (Summer 1980)

| Print Run | Original Works | Translations |
|---|---|---|
| | (per 10,000 copies) | |
| Up to 50,000 | 3% | 2% |
| 50,001–100,000 | 2% | 1% |
| 100,001–200,000 | 1% | 0.5% |
| 200,001–500,000 | 0.5% | 0.3% |
| 500,000–1,000,000 | 0.4% | 0.2% |
| Over 1,000,000 | 0.2% | 0.1% |

*Source*: Chinese Writer's Association, Beijing

judgment of the political leadership, not reader demand, is the crucial factor in determining the size of print runs,[49] both the fame and fortune of a writer are tied to the leadership's view of him.

The question of print-run payments is further complicated by the lack of a copyright system. In a time of political relaxation such as 1979–80, much reprinting of contemporary works occurred all across China, quite without the permission of writers or original publishers. This led some leading writers even to appeal for a "publication law." In China, where "law" is still commonly understood as hardly different from "control," and where writers, even in relaxed times such as 1979–80, have had to worry about the possible reapplication of tight controls on their own work, the call for a publication law implies a rather acute irritation.

Films are a source of ancillary income for a few writers, and whether or not to make a well-known work of fiction into a film is also a question that has required political review.[50] In 1979–80, the author of a piece of fiction from which a film was made received a one-time payment of 1,000, 1,200, or 1,500 *yuan*, at the discretion of the film studio.

In the great majority of cases, these various payments did not add

49. The leadership normally does consider reader demand, along with politics and other factors, in determining print runs. But given that reader demand for fiction usually exceeds supply (*far* exceeded it in 1979–80), whatever book the leadership decides to print or reprint is likely to sell. Thus the leadership's discretion is very important in determining not only which books are printed but which become best sellers.

50. Controls on film have been somewhat tighter than on fiction in China, presumably because the film audience, which need not be literate, is larger, because film's impact is more immediate, and because film audiences sit together in large groups.

up to very much. As an example, let us take the first story in this collection, "Eye of the Night" by Wang Meng. About 5,700 characters in length, it would have earned a "basic payment" of about 40 *yuan* when it was published in November 1979.[51] When it was republished in 1980 in a collection of Wang's works,[52] it would have brought another basic payment of about 40 *yuan* plus an additional 3 to 4 *yuan* in print-run payments for the 29,000 copies that were printed. But that amount, about 85 *yuan*, was probably all that this story brought the author. Certain other reprintings, done without the knowledge or permission of the author, brought no payments.[53] The unusual kind of work that did bring in large sums can be exemplified by the popular novel *The Second Handshake* (*Dierci woshou*) by Zhang Yang. Originally a "hand-copied volume" (*shouchaoben*) that circulated underground during the Cultural Revolution, *The Second Handshake* was published in 1979 by China Youth Publishing House. Within a year, 3.3 million copies had been printed, a record for the People's Republic, earning Zhang Yang about 2,000 *yuan* in basic payment and about 2,320 more for print-run payments. A film was made from the book, bringing 1,200 or 1,500 more, giving a total of 5,500-6,000 *yuan*.[54]

When payments grow this large, they do not imply commensurate material advantages for writers in China, where money by itself sometimes has limited utility. A few writers accumulated thousands of *yuan* in savings that they could not easily use. The most important material perquisites — housing, medical care, education for one's children — and even such relatively minor things as whether one rides first or second

51. This assumes, as may safely be done, that Wang Meng was paid at the top of the scale by *Guangming ribao*.

52. *Dong yu* (Winter rain) (Beijing: Renmin wenxue chubanshe, 1980).

53. An example of such reprinting of "Eye of the Night" is in a volume entitled *Zai Shehui de dang'anli* (In the archives of society) (Guilin: Guilinshi shifan "yuwen jiaoxue" bianjishi, 1980).

54. Zhang Yang's earnings in the thousands of *yuan* may have been small in comparison to the amounts that went to famous authors during the years 1949–66. According to a Red Guard newspaper called *Storm* (*Fenglei*), the People's Literature Publishing House paid nearly 230,000 *yuan* to Ba Jin and over 182,000 to Mao Dun in the first seventeen years of the People's Republic. More than a dozen other writers also received payments of between 30,000 and 70,000 *yuan* from this publisher during this period. (See Paul Bady, "Best Sellers and Writers' Incomes," paper presented at the Workshop on Contemporary Chinese Literature and Performing Arts, Harvard University, 13–20 June 1979.) If these figures are accurate, then either the print runs of Ba Jin's and Mao Dun's novels were many times what they were officially listed as in 1980, or there were other ways, or higher rates, used to pay such famous authors during 1949–66.

class on the railroad, or has access to good theater tickets and good restaurants, are determined primarily not by money but by one's official
status or unofficial connections. In 1980 the famous Cantonese essayist
Qin Mu lived in very modest housing, and this was neither by choice nor
because he could not afford a higher rent. (All rents in China are very
low, only a few *yuan* per month.) The problem was simply that his local
leadership either could not or would not assign him better housing.[55]
Cao Guanlong, the young author of "Three Professors," was apparently
short on both money and political status as of 1980. He lived in a tiny
garret apartment with four slanting roof slabs for walls. Inside there
were only a few square feet of space where an adult could stand erect.
Cao shared this apartment with six family members, who slept in the
crannies where the slanting roof met the floor. He composed "Three
Professors" sitting outside on top of the slanted roof. Writers who were
better off in 1979–80 included Wang Meng and Kong Jiesheng (author
of "On the Other Side of the Stream"), who lived in simple but quite
adequate quarters in one of the huge new rectangular cement buildings
lining Qianmen Avenue in Beijing. In Guangzhou, some of the older,
well-established writers, such as Ouyang Shan and Xiao Yin, lived in large
old colonial-style buildings from before the Revolution, in quarters that
were not luxurious but very comfortable and even charming.

## The Emergence of Individual Writers

It can be startling to realize how concerned contemporary Chinese
writers are about official recognition and prestige. This is not just an
expression of the jealousies normal in the literary circles of any country.
In a society where living standards and lifestyles (no less than writing
styles) must maintain certain uniformities, attention naturally shifts to
whatever markers *do* distinguish writers. Offices, prizes, and seminar
and delegation memberships become especially visible and coveted. In
1979–80, moreover, Chinese writers were consciously reacting against
the forced literary homogeneity of the Cultural Revolution years, when
individual literary reputations were nearly impossible to achieve. With
the exception of Hao Ran, writers during 1966–76 were practically
anonymous. To be sure, names were printed next to stories, but the

55. Qin Mu bears no responsibility for my happening to know these facts. Similarly,
Cao Guanlong, Wang Meng, Kong Jiesheng, Ouyang Shan, and Xiao Yin, whose housing
I comment on below, must not be held responsible for my observations.

stories were so nearly uniform in style and content that authors' names seldom stood out. Editorial boards divided responsibility for incoming manuscripts on geographical principles: one editor would read all the manuscripts from counties $A$ and $B$, another the manuscripts from $C$ and $D$, as if literary qualities corresponded to political subdivisions.

In 1979–80 editorial boards, while basically continuing to divide their responsibilities geographically, were much more flexible in what they would consider and much more sensitive to individual styles and reputations. Writers such as Wang Meng, Zhang Jie, Chen Rong, and Kong Jiesheng, as well as many others not represented in this book, could achieve national reputations for distinctive works (or sometimes types of work, such as Wang Meng's "stream of consciousness"). These writers were provincial neither in their perspectives nor in their audience appeal. They submitted manuscripts to magazines in every part of China, and would not hesitate to withhold their contributions from one province and send them to another whenever they felt they had encountered narrow-mindedness. At the same time they sought to revive and project their own distinctiveness as writers and as people. One young writer I interviewed in Beijing began the story of his literary interests with his great-great-grandfather, a Qing dynasty scholar-official. In other interviews, writers frequently enjoyed recounting their youth and the influence great literature had had on them. The lists of these great works, often led by *Dream of the Red Chamber* and *War and Peace*, themselves tended toward uniformity, which suggests that they may have been ideal lists rather than actual ones. But in any case, the wish to emphasize personal inspiration was clear.

## Chinese Writers and International Standards

It is interesting that Chinese writers in 1979–80 generally attributed half or more of their literary inspiration to foreign, especially Russian, tradition.[56] They were generally eager to have their works translated into foreign languages so that they could be evaluated by international standards. This book, whose main value is probably its revelation of Chinese life and ideas, also serves to give to some Chinese

56. In this paragraph, the writers I have primarily in mind were a group in Beijing that included Wang Meng, Zhang Jie, Chen Rong, Kong Jiesheng, Cong Weixi, Liu Xinwu, and Chen Jiangong. But the generalizations certainly apply beyond this circle. The Russian writers most commonly mentioned were the great nineteenth-century realists, especially Tolstoy, Dostoevski, and Chekhov.

writers that opportunity. Unfortunately, the impact will certainly be less than they imagine. Chinese writers sometimes assume that literature in the West, as in their own country, normally has a mass audience and a prominent place in society and politics. The ardency of their hopes may also lead them to overestimate the prospects for their works when measured by modern international standards. In this matter, they are particularly sensitive to the suggestion that writers from Taiwan such as Bai Xianyong and Chen Ruoxi[57] may have surpassed them — as, by modern standards outside China, they clearly have. Writers in the People's Republic tend to maintain as a matter of principle that they are the direct inheritors of China's May Fourth[58] tradition from the 1920s, and that theirs is therefore the Chinese literary mainstream. The notion that Chinese writers from Taiwan or overseas might have taken the lead is objectionable a priori, whatever may be thought of particular works.

While writers from the People's Republic in general do not do well by modern international standards (as Taiwan writers did not do well until the 1970s), to blame them for it is in many cases unfair. Does one blame the horse for the blinders? Or for blinking fitfully when the blinders are drawn back? What is surprising, actually, is that a writer such as Wang Meng, coming from fifteen years in remote Xinjiang Province, can write a story as technically good as "Eye of the Night"; or that Lao Hong, obsessed as he is by Chinese problems in "The Gap," so sensitively portrays the universal situation of awkward communication between parents and adolescent children. In the case of Cao Guanlong's "Three Professors," it would be a shame to ignore the raw brilliance of a young man for his sometimes obtrusive flaws. Zhang Jie and Kong Jiesheng have remarked that they will be satisfied if they can simply push Chinese literature forward a bit — they would be happy to see the next generation of Chinese writers render their own efforts obsolete.[59]

While their desire for progress in writing technique was certainly genuine, most writers in 1979–80 were nevertheless still guided by the more traditional concept of the writer as spokesman for the people and for the truth about China. These expectations were equally widespread

57. See *The Execution of Mayor Yin and Other Stories from the Great Proletarian Revolution* by Chen Jo-hsi (Bloomington: Indiana University Press, 1978); and *Wandering in the Garden, Waking from a Dream* by Pai Hsien-yung (Bloomington: Indiana University Press, 1982).

58. See note 3 above for books on May Fourth literature.

59. Interview, 30 July 1980.

among readers. A simple statement such as Liu Qingbang's "The Good Luck Bun" was admired, not as journalism but *as literature*, precisely because of its plaintive, unadorned authenticity. One of the best stories in this collection is Wang Zhecheng and Wen Xiaoyu's "Nest Egg," a poignant exploration of the problem of pride for an ancient and resplendent civilization that now finds itself "underdeveloped" in the modern world. This problem, which has lain at the core of Chinese thought and letters for about a hundred years, has seldom been treated so honestly or sensitively.

## Three Generations

It was standard in China in 1979–80 to refer to three generations of Chinese writers as old, middle-aged, and young. No generalization about the three generations can be entirely accurate, but many are sufficiently applicable to be worth making.

The formative years of the older generation were the 1920s and 1930s, when the May Fourth tradition emphasized the exploration of Western literature, the creation of a modern vernacular Chinese literature, and the engagement of the author in the historical crisis of modern China. Most of this generation turned increasingly leftward as China's situation deteriorated in the 1930s and early 1940s. In varying degrees, they became committed to the idea of political and social revolution. But at the same time, their literary experience and tastes were more Westernized than those of any generation before or after them.

In 1949 most of them felt basically loyal to the revolutionary leadership and stood ready to sacrifice some of their literary freedom for the sake of social progress. Very few left for Taiwan or elsewhere. But after 1949, successive campaigns effectively halted the creative activity of this generation. Some, such as Lao She, Ba Jin, and Cao Yu, attempted to write under the new terms of the revolutionary regime, but were far less successful than before. Others, like Shen Congwen and Wu Zuxiang, did not even try to write creatively, and turned to historical scholarship instead. The more politically involved ones, such as Ding Ling and Guo Moruo, essentially became literary officials. Ouyang Shan is unique in his generation for attempting substantial novels such as *Three Family Lane* and *Bitter Struggle* after the Revolution. That these works were eventually harshly criticized indirectly confirms why others in his generation were reluctant to write.

The older generation of writers continued not to write much during the thaw after the death of Mao.[60] Although pleased to be "exonerated" once again, most of them remained somewhat aloof from the excitement over "pathbreaking" works on the contemporary scene. Their literary identity was still rooted in prerevolutionary times, and a certain pride attended this fact. Not only was their generation, with its Western influences, more cosmopolitan than later ones; even their commitment to the Revolution and to leftist ideology was, at least as they conceived it, more genuine. They had experienced the Revolution from its beginnings, had understood its necessity, and hence could preserve a basic loyalty to it in spite of thirty years of vexing questions about Party control of writers. Whether one measured them artistically or politically, they could claim to be the high point in modern Chinese letters.[61] In the present volume, only Ai Qing and Huang Qingyun count as the older generation.

The middle-aged generation, represented here by Wang Meng, Zhang Jie, Chen Rong, Dai Qing, Lin Jinlan, Wang Zhecheng, and Wen Xiaoyu, were born before the Revolution but young when it arrived. Their consciousness of literature and society was formed during the civil war with the Nationalists (1945–49) and in the early 1950s, when optimism about the Revolution was at a high point. During these years, they were as devoted to the Revolution as most of the older generation, but the grounds of their commitment were different in important ways. The older generation, reacting to a severe national crisis brought on by war and domestic chaos, had supported a revolutionary movement in its nascent stages, when revolutionaries were an embattled minority; but the middle-aged generation was joining the Revolution at the high tide of victory and glory. Their enthusiasm came from participation in a great, centrally directed "progressive" effort. Unlike the older generation, their "hatred of the old society" came largely second hand — through instruction from elders and from peer enthusiasm that sprang

60. Some who did write were the novelist Ba Jin, whose collection of essays *Suixianglu* (Meandering thoughts) (Hong Kong: Sanlian shudian, 1979) is noteworthy, especially a poignant memoir for his wife, "Huainian Xiao Shan" (In memory of Xiao Shan); the playwright Cao Yu, whose new work *Wang Zhaojun* was produced in 1979 with great fanfare, but with decidedly mixed reviews among intellectuals; and the poet Ai Qing, whose poem "Roses and Thorns" is but one of the many that he wrote in the late 1970s and early 1980s.

61. The artistic and political standards both would appear to be implicit in a 1980 comment by Zhu Guangqian, an eminent Marxist aesthetician trained in the 1920s, that "no one [in literary circles] knows the first thing about Marxism these days" (interview, 23 July 1980).

from youthful idealism and was shaped to a considerable degree by the political slogans of the early 1950s. Though entirely sincere, the revolutionary optimism of this generation was partly artificial and, therefore, more vulnerable to the shocks that lay ahead. No generation was more shattered by the Anti-Rightist Campaign of 1957. The hard labor may have been more arduous for older writers, but the sting of rejection and disillusionment was strongest among this group, who were young in 1957 and middle-aged in 1979–80. Their disillusionment is apparent in stories such as "Nest Egg," "Anticipation," and "At Middle Age."

The younger generation of writers were born in the late 1940s or the 1950s and were educated entirely in the People's Republic. Too young in 1957 to be targets of the Anti-Rightist Campaign, the defining experience in their lives was the Cultural Revolution. Those with bad class backgrounds (see glossary under "five black categories") were cruelly stigmatized along with their entire families. They were allowed only the least desirable jobs, if any jobs at all; privileges such as Party membership or a university education were simply out of the question. The only hope for escape from their position lay in such drastic measures as public denunciation of their "reactionary" parents (called "drawing a clear line") and "volunteering" for labor in the countryside.

For those with good class backgrounds (or who did "draw a clear line"), there was the possibility of joining the Red Guard movement. There can be no doubt that the infatuation of Red Guards with the ideals of the Cultural Revolution was genuine. The slogan "Down with the New Ruling Class" seemed to signal carte blanche to attack arrogant local bureaucrats. "Bombard the Headquarters" added, for these starry-eyed youths, the romance of battle and the heady sense of being masters of whatever might replace the society they were wrecking. "Defend Chairman Mao to the Death!" gave them an article of faith whose fixity amid the chaos seemed as divine as ever a religious tenet has been.

But as the Cultural Revolution of the early and middle 1970s gradually turned counterproductive in important ways (see pp. 16–17), young people who had wholeheartedly espoused its ideals began to feel disappointment, followed in many cases by resentment and depression. The official denunciation of the Gang of Four in 1976 did bring some temporary relief, because it suddenly became possible to express certain resentments openly. But as the post-Mao leadership gradually escalated its denunciation of the Cultural Revolution, eventually calling the period "ten years of waste," it also — perhaps unwittingly — exacerbated the cynical mood of the young by confirming fears that they had been duped and their futures ruined.

The actual intention of the post-Mao leadership had been to rally the young to the new regime by denouncing the old. Yet in many cases youth's self-pity and cynicism were too strong to allow another rallying to *any* banner. In a sense, the Cultural Revolution had immunized them against such appeals. But, interestingly, certain mental habits from their formative years stayed with these former Red Guards, however strongly they repudiated the Cultural Revolution at the conscious level. For one, Mao had taught them "it is right to rebel," and many did not reject this principle when they rejected its famous formulator. They retained some of the Cultural Revolution's radical iconoclasm. Unlike the middle-aged generation, they considered nothing to be beyond question; they reasoned from the ground up, with little respect for anybody's "forbidden zones." Only among young writers, for example, was there a serious distinction in 1979–80 between advocates of "dismantling the system" (*chaitianpai*) and "repairing the system" (*butianpai*). The would-be dismantlers were not many, but their viewpoint was respectable even among advocates of repair. This intellectual irreverence among the young must be counted a positive legacy of the much-maligned Cultural Revolution, even if it has been only part of a larger negative legacy of cynicism.

The young people who cared enough to write fiction in 1979–80 were not among the most cynical in their generation. Ideals such as devotion to China, telling the truth for the people, and artistic self-expression remained important to them, despite the bitterness that pervaded their peer group and was locked, as well, in their own past. In the present volume, Liu Qingbang, Cao Guanlong, Jin He, and Kong Jiesheng represent the younger generation.

Of the three generations of writers, the middle-aged group generally wrote most perceptively during the post-Mao thaw.[62] The older generation, as noted above, tended to live in the past and did not write much; the younger generation wrote vast amounts but, untrained as they were, and obsessed with daring to shout their grievances, seldom

62. Besides the middle-aged writers translated here, I have in mind Liu Binyan, Gao Xiaosheng, Ru Zhijuan, and Liu Zhen.

wrote with much breadth of vision. But the middle-aged writers, who remembered the revolutionary optimism of the early 1950s, which now seemed a kind of "golden age," found themselves facing the question, "What went wrong?" Their role as a bridge between generations was significant not only among writers but, more importantly, for China's political leaders and their relations with educated youth. The top leaders were elderly (in their late sixties and seventies) and faced the very difficult problem of bringing the generation under thirty-five back from disillusionment and cynicism. To whom would they listen? It was no secret that the bulk of the readership of contemporary Chinese fiction were educated young people. They might sneer at slogans in the official press, but would read with respect a work by Zhang Jie, Chen Rong, or Liu Binyan. The leadership could not ignore the potential influence of the middle-aged writers, or the fact that, even when most critical of society, these writers were less cynical than many of their readers. Thus, without necessarily intending it, the middle-aged writers became extremely useful to the leadership during the post-Mao transition. Any move toward silencing them had considerable costs. It is significant that when literary controls were tightened in 1980, the first thrusts were directed at young writers, not at the middle-aged generation.[63]

## The Admonition to Consider "Social Effects"

For a year after the famous Third Plenum of the Party Central Committee in December 1978, the main question in the political control of literature was how much the scope allowed to writers would expand. Some writers became activists in the push for expansion. They wrote stories with the conscious aim of "breaking into forbidden zones"; when necessary, they sought alliances with like-minded editors and officials in order to marshal the political clout necessary to make difficult breakthroughs. Their progress was uneven, varying over both time and place. Winter 1978–79 was a generally favorable time, as was autumn 1979,

63. The three plays singled out for criticism at the "Conference on Playwriting" in Beijing in February 1980 were all by young writers. Then, in the ensuing months, the unofficial and semiofficial (student) literary magazines — which were important outlets for young writers — were shut down by official order. It is true that Bai Hua, who was conspicuously criticized in 1981, was a middle-aged writer; but the Bai Hua campaign was so generalized in its thrust that it affected all generations in all branches of literature and art. Bai Hua's alleged "bourgeois liberalism" was not intended or perceived to be a charge against the middle-aged generation.

with a temporary setback intervening in spring 1979.[64] Certain provincial centers, including Hefei, Guangzhou, Shanghai, and Shenyang, also tended to be more favorable than other places, largely because of more open-mindedness among the political leaders in these provinces. The writers and editors who were most active in the movement to expand the scope for expression also monitored one another informally, lest one of them get too far ahead and risk being singled out as a negative example for the others. The national situation of the interplay among writers, editors, critics, officials, and readers was fascinating and extremely complex. But at the same time, its very fascination was in a sense detrimental to an artistic renaissance. Too much of the attention of writers was focused on the drama of the shifting borderlines of the writer's permissible scope. Too much energy was expended in scuffles to press the borderlines further back, rather than in reflection on the profounder issues.

The official policy that eventually clarified a new definition of the scope for writers also constricted it somewhat. Unveiled in March 1980 with the slogan "Writers Should Consider Social Effects" (of their work), the policy meant that writers must take partial responsibility for the ideas and the behavior of readers who have read their works. The campaign utilized some dramatic negative examples — for example, a young boy murders his sister with a candlestick after viewing some foreign films — in order to demonstrate what happens if writers are irresponsible. Actually, of course, writers seldom can know, let alone control, their effect on readers' ideas and behavior. Thus Chinese writers, after the relative freedom of 1979, found the new slogan somewhat irritating. To attempt to obey in a literal sense would, in the view of many, have confounded the creative process fatally. No serious writer, they pointed out, can compose a sentence while imagining how a range of potential readers might react to it; honest writing is too intuitive for that. *Linggan*, or inspiration, is the writer's most precious resource, and *linggan* comes only when it comes, which is seldom on cue. Zhang Jie can write a story in one day when she feels *linggan*, and not write for weeks when she does not.[65] She and Chen Rong both feel that creative inspiration is so impor-

---

64. The setback of spring, 1979 was highlighted by an article titled "Gede yu quede" (Praise or shame?), *Hebei wenyi*, June 1979, by a young man named Li Jian, who held that it is shameful to criticize the great socialist motherland without also, and more basically, praising her.

65. Interview, Beijing, 30 July 1980.

tant that, far from calculating the reader's response, they cannot even design the shape of a story in advance.[66] In writing their longer stories, they even feel a sense of curiosity about what might happen to their characters next. By contrast Wang Meng, who liked mathematics in his youth, said he sometimes conceives an abstract structure for a story in advance, and finds aesthetic satisfaction in realizing it on paper;[67] but preconceived structures of this kind also come from personal inspiration and not from a survey of possible reader responses. Even Liu Baiyu, a powerful literary official in the Chinese army and a staunch supporter of the "social effects" slogan, admitted the problem. "A writer cannot fashion his own social effects,' according to Liu.[68] Asked what, then, the admonition that writers "consider social effects" might mean, Liu responded that "the key question is the individual writer's standpoint. If he stands on the side of the people, his social effects will naturally be good. If he stands against the people, his effects will naturally be bad."

None of this means that Chinese writers did not respect their readers or care about relations with them. Most writers cared a great deal. The problem was the simple impossibility of "considering social effects" and writing at the same time. And for Chinese writers in 1979–80 there was an additional reason why the "social effects" slogan was difficult to accept. Although writers could get into trouble for saying so explicitly, and hence confined themselves to roundabout expression, many clearly worried that the "social effects" slogan was a partial reversion toward Cultural Revolution policies. Under Mao's slogan "Put Politics in Command," Chinese writers in the Cultural Revolution had had to subordinate all personal inspiration to a calculation of the political expediency ("social effects") of what they put on paper. Editings and reeditings by others insured the elimination of whatever germs of individual flair may have been left. By 1979 Chinese writers had been able, to a considerable degree, to give more emphasis to their own inspirations than to external criteria such as reader response, political guidelines, and the views of critics and editors. The "social effects" slogan now seemed once again,

66. Interview with Chen Rong, Beijing, 7 August 1980.
67. The examples Wang Meng gave me (interview, Beijing, 3 August 1980) were his stories "Yanjing" (Eyes, 1962), which was inspired by the theoretical question of whether the "modelness" of a model worker can be described by looking into the person's eyes; and "Hudie" (Butterfly, 1980), whose inspiration came from the famous quandary of the philosopher Zhuangzi, who wondered, after dreaming about a butterfly, whether he was Zhuangzi dreaming he was a butterfly or a butterfly dreaming it was Zhuangzi.
68. Interview, Beijing, 11 August 1980.

gently but clearly, to demand that a writer's pen listen to outer voices rather than inner ones.

Some of the bolder writers and editors countered the "social effects" slogan with a number of rhetorical questions. How is one actually to determine whether the "social effects" of a given work are good or bad? Is it not obvious that only the masses of readers can decide this question? And, furthermore, that they will need time to do it? What alternative does an editor have, therefore, but to publish a piece and wait for the people's verdict? And suppose some problem in society does crop up: why do writers always get the blame? Aren't politicians, educators, and many others at least equally responsible? How is it that one "incorrect" idea of a writer can sometimes get more attention than a proven case of large-scale corruption by an official? These various parries, clever though they were, did not make much difference in the eventual resolution of the "social effects" question. It gradually became clear that the call to consider social effects really had nothing to do with investigating reader response; it was simply an oblique way of warning writers to stay within the permissible scope.

## The Absence of Explicitly Dissident Literature

Many observers outside China expected that the post-Mao relaxation would lead to the emergence of a significant underground literature, perhaps something parallel to the dissident tradition in the Soviet Union. But very little of this sort actually appeared. There were, of course, a number of "unofficial" literary journals in 1979–80, such as *Today* (*Jintian*) in Beijing and *The Future* (*Weilai*) in Guangzhou, as well as semiofficial student literary magazines on about twenty college campuses. But it is a mistake to describe these (as they have often been described in Hong Kong, Taiwan, and elsewhere) as "underground": they were bought and sold openly, were not officially illegal, and were often seen by their youthful contributors as stepping stones to the regular official press. Truly "underground," hand-copied manuscripts did circulate in 1979–80, but most of these were escapist adventure stories, murder mysteries, and love stories left over from the Cultural Revolution years, when they apparently were numerous.

The lack of an explicitly dissident literature had complex causes. Certainly a major one was that literary control continued to be effected not primarily through a censorship system, which one could try to skirt, but through writers' fears of official criticism. With memories of the Cultural Revolution, when public criticism could spell terrible disaster, still freshly in mind, Chinese writers in 1979–80 were understandably chary of criticism, even in its most oblique forms. Keen sensitivity to the literary "weather" led writers to censor themselves. "There are no forbidden zones for writers," as Party Secretary-General Hu Yaobang was reported to have said in early 1980, "but each writer should impose forbidden zones on himself."[69] Even the boldest writers were emphatic that they were different from Solzhenitsyn and thus should not be labeled "dissident." This term, whose standard translation in Chinese is the somewhat clumsy and overly explicit *chi butong zhengjian zhe* (literally, "holder of a different political view") could spell big trouble.

But the incentives to publish in the official press rather than underground or in the unofficial publications were not only negative. The official press, in addition to offering more safety, offered more prestige and influence. Its much larger circulations were more attractive to young writers who wished to establish their names. Writers who wished to make social criticisms or to "speak for the people" also felt, no doubt correctly, that their criticisms had greater impact under official imprimatur. Even more fundamentally, Chinese national pride colored the question. There was a sense that the official press does represent China, like it or not, and that China is not a thing to be skirted. The option of writing for an audience outside the country, as Soviet dissidents have done, was farfetched.[70] An international reputation could be a wonderful laurel, but only on the head of a writer who had achieved prestige and influence in a Chinese context.

In addition, the availability of a subtler, less open kind of dissent "within the system" made explicit dissent partially irrelevant. With this option, writers could make their views fairly clear by identifying with certain groups and their favorite slogans ("emancipate the mind" and "let a hundred flowers bloom," for example, or, on the opposing side, "consider social effects" and "stick to basic principles"). Such identi-

69. China's grapevine often carries comments from high officials about literature. Though impossible to document, these comments sometimes travel with remarkable speed and uniformity across China, and often presage policies that later appear in print. Even if a quotation such as the one here attributed to Hu Yaobang is inaccurate, its effect in pressuring writers is still an important fact.

70. It apparently occurred only to a few explicitly political writers in the "democracy" movement, which foreigners were already watching with great curiosity.

fication offered a writer a modest platform as well as the security of identification with others. Before attempting to publish a potentially controversial work, a writer often sought patronage — popularly called "backstage support" — from an individual or group with power in the literary establishment. This support best came from officials, literary or nonliterary, but could also come from editors, publishers, or other writers with established status and connections. Whether one could publish a potentially controversial work or not sometimes turned on the balance of power between one's own backstage support and that of the opposing side. The relations between writers and their supporters could be of many kinds, varying widely in terms of both the power of the supporters and the explicitness of their support. But the overall effect, especially in a time of political relaxation, was to allow considerable scope for oblique dissidence, while at the same time inducing writers to temper their expression to accord with group positions. To the vast majority of Chinese writers and readers, this partially encoded dissent was more interesting — and much better known — than any "underground" works. In sum, China's ancient cultural assumptions that a shared ideology brings unity and strength, and that the written word, including literature, is the vessel of shared ideology, has combined with the communist system to make explicit literary dissent a most remote and difficult alternative. How long it will stay that way is hard to predict.

# WANG MENG

# Eye of the Night

With this story and another, "The Barber's Tale" (*Chinese Literature*, 1980, no. 7), the reputation of Wang Meng (b. 1934) has risen again, like a phoenix, from the ashes of a heroic but ruined career in 1957. In 1956, when he was but twenty-one, he rose spectacularly to national fame with the publication of "A Young Newcomer to the Organization Department," a story apparently inspired by a Russian novel by Galina Nikolaeva, *The Manager of a Machine Tractor Station and the Chief Agronomist*. Wang Meng's story describes an idealistic young Party member's first harsh contact with, and defeat by, entrenched bureaucratic lethargy, incompetence, and corruption. Its publication refueled a debate that had been smoldering since the publication in Yan'an, in the 1940s, of Wang Shiwei's "The Wild Lily" and Ding Ling's "In the Hospital" and "Thoughts on Woman's Day." The issues raised in Wang Meng's story, and the issue of an independent role for literature that its publication implied, continued to smolder through the early 1960s, until literature itself was extinguished by the Cultural Revolution. Meanwhile, Wang Meng began a twenty-year exile in China's far west by taking up residence in a Uighur peasant village, where he settled down to learn the Uighur language and do translation and some editing.

Translated and introduced by Donald A. Gibbs. Originally published in *Guangming ribao* (Beijing), 2 October 1979.

"Eye of the Night" reflects the author's persistence in trying to shine a critical, moral light into the darker corners of China's new society. The story, in its juxtapositions, its lyricism, and especially its lack of plot, draws close to techniques developed by Lu Xun — in "A Little Incident," for example. But Wang Meng's narrative strategy is more contemporary in its use of cinematic description and interior monologue. Wang Meng draws readers into his narrative by furnishing his scenes with familiar universals of contemporary Chinese urban experience: the sensations of those who have just returned to the city after long years in the countryside, the use of back-door "pull," intimidation by strange surroundings, the ubiquitous construction clutter and government indifference to pedestrian hazards; and the most common human universal of all, imaginative flights whereby one does one thing while thinking just the opposite.

# Eye of the Night

Street lights, of course, are all turned on at the same time. Chen Gao knew that, but he still had the sensation that they were two rows of lights shooting out from his own head, two long, long streams of light so long that you couldn't see the ends of them. The locust trees overhead cast stark shadows everywhere. People on the sidewalk waiting for the bus also cast their own shadows, multiple shadows at that, some dark, some light.

Trucks, automobiles, trolleys, bicycles, horns honking, chatter, laughter. It takes nighttime for a big city to show off its energy and its uniqueness. At first the lights are faint and scattered, but then those attention-getting neon signs and devices like the revolving poles in front of barber shops come on. And you see permanents, long hair, high heel shoes, low heel shoes, short, form-fitting dresses, and there is the scent of cologne and face cream. Cities these days, like women, are just beginning to pretty themselves up, and already there are people who won't sit still for it. That's interesting.

For more than twenty years Chen Gao had not been back to this big city. For over twenty years he had remained in a small, remote provincial town where one-third of the street lights never came on at all, and of the two-thirds that did have good bulbs in them, a third of them never got electricity. Was this because of negligence or because the electricity allocation was haywire? A small matter in any case, for nearly everyone there lived by the old pattern of rural life anyway, working from dawn to dusk. By six in the evening all the offices, factories, shops and restaurants were closed for the day. Evenings, people stayed home cuddling their babies, smoking, doing laundry, or saying the kinds of things that are no sooner said than forgotten.

The bus arrived, a blue one, the long, articulated type. The conductress was talking through the loudspeakers. People squeezed their way off, and then Chen Gao and others squeezed their way on. There were no empty seats, but still it felt good just to get on board. The conductress was a young woman with a healthy glow on her face and a bright, clear, resonant voice. In Chen Gao's small, remote provincial town she would surely be picked as the announcer for the culture troupe programs. In a series of smooth, practiced movements, she deftly pressed the switch to close the electric doors, snapped on her shaded, gooseneck lamp for checking tickets, punched several tickets. Then "snap" again — and off went the lamp. Street lights, tree shadows, buildings and pedestrians all flashed by the windows until another stop was reached. Her clear, resonant voice announced the station. "Snap," on went the lamp, and again the crowds surged off the bus and a new crowd promptly surged on.

Two youths in worker's garb were among those who got on, keyed up in animated discussion: ". . .the crux of it all is democracy, democracy, democracy. . ." Wherever he had gone throughout the entire week of his stay in the city this time, Chen Gao had heard people talking about democracy. It was about as common as people in his small, remote provincial town talking about a leg of mutton. This was probably because food supplies in the cities were relatively plentiful so no one had to worry much over a leg of mutton. "How enviable," Chen Gao thought, smiling to himself.

But of course there really is no conflict between democracy and mutton. After all, if there is no democracy, mutton reaching the lips can always be snatched away. While on the other hand, any democracy that cannot help people in small, remote provincial towns get more and meatier legs of mutton is just so much hot air. Chen Gao had come to the city to attend a conference on writing short stories and plays. After the downfall of the Gang of Four, Chen Gao had written five or six short stories that some had praised as showing greater maturity and versatility, while others said, and there were even more of these, that he still hadn't achieved the level of his work of twenty some years ago. Having to pay disproportionate attention to the leg of mutton no doubt was regressive for writers, although one has to admit that gaining an awareness of the crucial importance and urgency of mutton is, in itself, a great advancement and a matter of personal benefit. The train bringing him to the conference had halted at a tiny country station for an hour and twelve minutes because a man who had no proper identity cards but who did have a high-priced leg of mutton to peddle was crushed under the wheels while trying to get the best price for it. In order to get a head start on selling his mutton, the fellow ended up risking his life by ducking under the car in order to make a shortcut across the tracks. Just then the brakes had slipped a bit, causing the train to roll slightly, killing the poor fellow. The event weighed heavily on Chen Gao.

In the past Chen Gao had always been the youngest to attend this sort of conference; now he was somewhat older than most, and also somewhat more countrified, more weathered in complexion and less refined. When the comrades of the younger generation whose shoulders were so much broader than his — tall fellows with large, prominent eyes — delivered their speeches, they always expressed fresh, bold, sharply defined, lively new ideas. They could really make one see the light, make one feel good all over, really fire a person up, stir people to action. This resulted in literary issues somehow never quite getting discussed, and no matter how strenuously the conference organizers tried to lead the discussion to the central issues, everybody ended up talking mainly about how the Gang of Four had got their foothold, how to oppose feudalism, or else they talked endlessly about democracy, law, morality, and the social climate, about how more and more young people were gathering in the public parks to dance together to the accompaniment of electric guitars, and how the park administrators were trying every trick they could think of to ward off such calamities, everything from announcing over the p.a. system every three minutes that dancing was prohibited to collecting fines from the dancers. They even tried clearing out the park two hours before closing time.

Chen Gao also spoke his piece at the conference. Compared with the others, his statements were low-key, things like, "Bit by bit, from our own individual efforts, we can get things done." How marvelous, he mused, if but half the things presented in the conference could be realized. No, one-fifth. No, even a tenth! The thought roused Chen Gao to life, but then, it also gave him pause.

The bus reached the terminus, still jam-packed with passengers. Everyone freely ignored the conductress's plea to show tickets as they filed off the bus, despite the note of irritation and impatience that had crept into her voice. Along with others who must have been newcomers to the city too, Chen Gao conscientiously held his ticket up high for the conductress to see, even though she never so much as glanced at it. As he dismounted, he tried to press the ticket into her hand, but even then she didn't bother to take it from him.

Under the bright lights of the bus terminus, he took out a small address book, folded back its blue-gray plastic cover, checked an address, and then began asking directions. He directed his inquiry toward one person, but to his surprise quite a few people at once began volunteering directions. In this respect, at least, he felt that city people had managed to preserve some of the traditional old respect for courtesy. Thanking them, he took leave of the well-lighted terminus, and after several twists and turns came to a neighborhood that was a maze of new apartment buildings.

To say that it was a maze is not to imply any great complexity; indeed, the confusion was precisely because of its simplicity — each building looked exactly like its neighbor. The balconies were all piled up with things. Pale blue light from fluorescent tubes and yellow light from ordinary light bulbs shone out from all the closely clustered windows of all the buildings in exactly the same degree of brightness. Even the sounds coming from the windows were identical. Apparently an international soccer game was on television — the Chinese team must have just scored, for a roar rose simultaneously from the spectators at the stadium and from those watching at home; people screamed wildly as applause and shouting rose to a crescendo, like a giant wave. The veteran sports announcer Zhang Zhi, so well known to audiences, was also shouting for all he was worth, although, as everyone knows, any description is entirely superfluous at such times. From still other windows came the sounds of hammers pounding on doors, vegetables being chopped, and children scrapping, with the threatening voices of their parents in the background.

All these sounds, lights, and material things were crammed together in these apartment buildings, which stood like so many matchboxes put on their ends. This sort of congested living seemed strange to

Chen Gao; it was really hard to imagine what it would be like, living here, and it even struck him as a little comical. The tree shadows, reaching as high as the buildings themselves, spread a thin layer of mystery over the strange lifestyle he now beheld. In his small, remote provincial town, the most you would ever hear at night was the sound of a dog barking, and so familiar was he with all of them that he could tell from the bark alone what color the dog was and who it belonged to. Beyond that, in his town there was only the sound of heavily laden trucks passing through the night, their headlights piercing the eyes with such brilliance you were blinded for a time after they passed by. All the houses and buildings near the road vibrated each time a truck rumbled by.

Chen Gao began to feel some regret as he walked here amidst this maze of identical apartment buildings.

"I never should have left that long, brightly lit boulevard, never should have left that noisy, packed but still cheerful bus, or that street where everybody was striding so purposefully along the sidewalks. How fine all that was." And yet, here he was in a place like this. Better never to have left the government hostel in the first place. Could have argued the whole evening with those young fellows. All of them struggling to make heard his own particular remedies for dealing with the problems left behind by Lin Biao and the Gang of Four. Always talking of Belgrade, Tokyo, Hong Kong, and Singapore. After dinner they invariably were good for a plate of shrimp-flavored chips, a plate of peanuts, and they'd order up liters of beer, too, to relieve the heat and give a boost to the conversation. But instead, he had ridden a bus for heaven knew how long, getting who knew where, fumbling around trying to find who only knew what kind of a place, looking up God only knew what sort of person, and all in order to take care of something that was none of his business in the first place.

Actually, there was no mystery at all as to what he was doing; it was a perfectly legitimate thing, an obligation, in fact, but the trouble was, he was simply the wrong person for the job. For him to take on something like this, well, you might as well have him go on stage to do ballet, to be the prince in *Swan Lake*.

As he walked along, there was just the trace of a limp in his step, something you wouldn't notice unless you were looking for it — a memento left him from the "Sweep Away Everything" period.

These upsetting thoughts brought to mind the time twenty or so

years before when he had first left this city. On that occasion, too, there
had been the sad ache of being set apart from others. It was because he
had written several short stories that at the time had been regarded as
too outspoken, and that were now regarded as having been too soft spoken, something that put him on a swing oscillating for a long time between being, as Chairman Mao had put it, one of "the 95 percent of the
people who are good," and one of "the 5 percent who are bad" — a dangerous game, certainly.

According to what they had told him at the bus terminus, the very
apartment house he was now approaching was the one he was seeking.
Quite clearly, however, construction was still underway; it looked as
though they were preparing to lay some sort of pipes. No, not only pipes,
because there were some bricks, tiles, lumber, and stone there as well.
Maybe they were going to put up one or two single-storied buildings, or
maybe dining halls. And of course they quite possibly could be public
toilets. In any event, there was a wide trench that he probably could not
jump across, not that he would have had any trouble with it before being
"swept away." Better search around for a plank to bridge it with. He grew
impatient as he walked the length of the trench without finding any.
Clearly, he had come here the wrong way. Go around or jump? Well, he
wasn't that old. He backed off a few paces, and then, one, two, three . . .
Bad luck. Soft sand ruined his footing just as he jumped, landing him in
the bottom of the trench. Fortunately there were no hard or sharp ob-
jects there. Even so, it was ten minutes or more before he had fully
recovered from the pain and shock of his fall. Smiling, he brushed off
the dirt from his clothes and slowly inched his way up out of the trench.
Once out, his very first step put him in a deep puddle. He extricated his
foot with a squish, but not before his foot and sock both were soaked
through, feeling gritty, like eating rice with sand in it. As he looked up,
his eyes were drawn to a light bulb fastened to a crooked, leaning post
beside the building, and forlornly glowing orangeish red in the surrounding darkness. This electric light, at this place, at this time, struck
him as a tiny question mark, or maybe an exclamation point, written on
an enormous blackboard.

As he walked closer to the light, again a great wave of cheering
swelled out from the windows, and this time whistles were intermixed
with the cheers. Probably the foreign team had just kicked in a goal.
He drew closer to the entrance to check the number over the doorway

more closely, wanting to be absolutely sure he was at the right building. Still not satisfied, he hesitated at the entrance, hoping to confirm the address from a passerby, even though just standing there idly made him feel awkward.

Before he had left for the city, one of the comrades in his remote provincial town, one of the local leaders he felt particularly close to, and whom he respected very much, had taken him aside and given him a letter and instructions to look up a certain leader in the city. "We're old army buddies," he confided in Chen Gao. "In the letter, I've explained to him that our Shanghai sedan is the only car we have, and that it needs repairs. Our staff and driver have been all over trying to get parts, but from the looks of it, there's no way we can get it fixed anywhere in the whole province. What we need are a few key parts to get it going. This old army buddy of mine is in charge of an auto maintenance unit. He's always said, 'leave anything to do with auto repairs up to me,' so go look him up, and after you get in touch with him send me a telegram . . ."

It was just a very ordinary thing. You look up someone you know personally, an old friend, someone in a position of authority, and you do this because someone else who also is in a position of authority, and who is regarded in his own local unit as someone of good character and prestige, wants to repair a car belonging to his unit, and the car, of course, is in any event state property.

There was no reason why Chen Gao should not have acceded to this veteran comrade's request. As someone who well understood the importance of a leg of mutton, Chen Gao never really developed any doubts about the necessity of having to convey this letter to the comrade in the city. Since he was coming to the city anyway, he naturally felt an obligation to do his best for his local unit. But after having accepted the assignment, he began to feel awkward about it, as if he were wearing shoes that didn't fit or trousers of different colored legs.

It seemed almost as if the comrades in that small, remote provincial town could read Chen Gao's mind, for shortly after arriving in the city, he began receiving one telegram after another from them, urging him to hurry up with the job.

"Anyway, it's not for myself. Besides, I've never ridden in that sedan, nor will I ever ride in it after this," he had encouraged himself, while making his way along that great boulevard with its two long streams of light, after leaving those friendly fellow passengers on the bus, after leaving the bus terminus that was lighted as brilliantly as a stage, and while he was winding this way and that through the dark side streets, falling into the trench, crawling out, wiping the dirt off his clothes, filling his shoe full of mud. And now, at last, here he was.

After verifying the street address and the building number from two youngsters passing by, he mounted the steps to the fourth floor, located the correct door, and stood before it gathering himself together, catching his breath. Then he gave the door as soft a knock as he could, a delicate, civilized rap, one calculated to be just loud enough.

No response. Yet, there did seem to be some sound inside. He put his ear to the door. Music, it seemed like. Stifling the split-second's urge to blurt out in relief, "Well, no one's home," he forced himself to give the door another good knock.

His third knock brought a response. Footsteps approached, "thump, thump, thump," from inside. The built-in lock squeaked as it rotated. Finally, the door was opened by a young man with unkempt hair and a bare chest. He wore only a pair of cotton undershorts, which revealed the thighs. On his feet he wore a pair of foam-rubber thongs. His body glistened with the sheen of the well-fed.

In a tone of voice that barely concealed his impatience, the young man asked curtly, "Yeah?"

"I'd like to speak with Comrade — —," Chen Gao replied, giving him the name written on the envelope entrusted to him.

"He's not home," the young man grunted, and would have closed the door had not Chen Gao so earnestly stepped forward. Making an effort to speak the city dialect as perfectly and as politely as he could, Chen Gao made a brief self-introduction, concluding, "And are you, may I ask, a relative of Comrade — —?" (He figured the boy must be — —'s son, and in point of fact, it was quite unnecessary, in addressing a member of a generation so much younger than himself to use the honorific form "may I ask?")

"Might I venture to have a few words with you to explain why I have come, and might I prevail upon you to convey a message to Comrade — —?"

In the dark corridor, one couldn't actually see the expression on the young man's face, but one could sense that he frowned and hesitated before answering curtly, "Well, come in." Turning on his heel, he receded into the apartment without so much as nodding or beckoning to the visitor, the way nurses do when they tell a patient it's his turn to go in and have his tooth pulled.

Chen Gao followed the flop, flop, flop of the boy's thongs, his own steps sounding a squeak, squeak, as they filed down the pitch black hallway into the apartment. A door on the left, a door on the right. Quite a few doors, actually. Think of that, one door opening into so many other doors. One door was opened revealing a soft light within. Soothing music was playing, and there was the warm smell of liquor.

A coil-spring bed, an apricot-colored silk comforter, neither made up nor folded back, but all bunched up in a heap in the middle like a wheat dumpling. A floor lamp had a metal stand issuing a cold, repellent glitter. Through a half-opened door on the bedside stand, he could see ball-bearing door stops. Any number of friends in his small, remote provincial town had asked Chen Gao to try and get some door hardware like this, but he could never find them for sale anywhere. Back home, big wardrobe chests with doors that needed those things were just coming into fashion in a big way. Then his gaze shifted slightly to take in the wicker chairs, a lounge, a round table, and on it a fancy tablecloth exactly like the one in Hatoyama's dining room in the fourth act of the revolutionary opera *Red Lantern*.

A four-speaker portable tape recorder. Imported. Hong Kong music. Soft voices, clear pronunciation — exaggerated even — and sensuous. Whenever you hear that kind of mushy stuff, you can hardly keep from laughing. If you took that tape back to his small, remote provincial town and were to play it for them there, why, it would probably frighten them more than a cavalry charge. Of all the things in the room, it was only a common drinking glass half filled with water that struck Chen Gao as something familiar, something close to his own life. Seeing it was almost like running into an old hometown friend in a foreign country. Even if you never were so very close at home, or even if there had been some friction between you, under such circumstances you'd become thicker than ever.

When Chen Gao spotted a worn stool near the door, he pulled it toward him and sat down. His clothes were still soiled from his fall. He began explaining the purpose of his visit, but halted after two sentences, thinking the young man would lower the volume on the tape recorder. He stopped and started several times until he realized the young man had no intention of turning it down. The strange thing about it was this: Chen Gao, who had always been a pretty good talker, now seemed to have lost his tongue. He spoke haltingly, in disconnected phrases, and sometimes his speech went completely awry, as when he meant to say, "We want to ask Comrade — — to take care of this for us," but instead heard himself saying obsequiously, "We would be honored if you could do us the favor of looking into it," almost as if he were applying to the young man for a pay supplement. At one point he intended to say, "At the moment, I just want to get in touch with him," but instead blurted out, "I want to line things up with you." And even his speech had changed so that it sounded more like a dull blade sawing elmwood than his own voice.

Having spoken his piece, Chen Gao pulled a letter from his pocket. The young man remained slouched in his chair, motionless, while Chen Gao, who was about twice his age, had no choice but to take that letter, written by a comrade in a position of authority, in his own hand, in a far-off place, and carry it across the room to the young man. As he handed it to him, Chen Gao got a better look at the annoyed, arrogant, ignorant expression on his acned and pimpled face.

The young man opened the letter, scanned it, and smiled contemptuously, all the while tapping his left foot in rhythm with the beat of the Hong Kong music. Tape recorders and Hong Kong music were new to Chen Gao, but he by no means found them disgusting, nor was he necessarily against that style of singing. On the other hand, he wasn't convinced, either, that music of that sort amounted to anything, so his own face also bore a contemptuous expression on it, even though he did not realize it.

"This fellow Y— — (the comrade in a position of authority in Chen Gao's distant and remote district who had written the letter), is he really my father's old army buddy?" (The young man had not troubled to introduce himself, so one could not be completely sure whom the reference to "my father" actually indicated.) "How is it I've never heard my father mention him?"

Feeling the insult, Chen Gao replied, "You're pretty young, you know. It's possible your father never told you about . . ."

"My father says anytime someone wants a car repaired he becomes an old 'army buddy,'" the young man interrupted.

"You mean to say your father doesn't know Y— —? Why, he went to Yan'an in 1936. Last year he published an article in *Red Flag*.... His older brother is the area commander in Z — — district . . ."

Chen Gao, despite himself, blurted out these credentials too hastily, and particularly, the minute he brought the prominent general into it, he suddenly felt his eyes blur and became conscious of beads of sweat running down his spine.

This time the contempt on the young man's face was twenty times what it had been before. Nor could he keep from laughing out loud. Chen Gao, feeling disgraced, looked down at his own feet.

"Let me put it to you this way," the young man said, rising to his feet, adopting a posture of authority. "If you want to make a deal these days, it takes two things. First, you've got to come up with something. What do you propose to offer?"

"Propose to offer . . . ? Why, I suppose . . ." Chen Gao replied, speaking more to himself than to the young man, "I suppose we have legs of mutton . . ."

"Mutton won't do," he scoffed, once again laughing.

By now, however, his contempt had run its course and had become pity.

"The second thing — and let me put it to you straight — you need to know the ropes on something like this. You don't really need to go through my father at all. If you can come up with something to offer, and if you have someone who knows how to handle it, it doesn't make any difference whose name you use to pull strings." Then he added, "My father's been sent to Beidaihe [an exclusive resort — Tr.] on the coast for a while." He was careful not to say "taking it easy."

Chen Gao found himself at the door unable to recall just how he had left the room. Just before stepping out into the hall, he hesitated and instinctively cocked his ear to one side. The tape recorder was now playing real music, a Hungarian waltz. In his mind he envisioned a single leaf dancing in circles over a dark blue alpine lake surrounded on three sides by tall, snow-covered peaks; beside the lake was his small, remote provincial town. A white swan had settled in peaceful repose on the surface of the lake.

Chen Gao raced through the dark hall of the apartment building and plunged down the stairway. Was the pounding in his ears his footsteps or his heart? Once clear of the building, he again saw above him that dim light bulb shining out like a question mark, or was it an exclamation point? But now it suddenly appeared bright red, like a devil's eye, a hideous eye able to metamorphose its beholder, reducing birds to rats, horses to gnats.

Chen Gao easily leaped the ditch. The television announcer was now speaking in a relaxed, intimate voice of the next day's weather forecast. In no time he reached the bus terminus. As usual, a large crowd had gathered to wait for the bus. A group of women night-shift workers were noisily chattering about the bonuses at their factory. One couple waited for the bus side by side, arms around each other. If the old fogey moralist "Mr. Siming" in Lu Xun's story "Soap" were to see this today, he would suffer yet another shock at the decline of Confucianism.

Chen Gao climbed into the bus and took a position near the door. This time the conductress was a woman already past youth. She was so bony and spare you could almost see her skinny shoulder blades protruding inside her thin blouse.

Through twenty years of frustration, twenty years of remoulding, Chen Gao had learned many valuable lessons and had also lost certain things that he should never have lost. Through it all, however, he had never lost his love for bright lights, his affection for night-shift workers, his love of democracy, bonuses, legs of mutton ... Suddenly the bell sounded, and shsss..., the three doors closed, one after the other; the tree shadows and street lights swiftly receded as the bus picked up speed ...

"Tickets? Tickets anyone?" But no sooner said, than "Snap!" out went her goosenecked lamp, long before Chen Gao could reach for his change.

"She must think all her passengers are night-shift workers with monthly passes," mused Chen Gao.

## WANG ZHECHENG
## and WEN XIAOYU

# Nest Egg

Writers everywhere are urged to write about what they know best. In the China of Mao Zedong's era, writers were urged to write about workers, peasants, and soldiers — subjects they certainly did not know best. During the thaw that began in 1979, when writers felt free to write about what they did know best — the life of urban intellectuals — the quality of literature rose dramatically. The present story is one of the best from this genre.

Much of the story is concerned with pride, both personal and national, and the facade that pride requires: the facade that all marriages show to the outside world, and the facade shown by China to outsiders. The story takes readers behind these facades so that they will not be like the overseas Chinese scholar in the story who, the narrator says, gets "a general impression but never really sees anything." Outsiders, he says, "can look all they want, but they're still blind to what's really going on."

There is an authenticity to the events and the dialogues in this story that has not been seen in Chinese literature for decades.

The authors are a husband-and-wife team. Both are 1960 graduates of Beijing University's Department of Chinese, where they studied under the famous fiction writer Wu Zuxiang. They now work in Huhe-

Translated and introduced by Donald A. Gibbs. Originally published in *Shouhuo* (Shanghai), 1980, no. 2.

hot, Inner Mongolia. Wang Zhecheng (b. 1936) is chief editor of the literary magazine *Grassy Plains (Caoyuan)*, and his wife, Wen Xiaoyu (b. 1938) is under consideration for promotion to associate professor in the Inner Mongolian Teacher's College.

# Nest Egg

Do you mean to say you really think there is something about our life that could possibly be of interest to a writer? There's really nothing to write about, you know. Really. Nothing at all. People of our generation, middle-aged teachers, I mean, are supposed to be the pillars of today's society, but we don't have much to show for ourselves, I'm afraid. We're certainly not in the same league with the great mathematician Chen Jingrun, nor can we match what the older generation achieved in their day. We're more like fruit that has frozen on the vine before it's ripened; and we probably never will get a chance to ripen. In ten years of turmoil, who hasn't lost something? We lost time, energy, our dreams, our enthusiasm . . .

I'll never forget back when we all had just graduated from college and I had just published two articles in an important national journal. Back then I seemed so full of promise, and after the articles were published I think people began to see me as someone rather special. But now? Well, I suppose all of us are in the same boat now. What do I teach? I teach classical Chinese literature, Tang and Song [Sung] Dynasties mainly. My lifestyle? Very simple: work, study, family. As for work, I teach two classes a week, do some advising, prepare my lectures. Occasionally students come to my home for a chat, but more often I visit them in their dormitory. It seems that except for three meals a day, a few chores around the house, and a very short time for sleep, I'm always at work. My wife always says that when our children some day write *their* version of "My Father's Back,"[1] it will be a description of skinny shoulders tensely hunched over a desk and a head buried in work. As for my studies, well, I read the daily newspaper, do the weekly political session, and study Japanese on my own. My family? Well, my wife is a secondary

---

1. A poignant autobiographical essay by Zhu Ziqing (1898–1948) in which he describes his last, lingering image of his father. Translated in *Chinese Literature Monthly*, January 1958.

school teacher, and she was also picked to be a homeroom teacher, which keeps her really busy and just wears her out.[2]

We have two "little devils" at home, too. Twins, in the fourth grade. We had an older daughter, but during the Cultural Revolution she fell sick, and for various reasons she just didn't get medical attention in time so she died. Anyway, we've ended up with two frisky little imps who are into everything.

So what else is there? Well, we have our pleasures and our problems, right? For me, the most pleasant part of a day is the deep stillness that comes late at night when the children are asleep, when all the little chores of the day are out of the way, and I can just sit down with a cup of tea, light up a cigarette and get on with my writing. I am doing a treatise called *The Underlying Basis for Literary Florescence in the Tang Dynasty*.

My problems? Well, I'll say this, there's no dearth of problems. As the saying goes, "Time grays the hair and grieves the soul." But my problems are all of the "chicken feathers and onion skins" type, as we say. They don't amount to anything special. I mean, who wants to hear about everyday things like soy sauce and salt?

I suppose the way some people see it, there is no connection between my kind of work and the Four Modernizations. But I feel my work can help somewhat in fostering patriotism. Judging from experience with my own students, I feel that young people today need some strengthening in their patriotism. Of course, one doesn't expect love of one's country simply to spring up from a pile of ancient texts. Certainly not. But you have to admit that an understanding of, and an enthusiasm for, a great cultural tradition constitutes a vital element in patriotism. You'll recall that Lenin himself warned that no amount of sloganeering was enough to establish communism. A communist, after all, can only be made by enriching the brain to the fullest extent with all the precious knowledge that has been produced by human creativity. Why is it that my generation of intellectuals, throughout this most devastating era, this terrible, terrible time, never lost its faith in our country or our people? For one thing, it's because we understand the long progression of our national culture, and because we bear in our hearts the memory of our historical poets. Men such as Qu Yuan, Sima Qian, Li Bo, Du Fu, Lu You, and Xin Qiji. A nation that has such a high level of cultural attain-

2. Homeroom teachers are responsible for students' moral instruction, including nearly all areas of a student's life both in class and out.

ment simply cannot atrophy or perish! And what's more, now that we have overthrown the Gang of Four, we must raise the cultural and scientific levels of all our people, for after all, people who know nothing of their own nation's history and civilization are hardly worthy of that nation's citizenship! Now don't get me wrong. I know my place. We're all like ants; we just move whatever little piece we can. Many ants together can move a flower, and if there are enough ants, then there will be enough flowers moved to decorate a whole garden. But look how I've digressed!

As for my home life, well, certainly a tempest has been stirred up. My wife has left me, dumping both boys in my lap, which means I have to do the laundry while I'm talking to you. Runs me ragged keeping up with things. You'll just have to excuse me. The worst of it is, work on my treatise has been slowed down by all this, but that can't be helped. Nor do I blame my wife. You see, I hurt her feelings, and now I have to pay for it. If you're interested, I'll tell you about it, but I'll have to begin at the beginning . . . Let's see now . . . Oh yes, *that* was the day it all began.

That was the day I nearly ran right into Jiang Wenhao downtown, face to face. I had heard he was back, but we hadn't actually met again. He used to be my best friend, during our university days, but now he was an American citizen with a professorship in Asian studies at some Canadian university. I spotted him from quite a distance, and even though we hadn't seen each other for all those years, I still recognized him right off. He was taller than everybody around him and heading right in my direction. Quick as anything, I ducked into a shop so he'd go on by without seeing me. Sure enough, before long he went right on by. I could see him clearly through the shop window, still the same as ever, very smartly dressed, even debonair, in a tailored, light khaki-colored plaid wool suit. He had kept himself in good shape and looked much younger than he was. Just like all the foreign tourists, he had a colorful bag of some synthetic material slung from his shoulder, and he was laughing and chatting as he walked, stretching his neck as he gawked this way and that, strolling down the sidewalk.

We had shared the same dormitory room all the way from secondary school through university, one of us in the upper bunk and the other in the lower. We always called each other by our nicknames. He called me Ahmao and I called him Haohao. He left China in 1957. Seems his grandfather in Indonesia left some money, and he had to go there to get the inheritance. His departure caused a big row between us. I called him a traitor, and I guess you could say there was a complete rupture between us after that. After he left, we never communicated. When Suharto became openly hostile to China, I worried about his safety, but later I heard from his aunt that he had already left Indonesia for America, that he'd probably got his degree already, and that he was going ahead with an academic career.

Actually, this was the second time I had avoided meeting him. The first time was in 1974, when he had returned to China to visit his relatives and was making a lot of inquiries about me, or so I heard. But since I had made some complaints about conditions at that time and had expressed opposition to our "three drops of water,"[3] and also because of my past friendship with Haohao, I was put under investigation. Then, when the "old crime" of knowing Haohao and the "new crime" of criticizing things were added together, I ended up branded a counterrevolutionary. I had to sweep hallways and empty latrines. Anyway, because of all this, no one told him anything about me when he made all his inquiries. That time, too, this very same street was where I ran into him. That time I avoided him by a much narrower margin, but I was really on my toes and ducked into a shop in the nick of time without his seeing me. Just like all the foreign visitors who come here, there he was, parading down the street, his eyes sweeping out over the scene every which way, getting a general impression but never really seeing anything—they can look all they want, but they're still blind to what's really going on.

Good. I made it. He went right on by, which meant I could slip out unseen. It was only then that I realized I had ducked into a shop selling ladies' wear. All kinds of garments were on display, and in all colors, from summer skirts to winter coats. A large crowd of women had clustered around the sales counter buying black woolen coats, trying them on and concentrating on making the right selection. I, too, began working my way into the crowd. My wife had been wanting a short coat like this for a long time. In the change of seasons from fall to winter, when it was too early to wear a hooded jacket, and when a thin padded jacket wasn't warm enough, she really needed a coat just like this. Especially when she went to school just after dawn to look after the self-study students. I looked them over closely. The material in the coats was quite

3. Mao's wife Jiang Qing (Chiang Ch'ing). "Three drops of water" refers to a graphic component in the Chinese character for Jiang.

nice, and they were the style in fashion just then. You had to admit they weren't priced too high, either, at forty-five dollars. But I realized she would never consent to spending that much money. These have been very lean years for us. You know as well as I do that virtually everyone in China in this day and age is in the same fix. That time in 1957, when they were after "rightists," we had no sooner graduated from college than they came up with the pay reduction for college graduates. They said at the time that this was to avoid any reemergence of anti-Party, anti-socialist "rightists," and was supposed to narrow the gulf between intellectuals and the worker-peasant class. So they cut our pay from forty-one dollars per month to thirty-seven. Our pay went down and household costs went up. On top of that, my wife's elderly mother was sickly and often needed help to tide her over. So, in spite of tightening our belts and cutting back on everything else, we had to borrow every month just to get through. The children's needs, apart from the basics of food and clothing, were also hard to satisfy. But even so, we did manage to come up with a tiny little nest egg. For this, we have our two little rascals to thank. Throughout the whole year, those two little brothers were able to overcome all kinds of simply unimaginable temptations, like not having so much as a taste of a popsicle even in the hottest weather. Every day they took a glass bottle of drinking water to school with them instead. Once, when something was being done to some steam pipes near our dormitory and the road was all torn up and rough, the younger boy was a bit careless and bumped his jar into one of the concrete hatch-covers. "Crack!" the bottle smashed to pieces, water came pouring out, and the jagged glass cut a long gash in his hand. Right away blood oozed out, and he began to scream. By the time he got home, with his brother's help, he was in such a state that one look at him drained all the blood right out of his mother's face. Well, when we finally got to the bottom of it, you can imagine how we felt as parents. We cleaned his cut, got some medicine on it, and bandaged it up, all the while blaming ourselves for what had happened.

"All right, enough is enough. From now on you boys won't have to carry water to school. We'll go back to giving you each ten cents a day spending money so you can buy yourselves popsicles when you're thirsty, how's that?" So saying, I pressed a ten-cent coin into each of the boys' palms.

"No, Papa! No! I don't want it!" the older twin protested. No matter how we coaxed him, he just wouldn't take it. He pointed to his brother and said, "He cut his hand — so he can eat popsicles if he wants. I'm still going to take a jar of water to school." At this the younger boy, ten-cent piece held tight in his squeezed little fist, looked first at me, then at his mother, and finally at his brother. He hesitated a bit, then looked up at me with his little face still wet with tears, and said, "Find me another jar, Papa. I'll take a jar to school too."

So that's how it was, all year long. All of us struggling to save money so that now, well, we've finally got fifty-seven dollars saved up in the bank.

I'm not ashamed to say that this tiny little nest egg of ours has played an enormous role in our planning. If any of these plans had been carried out, well, we'd have spent that fifty-seven dollars many times over. For example, I wanted to get my wife and the boys some presentable clothes; my wife, on the other hand, wanted to get some furniture. Really, you know, we don't have even the crudest kind of a dresser. For twenty years now, we've just been stuffing clothes into cardboard boxes, and we really can't keep on like this. And those two little tyrants of ours? Well, long ago they set up a howl for a television set, you know, just one of those little black and white sets with a small screen. They made it plain to their mother and father that this was money they themselves had been saving up, so in the future we simply had to keep from spending it until there was enough for a television set for them! It was true that they had scrimped for it all right; and then it was also true that when they went to someone else's place to watch television, it tended to crowd people up, which was an imposition we felt awkward about.

The minute I thought of their so highly cherished hopes and their stern admonitions to us, I simply had to turn from the coat counter and walk away.

Why didn't I want to meet Haohao? Do you think it was fear of that old stigma attaching to those with so-called "foreign connections," the thing that got so many of us in trouble during the Cultural Revolution? No, of course not. Not any more. And I, for one, firmly believe that no civilized country is afraid of its people making friends with people of other countries, not to mention the fact that scholarly exchanges and contacts are useful for the Four Modernizations. All right, so then it must be the fact that I can't put out of mind that last rupture of ours, that I continue to hold a grudge. Well, that's not true either. After all, our two lives are like two widely separated highways, each going in its own separate direction, so I really no longer have any strong feelings one way or the other about him. Then it must be envy for the fact that he has established a reputation for himself and has something to show for himself, right? A case of being ashamed of myself, right? Well, perhaps, but that's not the whole story. My feelings are very complicated, and while I don't want to admit it, still, I must face the fact squarely that the main reason why I don't want to see him is simply that I don't want him to see how miserable our household is. And I especially don't want him to see my wife, because she's the one Haohao really wants to see. She's the reason he has tried so hard to look me up.

Ah! Twenty years ago, just think what my wife was like then!

It was winter and the lake on our campus had frozen over, signaling the beginning of the skating season. To those of us who were students up from the south, people gliding about on that mirror-smooth surface seemed like magic. As soon as classes were out, we'd break for the skating rink on the pond as fast as we could. The loudspeakers would play a waltz or some light music, and, well, the whole mood was both exciting and soothing all at the same time. Students would skate by, bent over sharply at the waist, hands joined behind their backs, skating vigorously, one pursuing the other, racing round and round in broad, sweeping circles. Others would skate in pairs, hand in hand, performing all kinds of graceful maneuvers in the center of the lake, even leaps and pirouettes. But so far as that kind of skating is concerned, I was a hopeless case. I wobbled and swayed even when I was just standing still on the ice, and made an awkward spectacle of myself when I tried to take steps. I'd lose control completely, getting into people's way and even crashing into them. Often enough, I'd end up sprawled on the ice, flat on my back, staring at the sky amidst a roar of laughter from the crowd.

Haohao had done some roller-skating in Shanghai before, so he caught on to it quickly. Before you knew it, he was using figure skates and had become one of the stars of the rink. One day, I don't know why, but I suppose he just took pity on me or something, he came over to give me a hand. He was very enthusiastic about it, putting his shoulder right next to mine and skating very slowly and gently. Just as I was really concentrating on getting the hang of it, going along one step, one push at a time, along came a girl gliding like a swallow, right between us, catching me completely by surprise and scaring the wits out of me. The minute I lost concentration, my feet got tangled and down I went in an awful clatter, flat on my back. Haohao almost went down, too, but he regained his balance with a lot of arm cranking, the way a big bird looks when it's startled into flight. Of course, all this got everyone around us laughing. The girl skated back around to us again, smiling mischievously and saying over and over again, while she helped me to my feet, "Oh, I'm sorry, I'm so sorry."

Haohao and I both were struck dumb. The girl was simply dazzling. So slender, lithe, and agile. She was wearing a bright red sweater made of nice thick wool, and a bright red skating cap. Her cheeks were flamered and her eyes sparkled like stars. No, she wasn't really a girl at all, she was more like a ball of fire, a bolt of lightning, a bouquet of flowers!

She apologized, and then, seeing us both so dumbfounded, simply smiled at us sweetly as she was swept into the circle of swift skaters as if by magnetic pull.

We were unusually slow leaving the ice that day. By the time Haohao and I went over to turn in our skates, the gym was deserted. We went up to the skate check-out window and again were put under a spell. There in the square outline of that window was the charming face that had so bewitched us, looking exactly as if it were a framed portrait.

"Don't just stand there! Hand in your skates!" she demanded, flipping onto the counter the last two student I.D. cards from her check-out board.

We took care of the forms for checking the skates in, but as luck would have it, the laces on our skates had become a tangled mess. She fixed us with a sort of amused look while we worked frantically to untangle them, feeling pretty uncomfortable, I must say.

It turned out that she was the daughter of the gym custodian. Her father had to leave early that day, so she took over his job of dealing with stragglers like us. She was a student in a teacher's college and was two years junior to us. She also had a really lovely name: Ye Ru-ying,[4] which means, as you know, Sparkle.

It goes without saying that both of us fell head over heels in love with her. What a time we had those days when the two of us were both doggedly pursuing her at the same time — quietly, each in his own way. In agony, ecstasy, and despair, with ever rekindling hope, never abandoning courage, ever persisting with fresh vitality, full of a kind of conquering, demanding, competitive sort of spirit, we pursued her.

4. Here spelled in exception to standard *pinyin* for aesthetic reasons. —*ed.*

Haohao's advantages were all too apparent. He was good-looking and charming, and he could take her out on the ice and do all sorts of dazzling things there with her, attracting quite a crowd of envious admirers around them. He was able to take her to dances on weekends, and could keep her whirling and twirling right from the beginning of the music to the end, always overflowing with the enthusiasm and energy of youth. I couldn't do any of that. I was just too awkward, but I couldn't bear not to watch them either. Whenever this happened, I would always force myself to endure the enormous, indescribable pain it caused, and I would keep quietly to myself, off to one side, until the music came to an end.

Once, right out of the blue, she came to borrow a book from me, saying she had become attracted to Tang and Song poetry. This, for me, was an unexpected windfall. I can't begin to tell you how elated I felt. It was just as if some great treasure had been handed to me. I poured out to her everything I knew about Du Fu, spouting off some of his greatest lines. Oh, things like:

> Behind those lofty, vermilion gates,
>> fine wines and meat grow rancid,
> While on the nation's roads lie bones,
>> of those who die of cold.

And Bai Juyi's:

> Could I but command a fur so huge,
>> that within its mighty folds,
> Our frozen homeland warm shelter find,
>> from all the surrounding cold.

And some patriotic lines from Lu You:

> My whole life through I've hardened my heart
>> to naught but steel and stone,
> Abandoning home, forgetting my family,
>> and all for the sake of the nation.

And:

> To perish in battle!
>> Is the stuff true men are made of.
> How shameful am I,
>> To come back home and live with wife and child.

I kept reciting lines from these great poets who had wept for our country and for our people, and, well, I was so carried away my eyes welled up with tears as I recited them to her.

"Aren't there other kinds of poems you could recite to me?"

"What kind do you have in mind? Do you think anyone in Tang and Song literature is better than they?"

"Well, I was thinking of lighter things like music lyrics from the Tang or the Five Dynasties, or some Song verses. Couldn't you let me hear some lines from Zhou Bangyan? Oh, and there's Chin Shaoyou, and there's . . ."

I exploded before she had a chance to go on.

"But all that stuff is called 'carving of insects'! It's . . . it's so insignificant compared with the others. Frivolous! Don't you see?" I was practically shouting at her. My voice had become thin and high-pitched. I had begun to stammer and must have sounded awful. I couldn't help it. It always happens to me when I get emotional. Usually I can control it, but this time I was so worked up that, well, it happened, and it *would* happen with her, of all people.

"But there's that old saying," she said,

> "Writing accords with the times,
>     the right work for the right time.
> Songs and poems accord with occasions,
>     the right work for the right occasion."

"But . . . But . . ." I stammered, almost shouting, "Du Fu, Bai Juyi, Lu You . . . Why . . . Why . . . Their works were the best . . . the best that realism has to offer, perfectly in accord, perf . . . Their poetry not only gives us a strong feeling for their times, but also reminds us to think of the common people, to think of the whole nation. It, it, well, it's elevating, that's what it is! Elevating! Their poems are the distillation of our great culture, the essence of Tang and Song literature. Anyone who masters this poetry can say he commands the mainstream of Chinese literature for the whole epoch, don't you see? Any other view of it," and here I lapsed into my classical way of talking, "just fails to distinguish the primary from the ancillary . . . ignores the root to cherish mere twigs."

Ru-ying heard me out, all the way to my "roots and twigs" doctrine, then nodded her head as if in assent. But then she suddenly shook her head, heaved a sigh, and turned to leave.

Soon after that, Jiang Wenhao went abroad. There were quite a few reasons behind his decision to leave. My attitude toward leaving China is the same now as it was then: no one should leave his native country at just any time and in any way he pleases, for no matter how poor his country may be, how backward, no matter how unstable and unpredictable things may be, one's country, after all, is a mother. It has given us life, has nurtured us all these years, and it's a real flesh-and-blood mother to us. So no matter what takes place, we should always stand by her. But of course none of what I had to say had the slightest effect on Jiang Wenhao. The only thing that made it hard for him to decide whether to go was Ru-ying. If Ru-ying loved him and had agreed to leave with him, he would have left without a moment's hesitation. If Ru-ying had declared her love for him and had begged him to stay, then I suppose he would have stayed.

In those days, I was really on edge, worried that Ru-ying would be taken away. But at the same time, I was paralyzed from doing anything about it, since I had no right whatsoever to interfere. It dragged on like that, day after day. Every day Haohao would go to see Ru-ying, be it at home or at school, and every day he would return very late at night, sometimes elated, sometimes dejected. All this time, I never dared to ask how things were going, but in my heart I suffered the awful torment that only those who have suffered unrequited love can understand. It would be very difficult for an unsophisticated young woman like Ru-ying to withstand the kind of sudden pressure that Haohao put on her. Finally, I resolved to put the whole thing behind me. I would forget all about this adorable but ephemeral illusion. I would bury myself in studies; I would start all over again to make a new life for myself.

Then, late one night when I was, as usual, the last to leave the library and head back to the dormitory, I was surprised to see a figure standing in the shadow of a fir tree beside our dormitory. Seeing me approach, the figure stepped out onto the pathway and stood there, bathed in the moonlight, quietly waiting for me. I couldn't believe it. Ru-ying! Had she come to say farewell? When I saw how her eyes sparkled in the moonlight, my heart seemed to jump right into my throat. I even stopped breathing.

"Why haven't you come to see me?"

"Wh . . . Why . . ." For a moment I couldn't find anything to say.

"Cast me off, just like that, making a girl have to withstand pressure like that all alone. I suppose *that's* your idea of how the great patriot-poet

who 'thinks of the nation, thinks of the common people' is supposed
to act?"

"But, I . . ."

"*You*! You sure know how to cause someone a lot of grief, that's
for sure."

"Ru-ying, listen to me . . ."

"I'm not in the mood to listen to anything right now." Then she
lifted her gaze to meet mine and searched my face with those sparkling
eyes of hers. Silently, two lines of hot tears streamed down her cheeks.

"What do you mean, Ru-ying?" This was the first time I had ever
seen her like this, so emotional and so hurt. "Tell me, Ru-ying, tell me,
what's come over you?"

"Up to now I just couldn't make up my mind . . ."

"About what, Ru-ying?" Steeled for her reply, my voice lowered almost to a whisper, and was quaking.

"I . . . I just couldn't make up my mind whether you were willing to
teach me Tang and Song poetry or not."

"Good heavens, Ru-ying . . ." I rushed to her with my arms outstretched, heedless of the books held under my arms that now clattered
to the ground. "Oh, Ru-ying, stop tormenting me. Whatever makes you
think you'd have to ask me? Of course I will!"

She drew me close to her and we hugged as tightly as we could. To
this day I can still hear her soft whisper in my ear, "I've already told him
. . . that I've given my heart to you . . . that I'll always be yours . . ."

All of this quickly slipped into the past. Who would have thought
that twenty-two years would pass so quickly? It's like the old poem describing the poet who labored all through the night unmindful of the
time until he saw the dawn:

> Searching for phrases, choosing just the right words,
>     polishing, polishing, his carvings of insects.
> Then lo! Framed by the window, the moon hung suspended,
>     a frail thin bow of silver white jade.

So, here we are, entering the autumn of our life.

Ru-ying has suffered a great deal as my wife. After the Cultural
Revolution broke out in 1966, it was discovered that some of us had de-
veloped into "incipient revisionists" in the seventeen years since New
China's founding. Suddenly, it seemed there was a poised sword above

our heads and thin ice beneath our feet. Our days were filled with tension and fear. We suffered many setbacks because of my ineptitude, and several times I nearly brought ruin down on our heads. It was right after the first time I was paraded through the streets to a struggle session and put in solitary confinement that our baby daughter died. This affected Ru-ying far too much. Her face lost its luster after that, and all the sparkle left her eyes; she had aged overnight, it seemed. Later the twins were born. Things were bad for us financially, and then there was all the housework to do, so she became terribly fatigued from overwork. I have to confess that I felt very remorseful about all this, and so the fact is, you see, it was precisely because Ru-ying was so far from her old self that I couldn't bear to face Jiang Wenhao again.

Ru-ying has never blamed me for what's happened to us. She's been very clear-minded about it all, about where we've stood, I mean, and the situations we've been in, realizing that in China how one fares is not related in any way to how hard a person works. There wasn't anything at all I could do to improve our miniscule income. But as time wore on, and with day after day of strategies for coping, and after all the tension over whether we were going to make it through or not, well, it wore on us, and inevitably it ruined her good disposition. She became edgy and impatient. Flaring up at me over the slightest little thing became common practice. Once, she really flew off the handle just because I happened to have bought a few too many books and somehow managed to upset her careful budget. Another time I wasn't cautious enough when I went out and a pickpocket got away with some pocket money. She cried over that. But the most serious instance came just six months ago when that "40 percent policy" went into effect, giving promotions to just 40 percent of the faculty and staff. There were five of us in exactly the same set of circumstances, but since we were given only two slots for promotion, I naturally let the others have it. I mean, how could I not let them have it? We were all classmates, we had all been colleagues for a long time, they were older than I was, and they were somewhat more hard-pressed than I. We all work so hard it's practically impossible to say who's accomplished a little more or who's got the edge on anyone else. What I did was perfectly rational, so my mind was at ease about it. Simply put, it was the right thing to have done. But I hadn't counted on how outraged Ru-ying would become over it, what with her crying, screaming at me, and really having it out between us something awful.

"My, aren't you generous, I must say! I mean we've gone twenty years now without a raise! Other people see a chance like this and they can't wait to get in there and fight for it, but no, not you!"

"Fight? You think I can fight with these people?"

"Even if you don't put up a fight, that still doesn't mean you have to go right out and hand it to them, does it?"

"But Ru-ying, it all was so clear-cut . . ."

"Clear-cut, was it? Prices going up all the time, are you clear on that? If a person doesn't get a raise then it's the same as getting a cut in pay, that's what's clear-cut!"

"Ying, dear, what's got into you? Just for the sake of a paltry four or five dollars a month . . ."

"So I've become nasty, right? Petty, right? I'm so nasty and mean that all I care for is money, right? Well, I'll tell you something. That four or five dollars is very important to me. Very important."

"Ying, dear, suppose I smoke less. How about that?"

When she saw I had no fight left in me, she fell silent, maybe feeling sorry for me. And for herself, too. Then she threw herself down on the bed and began sobbing.

I went over and stood by the window, complete turmoil inside me. The image of the writer in Lu Xun's famous story "Happy Family" some-how came to mind — that poor fellow who found his attention distracted by the stack of cabbage in the room where he was trying to write crea-tively — and I just figured that the girl to whom I used to recite some of the most beautiful lines in Chinese poetry was gone forever. We used to savor Li Shangyin's line, addressed to his old companion:

> When shall we two
> Trim the candle again
> In the wee early hours of the morn,
>
> Talking all night
> in a tiny thatched hut
> on the forested mountain slope?

But to be honest with you, right then and there I must have puffed away a half a pack of cigarettes, one after the other. So far from cutting down, I was becoming more extravagant.

So you see, what point would there be in seeing Jiang Wenhao again?

But as it turned out, ducking him on that one chance encounter wasn't the end of it. Two days later, I received a formal written invitation.

The Pleasure of Your Company is Requested on _____ month, _____ day, at 5:00 P.M. for a Reunion Banquet with Classmates at _____ Restaurant. Please bring your wife.

Jiang Wenhao

When Ru-ying saw this invitation, she was indescribably happy.

"We'll go. But of course we'll go! It's been such a long time since we've seen him, and now that he's an overseas Chinese scholar we'll have to see what's become of him."

But that very night she changed her mind completely. I watched as she opened the cardboard box she kept her clothes in, and one after another flung them onto the bed. Then, plumping herself down, she stared vacantly.

"So now what is it?"

"I've nothing at all to wear. They're all so old."

One by one she held them up for me to see. Well, she was right about that, all right. They were good enough if you were going to be surrounded with chalk dust all day teaching classes, but they certainly wouldn't do for a banquet. It was hard for me to have to sit there and see how much this worried her.

"I don't know what to do," she sighed. "I suppose I'll just have to go borrow something to wear."

This was a challenge to my self-respect, so I couldn't suppress a sardonic smile. "Just like the wife in Maupassant's *The Necklace*, right?" I chided.

Ru-ying swung sharply around, fixed me with a stare, and although she said nothing, there was a kind of fury in her eyes. Then she slowly began putting her clothes back in the box, one by one.

"Angry? I was just kidding, you know."

She slammed the cover down on the box with a loud "frump."

"I won't go."

"You don't need to go to that extreme."

"But you're right. The age of *The Necklace* is long past."

"Right. So we go the way we are. Whatever we are, we are, and that's the way we'll go. What difference does it make?"

A sad smile came over her face. "It does make a difference! Just look at me! And look at yourself, too! I won't have you looking any less than he does. You always were better than he was, and when you go out, you should show it."

I saw tears welling in her eyes, I saw the blush that had come into her cheeks, and in that instant I again caught sight of the girl who was waiting for me that night in the dark shadows under the fir tree. I opened my arms and wrapped them around her, pulling her close to me, and she held on to me tightly, sobbing.

"What makes you think in those terms?" I asked gently, trying to soothe her. "You can't judge people by what they wear or by their money."

"But now, in his career, he's gone ahead of you. He has things published, he's a full professor, and here he is coming back home as a 'returning scholar,' getting a big welcome and red carpet treatment everywhere he goes."

"That's not my fault, is it?"

"Of course not. But I can't help thinking you're still better than he is. In your student days you always were better than he was — far better, in fact."

"It's pointless to talk like that. The fact is, when an arm is broken you hide it in a sleeve. We both know what our situation is here, but that doesn't mean we have to parade it in front of him. We can find some polite excuse to turn him down."

But this did not bring the matter to a close. It seemed as though Jiang Wenhao had sensed there was something behind our refusal, so he persisted in trying to see me. First he tried to reach me through telephoning the department. Then he had someone bring me a hand-delivered letter saying he would like to pay us a call "in our residence." His letter was very sincere, full of talk about our friendship in the old days and all that, and he mentioned, too, that he was preparing a paper to give at a conference and wanted my advice on several points. But finally, at the end, he went straight to the point and without beating around the bush said he looked forward to seeing Ru-ying again.

This set both of us to worrying all over again. To tell the truth, so far as academic exchanges were concerned, we could get together right there in the department offices at school. But what with the three-way connection among us, well, you know, it would be too awkward.

Or could we invite him to our place here in faculty housing? Our eyes swept around our one room of twelve by thirteen feet: a big bed and a smaller bed took up over half the room, and in the space left over, after you allow for a bookcase, cardboard cartons, and a cupboard, there was just barely room for a desk. Now this desk of ours, well, when it came to preparing for classes, that was the desk I used; when my wife corrected her homework papers, that also was the desk she used; and that was the same desk that the twins used, too, for their homework — everyone in the family was after that desk. But when "dinner's ready" rang out, no matter who had the desk at that moment, well, there was no question but that they'd give it right up, because, you see, for dinner, that was also the table we used.

So that's what our place is like. I don't have to tell you what the typical hallway in this type of mass housing is like: dark and creepy enough to scare you out of your wits, and piled high on both sides with all kinds of wicker tubs and bamboo baskets, messy coal bricks and clay firepots for cooking, and even pickle urns and bicycles are there — stuff lining both sides so that only a narrow opening down the middle is left for you to struggle through. Anyone trying to make his way down that kind of hallway has to go sideways, and he'd better concentrate on what he's doing or else one misstep will bring disaster.

"No. That won't do." Ru-ying shook her head at the idea. "That hall-way out there is enough to give anyone a fright, and our room here isn't much better. On top of that, after he does get here, we'd have to invite him to stay for dinner, and what could we offer him?"

"Better just invite him out to eat!" I blurted, without having thought it through first, and just leaving it at that. Ru-ying's eyes swept over my face questioningly, for we both had the same unspoken question. How would we pay for it?

After awhile, instinctively, we both turned to look at the two boys, who were sleeping soundly. In this way, too, we avoided looking at each other, for you see, both of us had thought of that nest egg of ours.

I pretended to resume reading, with my back deliberately turned toward everyone. Actually, there was a fierce struggle in my mind, for it was only yesterday that we had come to a tacit understanding: next month for sure we would buy a television set.

A squabble the younger boy had with a plump youngster whose family owns a television set is what set it all off. The older boy was grum-bling and blaming the younger boy, saying that this time he'd really done it, and now they couldn't watch that family's TV any more. The younger boy had flared up at this, shouting, "If we can't, then we can't! Not watching TV isn't going to kill you!"

"You should've known better than to argue with him. Beggars can't be choosy, you dummy. 'When you live in a house with low eaves, you keep your head bowed low.' Everybody knows that."

This was like a slap in the face to both of us when we heard it.

"What did I hear you say?" Ru-ying shouted, whacking the older boy on his backside. "Whoever told you to bow your head low? We can buy our own television set anytime we want!"

Both boys were struck dumb at this.

"Can we really buy one?"

"Of course we can," I put in. "Even if we have to borrow the money, we'll still get one."

Both boys came over and hugged me and gave each of us a loud kiss on the cheek.

Then we got to figuring it all out: if we tightened our belts a little next month we could squeeze twenty dollars out of our two salaries for that month. I could borrow twenty dollars from the cooperative. Ru-ying could borrow sixty-five from her brother, and when all this was put with the fifty-seven we had saved up in our family nest egg, it came to one hundred and sixty some. We'd get the set and worry about how to pay it off later.

But now here I was, like a criminal, plotting how to relieve my own two children of their wealth, with the result that all their plans and hopes would come to nothing. And yet, on the other hand, whether we invited this guest or not was really tied in with my position as one of our country's intellectuals; it was tied in with issues of honor, prestige, and the self-respect of all of us. I mean, after all, for the sake of our country's national honor, I couldn't very well not show at least this much self-respect, could I?

I never read another word that night. Instead, I just sat there and smoked one cigarette after another, sitting at the desk until deep into the night. It wasn't until I began getting ready for bed that I discovered that Ru-ying, who had gone to bed long ago, was still lying there with her eyes wide open, staring at me.

"Why haven't you gone to sleep?"

"Ahmao, this business of hosting a dinner—we have no choice but to go through with it."

I kept my eyes downcast. I was terribly grateful to her for this. The decision, after all, was much more difficult for her to make.

After that, all that remained was to discuss the menu and settle on a guest list. In addition to Jiang Wenhao, there would be his aunt. On our side, there was a couple we were especially close to, classmates actually, who were fun to be with and who could talk intelligently about our field. There would also be Ru-ying's older brother and his wife — we had depended on them for a number of things over the years and had long felt the need to do something to show our appreciation. With the four of us, that would come to a dinner for ten. We'd reserve one large round table at a first-rate restaurant.

"Thirty dollars ought to be enough, don't you think?" I asked Ru-ying.

"I should think so, but take a little more just in case."

"All right. I'll go withdraw forty."

But I didn't do that. I withdrew the entire nest egg, thinking I'd also buy a nice between-seasons blouse for Ru-ying.

When classmates have a reunion, it ought to be a happy get-together. This time, however, after the polite greetings were over and we were all seated at the table looking out over a pure white tablecloth, there was some tension, for despite the fact that Haohao was still his same old self, easygoing and unaffected, still, none of us could rid our minds of the notion that this dinner tonight was for an outsider.

I stole a look at Ru-ying. As if by magic, a transformation had come over her. She was wearing a silver-gray jacket with a pure white blouse, on the collar of which she had neatly embroidered two tiny dark gold flowers (she had stayed up half the night, before the banquet, doing them), and her hair had a little something done to it so that there was a slight wave in it. All this gave her an elegant look, an air of refinement and feminine grace. She smiled at Jiang Wenhao proudly, and looked after all her other guests very attentively, appearing for all the world like the mistress of a prosperous household — vivacious, attractive, and radiant.

Jiang Wenhao simply couldn't take his eyes off her. It was obvious how much he envied us!

"Ahmao, to tell you the honest truth, I've been worried about you two these years, thinking that things weren't going well here. I'd heard you were in trouble a few years back and that you'd had a hard time of it."

I smiled, not quite knowing just what to say. Ru-ying quickly picked up the lead, saying, "That's all in the past now. No point in even mentioning it. What do ten years amount to? Just a snap of the fingers, really."

We all laughed and drank a toast to our gallant hostess.

Then Jiang Wenhao went on to say, "You're right about that. You two look just as good as you did back then. That's certainly worth drinking to, I'd say. You know, coming back this time I thought for sure it would be like that poem:

'Grandeur flourishing all over the capital;

He, alone, sits wan and sallow.'

And yet . . . and yet . . . here you are . . ."

"I'd say it's more like the line that goes:

'Not even a prairie fire can destroy the grass;

Spring breezes restore life every year anew,' "

Ru-ying responded. This brought another round of laughter from everyone and another round of drinking.

Ru-ying was in her element tonight, with lines coming to her almost as though from divine inspiration.

Plates of food, one after the other, were brought out from the kitchen. Ru-ying kept everyone's wineglass full and was always putting choice morsels onto their plates. The menu had been selected for us by Ru-ying's brother. The wine and the food we'd ordered were about right, I'd say, not too cheap, but not ostentatious either: a platter with seven varieties of cold cuts to start with, then eight dishes of various things, plus four more that were specialties of the house — things this restaurant was supposed to have made its reputation with — and finally, a shrimp-ball soup.

"It's hard to eat like this abroad," Jiang Wenhao laughed. "When it comes to eating, no country on earth can beat China."

"In that case, here, have some more," Ru-ying urged, putting a nice piece of fish on his plate. "It's called 'squirrel fish' and it's one of the dishes this restaurant is famous for."

She was right. It was a big kingfish that had been split along the bottom and placed on the platter with its spine up and the two sides splayed out. The way it had been scored with a knife and fried to a crisp with a brown sweet-and-sour sauce on top, then served with its back up in the air like this, did make it look something like a squirrel.

The conversation turned to academics.

"At school, among all of us in Chinese literature, Ahmao here was always right on top. I'm not kidding when I tell you my Ph.D. thesis had a lot in it from his papers."

"My papers?"

"Sure. From those essays you published right after graduation: 'The Literary Atmosphere in Mid-Tang Times,' and the one called 'Proleptical Survey of the Schools of Tang Poetry.' Here was somebody hardly twenty years old doing work based on good, solid research, making some excellent points, and presenting them very eloquently. I mean this was work that drew the attention of scholars outside China. We all used to swear that you'd be a full professor before you were thirty."

Again, I had no idea how to respond. Ru-ying smiled at me and said, "As far as he's concerned, those two pieces were just his schoolwork, done when he was just a beginner."

"Of course, of course," Jiang Wenhao broke in. "And now that the Gang of Four has been set aside, and with you two at the peak of your careers, you can really show your stuff. You'll have a lot to show for yourself. What are you working on now? Do you have a manuscript?"

It was Ru-ying who replied, "He's writing every day, grinding away at it every minute."

"What are you writing on?"

I had no choice but to tell him the topic of my new work, which, to tell the truth, had only just begun to take shape in my mind quite recently.

Jiang Wenhao was so happy when he heard it that he smacked his hand down on the table.

"Why, that's wonderful! That's a great topic, a big topic. When you get it done, it should be a masterpiece. Say, I'll be going to Dunhuang this trip. How about joining me? Right now I'm working on the influence on Tang literature from Central Asian trade routes and the introduction of Buddhism to China. If we go to Dunhuang together you can use the opportunity to gather material for your work."

Here he really touched a responsive chord, for to go to Dunhuang was one of my most secret yearnings. The study of Dunhuang wall paintings and the influence of religion on Tang art and culture are of pressing importance for my treatise, *The Underlying Basis for Literary Florescence in the Tang Dynasty*. A trip to Dunhuang is what every Tang specialist holds dearest to his heart! But it was, of course, out of the question for me to finance such a trip myself. Such a thing is utterly beyond our means.

"Listen, I've brought with me some first-rate photography equipment. Really, do come along with me."

I kept silent, forcing only a smile to my lips. It was too true; even if I could come up with the travel money, I still wouldn't have the necessary equipment for the trip. No, I'd have to yield this time to Jiang Wenhao, someone who comes here all the way from far overseas, and let him go ahead of me.

"Where would he ever find the time to go?" Ru-ying put it.

Once again she was the one who smoothed things over for me. I don't know how I managed to blurt out, "Right. Right. Here in China it's easy enough for us to go there any time we want. In fact, I've been planning to make the trip next year if I can find the time."

Now, dear comrade, I suppose you're going to chastise me for telling a lie? But what could I do? Do you think it would do for me to set forth all our miseries so an outsider could see just how shabby we are? I don't care what you say, I just couldn't do something like that. Why, even my two young generals here know better than that. Incidentally, their behavior that night was far beyond anything we could have expected. They were both dressed up nice and tidy as could be. They didn't just sit there like a couple of wood carvings, but they didn't fidget around a lot, either. The dinner table was piled with all kinds of things they don't get much chance to eat, I dare say, but still they held back very well and only took whatever their mother put on their plates. A minute ago, when their Uncle Jiang from overseas gave them a big box of chocolates, they used English to say "thank you," and then dutifully handed the box over to their mother. All through the dinner, too, they kept themselves from staring over at the colorfully decorated box. Now, having finished eating, they wiped their hands clean and went off to play. Naturally, all of this, from beginning to end, is to Ru-ying's credit. She's the one who formulated the rules and worked them out with the boys.

"Ru-ying, I'm very happy to see you having such a good life." Jiang Wenhao leaned over the table to say this directly to Ru-ying. "And especially those two youngsters of yours. They're wonderful. I really envy you."

"How about your own wife and children? How is it you didn't bring them back to China with you this time?" Ru-ying asked.

Jiang Wenhao was speechless. His eyes searched Ru-ying's face for the longest time before he stammered incoherently, "You mean no one ever told you . . . you weren't aware that . . . you didn't know that I never . . . married?"

A silence came over everyone as they all looked at the three of us. My heart began beating wildly and I looked down, eyes fixed on the small plate in front of me. I didn't dare look at, and had no desire to see, the expression on Ru-ying's face.

"Wenhao! You've had too much to drink!" His aunt broke in hastily, trying to change the subject. "We still have a performance of Peking Opera to see tonight!"

"Oh yes, auntie, I realize that, but never mind for now. For years now I've been wanting to see them, and this time I really had my heart set on getting in touch with them. Besides, we're all close friends here. You all know me well enough. It's true, I suppose, that there is no shortage of female companions overseas, but it's just that, well, I've never been able to forget how, twenty years ago . . ."

"Jiang, old chap, you've had too much tonight. Here, get some more food into you!" The two classmates, who were really good friends of ours, both had leaped to their feet, trying to stop him from continuing.

"No. No. I haven't had too much to drink. Let me go on. I won't say anything out of line, and Ahmao here won't hold anything against me anyway. But to tell you the truth, if I'd come back this time and found Ru-ying not as well off as she is, then I'd have hated you for it! But as it is, Ahmao," and here he stopped to fill our cups right to the brim, "let's down a cup together and drink to your happiness! Drink up, old chap!"

I was very touched by this, and raised my eyes to look at Ru-ying. She smiled at me, completely at ease. Both our cups were filled to the brim with glistening red grape wine. Ru-ying and I brazenly squeezed each other's hands as we stood up to drain our cups to Wenhao's toast.

It would be fine if I could say the dinner and Wenhao's visit went off as smoothly as this, and that was the end of it. But surprisingly enough, this dinner of ours stirred up a tempest that very same night.

After the dinner, I just couldn't get my research work off my mind, so I sat right down and read straight through the rest of the evening. I had made an appointment for the following day to call on a senior specialist in the Institute for Religious Studies, so naturally I felt an obligation to go over all his works that had a bearing on my topic before I went to see him. Since I couldn't go to Dunhuang myself, I had to make the most of whatever resources I had at hand. But those two boys of ours, well, I have no idea what got into them, but they simply would not settle down. One minute they were all keyed up and the next they would sit there and mope. It seems the older one had heard somewhere that a television program they had been looking forward to for a long time was playing that night, and if only the younger boy hadn't had a falling out with their chubby playmate then they would be watching that show this very minute.

"What difference does it make? We've only got another ten days or two weeks at the most," the younger one declared with supreme indifference. "Papa and Mama already promised we'd get our own set by next month and then we won't have to be goody-goody to those people anymore. When that happens, if we want to watch a little longer, we can do it, and we can watch whatever we want to!"

Precisely when the two little fellows' chattering had reached a crescendo, Ru-ying, who was busy washing dishes and scrubbing pans screamed at them in a voice that was choked with emotion, and yet also seemed to be imploring them, "Won't you two leave anyone in peace for just a little while? You're driving me crazy with all your talk, talk, talk!"

She was boiling mad — I could see it in her face — and she seemed so tired she could hardly stand up.

"All day long it's nothing but TV this, TV that. I mean, is there no end to it?"

I hurried to signal the boys to say nothing. I realized that at this time in particular all their talk about television sets was cruelly gnawing at that mother's conscience of hers. But before you knew it, the two boys, who had poured out a basin of hot water to rinse off their feet, had again got to chattering away. They were simply overexcited about the prospect of our family having its very own television set, skipping around swinging their arms and the like, and, well, they accidentally knocked over a hot-water thermos. It hit the floor with a crash and instantly water spread all over the floor and there were glass fragments scattered about, too. Talk about chaos and confusion! Well, this really threw oil onto the fire. Ru-ying flew over to the children like a madwoman and gave each of them a whopping smack. Then she turned to me and screamed, "How can you just sit there and not take a hand in anything here at all! Are you so lazy you can't even help them pour out hot water! It's as though the whole household existed just for you alone!"

Everything seemed to fall apart all at once, and by now, of course, the children were bawling their heads off.

Ru-ying regretted her outburst, I'm sure of that. But because I sheltered the children and held them close to me, playing the role of guardian, you see, she became even more furious and tried to jerk them away from me to give them another whack.

I had to use all my strength to pull them back to me and to hold her away.

"How can you get so raging mad over an old beat-up thermos?" I asked.

"An old beat-up thermos, is it?" she shouted, now directing all her fury at me. "It's so easy for you to say that, but even an old beat-up thermos takes money to buy, you know!"

"Ru-ying!" My voice begged her in earnest, and yet there was . . . yes, there was a threat in it. "Quiet down. That's enough!"

"No! I will not be quiet! I suppose you think that the money to buy that thermos bottle came easily, don't you? Well I'm just not the big spender you are, that's what, just not as high-class. You won't even press for a raise, and still you let the children get away with wasting things!"

"Don't get so carried away, Ru-ying!" I shouted, trying to quiet her down.

"Why are you shouting at me? Go shout at your department. Go shout at your department to give you a raise! God, you're so *hopeless.*"

Here, I lost patience with her. I had my work on my mind and I was anxious to get back to it. But I stopped to look around me at this household of ours. There we were, cramped into a place no bigger than the palm of a man's hand, water spreading all around and things dripping wet; the children bawling, the parents shouting; I standing accused of being "hopeless" and having "no future." Well, it certainly took away whatever cool detachment and clear thinking I may have had left in me. I lost control of myself and joined the shouting match.

"No . . . No . . . future? You're saying . . . you mean to say I have no future? Well . . . well, for God's sake, right at the beginning then, right then at the very beginning, why didn't you marry your Jiang Wen-hao then?"

Ru-ying stiffened. She trembled all over and looked at me in a way she had never looked at me before. She stood there like that for the longest time. Then she roughly pushed the children toward me, covered her face with her hands and ran out the door.

It never occurred to me that this storm in our household would spill over into the university administration, but it did. The Party Secretary became involved, and in fact has already gone to see Ru-ying twice. He even criticized himself for having neglected the people's welfare, indicating he would do his best to try and find a solution to our problem. Ru-ying, for her part, had already indicated to the Party Secretary that my behavior that night was caused by anxiety, that I had wanted to get some studying in so that I could get ahead of Jiang Wenhao. For my part, I do admit I was out of line in the things I said that night. But you see, a Chinese intellectual in this time of the national buildup for the Four Modernizations really ought to press forward with his work on China's national culture, and really ought to make new contributions. One really should try to understand this, don't you think? What do you think, am I right or not?

# LIU QINGBANG

# The Good Luck Bun

It is often said that literature is the diary of a nation. But in China, where topics are sometimes assigned to writers, and some topics are forbidden territory, the "diary" has missing pages. The present story helps fill in one conspicuously missing page: the massive famines that struck many areas, killing millions, during 1959–61.

The cruel hardship of a harsh winter and a severe food shortage is the centerpiece of the story, but there is more that is furnished obliquely: the pettiness and meanness that grinding poverty and hunger provoke when the human ability to bear frustration is worn to nothing; the ultimate goodness and mutual concern of people who share a common fate; and, of course, the tyranny of commune bosses and the revelations, through the voice of the old aunt, that waste and bad farming practices occur in the rush to meet deadlines imposed by arbitrary and distant leaders.

The meaning of a personal name in China is important. The fact that the three children in the story all have names related to food — Maizy, Wheatly, and Beansprout — is not extraordinary, but merely reflects a country family's preoccupation with the basic sustenance of life. Names are also thought to have power over real events; hence the names are meant to be auspicious as well.

Translated and introduced by Donald A. Gibbs. Originally published in *Benliu* (Zhengzhou), 1980, no. 3.

Liu Qingbang (b. 1951), who as a boy lived through the famines in rural Henan, near Xinyang, eventually finished junior high school there at age sixteen. He now works in Beijing at the Ministry of Coal, where he is an editor of the ministry's publication *The Coalminer*.

# The Good Luck Bun

## 1

February 1960. Normally the weather should have turned warmer by now, but South Willow Village was still gripped in ice. A scrawny crow among the bare branches of a tallow tree, stirred by the chill early morning wind, opened its beak to caw, as if in protest at the cold. Sparrows with nowhere to search for food were perched on the rooftops in twos and threes with their heads pulled down into their bodies, and now and then emitted a "chirp, chirp."

Because yesterday's snow had not yet melted, there would be no work in the fields today. This made people reluctant to stir about; they preferred instead to remain behind tightly shut doors, bearing the cold by staying bundled in their warm nests of quilts. The older people already had considerable experience with hunger. They always said, "The stomach is like a grindstone; but when you sleep it stays still and you don't feel the hunger." So they all stayed inside, and they kept the children in too. The dull, smudgy winter sun had slowly climbed as high as the rooftops, but still the village remained locked in stillness.

Suddenly the commissary bell broke the silence. Representatives from each household scrambled out, each hoping for a front position in line, running pell-mell in dread of being last. Breathlessly they rushed in. Then, later, they filed outside, now walking slowly, with their steps crunch, crunching in the snow.

A girl of perhaps thirteen or fourteen emerged, her hair in two rather fuzzy braids. She was somewhat sallow in complexion, and her eyes seemed unusually large. Both hands had disappeared into the opposite sleeves in search of warmth, and a small basket woven from willow twigs hung in front from her sleeved wrists. Rolling from side to side in her small basket were three tiny steamed buns, hard as clay. As she trudged home, people heard her singing to herself the little chant she had picked up only the day before:

> What do we eat? Why the commissary bun!
> It fits in a matchbox when it's done.
> Grownups two; kids just one.
> Tiny tots? Well, they get none!

As she looked down into her basket, she thought to herself, "Well, that's sure no lie. They're tiny all right!" Just then, a tall, thin woman overtook her from behind, eyes fixed on the girl's basket.

"Just a minute there, Maizy! Let me see what you've got there," she demanded, reaching in to take out one of the buns.

"Aha!" she announced triumphantly, holding the bun close to her nose for a sniff and then placing it in her own basket for comparison. As if she'd made some great discovery, she shouted to those behind her, "Look here! I thought there was something fishy when they were handing out the buns. Those commissary people eat better than the rest of us, and even their family members do, too. No wonder people say,

> 'Rations slashed to an ounce a day.
> But never a cut in the bosses' pay.
> Cut rations again, down to a dram,
> But cooks in the kitchen gobble what they can.'

Any family that's got someone working in the commissary kitchen is going to survive all right. The only thing people like us can do is wait around for starvation to get us."

Perhaps because she drew such a bleak picture, she had to keep wiping away tears with her sleeve.

People filing out of the commissary came up behind them, drawn by the commotion. A crowd soon gathered around and grew larger all the time. Since no one knew quite what the trouble was, one person asked, "Gao Lanying, what's got into you so early in the morning?"

Bolstered by the crowd's interest, she shot back, "What's got into me! Have you no eyes in your head? Look at this bun. It's as yellow as can be. Tell me, does it look like the ones we all got?"

The bun was passed around for others to see, to sniff, and to compare with the others. One even pinched off a bit and put it in his mouth to taste it.

"It *is* different. The ones I got are black as a skillet, but this one's got some yellow in it, all right."

"Mine are made from mildewed sweet potatoes, bitter as all get out. But not this one. In fact it tastes as though it's got a bit of soybean flour in it."

The bun was passed from hand to hand, each person adding his own opinion to the general discussion.

"Give it back," Maizy asked anxiously, "Give me back my bun. My brothers are hungry and they're waiting for me to bring it back to them."

Gao Lanying, suddenly afraid the girl might run off with the evidence, hastily snatched the bun from someone's fingers and declared, "In bad times it's always share and share alike, I say. This dumpling business has to go to the brigade leader if there's going to be any justice done."

"Let it go, Lanying," someone cautioned. "Give it back to her. Live and let live, Lanying. You don't have to be as strict as all that."

"Not on your life am I going to let it go! I'm going to do something about this. It's just not right for the commissary people to stuff themselves while the rest of us starve to death." So saying, she pushed her way through the crowd, heading for the brigade leader's office.

Maizy stood there helpless, wiping the tears back from her eyes, and then slowly made her way home.

## 2

Just after New Year, Maizy's father had gone off to dredge a river eight or ten miles away. Her mother had been assigned to work in the brigade's kitchen, leaving Maizy home alone with her two little brothers. The oldest, Wheatly, was ten, and the youngest, nicknamed Beansprout, was eight. When Maizy had gone out to get the family's rations, both her brothers were still snuggled deep in their quilts. Now, just as she was returning to their quarters, she heard them saying, "I can eat a *hundred* of those buns."

"I can eat a *thousand*!"

Hearing her steps approaching, both boys quickly squirmed out of their quilts and stuck their heads out to peek inside the basket when she entered the room.

"Hey! Only two buns?" Beansprout asked.

"I ate mine already," Maizy replied.

"So fast? I bet you picked the biggest one, didn't you?"

Maizy was silent. Her throat tightened and she was afraid she might cry.

"Ugh. Still bitter," Beansprout winced.

"Try not to taste it, Beansprout," his brother counselled. "Just press it with your tongue and swallow it straight down. Here, watch how I do it." He then stuck out his neck and swallowed a piece to demonstrate his technique.

Watching her two brothers eat made Maizy's stomach growl, and she began to think of what had happened to her own bun. It was her mother who had been handing out the buns, all right; but when she had given Maizy hers, Maizy saw quite clearly that her mother had simply taken three buns out of the basket in order, without any picking or choosing. At the time, Maizy had not noticed that one of the buns was a different color, but Gao Lanying was very sharp-eyed and had spotted it at once. Then look what had happened! Maizy still couldn't quite figure it out. Had her mother really made two different kinds of buns and taken the opportunity to slip a special one into her basket? Maizy sat on a footstool by the bed, chin resting on her fists, lost in thought. Little did she suspect that the bun with just a tiny little bit of yellow in it was at that moment stirring up a big fuss in the commissary.

The brigade chief, Liang Shan, stalked into the commissary surrounded by a crowd of people made up of Gao Lanying and others. Carrying the bun behind his back, he strode up to where Maizy's mother was still handing out buns, addressed her with grave and stern mien, "Liu Caiyun, you're to stop handing out buns."

Liu Caiyun, caught by surprise, stood there dumbfounded. She saw the fury on the brigade chief's face, and she noticed that those who had lined up to receive buns were glaring at her in a way she had never seen before.

"What on earth has happened?" she asked. Her face turned pale and her heartbeat suddenly quickened. She timidly raised her eyes to meet the brigade chief's glare, as if to ask, "What's this all about?"

The chief then issued an order: "You're to stop working in the commissary, and as soon as the fields dry out you're reassigned to work in the fields."

Liu Caiyun was now even more confused. She sensed that something big had happened. She was very alarmed, but replied with her characteristic docility. "All right, I'll work in the fields. But what's this all about?"

"Playing dumb, eh? No idea at all what you've done, is that it? You want me to recount what you've done so everyone can hear, is that right? Now, out! And your whole family is fined one day's rations. We'll give you a taste of hunger and see how you like it."

At this, he took the bun that had been clenched behind his back and threw it into the steam cage, then turned on his heel and left.

This had all happened so unexpectedly that to Liu Caiyun it was like a clap of thunder breaking right over her head. She stood in place woodenly and thought she might faint as darkness seemed to overwhelm her. After a moment, with trembling hands, she slowly picked up the bun that the chief had thrown into the steam cage and turned it around in her fingers studying it. She compared it with other buns, and then seemed to grasp what had happened. She heaved a sigh, loosened her apron, brushed the crumbs off herself and was just about to head homeward when several kitchen helpers came over to her.

"Why do you let them pick on you like that? You haven't anything to hide, and anyways, nobody'd believe you would make two kinds of buns."

"Caiyun," said another, "this whole batch of buns was made by Yuxiang and Lianhua's mother early this morning. When they finished, they said they had to go to North Village today. As soon as they return, we can get to the bottom of this. Everybody is responsible for his own actions, so nobody's going to blame you for anything. You'll see."

Liu Caiyun gave this a wry smile. "It's all right. I was thinking of going back to field work anyway. We all have a conscience to listen to." Then she turned to leave.

Another young woman in the commissary came over, took two buns from the steamer and pressed them into Liu Caiyun's hand, saying with great concern, "Here, take these. These are your regular ration. Remember, you've worked hard all morning and you haven't had anything to eat."

Liu Caiyun looked down at the two tiny buns, then turned to put them back into the steamer. "I'm not hungry," she said, then turned and quickly left the commissary.

Discussion of what had happened continued long after she left. Some believed she actually had made two kinds of buns. Otherwise, they argued, why would she have left the commissary without putting up a fight? Others pointed out that it had been some fifteen or sixteen years now since she had married into South Willow Village, and everybody in the whole village, young and old alike, knew she wasn't one ever to do anything dishonest.

Apart from the issue of whether or not Caiyun had really made two kinds of buns, and apart from the deliberations on the matter, she seemed to weather the tempest quietly and easily. Had she been any other woman, she probably would have cried her eyes out and shouted her innocence. She might even have threatened suicide to gain exoneration right on the spot. But Liu Caiyun had always taken whatever life handed out to her, and she accepted it without protest.

That's just the way Liu Caiyun was — a timid, fearful, easily intimidated countrywoman. She was used to keeping things inside. In fact, one rarely heard her speak, and such things as delight, anger, grief, or joy were never clearly registered on her face. She always appeared calm — wooden, even — and was like that from one end of the year to the other. Several years earlier, when her husband was still a primary school teacher, he used to get so fed up with her lack of playfulness that he would say you could squeeze her for all you were worth and still not get so much as a fart out of her. He even complained that she couldn't cry, and said she was no better than a dead sow. But no matter how hurt she might have been, she never argued with her husband. She always took good care of the children and always silently went about all the wifely duties of washing clothes, making beds, heating water, and cooking meals as nice as you please. In 1957, when her husband was attacked as a rightist, they sent him back to his native village, with only a bedroll on his back, to serve as a laborer. When that happened, her husband had thought she would desert him for sure. But she treated him better than ever, and comforted him calmly. "Don't take it so hard," she said. "It doesn't matter where one lives. The thing is just to go on living." Not until this moment had her husband appreciated her virtues. Feeling deeply ashamed of himself, he held her closely in his arms and sobbed loudly. Liu Caiyun's own eyes were dry.

True enough, no one in the entire village had ever seen Liu Caiyun cry. Someone said that, before Liberation, Liu Caiyun's father had died when she was still a tiny girl. The hard times she had suffered while following her widowed mother around begging in the streets had drained her of every tear. But others said she was just born like that, so wooden she couldn't cry if she wanted to. Except for her inability to cry, though, no one could find any other fault with her. In the village of several hundred people, no one could match Liu Caiyun when it came to getting along well with others. She was always yielding and was never known to squabble; any time you asked for her help, she always pitched right in. She was a good field hand, too; not even the younger women could do more than she did in the fields.

Word of Liu Caiyun's two kinds of steamed buns swept through the village like wildfire. People had always been dissatisfied with the commissary and had always hoped to lay their hands on what they called "a gorging house rat." They would teach this person a good lesson. Who would ever have dreamed that they would be catching someone so well known for her goodness as Liu Caiyun? When word of this reached Liu Caiyun's aunt, the old lady became furious.

"It's just like persimmons; people only squeeze the soft ones! So now they're picking on my niece, are they? You can tell me anybody you please was making two kinds of buns and I'll believe you, but nothing in the world will make me believe Liu Caiyun was up to something like that. So what if she doesn't talk much? She's got gumption, that girl does."

With this, leaning heavily on her cane, she went straight off to see Liu Caiyun.

## 3

Liu Caiyun's family lived in a three-room house with tamped earth floors and a thatch roof. Patches of unmelted snow glistened in the sunlight here and there on the roof. No strings of peppers hung from the eaves, and there were no strings of dried corn-on-the-cob either. Only the long, uneven icicles hung from the eaves, chilling the air around them.

The two boys had gone off to school. Liu Caiyun was sitting in their only chair, her cheek resting against one hand. She was staring at the floor. Maizy wriggled up onto her lap, tears glistening in the corners of her eyes. Liu Caiyun was at that moment thinking that it surely must have been Yuxian and Lianhua's mother who had added the soybean flour to that bun. "They shouldn't have done that," she thought to herself, "but if I try to clear it up, I'll cause bad feelings. And yet, if I don't get it ironed out, I'll have to take the blame. What's really bad is that our rations are gone for the day. What will the children eat? If they should fall ill from lack of food, what will I say to their father? When things were better, it wasn't so awful to miss a day's food, but the way things are these days, a single meal is just barely enough to hold off starvation. And it's so much harder on the children. How can they stand it?" The thought of her little children having to suffer was almost more than Liu Caiyun could bear.

"Mama, let's go find daddy." Maizy suggested.

Liu Caiyun caressed her daughter's hair. "Silly girl, it's the same everywhere. No one has enough to eat. Think of the hard labor they've got your father doing, and they're putting him through struggle sessions too. How can we take any of his rations from him?"

Maizy's eyes again began to fill with tears.

At that moment, they heard old auntie, who had come hobbling up and had begun shouting before she reached the door.

"Caiyun! Let me have a look at you, girl. They always pick on the good ones, don't they? They won't be satisfied till they hound you to death, I suppose."

Liu Caiyun rushed to the door to help the old lady in, while Maizy hurried to get her a straw cushion.

This old aunt of theirs was always blunt and never one to hold back on words. Once she started talking, it was like a ball of yarn unraveling — never an end to it.

"Well, I said to myself, Maizy's mother must be taking all this pretty hard. Go on and have yourself a good cry, you hear? When something eats at you, don't you go and keep it all inside. Makes a person sick if you do. All right. So you folks don't have anything to eat. Don't let that get you down. At noon you take one of my bun rations and give it to the children." Then she added in a whisper, "We're still better off than some, you know. We at least get a mouthful of sweet potato bun. I hear that over on the south side the food shortage is a lot worse than ours."

Maizy's eyes widened at this, and she could feel her heart racing. Her mother, also alarmed, interrupted, "Don't talk like that! If they hear you, we'll be in real trouble!"

"I'm not afraid. I don't have many more days to live anyway. Besides, we were all given a mouth, weren't we, so what's wrong with using it? And anyway, it's the truth. I'm not like those two-faced, double-talking

damn cadre people, always talking so big, and half the time they don't
know what they're talking about. 'So many thousand catties of rice from
this field, so many thousand catties of wheat from that,' and when anybody tries to reason with them, the first thing you know they've got a
struggle session turned on you. The more we produce, the more we just
have to hand over to fill the commune quota anyway. This year, even
after adding in the old grain stored up last year, we still didn't have
enough to satisfy them.

"But never mind that. Giving grain over to the state isn't all that bad,
but what really tears a body up is all that food that goes to rot in the
fields. I don't suppose you know anything about it, but over in that western section where we put in almost twenty acres of yams, they said we
had to get them all dug up in just one night. Anyone who didn't pitch in
was a rightist or a backslider. Well, they plowed through the field that
night, so dark you had to do everything by feel, and all they gave it was a
quick once-over. I tell you, there were yams as big as rice bowls still left in
there, just left there to rot. I tell you, a body could live through eight
lifetimes and still not see anything as crazy as that.

"And then they go on and on with their slogans:
　　　'Three meals a day, three days straight.
　　　Each meal good, the best you ever ate.'
"Crap, it's all crap. If they go on this way we'll all starve to death,
that's for sure."

The old lady would have gone on forever, but Liu Caiyun, sitting
beside her, grew apprehensive. She had heard her husband say that it
was because he had expressed some dissatisfaction with the leadership
that he had been labeled a rightist and sent home with a dark cloud
over his head, and that was why he had to be under surveillance and
"remoulded by the masses." These things that auntie was saying were
forbidden. Gently she tried to divert her.

"Auntie, why don't you just relax now? Even talking eats up a lot of
energy. Don't worry about me, I'll get over it . . ."

"If you can get over it, that's fine. For the children's sake, try to keep
yourself above it all. I'll be off now. Come noon I'll bring my bun ration
over for the children."

She stopped when she reached the door and turned again to Liu
Caiyun. "I hear some of those yams buried over on the west side are still

edible. Send Maizy over there to bring some back and boil them. No matter how bitter and puckery they are, it beats starving."

Liu Caiyun promised she'd send Maizy over, and saw auntie out to the front gate.

## 4

Night came, and a great darkness enveloped the land. The entire village sank into a deathlike solitude. None of the villagers could afford to buy lamp oil. All the lamps were dark, all the stoves were cold, and although it was still early, the people were deep in slumber. There was the occasional militia patrolman, rifle slung from the shoulder, walking back and forth through the village. This was because recently some of the people from the south side, starvation gleaming in their eyes, had taken to stealing livestock, prying open granaries, and even robbing people on the small bypaths.

The little family of four in Liu Caiyun's house was not asleep, however. Liu Caiyun was sitting on the bed hugging little Beansprout close to her, while by the window, in the darkness, Maizy and Wheatly worked together, brother and sister, at skinning a tiny little suckling piglet.

Just after noon, auntie had brought over a bun and Liu Caiyun had given the two little boys half a bun each. Both of them were well-mannered: one wanted to give part of his half to his mother and the other wanted to share his with his sister. Maizy was so touched by these gestures from her thin, bony little brothers that she once again could not hold back her tears. Liu Caiyun put her arms around her daughter and held her tightly. The grief she felt for her children would not go away.

That afternoon, the two boys again had dragged themselves off to school while Maizy went off to the western fields to dig up yams, basket slung on her arm. All the yams had long since rotted, but still Maizy dutifully searched for a long time. A noisy crow overhead swept back and forth screeching an ugly "caw, caw" that frightened her. Just when she was about to give up, she noticed two men at the far edge of the field who seemed to be burying something. When they left Maizy went over to rake up whatever it was they had buried and discovered several tiny little suckling piglets.

The piglets had been buried by people in charge of the brigade's pig farm. There was a rule in the brigade that no pig that died of disease was to be eaten, because this was bad for public health. Anyone who violated the rule was subjected to intense criticism. But Maizy reasoned that there would be no harm in eating them so long as no one saw you doing it. Making sure no one was around, she scooped one of the tiny piglets up into her basket, and cautiously hurried home with the basket under her arm.

When Liu Caiyun saw the piglet her child had brought back — no more than a little bag of bones really — it heightened the grief she felt for her children and produced a dilemma for her.

Eating the dead piglet and lighting a private fire to cook it were two violations right there. If they were discovered, this would add to the trouble she already was in. And yet, it tore at her heart to see them so famished. All day long, poor Maizy hadn't had a bite of food of any kind. She herself was an adult and could stand it, but how much longer could Maizy hold out? After all, she was still just a little girl!

Maizy had wanted to skin the piglet the moment she got home, but her mother cautioned her. "Wait until it's dark out, Maizy." Maizy nodded her head knowingly and laid the tiny carcass out of sight in one corner of the room.

Darkness finally came and a stillness gradually spread everywhere. Standing by the window, one could feel only the frigid night wind on one's face. There was not a flicker of light anywhere. This was the moment Maizy and her brother had been waiting for. All they had to do was skin the piglet, remove its innards, and plunge it into boiling water. But they needed a pot. Where could they find a pot? Two years before, during the great movement to make steel [the Great Leap Forward campaign — Tr.] large *woks*, small *woks*, skillets — anything at all made of iron — had to be turned in to be beaten into pieces for the smelters. You couldn't hold back so much as a spatula. Fortunately, Maizy had buried an iron washbasin in the privy. The iron basin had been allocated to them when the household property of the landlords was being divided among the poor during land reform. Tonight they propped this lucky survivor of the steel smelting movement on top of two bricks, and beneath it, for kindling, stuffed some wood scraps they had ripped from their fence. The fire caught on and flames began licking the sides of the basin.

Thus a "hearth" in this very ordinary peasant household of Liu Caiyun's, where no fire had brightened the interior ever since they had joined the commissary, now once again shot out flames — flames that were dazzlingly bright, and smoke that was tantalizingly aromatic. In the flickering light, the soft features of Liu Caiyun's peaceful countenance revealed the faint traces of a smile. And each time little Maizy reached forward to shove more wood bits under the basin, the firelight imparted an especially bright and rosy hue to her adorable face. Wheatly's face was even redder. But wait a minute — the redness in his case came from the smelly pig's blood he was smeared with! He was the one who had peeled the carcass off and had served as "butcher." But he had also, from time to time, stopped his cutting to scratch his face. The "rosy complexion" had arrived on his face long before any fire had been lit.

Little Beansprout also was wide awake that night, but every time he tried to wriggle out of his quilt, he had to be restrained by his mother.

"Mama," he pleaded, "I want to watch too."

"There's nothing to see, Beansprout. It'll be a while yet before it's done," his mother would say, raising her head to peek over at the basin. Suddenly, with a fright, she remembered they hadn't covered up the window. How could they have forgotten something as important as that! In a frenzy she snatched up a bedsheet and draped it over the window. Unsure that this would do the job, she opened the door and stuck her head outside to check. Good, pitch black. Not a sliver of light. In her heart she prayed, "Oh God, please, please this once. Have mercy for the children's sake."

The faint aroma of meat wafted from the basin, ever so faintly, but soon it filled the room and went straight to the children's innards. Wheatly and Beansprout had such a craving that saliva practically leaked from their mouths. Even Maizy, usually better at keeping possession of herself, could not keep from lifting the cover off the basin now and then, blowing at the billowing steam to get a good look inside.

"Mama," she reported, "there's even some fat in it! I can see bubbles of it floating on the top."

Then, a little later, another report: "It can't take much longer. You know, mama, if you don't like the bad smell of the meat, you can just eat the best part, the liver."

Liu Caiyun smiled wryly to herself. Here was a piglet no bigger than your hand, one that probably had died the minute it was born, and was no more than a tiny little bag of bones weighing nearly nothing. Yet here it was in a pot of boiling water without a speck of salt in it, and still it had the children all worked up like this. But then, could she really blame them? Last year, and this year again, what meat had they ever tasted? At New Year who had got so much as a whiff of meat cooking in a pot? There mere thought of it made her sigh.

"Maizy, dear, it'll take three times as long when you peek at it like that. Stop your peeking and keep the lid on tight if you want to hurry it up."

Maizy had just shifted the lid to cover the basin more securely when Liu Caiyun suddenly heard the loud crunching of approaching foot-steps on the ice outside their door. She jumped from the bed, swiftly scattered the fire with her foot, then stamped on it frantically to put it out. But too late. Brigade Chief Liang Shan and a militiaman, who had a rifle slung over his shoulder, had already kicked the door open and en-tered. The round shaft of light from their flashlight shone directly on Liu Caiyun's drawn face.

She was scared speechless. She just stood there rigidly, even when the fragments of the scattered fire burned her shoes.

"Lighting fires, are you?!" the brigade chief shouted fiercely.

"It's . . . it's just the children, you know," pleaded Liu Caiyun, trying to duck out of the light which was shining in her face. "They didn't know it was wrong. They found a little piglet dead somewhere and brought it home. They insisted on eating it. They haven't had a bite to eat all day. You could let it go just this once, couldn't you?"

The chief said nothing. He reached over to raise the lid on the basin.

Maizy, terrified that she had again brought disaster upon them, be-gan to cry.

"Don't cry, dear. Your Uncle Liang here won't harm us. Way back when they were little boys, your father and Uncle Liang used to beg for food together. Why, they're good friends!"

"That's enough out of you!" the chief interrupted. "Who'd ever be friends with a rightist!" He tipped over the basin with the tip of his foot, spilling the half-cooked piglet out onto the dirt floor. Turning to the militiaman with the rifle slung across his back, he ordered:

"Take that basin."

At this, Maizy broke into deep sobbing. Wheatly bit his lip, hatred flashing in his eyes. Little Beansprout's eyes widened in fright. Liu Caiyun lost her temper. "Mr. Brigade Chief," she seethed at him, "we're a poor peasant family here. You can't treat us this way."

"So what if you're poor peasants? Look at *me* — I'm a Party member and people can get up a struggle session against me anyway. It is not permitted to light kitchen fires. Do you know that or don't you? It is not permitted to eat pigs that die of disease. Do you know that or don't you? And was it you or wasn't it you who made two kinds of buns? One crime after another. It looks to me as though you're tired of living. Tomorrow you're going to confess in front of everyone at a mass meeting, you hear? And you're fined another day's rations for the whole family."

There was nothing Liu Caiyun could say. She felt like she'd been hit in the stomach and could not stand up. The room began spinning around her, making her stagger to the bed where she crumpled in a heap.

The chief strode out. The militiaman, holding the basin in one hand, stopped to pick up the half-cooked piglet between the fingers of the other. He raised it to his nose, sniffed twice, and carried it out.

## 5

Their basin was gone and their pork was gone. Liu Caiyun felt that an enormous disaster had befallen them. She was numb all over, and her chest felt as if a millstone were pressing on it. A rainbow of colors flashed into her consciousness and seemed, in wave after wave, to completely engulf her until finally she felt at the verge of oblivion.

Maizy was clinging to her mother's arm, crying in whispered sobs that wracked her whole body. This young girl, mature before her time, was doing her best to suppress tears, but was now just about overwhelmed.

"Mother, it's all my fault. I just never seem to learn . . . But I promise, Mother, oh I promise I won't do anything bad ever again . . . I promise, Mother . . ."

Each spasm of tears stabbed at her mother's heart. Such deep, convulsive sobbing! Liu Caiyun's despair at the fright and the misery that had now been heaped upon her helpless, vulnerable, dear little children was greater than any she had ever known. Her throat tightened, and tears, so long dried up within her, almost found release. Groggy and overwhelmed, the mother managed to say only, "Maizy, dear, go to sleep."

Gradually, the tiny room settled into the deepest depths of stillness.

Later that night, a fierce wind arose. The frigid, howling wind caused the tattered paper that covered their window to make a flapping noise with each strong gust. The passing of time and the icy wind's sudden incursion into the room gradually stirred Liu Caiyun into wakefulness. She became aware of a chill over her whole body. It was only then that she realized she had no quilt over her. Were the children covered? She tried to get up, but Maizy was still clinging tightly to her left arm. Though sound asleep, the girl occasionally gulped a deep sob. Liu Caiyun stretched out her right arm to stroke Maizy's face. It was cold, but the child's still-wet tears were even colder. Gently she wiped the tears with her hand. Then she extricated her left arm, pulled Maizy's quilt up over her, and tucked it in. She groped in the darkness for Wheatly and Little Beansprout. These two little fellows had also fallen asleep with their clothes on, without covering themselves up. Wheatly had his arm around his younger brother and had pulled him close. Liu Caiyun covered them both up, and as she did so heard little Beansprout, her youngest, smack his lips and mumble in his sleep, "Gosh, it smells so good . . . It's delicious . . . I want some more . . ."

Hearing the child talk about food made Liu Caiyun's stomach growl and rumble; she was terribly, terribly hungry. She was so hungry she could hardly stand it, and it frightened her. Somewhere she had heard that one kernel of rice was enough to keep a person going for three hours. Right now she'd settle for that one kernel, but where would she find even that much in their house? Why, they didn't even have so much as a tree leaf to eat. Her thoughts turned from herself to her children, and to the thought that the next day they once again would have to go without rations. Even more terrifying was the thought that in the morning she would have to stand in front of the masses and make a confession of all the things she had done wrong.

She had attended confession meetings before. When was there ever a time when the confessor got off without a beating? You have to stand there and take it, without moving a muscle, all the while saying, "Help me out, everybody. Teach me a lesson." The "help" of course was pulling your hair, pushing your head down, spitting on your face, making you kneel on bricks . . . Liu Caiyun couldn't bear to think of all the things they did.

When the first faint light of dawn appeared, the wind had died down, but a rasping sleet still scattered from the sky.

Maizy was suddenly awakened from her sound sleep by a strange ka-chunk sound, and the roof beam in the house began creaking at the same time. She sat up, rubbed the sleep from her eyes and reached over to shake her mother. What? Not there? "Mama. I heard something strange," she called out. But no answer.

She quickly scrambled off the bed, went to the outer room and stuck her head inside. Her mother was hanging stiffly from the roof beam overhead, and under her there was a table upon which rested a small stool that had been kicked over on its side. Maizy screamed and ran outside. "Hurry, somebody! Hurry!" she shouted. "Help! Help! My mother is hanging herself. Help! Help!"

Her high-pitched, shrill voice pierced the open air, now filled with thickly falling snow. The neighbors, hearing her shouts, rushed outside without buttoning up their clothes and raced over to Maizy's house. They leaped up onto the table and held Liu Caiyun in their arms while they unfastened the cords from the roof beam. Then they carried her into the inner room and stretched her out on the bed. Maizy, nearly hysterical, flung herself atop her mother's body, crying, "Mother! Oh Mother! You can't die, Mother. You can't leave us alone!" Wheatly and Beansprout, thoroughly frightened, were now also wailing.

The tiny rooms filled to overflowing with people who were responding to Maizy's cries for help.

"Quick, send her to a hospital," someone said.

"Hurry up and get a goose. A goose can get her breathing again," advised another.

"Better hurry over and get Gao Lanying. Her father was an old herb doctor so she knows all the pressure points."

But before anyone could go and get her, Gao Lanying herself appeared, out of breath, her jacket unbuttoned and without even stockings on her feet.

"Hurry, hurry," everyone shouted. "Let her through, let her through." Without a word, Gao Lanying pushed through the crowd and went straight to Liu Caiyun's side, quickly felt her pulse and then supported her from the back into an upright position. She pressed down very hard with her thumbs on points between Liu Caiyun's shoulder blades. This done, she deftly pulled a pin from her lapel and jabbed it firmly into the septum of Liu Caiyun's nose. All of Gao Lanying's movements were smooth and practiced.

When she was satisfied that Liu Caiyun was going to live, Gao Lanying relaxed and heaved a sigh. Then she enlisted Maizy's assistance.

"Stop your crying now, child," she said. "If you want to save your mother, say 'Mother, hurry and wake up.'"

Maizy at once did as she was told, and her two little brothers joined in. "Mother, hurry and wake up!" they shouted over and over. Seeing the children so frantic and intent brought tears to the eyes of all who were crowded into that tiny room.

Gao Lanying was even less able than the others to fight back her tears. She had no idea, of course, what had happened that night.

"Caiyun, to think that all this is just because of that steamed bun. I'm a beast for what I've done. I shouldn't have found fault with you. You can't die! Think of your children! You mustn't die, you hear? Give me a good slap, go ahead, give me a good slap." She actually picked up Liu Caiyun's hand and would have slapped herself with it had the others not intervened.

By now a little color had returned to Liu Caiyun's face and her nose quivered slightly as it drew in air. But her eyes were tightly shut and she otherwise was perfectly still.

At this point, her old aunt hobbled up beside the bed and took Liu Caiyun's hand in hers. "My poor little girl," she said. "You took it all so hard, didn't you? Now you have yourself a good cry, you hear? A good big cry." But Liu Caiyun lay as mute and lifeless as ever.

Outside, the snow fell more heavily, and inside, the crowd grew larger. The rooms were jam-packed, and quite a few people were standing outside in the courtyard as well. There was speculation as to just why Liu Caiyun had tried to end her life, and naturally everything went back to the controversy over the steamed bun. Yuxiang and Lianhua's mother had just returned from North Village, and upon hearing that Liu Caiyun had tried to hang herself, they rushed over and joined the crowd in the courtyard. In response to everyone's questions, they told how they had got up especially early the day before and made the batch of buns that Liu Caiyun had handed out.

"Aiya, so that's what happened!" people exclaimed. "Hurry in there and tell Maizy's mother. Tell her how she nearly lost her life over that steamed bun."

Yuxiang and Lianhua's mother agitatedly threaded their way through the crowd to Liu Caiyun's bedside. Lianhua's mother brushed the hair away from Caiyun's eyes and said, "Caiyun, wake up now. Wake up and listen to me. God be my witness that I am telling you the truth.

Nobody made a different kind of bun on purpose so they could eat it themselves. You know how we dust a little soy bean flour on the board when we knead the sweet potato dough for the buns? Well, yesterday when we were finishing up, I swept up the flour with my hands and mixed it into the last bun. Yuxiang told me I should mix it with the starter yeast instead, so that nobody could suspect the commissary people of making two kinds of buns. But I figured it was such a tiny bit nobody could possibly tell the difference. So I said to her, 'Why don't we just mix it into one of the buns made of rancid sweet potato dough and let that bun be something extra special? Who knows how long we'll have to go on eating these bitter old buns, so why not steam this one and whoever gets it just gets it by chance. It'll be a good-luck bun, don't you see?' Caiyun, I'm so sorry. *Please* wake up, Caiyun." By now, Lianhua's mother was crying so hard she was drenched with tears.

Yuxiang, speaking through tears, also pled with her: "Say something, Caiyun."

Liu Caiyun had heard everything Lianhua's mother had said, and it became clear she was moved by it. She was biting her lower lip, which had begun to tremble, when a torrent of silent tears flowed down her cheeks, as if a dike had broken.

When she saw this, Maizy shouted, "Mama, speak to us, mama!" Others shouted the same thing.

Her lips seemed to move before any sound came out, and then, in a hoarse whisper, they heard her say, "This . . . this . . . is our good luck?"

# LIN JINLAN

# The Transcript

The admonition to writers in China to "experience life" and limit their themes to what they knew firsthand came to bear ironic fruit after the Cultural Revolution, when many writers emerged from labor camps or prisons. Although their sojourns had hardly been intended as material for future creative writing, "life" of a significant kind had nonetheless been "experienced." What is surprising, actually, is that so few stories about the camps and prisons emerged, given the large number of writers who had direct experience of them. But publication on this topic was not easy; and besides, many writers were loath to recall extremely painful experiences and to subject themselves to the further involvement in politics that submission for publication entailed. A frank and detailed account of prison life such as Wang Ruowang's "Hunger Trilogy"[1] is as unusual as it is powerful, describing physical circumstances of poor food, punishment, and crowding, as well as the prisoner's inner musings on hunger, friendship, jealousy, loneliness, and plain stultifying boredom.

Translated by Howard Goldblatt. Originally published in *Renmin wenxue* (Beijing), 1979, no. 11.

1. "Ji'e sanbuqu," *Shouhuo* (Shanghai), 1980, no. 1. Unfortunately the work as a whole is too long for inclusion in this collection and excessively wordy. The contrast between the Cultural Revolution prison described in part 3 and the Nationalist prison of the 1930s described in part 1 is made only implicitly, through plain juxtaposition of factual accounts. But it obviously contains a message from the author, himself a devoted communist and a veteran of both prisons, about the progress of the Revolution.

Cao Guanlong's "Fire," included in this volume, tells a prison story whose spectacular elements may seem to deprive it of credibility for an outsider, but that conjure up an entire range of memories — of events similar, if less extreme — among returnees from Cultural Revolution prisons.

Other writers, while choosing not to face the prison or camp experience as squarely as Wang Ruowang or Cao Guanlong, have drawn upon its dramatic power in oblique, but no less telling, ways. The specter of the camp experience haunts Liu Binyan's 1979 story "The Fifth Man in the Overcoat,"[2] about the contemporary problems of a returnee from the camps who wore a crumpled overcoat passed along, we are unobtrusively informed, by four others who had died. Yang Jiang's vignettes on a camp experience, called "Six Chapters from My Life 'Downunder,'"[3] suggest the proportions of her suffering only in extended metaphors and occasional arresting details.

"The Transcript" is another story that treats the incarceration experience in a limited way, in this case by presenting just one of its features: the interrogation. The author buffers its harshness by poking fun at the interrogator—a luxury, of course, that no one actually living the experience could have afforded. The jokes also serve to make the story more politically acceptable, not only because of the softening effect, but because they represent a kind of joke that circulated widely after 1976 with overt official approval. These jokes, which pointed out the glaring illiteracy of Cultural Revolution authorities, are represented in this story by the interrogator's failure to recognize a famous literary figure or even to read his own instructions.

Lin Jinlan (b. 1923) has published four collections of stories, essays, and plays, many about socialist movements in the countryside in the 1950s, and some about intellectuals. In 1979–80, he was a professional writer in the Beijing municipal branch of the Writers' Association.

## The Transcript

A transcript of the type that follows was, at the time of its recording, called "trial proceedings." Yet this particular transcript originated nei-

2. "Diwuge chuan dayi de ren," *Beijing wenyi* 1979, no. 11. Translated by John Rohsenow in Liu Binyan, *People or Monsters? And Other Stories and Reportage from China after Mao*, ed. Perry Link (Bloomington: Indiana University Press, 1983).

3. "Ganxiao liuji" first appeared in the Hong Kong magazine *Guangjiaojing* [Wide angle], no. 103 (April 1981). It is translated by Howard Goldblatt in *Renditions* (Hong Kong), no. 16 (Autumn 1981).

ther in court nor in any public security office, which makes finding a proper label for it today difficult. I'm told that it will be some time yet before any light is shed on the subject.

Interrogator: Ran Agang, are you familiar with Party policy?

Ran: Yes.

Interrogator: Let's have it.

Ran: Leniency toward those who acknowledge their crimes and severity toward those who refuse.

Interrogator: And . . .?

Ran: Resisting confession is the road to ruin.

Interrogator: All right, you've got the idea. (*lightly pounds the table*) So why not confess?

Ran: Already did.

Interrogator: Subject, let's have a subject! *Who* already did? You trying to bully us because of our lack of experience in analyzing evidence, or what? Why no subject in your response?

Ran: (*in hushed tones*) Because there was none in the question.

Interrogator: What, what's that? Speak up . . . I'm conducting this interrogation, so don't you tell me about subjects. Don't think that just 'cause you're a girl, you're mature enough to know what's goin' on. Don't try to pull any of that crap on me.

Ran: (*Although her lips move, no sound emerges, as though she were chanting incantations.*)

Interrogator: Ran Agang, on your feet! You — subject . . . trying to bully us around.

Ran: (*gets to her feet, but continues to speak in hushed tones*)

Interrogator: Speak up. Didn't you say you wanted to come clean? You tryin' to see how stubborn you can be? Or how heroic? You think you're as hard as granite or somethin'? What's with all the mumbling?

Ran: (*in full voice*) I've got nothing to confess.

Interrogator: Aha! So it's arrogance, is it? You wanna go off half cocked, eh! Too bad we're almost outta time, 'cause today we're gonna settle accounts with you once and for all.

Ran: (*Mumbles something unclearly . . . this is a device that has become second nature to her. She seems to have grown up pampered by someone.*)

Interrogator: (*in a tone of supreme tolerance and patience*) Those two classmates of yours, the ones you're so cozy with — like sisters — have already made a clean breast of things, and leniency has been shown them. Now listen carefully, and stop that mumbling — we've taken all of that we're gonna take. They've already been released and returned to the masses. You're the only one left. What makes you think we don't know how to handle someone like you?

Ran: Xu Youying is not my classmate, not even my schoolmate. We've never exchanged more than a few words. As for Mei Shitao, we shared the same dormitory room for the first semester, but since we couldn't get along, we split up the following semester.

Interrogator: Okay, okay, you say you barely spoke with Xu and couldn't get along with Mei. That's pretty convincing, don't you think? But we're not interested in hearing about who you did and did not room with. Piddling affairs like who you shared your bed with are no concern of ours. We don't care about that kind of trash — that's your own shameless business. Stand up straight, lower your head! Who do you think you are! You're being interrogated here, so let's have some concrete details. Were you telling the truth just a moment ago?

Ran: I've never been a member of any spy organization, inner or outer circle, concrete or abstract . . .

Interrogator: I'll tell you one more time, this ain't the time for any tongue-in-cheek show. Don't underestimate the seriousness of the situation. (*He suddenly pounds the table so fiercely that the windows rattle.*) What about that metal box of yours?

Ran: You're the ones who dug that up.

Interrogator: Are you saying we forged evidence? That we're being tricky? That we're tryin' to frame you? Okay, okay, you are so brilliant! (*every syllable a shout*) You — are — out — to — get — us!

Ran: On the seventeenth of November . . .

Interrogator: So you're gonna switch dates on us, huh?

Ran: You wanted concrete details, didn't you?

Interrogator: Go on, finish what you were saying. Spout your shit.

Ran: (*speaks very softly*)

Interrogator: There you go, mumblin' again. You didn't like what I said about spouting shit, eh? You eggheads, you dainty folk with your lily-white hands and soft skin . . . pardon me all to hell, go ahead and speak your piece. Just don't spice up your account too much.

Ran: On the seventeenth of November, I was interrogated all morning,

then without a noon break, you brought in a new team of interrogators and kept it up all day. Then you got me up in the middle of the
night and interrogated me till dawn. All you talked about was a
metal box, until I finally confessed to owning one — round, square,
flat, whatever you wanted me to say, I said it.

Interrogator: Had you 'fessed up before that?

Ran: No.

Interrogator: Why not?

Ran: The metal box isn't the only thing I didn't " 'fess up" to — there's the
soy sauce bottle, vinegar bottle, pickle jar, sugar bowl . . .

Interrogator: Go ahead . . . why stop there? Give the whole opening
spiel — firewood, rice, oil, salt, soy sauce, vinegar, tea. Today's such a
nice day — not too cold, not too hot — and since you've got plenty of
time on your hands, let's take our time and just chitchat awhile . . .
(*raises his voice*) But I will ask you to lean over at the waist, keep your
legs straight, and raise your butt a little higher . . . you shameless
creature. Tryin' to bully your way around here. Come on, let's hear
the opening spiel. But how come I don't hear no closing spiel? When
the People's Liberation Army surrounded the city, your imperial
court began to crumble. The closing down of your school frightened you people right outta your skins. So in the dead of a windy
night, you snuck into the schoolyard like the sinister, disgusting
creatures you are, found a likely lilac bush, where you dug a hole
and buried your metal box, like you were planting a revered ances-
tor, or somethin'. Just like everyone else on the rubbish heap of history, you've made the mistake of misreading the situation. You
figured that the PLA couldn't hold their position. But things never
change: a rabbit — no, not a rabbit, a leopard — can't grow a long
tail. You weren't gone more'n a couple of weeks before your treasure
was dug up and the mummy was brought back to life. That spring
dream of yours, that lovely, lovely pipe dream burst in your faces.
Now whaddya have to say? Cat got your tongue?

Ran: I'm listening to your analysis.

Interrogator: That's another mistake on your part. Analysis? The stack
of material we've dug up is all the circumstantial evidence we need.

Ran: I've got no secrets. It was just a bunch of schoolgirls burying a box
in a schoolyard.

Interrogator: Whatever you say. Every mouth has two lips, whether they're horizontal or vertical. But the interrogation goes on as new evidence pours in. I personally took four people with me to check things out. We went by train and by ship, and we were flown back afterwards. In every city along the way we stayed at first-class guest houses. All this talk about outside interrogators not being welcomed any more . . . is nothin' but reactionary rumor mongering. We just refused to stay at guest houses that didn't have bathrooms. That's quite a nice place you've got there, with its green hills and blue waters. I always used to ask myself why I'd never seen any of the scenery in all those famous paintings — now I know it's 'cause you've got it all down south. Your mountains are loaded with timber, your streams stocked with fish. But don't think you can pull the wool over our eyes. You can't make a silk purse out of a sow's ear. When we got to your schoolyard, each of us took a spade and picked out a lilac bush. But with the cold weather and frozen ground, the spades just sort of scratched the surface . . . What's so funny? All right, back to your "flying position" and see how you feel.[4] Stretch your arms a little more, huh! Tryin' to bully us around! The day'll come when you won't even be able to cry. We dug so damned hard we were covered with sweat — Just talkin' about it now makes me sweat. (*mops his brow*) This is another account we'll be settling with you.

Ran: Did you finally manage to dig anything up?

Interrogator: Okay, so you think we're just a bunch of freeloaders, eh? That all we're good for is hangin' around guest houses? That we're all fun and games? I want you to know that two of those people were military men, so we went to the local garrison and enlisted their help. They sent a platoon of soldiers from the engineering battalion, along with some mine-detecting equipment. You talk about mass mobilization; I'll tell you, we mobilized officers in the service of the dictatorship of the proletariat and troops belonging to defense forces of our revolutionary line. We turned that schoolyard of yours upside down. And that's another account of yours that'll hafta be settled. We dug up a ton of rusty old water pipes, plus an oval box

---

4. A common method of persecution during the Cultural Revolution was to interrogate a victim while forcing him or her to "ride an airplane": to lean forward at the waist with arms stretched backward, parallel to the ground.

with carvings all over it. When we opened it, all we found inside was a bunch of dried-up rose petals. Now what the hell is that all about?

Ran: You can blame that on Lin Daiyu.[5]

Interrogator: (*He thinks, "we old hands at these special investigations are especially sharp where people's names are concerned. No need to check through the dossier for that name — I'm positive this is the first time I've heard it. But I'll keep my composure."*) What grade's she in?

Ran: Huh? Who? (*noticeably startled*) Oh! Her! (*masks her astonishment with a smile*) She's long dead.

Interrogator: (*takes the offensive*) How'd she die?

Ran: (*venomously*) Broken heart.

Interrogator: (*pressing for the kill*) What was her problem?

Ran: (*cunningly*) One of life's problems.

Interrogator: (*continues taking the fight to her*) When did it happen?

Ran: (*paying close attention: bites her lip*) Some time before Liberation.

Interrogator: (*a fortress is most vulnerable to an attack from within*) We've got the goods right here. See, here it is — Wanna take a look?

Ran: I don't need to. There's enough "goods" from her to fill a book.

Interrogator: Crap! Nothing but trash! There ain't a single decent one of you in the lot.

Ran: Are you talking about Miss Lin?

Interrogator: Miss Lin ... (*He thinks, "I can't let down my guard for an instant!"*) Okay! Even in the "high-flying" position, you've still got time for planting tacks and timebombs. I'll put all these on your account, too.

Ran: Boy, this is sure going to be a tough account to settle!

Interrogator: Well, you've got a mouth; let's hear about that metal box. What was in it?

Ran: Student I.D.'s and a few letters.

Interrogator: Student I.D.'s only?

Ran: If I'd had any other I.D.'s, I would've put them in, too.

Interrogator: How about a secret-agent I.D.?

Ran: Sorry, I didn't have one of those.

Interrogator: You're sorry?

Ran: Yes, I'm sorry. If I had, I would've come clean about it long

---

5. Lin Daiyu, the fictional heroine of the famous eighteenth-century novel *Hongloumeng* (Dream of the red chamber).

ago. Then I'd've been set free and would already be back with the masses.

Interrogator: Bend over! Who said you could straighten up? Who're you tryin' to bully? Ran Agang, we're at a critical stage here. Don't dig a deeper hole for yourself. You say they were only student I.D. cards, huh? Why would you bury somethin' like that?

Ran: At the time we were of one heart and mind to join up with the PLA as soon as the soldiers entered the city and go south with them to liberate my hometown — to liberate *all* of China. We buried our student I.D.'s and a few letters to serve as a sort of memento. (*sighs*) Young people often have silly thoughts and do silly things.

Interrogator: Well, all right, now we're gettin' somewhere: after all this time we've got you to admit to being "silly." Even though it's got absolutely nothin' to do with the matter at hand, it's welcome anyway. I'm a man of my word, so you can straighten up. Sit down.

Ran: (*Sits down, but reverts to her old trick of mumbling to herself.*)

Interrogator: (*in a tone of supreme tolerance and patience*) Your brow needs mopping — let's both mop our brows. (*He has temporarily dropped his stormtrooper tactics and adopted a more roundabout approach.*) Ran Agang, have you come to your senses yet? Have you finally realized what's going on here today?

Ran: Yes, I'm being given my fifth final chance.

Interrogator: Okay, as long as you know — and there'll be no sixth chance. In just a moment I'm gonna bring out a piece of evidence, and not just any old evidence, but somethin' as solid as the Rock of Gibraltar. Experience has shown us that no matter how tight-lipped he is, evidence like this'll make a man grovel every time.

Ran: I'd like to see your evidence.

Interrogator: No hurry. First, listen carefully: when I bring this piece of evidence out — when ... I ... bring ... it ... out ... your number's up — you'll be sent someplace else. You know where that someplace is?

Ran: I doubt that you're talking about some foreign country.

Interrogator: Okay, okay. If it comes to that, all the tears and wails in the world won't do you a bit of good.

Ran: I'd like to see your evidence.

Interrogator: I'm gonna give you exactly three minutes to think it over carefully.

Ran: I'd like to see your evidence.

Interrogator: Okay, fine, it's your funeral. I can see you're tryin' to turn the tables on us. Who — are — you — trying — to — bully? (*turns silent*) (*pounds the table hard —like a peal of thunder; shouts a command —more thunder*) Stand up! Two steps forward —one, two —halt! (*opens a notebook*) This criminal item in the dossier has been verified and reverified. Here, see this sentence? Read it aloud.

Ran: "Xu Youying, Mei Shitao, Ran Agang signed petitions and joined a restoration society."

Interrogator: Well, what've ya got to say about that?

Ran: Let me read it again.

Interrogator: Go ahead.

Ran: (*Reads softly . . . this is the girl's standard device when faced with a serious matter or critical situation like this: as though chanting an incantation, she speaks softly with a mysterious sparkle in her eyes.*)

Interrogator: I have here an arrest warrant; up until now it has remained blank . . .

Ran: (*explodes into loud, uncontrollable laughter*) Ha, ha, ha . . . (*with a wild look in her eyes, she says almost hysterically*) This Ran Agang isn't me. Ran Agang isn't anyone. What this says is "Xu Youying, Mei Shitao ran a gang, signed petitions, and joined a restoration society."

Recommendation: Hand over to a mental hospital for observation.

Physician's Inquiry: Who is the patient?

# CAO GUANLONG

# Three Professors

Fiction in 1979–80 dealt with the problems of intellectuals more than any other social group. This is hardly surprising, given that intellectuals had suffered greatly in recent years, and that most writers were, of course, themselves intellectuals. "Three Professors" is a trilogy presenting cases that, while very different, are symptomatic of a large and well-known pattern of abuse of intellectuals during the Cultural Revolution. Tales such as "Cats" (part 2 of the trilogy) are entirely common in recollections of the Cultural Revolution. "Locks" (part 1) depicts a more distinctive individual character but still an all too familiar general situation. Only "Fire" (part 3) seems farfetched (the author does not increase our credulity with his nearly supernatural ending); but even "Fire" is based on the true story of a young man named Tan Yuanquan, who was shot by firing squad in Shanghai about a month after he had dared, in August 1968, to make minor changes in the revolutionary model opera called *Shajiabang*.[1] While assuredly an extreme, the case of Tan's planned dismemberment lends symbolic power to the author's message about the Cultural Revolution generally. That such events are not entirely incredible is further confirmed by the protest that "Fire" elicited

Translated by John Berninghausen. Originally published in *Anhui wenxue* (Hefei), 1980, no. 1.

1. Cao Guanlong, letter to the editors of *Anhui Literature*, 27 October 1979, published in *Anhui Literature*, 1980, no. 1: 31.

from surgeons in Shanghai, who complained that they, as medical professionals, were never *willing* accomplices in such cynical cruelty.

Cao Guanlong (b. 1945), from a "landlord" background in rural Zhejiang, was an "educated youth" working as an automobile repairman in Shanghai in 1979–80. After writing "Three Professors" in the winter of 1978–79, he posted the stories in manuscript form on a wall at Fudan University, where they were received with excitement and high praise by students. Nearly a year later, after their publication in *Anhui Literature*, they received enough public attention to warrant a comment from the Ministry of Culture in Beijing, where they were pronounced "literature of despair." This charge did not mean that the author lacked idealism — since it is too obvious that he wrote from an indignation born of high idealism — but that his stories were too pessimistic. He had failed to balance his grim accounts with appropriately upbeat endings.

The distinctive style of this young writer combines a flamboyant imagination with a rich terseness. One wishes he could have had a good editor, who, without changing his stubborn truth-telling, could have excised his jejune chase scenes (in both "Locks" and "Cats") and exaggeration (the end of "Fire") while cultivating his remarkable gift for imagery and metaphor.

# Three Professors

## Locks

"According to our reports, Master Numbskull has been buying quite a few locks recently and seems to be spending a lot of time in his room fiddling around with them in a very suspicious fashion. No one knows what in the world he's up to!" One of the investigation case workers was flipping through the folder of materials gathered from informers as he conscientiously presented his report. The Special Investigation Team attached to a certain university was right in the middle of the regular meeting it held each week to exchange intelligence. But his report seemed to disappear into the hum of murmuring voices, failing somehow to attract any attention from the others who were sitting around the office in small clusters, some cracking watermelon seeds between their teeth, others absorbed in paring their fingernails. Nor was this lack of response surprising, considering that this particular Special Investigation Team had already made quite a name for itself throughout the city. Having become accustomed to handling the really big stuff, who could expect them to show any interest in this kind of small potatoes?

"Are you trying to tell us that that old duffer is attempting to pull something off? You must be kidding." Somebody finally responded after a long while. "Oh, I guess you probably haven't ever heard the story about him, quite a funny story, too. It seems that a few years back, a burglar jimmied the door to his room and made off with his radio. Master Numb-skull was, in fact, wide awake at the time, but he was so scared he couldn't even croak out a sound. Well, the burglar was long gone, vanished into the night by the time the old boy had climbed out of his bed and crept over to close the door, trembling every step of the way. *That's* when he began scampering around the room yelling 'Stop! Thief!' . . .!"

A burst of raucous laughter engulfed the room.

The chief investigator of the Special Investigation Team sat back comfortably in his handsome swivel chair of glossy walnut, taking in his staff's reports with complete aplomb. The old saying, "you can't play with ink without staining your hands," certainly has something in it. This intrepid and battle-tested "pebble" [see glossary], having been immersed in the slimy mire of intellectuals for quite some time, was actually becoming a little refined in his gestures and choice of words. A dangerous sign. From among a big heap of "the spoils of war" stacked up beside him, the chief investigator casually plucked out a faded brown copy of the earliest extant edition of the *Zhoubisuanjing*, a Zhou Dynasty treatise on astronomy and trigonometry printed under the Southern Song Dynasty [A.D.1127–79]. After absentmindedly flipping through its ancient pages, he took this work, written before the Qin Dynasty [221–210 B.C.], the first Chinese work on mathematics, and blithely, even jauntily, tossed it into the fireplace. Truly it may be said that heavenly justice is all-encompassing, and though its millstone may grind slowly, it grinds exceedingly fine. This classic work on mathematics somehow escaped the large-scale book-burning by the dictatorial First Emperor, Qinshihuang—but have no fear, for after two thousand years, it had in the end been brought to bay and exterminated by the iron hand of "total dictatorship." The chief investigator, having served as the executioner privileged to carry out final justice, watched appreciatively as the pages of that irreplaceable book writhed painfully in the flames. At the same time, he demonstrated his command of that bureaucratic jargon, an amalgam of Shanghainese and Mandarin favored by Party officials, unctuously summing up the discussion by delivering this drawled-out pronouncement: "Master Numbskull, ahh, fancies himself the proponent of some theory of, umm, what was it, uhhh, oh, yes, I've got it, he concocted some theory of probability. Let's see now, didn't he propound some universal, ahh, some universal law?"

His female secretary immediately picked up this thread. "Yes, he once propounded 'A Series of Most Refined Mathematical Formulae Governing All Changes in the Universe from the Movement of Galaxies to the Propagation of Mosquitoes, from the Ebb and Flow of Oceanic Tides to the Rise and Fall of Continents,' or something along those lines."

"Um-hmm." The chief investigator nodded approvingly and continued, "During the past several years, he has been in no position to do any teaching or to carry out any research, since he spends all day in custodial work. Naturally he can't help being a little bit out of it. I would imagine that, quite possibly, he's now taken a wild notion that there is some great mathematical law to be derived from studying the inner workings of locks!"

Another big outburst of sycophantic and scornful laughter.

"However, there's another aspect to this, and that is that recently the old boy has been toeing the line and behaving himself a lot more the way these people ought to." Adopting a magnanimous tone, as if graced with that certain generosity of spirit and tolerance politicians ought to have, the chief went on to amplify his remarks, "He now seems to be quite well disposed toward all of us here in the Special Investigation Team office. Why, this week alone he's come round six times already to report to me on his ideological progress. That's not to say that the old muddle-head doesn't run off at the mouth and spew out a lot of jumbled nonsense, but still and all, there's no denying that this kind of attitude is pretty good, isn't it?"

Master Numbskull was, in fact, surnamed Dài. But during the time when all intellectuals were subjected to relentless attack for being "unable to tote a rifle, plow a field, or swing a hammer," people started intentionally mispronouncing his name as Dāi ["slow-witted" —Tr.]. It was thus that he became "Professor Numbskull." Then with the campaign in which Master Kong [Confucius] and Master Laozi [Lao Tzu] were selected for a flood of public invective, "Professor Numbskull" became "Master Numbskull."

Master Numbskull actually was a bit numbskulled when you come right down to it. Take that incident last year, for instance. The Special Investigation Team had just received glowing commendations from the city's revolutionary committee and from senior officials in the central government for having broken up an enemy intelligence network in which several hundred intellectuals working in more than a dozen institutions of higher learning and research had been implicated and arrested. The entire Special Investigation Team, along with various big shots and lower officials of the university, had organized a celebration banquet. Professor Dai, now known to everyone as Master Numbskull and still under detention for further interrogation at the school, was pressed into temporary service as a waiter. After three rounds of toasts, all of the brave "gestapo," well-renowned for their derring-do, were already muddled with drink. According to the customary order of things at such banquets, a course of fresh fruit was supposed to have been served at this point to help the revelers sober up.

"Hey, Master Numbskull, run out and buy us a few pounds of tangerines!"

An hour or more went by, but Master Numbskull was still nowhere to be seen. Eventually the sleuths, now sprawled and lolling here and there throughout the banquet room, suddenly recalled having sent him out for tangerines. They leapt to their feet in consternation. Almost sober, they grabbed their long lances and charged out through the door, each one screaming curses and dire threats against the old scoundrel for having proved himself unworthy of the trust they had placed in him. Just who did he think he was, trying to evade his well-deserved punishment?

In hot pursuit, the revelers got no farther than the main gate of the university when they were greeted by the sight of a large crowd of people gesticulating and laughing in front of the nighttime shop across the street. Master Numbskull's pursuers dashed across to see for themselves what was going on. The crowd, catching sight of glinting spears rushing their way, supposed this to be yet another bout of armed struggle. They scattered shrieking in all directions, thereby revealing the singular object that had been the center of their attention. A man was sitting underneath the shop window, all scrunched over, tangerines strewn and rolling on the ground around him. As the advancing spear carriers drew near, they could see it was none other than Master Numbskull!

The paper bag in which the tangerines had been sold to him was spread on his lap. He was bent over it, availing himself of illumination from the shop's electric lightbulb, totally absorbed in the tiny symbols and words that covered its every inch. His bald head bent down so close to that old paper bag that he was the very image of a round-shelled snail obliviously devouring a leaf, bite by bite, greedily munching away on it, savoring it, digesting it. His ears did not register any of those vicious curses, much less did his eyes observe the welter of shoes surrounding him. It was not until a hand suddenly cuffed him a good one on the back of his head that Master Numbskull blankly looked up. The cold metallic glean . of a spear tip flashing right in front of his nose abruptly reminded him of the errand on which he had come. In a panic, he frantically tried to gather up all the loose tangerines. One of the spear carriers rudely snatched the paper bag away, and holding it up to the light for a look, flew completely off the handle, screaming with rage, "It's that same fiendish obsession of his!"

It just so happened that the paper out of which this particular bag had been fashioned was a page from some unknown mathematician's handwritten manuscript, its title running straight and true across the top: "Applying Optimization to the Refining of Pharmaceuticals."

Back in his room, our friend Numbskull was now writing out this week's seventh report on his ideology. This man, who could frolic freely and dive to spectacular depths in the ocean of numbers, found it an altogether different matter when faced with stunts such as "carrying out revolution in the depths of one's soul." Trying to cope with this type of thing, he was just like a carp who has flipped out of the water into an ash heap; the more he thrashed around, the more flummoxed he became. Nonetheless he kept at it, slowly and laboriously filling up the paper with words.

He wrote, first of all, that his being confined in isolation and undergoing investigation completely proved the concern and care shown him by the Party organization; then he wrote some more, saying that the instruction he had received from the chief of the Special Investigation Team far outweighed the ten lean years he had spent as a poor student struggling to become educated; and he went further, writing that now there really and truly was a gratifying springlike warmth and gentleness in the office of the Special Investigation Team, and so on and so forth. Resorting to characters almost as large as the standard script of Liu Gongquan [famous calligrapher, A.D. 778–865 — Tr.], he finally managed to fill up five or six pages of this latest report on his thinking.

Quickly scanning it once, he folded it up and slipped it into his pocket. Then he pulled open the drawer of his desk and took out six separate bunches of steel wires of various lengths and shapes, each with a hook or twist on one end. His hand reached out to turn off his desk lamp. This left him sitting in the dark, just like a Buddhist monk meditating as he counts his beads. Reciting words and numerals under his breath, the professor concentrated on carefully feeling each wire with his fingertips. This done, he slipped each packet cautiously into an inside pocket and then patted them to be sure they were in place. He sat there in the silence of his room, his accelerated respiration rasping extraordinarily loud and distinct in his ears. All of a sudden the table clock struck nine. The professor jumped to his feet and was gone out the door.

His pallid face was illuminated by the street lamps, and the corners of his lips tightened into frequent spasmodic grimaces. A cold chill ran down his spine, while his forehead exuded drops of sweat as large as beans. Stealthily ducking into a line of stumpy trees and scrambling through a hole in the fence around the university campus, the professor then crept silently along a wall until he could slip inside a small French-style building. He brushed off his clothes and began to climb the stairs to the second floor. Although he stopped time and again to take in deep breaths in an effort to calm his nerves, his legs simply refused to stop their wild trembling as he climbed the staircase.

There was no light upstairs and the whole corridor was pitch-black. Starting from the head of the stairs, the professor counted out five paces, then reached out and groped around in the dark. Sure enough his hand soon came into contact with the labyrinthine keyhole of the "Empress" brand lock with which the door to the Special Investigation Team's office had been specially fitted.

With the latest installment of his "thought report" in his left hand, he rapped lightly several times with the knuckle of his right index finger, pressing his ear against the door. No sound came from within. Then he beat several times on the door with the open palm of his hand and still there was no response. Without further delay, the professor wadded up his "thought report" and stuffed it into his pants pocket. Quickly

fishing out those packets of wires, and softly repeating a six-digit number to himself, he pulled out a specific hooked wire from each of the
packets according to a predetermined sequence. Next he combined
these into a certain configuration and inserted them by feel into the
keyhole. Holding their ends tightly between his thumb and forefinger,
he twisted and jimmied these springy wires rhythmically back and
forth, in and out, but the mechanism of the lock simply would not
budge. Thereupon he recited another sequence of numbers and tried a
different set of six steel wires, again to no avail.

Time slid by in perfect silence, nothing to mark its passing, as the
professor stuck to his sequence and methodically tried one configuration after another. As he worked, he gradually entered a different state
of mind, akin to euphoria or dementia. Cowardice, anxiety, trembling,
giddiness had all vanished into the night, leaving him fully concentrated
on the job of picking the lock. It seemed his other senses and every part
of his nervous system not employed in this task had ceased to function
for the duration.

Had the professor's skull turned into a transparent glass dome right
then, we could most assuredly have seen a miraculous sight: the bulging
surface of the professor's brain would have appeared to us as the fluorescent screen of an oscilloscope with a single point of light glowing and
sparkling on it there in the dark. That nodule of light would be the
supreme center of stimulation among the many functional areas of his
brain. The "fuel" supplied to the brain calls to stoke its cogitational ac-
tivities—those high-energy phosphotidic acids—would have nearly all
converged at this hot point and be intensely metabolizing, reacting,
combusting, emitting a dazzling glow. But the tens of billions of nerve
cells surrounding this one center of stimulation were all inactive, temporarily held in check; they would have shown up as nothing but an inert
gray mass on the fluorescent screen.

That glowing point of light would be the quintessential nature of
the professor and would represent the crucial characteristic of many,
many other scientists who lose themselves so completely in their work. It
is this temperament that has accomplished so many great discoveries
and inventions. But in this particular environment, with danger lurking
all around, what would this special temperament bring to the professor?

Everything was proceeding according to his preestablished plan of
attack. The professor himself was calm and collected, his movements

sure and deft. He was totally oblivious to the fact that he was in the middle of a very dangerous and tricky piece of business. He was like a superbly skilled surgeon performing a delicate operation to set the stirrup bone in the middle ear.

The eighth configuration of wires finally did the trick, turning the mechanism of the lock around twice with the faint sound of metal springing into place. The professor turned the door handle and the door slowly opened to him. He nipped in through the door, immediately closing it behind him, then leaned back against it to catch his breath before setting off through the darkness. "Three steps forward," he muttered. "Now three to the left, now two to the right, here we are!" He reached out to touch the chief investigator's office desk. It was right where it was supposed to be. Detouring round the chief's chair, he brushed up against a pile of books stacked in the corner. He then squatted down and felt around with his hands until he found what he was groping for—a square bundle of papers tied up with four crisscrossing pieces of twine.

"Right, this is it!"

Everything had gone off without a hitch and the object he was after was now in his hands. After a few seconds, a sudden thought struck Professor Dai just as he was about to clear out of this frightening place. "Could I have gotten the wrong one?" So he put the bundle of papers down on the desk and, bending over it with the window at his back, struck a match, which clearly illuminated the title on its wrapper: "An Inquiry into the Criteria for Uniqueness in the Q Process."

"That's it! That's it!" A tremor of delirious joy swept through his body; his legs went weak at the knees and then gave way as he sank backward into the chief investigator's upholstered swivel chair. The flame from the match quavered, calling forth dim shapes of desks looming all around, ever so like wild beasts lurking in a mountain cave, peering malevolently at this uninvited guest who dared to trespass within their lair. The match burned down and began to singe his fingertips, but the professor was unmindful even of this.

"I wonder how he begins his argument," mused the professor. "The opening argument generally determines the whole exposition. Just a quick glance. I'll just take a peek at the first page and then get out of here." With two final quavers, the match flame went out. Incredibly, the professor's hand now inched through the darkness toward the switch on the desk lamp. *Click!* The room was suddenly filled with eye-piercing light.

Please don't blame the professor too harshly for his foolhardy self-indulgence. If we could comprehend the far-reaching and decisive significance that the content behind that abstract and peculiar title had for the future of ballistic accuracy, earthquake prediction, meteorological forecasts, plant and animal genetics, and so on, or if we had any conception of the history of probability studies during this past half century, in which so many experts have expended so much effort on this very topic, about which to this day they are unfortunately still groping in the fog, perhaps we would then be able to appreciate the nearly magical allure of this manuscript for the professor.

Just as the pearl diver who has gone through great hardship finally to get his hands on a large and promising oyster shell, and who needs only to pry that shell gently open in order, perhaps, for a pearl of breathtaking lustre to come into view, likewise the professor could not resist the hope that out of that bundle of papers would emerge a pearl of wisdom to rise up into the limitless starry firmament of knowledge, there to radiate its light and guide mankind's eternal voyage in search of truth. When one thinks of it this way, even if you were risking your neck in a wildly pitching sampan, do you think you could have withstood the intense desire to take one little peek?

The first page had long been turned over; the professor had not kept his promise to himself. The second page had followed, and the third . . .

It was just like the good old days when he used to sit beneath that pale yellowish light, so warm and cheerful, back at the faculty room correcting graduate students' papers in the dead of night. He ran his eyes rapidly through pages filled with line after line of abstruse and monotonous numbers, signs, equivalences, equations. He resembled the conductor of an orchestra silently poring over the score of a colossally complex symphony; merely from notes, dots, and lines on paper, the maestro can hear in his mind's ear the forceful, surging resonance of the piano, the dolorous tremolo of the violin, the soaring clarion call of the trumpet, the heart-stopping barrage of the kettledrum's roll . . .

The professor was intoxicated, his whole body and soul intoxicated. He couldn't help slapping the table in delight at the incisiveness and boldness of the thesis, he whistled to himself and exhaled repeatedly in admiration of the finely honed and tightly argued proofs. Again like a conductor, who detects a few faint discordant tones present somewhere in the orchestra's harmonious chords, the professor also had to shake his head and sigh at the occasional oversight or mistake in the thesis. He reached out to take an old-fashioned steel pen from the penholder on the desk, the very same pen that had split countless good and innocent couples asunder, that had separated children from parents, destroyed homes, sent good people to their deaths. Dipping the nib into the inkwell, he painstakingly set to work refining the manuscript with a mark here and stroke there . . .

Those amazing spies in thrillers and detective stories are often depicted as possessing a sixth sense. In tight spots, they are always able to maintain all six senses in a state of heightened alertness so that they absorb and process the slightest bit of data captured from their surroundings and thus prevail over their opponents and protect themselves. Although our good professor had mastered the art of picking locks to a degree that probably would have left Sherlock Holmes wideeyed and gape-jawed, what happened to him next further demonstrates, unfortunately, that he really was not in the same league as the great detectives and spies.

The sky in the east was beginning to turn fish-belly pale, but he did not notice. The early morning sun began to shine in through the iron bars on the window, but he was completely unaware of it. Nor did he perceive the peal of voices as people did their collective morning exercises on the playground outside. He didn't even know what to make of the earsplitting cry of surprise from the woman secretary as she opened up the office that morning.

Several items of incriminating evidence were collected when they searched the professor's room:

First, there were all those disassembled, shiny metal parts of door locks found in his desk drawer.

Second, there was a small notebook chock-full of numbers, plus a great many sketches and diagrams of hooks that looked like steel wires.

Third, there was a blurry letter written on coarse straw paper. It read:

To my esteemed teacher, Professor Dai:

I'm afraid I haven't much longer to live. They want me to confess to being an enemy intelligence agent and several shifts of them are interrogating me around the clock; they persist in smashing my head — very hard — against the concrete wall in the air raid tunnel. This happens every day!

My capacity for logical thinking has been ruined. There was a time when you used to praise my memory, but now I can't even recite the multiplication tables! When you're a mathematician and you have your cerebrum destroyed, then what's the use of living, anyway?

Since I'm an orphan and you were my teacher, I have to be counted as one of your children. Permit me to unburden myself and leave my last words to you as to a loving father.

Some years ago I wrote "An Inquiry Into the Criteria for Uniqueness in the Q Process." But even though I completed the manuscript, I didn't publish it because there were still certain places that needed further consideration. Who would have imagined that the manuscript and I would come to grief simultaneously?

The last time I was taken into the Special Investigation Team's office for interrogation, I noticed that my manuscript had been thrown into a corner near the chief investigator's desk where all kinds of books lay in a big pile.

This body of mine is now nothing but a worthless piece of junk waiting to be discarded; whether it is buried or cremated doesn't matter. But what I've written could conceivably offer some useful leads that would contribute to the eventual solution of this major mathematical proposition. Just the thought that those pages might wind up being used as kindling or burnt as waste paper makes my head whirl and throb in the most horrible way . . .

"Goddamn! The creep was about to die and he still tried to pull a fast one right under my nose!" The chief investigator, feeling that he had been duped, finally dropped all pretense of refined civility and vented his ire in loud cursing. "I know this handwriting! This letter was written by that bastard who killed himself last month by slitting open his carotid artery. That's it, no mistaking it!"

Those several sets of steel hooks, the miscellaneous contents of the professor's desk drawer and the indecipherable notebook were all sent to the responsible unit for analysis. After a long time, they came out with their formal appraisal:

> The pieces of metal found in the drawer are all parts of "Empress" brand door locks. Furthermore, each metal part bears clear traces of having been sawed, filed, chiseled, hammered or otherwise manipulated in the process of being taken apart and broken down for analysis.
>
> The numbers recorded in the notebooks represent the nearly ten thousand possible states of the cylinder of said lock as constituted by the permutations of the sequence and lengths of its six tumblers; and, the general formula for opening the lock as derived from the above. The hook diagrams are the simplest key components derivable from the formula.
>
> Following the sequences prescribed for each set of six-digit numbers in the notebook, we have grouped the six sets of steel wire hooks into all possible combinations and then experimented with them on all the "Empress" locks we have in storage. The results have yielded success in opening every lock without exception.
>
> The "Empress" door lock is a new type of lock reserved for official use in China after the incorporation during the last few years of comprehensive improvements over its model, the 1940 German product called the "Swastika Brand" security lock.

## Cats

It was past eleven o'clock one night in a certain apartment building in Shanghai; a white head slowly circled its way up some dimly lit stairs, turning at each flight of steps until finally reaching the fifth floor. An old man shuffled unsteadily along until he reached the door of his studio apartment, where he fumbled a long time for his key. As he pushed open the door, a pure white cat scampered out and rubbed against his legs, meowing as it curled in and out between his feet.[2] The old man lovingly bent down to pick up his cat and then, breathing heavily from his exertion, entered the room.

A little stooped over at this late hour, he had returned from work

2. In the Shanghai dialect, the word for "cat(s)" and "Mao" as in Mao Zedong are homonyms. The significance of this fact emerges in the story.

still wearing his apron of black vulcanized denim and a pair of oversized galoshes. He also was carrying a rusty iron kettle full of fish heads, fish tails and the like. Dressed in this getup, he resembled the men who scale and clean fish at the market; but he was, in fact, a professor.

For the past several years, he had been assigned the duty of cleaning out all the toilets at the academy. There were more than a dozen of them scattered through several buildings. This was plenty to keep him fully occupied, yet he was also frequently plagued with unforeseen interruptions. For instance, this very day, when it was time to finish up and go home, he had suddenly been called before the political control team and questioned for three or four hours. In the end, his interrogator had tossed him a letter with "imperialism" stamped on it. It turned out to be an invitation from an international scholarly organization inviting him to take part in a conference. The professor was sent home with orders to write out a full confession detailing any and all foreign organizations with which he had ever had contact. A cold front had suddenly set in and it was raining, so the professor went straight home, still in his workaday outfit.

In point of fact, the word "home" was an empty term when applied to the apartment in which he resided. His wife had been a high-school principal, but, after several months in the "cow shed" [see glossary], had escaped back home one night in a state of complete distraction. After a last look at their children, she had thrown herself from their balcony.

This balcony was quite spacious. In former times, the old man would rise very early each morning and go out on the balcony to water their many flowers and plants. Then he would enjoy waving his arms and legs through a set routine of dumbbell exercises. But after the death of his life's companion, the old man had used a piece of thick wire to bind shut the steel-grating door to the balcony, and had closed the balcony from view with a thick curtain, which he never opened. He could no longer bear the sight of that balcony.

One by one, the children had grown up and moved to distant places, leaving him alone with no one but this cat. Before his wife's suicide, the professor had never much cared for dogs or cats. Tonight he leaned back in his rattan chair and stroked the soft, silky fur of the little white cat that lay in his lap. He could not help surrendering himself to a happy illusion that floated up before his eyes: his wife knitting in the sunlight, the little cat tumbling and rolling around, flinging itself this way and

that as it played with her ball of yarn. This reverie was abruptly dis-
solved by a sudden recollection of that order to write out a confession;
his whole body began to shiver as a chill came over him. Most likely that
wool sweater of his was packed away in the case on the upper shelf of the
closet. The old man pulled a square stool over to the closet and gingerly
climbed up on it. As ever, his little cat followed him wherever he went in
the room; this time it lay down to wait quietly beside the stool upon
which its master was standing.

The old man gave a hard tug at the case, which was high up on the
closet shelf. A dark object hurtled down from the shelf to land below
with a dull thud. He looked down. It was one of his dumbbells, which
had rolled out and fallen directly onto the little cat's head. This happened so fast that the cat had not even had time to gasp. It just lay there
with its legs twitching spasmodically.

As he leaped down from the stool in panic, the old man's feet
slipped out from under him and he fell sprawling on the floor. Having
righted himself, he picked up that poor little thing with the smashed-in
head, and held it in his arms. Then he sat there, gape-jawed and dumbfounded, his chin trembling.

More than an hour went by and still the old man sat on the floor,
benumbed as one suddenly fallen into a boundless expanse of nothing-
ness. The table clock struck one with a frightening clang and the old
man was finally startled back to consciousness. The white cat was still
lying peacefully across his legs, but it had already grown cold. Hunting
up a piece of white cotton cloth, the old man wrapped his cat up in it
and, cradling the tiny corpse in his arms, made his way in a daze back
down the five flights of stairs.

After walking a few blocks, the old man halted across from a trash
bin in a dark corner. A bunch of street cats were hissing and biting and
making a terrible din as they tumbled and wrestled with each other atop
the trash heap. But as soon as the old man walked over to the bin, they
shrieked and ran in all directions. As if fearful of jarring his little cat's
wound, the old man gently placed his white bundle on top of the trash
pile. He then stood for a long while, the very image of dejection, before
he turned and heavily dragged his feet back home.

The next evening, while cooking dinner in the kitchen he shared
with several households, the professor overheard two of his neighbors
conversing quietly.

"Say, 'dja hear 'bout it? Wouldja b'lieve it but a counterrevolutionary deed's been committed right on our street, and I mean something of a serious nature, I do!"

"Huh? Howd'yah find out 'bout it?"

"Today the Red Guards had an emergency meeting of their 'Attack with Words, Defend with Weapons' task force. My husband was there."

"So, what's the story, what actually took place?"

"It was a cat." The first woman lowered her voice and spoke with a very mysterious air. "A cat was murdered last night in the most horrible way. Somebody smashed its head to a pulp. According to the postmortem by the medical examiner, some blunt instrument had been used to bludgeon it to death. It counts as premeditated murder! The murderer tried to escape responsibility . . . he wrapped the body up in a piece of cloth and threw it into the trash."

"A cat? Just a cat? A counterrevolutionary deed?" The second woman's level of political consciousness was obviously low; she was having trouble believing her ears.

"Oh, goodness gracious, how dense can you be!" The woman with the special news sources did not conceal her derisive attitude toward anyone so obtuse that she would fail to recognize the Buddha even while burning incense to him. "Even the leaders in the city government have intervened to order that the case be solved in due time. They called it a fiendish attack . . ."

"Ahhh?" Interjections of surprise burst forth simultaneously from the stupid woman *and* the old professor. The lid of the professor's rice pan fell from his hand and went clanging to the floor. The two women spun round at once to see the old man crouching to retrieve the lid, frantically trying to cover up by muttering loudly, "Ouch! Ooh, that's hot! Burn your fingers right off!"

As he picked up the lid, his ears caught another bit of inside info that the official's wife let slip. "Bright and early tomorrow morning, they're going to spring a big house-to-house search. They'll call it a sanitation inspection, but actually they'll be taking an inventory of the neighborhood cats!"

Without even waiting for his rice to boil, the old man picked up his kettle from the stove and rushed back into his room. He leaned weakly against the door, his heart pounding. A minute ago, he'd been pretty hungry, but now he had an acrid taste in the back of his throat and felt like throwing up.

"Cat! Counterrevolutionary! Vicious attack! Of a serious nature!" The words pounded violently at the old man's eardrums, echoing and reechoing. His fifteen-watt lightbulb seemed extraordinarily bright, and his eyelids blinked rapidly from the discomfort it caused him. He switched off the light but then felt oppressed by the heavy, stultifying darkness. "A big search first thing tomorrow!" Beads of sweat were now popping out on his forehead as he pulled open the door and rushed down the stairs.

It was the middle of the night again when he returned to the same trash bin he had visited the night before. Its iron door was wide open but inside was as dark as a cave; cats of every hue and stripe were prowling and pacing around the bin's open door. A pure white cat came slinking along the base of a wall and slowly climbed into the bin. Suddenly a giant dark form came hurtling in through the trash bin's open door and pinned that white cat to the floor. A man! With his full head of white hair, he now clumsily pulled himself up out of the trash heap. It was the professor! Taking a quick glance around and seeing no one, he stuffed the cat into his coat and limped away. The cat screeched and struggled wildly beneath his coat but the old man held on, patting and caressing it, even humming to it as if he were comforting a baby. But the street cat was having none of this; its caterwauling grew louder and louder until the old man was so agitated he broke into a cold sweat. Drawing near the entrance to his apartment building, he looked around furtively and then, hardening his heart, clamped down on the cat's neck and managed to choke off that terrible wailing. Even so, the cat continued to thrash around for all it was worth, taking full advantage of its rapierlike claws to scratch and rip at the old man's chest until it throbbed with pain. He ignored the pain and tiptoed stealthily upstairs, almost all his strength concentrated in his fingers. No matter what, he could not risk any sound from that cat!

Finally he was back in his room with the door safely shut behind him; his two arms fell weakly to his sides and the cat slid noiselessly down from his bosom to drop heavily onto the floor. But there it lay motionless! In panic, the old man knelt beside it and lifted up its head. Hopeless! Its tongue was hanging out of its mouth; this cat was gone, too! His brain felt a savage jolt, as if someone had used a stick to fetch him a mighty blow to the head.

"A big search first thing tomorrow!" The horrifying words rang again in his ears. He rushed around in a frenzy, pulling out some old newspaper and clumsily wrapping the dead cat in it. He stuck this packet under his arm, and again hurried out. Stumbling through the night, he hastened back to the trash bin. Just when he had discarded his parcel, and was intending to steal back to his room, the snowy white beam of a powerful flashlight shot out at him.

"Identify yourself!" A harsh voice yelled at him from a distance. The old man whirled and ran, blindly twisting and turning through the maze of lanes and alleys until he finally gave his pursuer the slip. He rushed frantically up the stairs and burst in through the door to his room to fall full-length onto the floor. His heart pounded, pounded as if it would jump out from his throat. His mouth was parched, as if on fire. With great effort, he crawled across the floor into the bathroom, where he managed to pull himself upright and turn the faucet. He gulped down mouthfuls of water, pausing only for labored gasps to catch his breath. He saw streams of stars rush before his eyes like phosphorescent wisps of ghost fire fluttering and scurrying in a graveyard of a summer's night. These everchanging streaks of light abruptly transformed themselves into the heads of cats—black ones, white ones, yellow ones, spotted ones, even the head of his cat that had been smashed flat, and that one with its tongue hanging out—and all of them, jostling, scratching, biting, howling, came rushing at him. The old man stumbled around his room in the dark, terror-stricken, desperately trying to hide. But from under the bed, from the top of the closet, from behind the door came nothing but pair after pair of burning greenish eyes . . .

The night patrol of the task force may have failed to seize the man who had thrown away the bundle wrapped in newspaper, but they had succeeded in discovering his name and work unit, since these were clearly written as the subscriber's address on that sheet of newspaper. It was then only a matter of calling his work unit to learn the full particulars of his situation: "reactionary academic authority"; "wife committed suicide to escape justice"; "close connections with foreign organizations"; "drafting a full confession of his criminal behavior . . ."

"It all stems from a reactionary class-nature!" was the logical conclusion they immediately drew. The task force immediately cabled the

Municipal Revolutionary Committee, who wasted no time in sending back an unequivocal directive: "Arrest him without delay!"

A truck loaded with men in wicker helmets and carrying long spears braked to a halt in front of the old man's apartment building sometime after three o'clock in the morning. They had the building surrounded in short order. Then a small detachment of spear-wielders went pounding up the steps. The one in the lead was carrying a "type-54" police revolver. Just as the detachment reached the fourth floor, some loud noises issued from the floor above: a heavy object smashing against something; then the breaking of glass and a loud shriek something like, but not exactly like, the screech of a cat.

"Charge!" ordered the leader, and the group of men rushed toward the fifth floor. There came another sound, of pottery being smashed. It seemed someone inside was desperately struggling, resisting. A big leather boot smashed against the outside of the door and forced it open. Several flashlights stabbed into the dark room. Inside was a complete shambles, broken glass all over the floor. The steel grating over by the balcony had been wrenched open.

Probing the balcony with their beams, those flashlights picked out and revealed an old man, crouched over, every white hair on his head standing erect like a hedgehog's. An eerie gleam shone from his blood-shot eyes. The flesh on his face, swollen and purplish like pork liver, was covered with goosebumps. His white shirt hung in tattered shreds, tangled and bloodied and virtually indistinguishable from the mangled skin of his lacerated chest.

His mouth was contorted into a toothy grimace as the frightfully crazed old man let out those cries of terror, rage, and despair that reminded one of a cat, yet were somehow different. The cries began low down with a hoarse panting, a muffled moaning, then would start to quaver and rasp higher and higher, up and up to the highest possible pitch until they turned to mad wails and piercing shrieks.

He was like a wild animal driven into a corner. Stretching out his bloody hands, the old professor lashed out, clawed, and struck wildly at the night, looking for all the world like someone locked in a life-and-death struggle with a disembodied spirit. He appeared to be totally unaware of the intruders who had come to arrest him. His glazed eyes were fixed on that nonexistent thing with which he fought, at which he yelled, and from which he retreated ever closer to the edge of the balcony. Even when the railing of the balcony pressed him in the small of the back, he still tried to back away. His upper body leaned farther and farther back over the railing until finally he fell backward over the edge. A bone-chilling scream receded quickly into the darkness below...

Everything once again was silent.

However, that same disembodied spirit is still abroad in the land, haunting, haunting...

### Fire

"Glass" moved in.

Scarcely over twenty years old, Glass had sunken cheeks because of his skimpy rations. Yet the appeal of his handsome, finely chiseled features could not be vanquished by his starved condition. The dark circles around his eyes, put there by anxiety and lost sleep, only served to highlight that extraordinary pair of sparkling eyes.

Indeed this pair of eyes shone like glass! Whenever he fixed something in that reflective gaze of his, the crisscrossed lines of an interlocking grid would appear clearly and crisply reflected within those jet black pupils. A poet would probably liken these crisscrossing lines to willow branches trailing down over the still waters of a pool. In fact, they were reflections of the bars over his prison window.

These bars would bend, undulate, and melt away, and with one blink of his long eyelashes, two crystalline pearls would spill out from his eyes. Then the iron bars would gradually take shape and converge to form again the tightly wrought net over those limpid eyes, which once again shone clear and bright!

Of course, Glass did have a long "prisoner's number," but his cellmates disdained it as both hard to remember and awkward to use. Thus they came up with the elegant and perfectly fitting nickname of Glass.

Among these cellmates was one who had rifled a cash box, one who had committed armed robbery, another who had murdered his wife, yet another who had raped a young girl; indeed it is fair to say that the prison held everything: every faith and pursuit, evil fiends of all varieties. Yet, of all the inmates, Glass had the worst crime of all on his record.

It really was a terrible crime. Not long after taking up a job in the factory to which he had been assigned, one of the amateur Mao Zedong

Thought Propaganda Troupes in that district of Shanghai had taken a shine to him, and he was almost immediately tapped for the leading role of Guo Jianguang in the Propaganda Troupe's production of the revolutionary model opera *Shajiabang*. The only trouble was that Glass, though a gifted actor, you might say was even more talented as a playwright. Less than a month after he had started performing, he suddenly hit upon the idea of inserting a new twist into the performance. The public health worker would give subtle signs of a secret crush on the army officer. Glass felt this slight revision in the script would help to flesh out the character of Guo Jianguang as well as add a touch of romantic appeal. But in the end this little twist, this tiny pinch of romantic spice, turned out to be the most heinous of crimes.

Of course! Everyone knows that "lust is the origin of a thousand disruptions and lewdness the leader among ten thousand evils." We should recall that it was the year in which some would-be lovers in fiction were stripped of all affection and desire, and, pledging themselves to "model" behavior, swore to cleanse their minds and be good boys and girls. At the same time, characters such as Li Yuhe and Tie Mei in *Red Lantern*, Yang Zirong in *Taking Tiger Mountain by Strategy*, Lei Gang in *Azalea Mountain*, Fang Haizhen in *Seaport*, Jiang Shuiying in *Ode to Dragon Mountain*, and so on, appeared as pristine and sexless as if they were Buddhist monks and nuns made of iron. How in the world could we tolerate a poisonous serpent to come slithering into our perfect and pure Garden of Paradise, there to tempt Adam and Eve? When we see things in this light, can there be any doubt that the relentless and overwhelming attack by the dictatorship of the proletariat upon this fanciful young playwright and actor was exactly what he deserved?

Eventually Glass was tossed into jail on the fearsome charge of having distorted a revolutionary model opera. Once among the pack of common criminals who were his cellmates, he became subject to their supervision and remolding.

Some of our compatriots are possessed of the virtue of flexibility, of knowing when to be tough, when to be soft, when to lord it over others, and when to bow and scrape. We might define this particular virtue as our "canine quality."

Dogs, who have grown accustomed to slavery, will grovel and lick and crawl on their bellies in the most shameful fashion at the feet of a stronger creature. However, dogs also carry the genes of the wolf in their blood. They will snarl and bare their fangs, and lunge and bite at anyone over whom they have gained an advantage; they will commit any act of brutality or tyranny against those weaker than they. These dregs of society in whose midst Glass now found himself were mere curs under the heels of the guards. But just as soon as they got the chance to bully Glass, they instantly turned into wolves. They were well aware that the remanding of such an important political prisoner into their charge was an unmistakable sign of great trust placed in them by the political leadership. Had their guard not spoken of theirs as an important political mission? "Political mission"! What glory! What stature it gave them!

So Glass was not allowed to sleep anywhere but beside the piss bucket, and was given only half portions of food. When it was cold, he had to hug the feet of the "cell boss," and when it was hot, he had to fan the "chief." Glass had become a slave of slaves. It was as if he were to remain eternally, with no hope of redemption, in an air raid shelter dug beneath the eighteenth and lowest level of hell.

But suddenly the golden light of deliverance shone forth, and things changed for the better. One day the warden was personally escorting about a dozen physicians, all wearing surgical masks, on a tour of the cell block. The gist of the pretty little speech he delivered to them out in the corridor was that the prison director was so concerned about the well-being of the prisoners that today he would show his magnanimity by ordering a physical exam for everyone. Thereupon blood and urine specimens were taken, and the examination of everyone's hearts, lungs, eyes, noses and throats, and so on, was so rigorous it made you wonder if they did this even when selecting airplane pilots. Glass was transferred almost immediately to a private cell upstairs that faced south. When the puffs of cool fresh air wafted toward him through the window of this new cell, they seemed to him even sweeter than ice cream!

The next day, another physician came to visit Glass. He said the general examination the day before had revealed that Glass was afflicted with a mild eye condition, and that they wanted to make further efforts at diagnosis and treatment.

Of rather gaunt appearance, this doctor had kindly eyes and wore a long white physician's coat that was immaculately clean and starched. He deposited some glistening greenish drops of medicine into the young prisoner's eyes and used peculiar-looking instruments to peer into his pupils. At the same time, he kept making quick notes on his findings in the sprawling, squiggling lines of some Western script. To take the patient's mind off all this, he kept chatting with Glass in a friendly fashion; he expressed great sympathy for the prisoners' hard lot and said he might take the matter up with the authorities concerned.

"That's fine." The doctor patted the youth's shoulder when the examination was finished. "This is a vial of cod liver oil. It's very good for the eyes. Take a dose of it three times a day. Don't forget. Once after each meal."

"But I only get two meals a day!"

"What? Still only two a day? Don't they realize what you're worth? What a shame!" The good doctor seemed almost overcome with pained indignation. "Don't worry, young fellow, you're somebody with a future. I'm going to see to it you get your three meals a day. You can count on it!"

Glass choked back his sobs of gratitude.

In the past, when the guards had manacled his arms behind him and hung him from the bars of the window with a heavy stone suspended from each foot (they called this "eating hanging noodles with two stalks of garlic"), he had never cried. Nor had he wept when his cellmates wrapped him in a quilt and ganged up to pummel and kick him, then pried his mouth open and poured urine down his throat (called "stuffed dumplings washed down with a bowl of yellow wine"). But now, like a long-suffering child who suddenly spies the loving face of his father, Glass could not hold back the tears that came streaming down his face.

He wanted terribly to throw himself into the arms of that doctor, but, suddenly realizing that he was a criminal, he checked himself. How could he contaminate the clean soul of that physician by contact with his own sinful body? Thus he could do nothing but cling tightly to the iron bars, wailing and sobbing. He was weeping from humiliation and hatred, yes — but also in gratitude for the doctor's comforting words. He was weeping from bitterness and loneliness, but also for his hopes and dreams. It seemed this normally articulate young man had been driven to monotonous, ear-piercing wails as the only means to deliver himself of his complex, conflicting emotions.

"All right, all right, son, don't carry on so," the physician urged solicitously, while putting away his instruments. "Too much crying can hurt your eyes."

The next day, the slender doctor came again, but this time a large troop of people were following along. The warden, security men, guards, administrative cadres, and the like were all bustling and circling around self-importantly.

"Here, Director, have a look, sir, this is the one." The thin doctor spoke softly and deferentially as he pointed to Glass inside his cell. The retinue then parted to reveal a tall, fat man with a florid face. This man stretched out his arms imperially, allowing two nurses to help support his bulk. He slowly turned his ponderous head in the direction of Glass, but somehow failed to catch sight of him. At this, the thin doctor beckoned to the prisoner. "Come here," he said. "The director wants to see you."

Glass walked hesitantly over to the bars of his cell and stood there blankly. The nurses helped the director to move nearer. Finally, the director of the Public Security Bureau and an incarcerated criminal were looking into each other's eyes with only iron bars between them. What a frightening pair of eyes! Glass was gazing into eyes so cloudy they looked like two pickled eggs gnawed rotten by flies. The director's corneas were covered with lines and blotches of nebulae that reminded one of countless squirming, twisting maggots. This pair of eyes had fixed him with an unblinking, cold stare. Perhaps they still couldn't see him clearly, for they opened even wider and leaned closer and closer until that fat nose was sticking between the bars. The sight made Glass's blood run cold and his scalp turn numb and prickly. He felt as if a huge bear had just bowled him over and lay on top of him, but even with those steamy puffs of breath hitting him full in the face, Glass dared not move a muscle.

"Hmmm —" Finally, a deep and powerful grunt came from those nostrils.

"However, Director, there is a small problem of inadequate nutrition." The thin doctor moved closer to the director and quietly offered this observation.

"Well, Warden, did you hear that? His nutritional intake will have to be increased!"

With that the director slowly made his way back downstairs, with the same retinue clustering around him. Back in the warden's office, the director, somewhat worn out from his exertions, lay back on the warden's sofa with his limbs sprawled out and his eyes closed.

"Well, Professor, what do you think?" he asked. "When can you perform the operation?"

"Uhhh, well, Director, as I see it," responded the slender doctor eagerly, "this is the hot season, when wounds are most easily infected; I would also rule out the winter, when it's more difficult for them to heal up properly. The fall would be best, sir, yes, the period of crisp, cool air in autumn would be the most suitable!" The professor's explanation was delivered in the sweetest and softest of tones.

"Very well then." The director of Public Security inclined his head slightly toward an assistant sitting at his right, and gave him his instructions. "You may inform the Special Investigation Team that I have gone over their report, but that their recommendation is not acceptable. The facts in this case of distorting a model revolutionary opera are very serious, and if we were to handle such a case with the excessive leniency they appear to favor, well, that would be tantamount to disregarding our responsibilities to the masses. We are public servants who must place the interests of the people first in every instance!" The director's voice then took on a pained tone. "These comrades of ours, ahh, despite all the years they've worked in the administration of public security, prosecution, and justice, they've never quite gotten the guiding principle of class struggle through their thick skulls. Why is it that whenever we decide on a sentence, they're always raising a fuss about so-and-so's father having served as such-and-such a cadre, yet somehow they always conveniently neglect the grandfather, whose whole life history was one of serious political transgression? Now why is that? The grandfather may be dead, but the reactionary class roots are very much alive!"

His right-hand man transcribed everything the director said with lightning speed, scrupulously including every tiny inflection and evocative grunt or sigh. It would be a great mistake to dismiss those little "ahhs," "hmms," "wells," "tsks," and so on. These little noises would be of inestimable value to all the subordinates in their efforts to puzzle out and fully comprehend the head man's thinking.

At this moment, the professor had secretly decided to pull a little stunt of his own. He took a step forward and, in a moderately loud voice, addressed the director's right-hand man apologetically.

"Hm'hmmm, I'm terribly sorry, but I think I have to excuse myself now." So saying, he stole a peek at the director, who, sure enough, was reacting just as he had hoped.

"You have something urgent to attend to?"

"Oh, not exactly, Director, it's not what you'd call urgent, it's just that my useless son is trying to get into university, but he's still pretty hazy about even such simple things as basic arithmetic. So I've been trying to find a little time each day to help him review at bit."

"Wants into college? To study medicine?"

"Ahh, no, Director, I'd like him to study politics, then in the future he could work under you."

"Politics, going to take up politics? Excellent! That's the ticket! Politics in command, right?[3] Well done! Come on, come over here and sit beside me, come on!" The director patted the sofa and laughed jovially. "Damn few intellectuals are anything like you, most of 'em completely out of step with the times! But it seems to be quite unnecessary for you to spend time helping your son with his lessons. You should be devoting all your energies these days to the most careful preparation for this operation. You should go over every detail of the procedure, and grab every chance to do tests, in order to ensure absolute success for the operation."

"Precisely. This is a very important political duty!" The director's right-hand man was going out of his way to emphasize the point. "As far as your son is concerned, you may set your mind at ease. After the operation succeeds, I of course will fix everything up for you."

With a respectful maneuvering of his slender frame something like the prancing horse step in Chinese shadow boxing, the professor propped his skinny buttocks on the very edge of the sofa and sat there on the left side of the director in the most deferential fashion. Even though his rigid posture deprived the professor of the normal comforts of sitting on a sofa, he actually felt on top of the world as he perched there basking in the warm glow that comes from getting in thick with a big shot. Indeed, was not sitting there at the director's left virtually equivalent to being his number two assistant? Adopting the tone of voice of the director's number one man, the professor now gave *his* instructions to the warden:

"As for that prisoner, you must not only improve his diet but, even more important, take steps to lift his spirits. You must keep him happy. To do this, it seems to me it wouldn't hurt to employ a little ruse, mmhhh —" Now the professor's voice was beginning to sound more and more like the director's. "For instance, you might tell him that his case is

3. A Cultural Revolution slogan closely associated with Maoist revolutionary zeal.

about to be cleared up, and that it won't be too long before he'll be released, and so forth. You must realize that the health of the donor has a direct influence upon the success or failure of such operations."

"That's right, that's right!" The director nodded repeatedly in full concurrence. "Now then, Warden, I know that you'll be careful to follow the professor's guidance in this matter!"

By the end of September, the professor had completed all the necessary preparations. Thereupon the director of the Public Security Bureau, from his suite in the hospital, officially signed the following directive:

"The criminals whose names are listed below are to be transported under guard to the appointed site and there to be executed by firing squad . . . "

It was very foggy.

Those wispy strands of morning mist curled silently through the bars and into his cell. Gently they caressed the solitary prisoner, as if someone had lit a stick of incense in honor of this unfortunate soul. This was to be Glass's final morning.

He sat on his bed with his knees pulled up to his chest, his body slightly hunched over, looking as if he were still unable to shake off the night's dreams. As he stared blankly into the ever-changing wisps of fog, he seemed to see a host of angels trailing lacy ribbons of pure white. Weightlessly, gracefully, they circled through the air without the slightest sound, slowly pirouetting in the mystical dance of the Celestial Realm.

Glass went on sitting there as if carved from stone, while events from the past overtook time and space to float up one after another before his eyes . . .

From the ventilation duct of an air raid shelter, a face, pallid and swollen, stared out expressively at a group of children in the school yard.[4] At that time, Glass had been a Red Guard along with all the others, and had hurled clods of earth at that face screaming, "You cow, you cow!" . . .

. . . "Yes, when I get out of here, I swear I'll go back to my old school and stand before that very air raid shelter where our teacher met her terrible end. I shall lift my face toward heaven and shout, 'Dear teacher,

4. During the Cultural Revolution, air raid shelters dug beneath schools, factories, and other buildings were used by Red Guards as detention cells in which "class enemies" could be imprisoned.

just when you were suffering the most, I, too, was among the attackers!'"

Perhaps it had been as far back as his nursery school days that he had once caught a dragonfly and tied a thread to her tail. Oh, how she had bled! A drop of translucent, pale green blood had hung there quivering from the end of the tail. How she had strained against the thread, her diaphanous wings beating the air as she struggled to fly into the freedom of the blue sky, but her efforts had only pulled the thread tighter and tighter. Oh, how that poor little creature must have suffered, thought Glass. And afterwards, afterwards, uhh . . . what had happened to her? Had she died or flown away? Remorsefully Glass went over and over this memory, but just could not recall the fate of the dragonfly. . .

A sudden clang, and into his cell stormed several bailiffs who, without a word, expertly carried out their set plan to truss up Glass so that he could hardly move. First they tied his ankles with rope. Then, fiercely twisting his jaw, they dislocated it so that he couldn't get it back in place. With the spittle dripping out the corners of his mouth, Glass could no longer talk, but only grunt in pain.

Yet even this was deemed inadequate. As an additional safeguard, they fitted a noose of extremely fine nylon filament around his neck. Actually this new use of thin nylon cord represented one of the more important technical innovations to have occurred in their line of work during the past several years. Formerly, they had used a piece of hemp rope, which, though sufficiently devastating to its victim, had the distinct disadvantage of unsightliness. Now, with this transparent, yet very strong, nylon line, which was nearly undetectable by anyone not in the know, mere tugs on the noose by the bailiff behind could prevent even titans and heroes from uttering a sound.

Transparency often harbors great strength.

The strands of a spider's web are transparent, but think how many naive and foolhardy moths have met their ends by straying into those painstakingly woven webs of such intricate design. Snake venom is also transparent, but a fraction of a milliliter is enough to make a shepherd girl fall dead into the underbrush in less than seven paces. Can you see electricity? Yet in the wink of an eye it can convert a living, breathing, active child into a charred mass — just like that, no muss, no fuss! And gas, why, gas is even more marvelous. Besides being able silently to snuff out a life without the slightest disturbance, gas can make the dead seem wrapped in sweet repose! The mysterious thing we call "God" is practically invisible, though He has dominion over the entirety of human life.

Ah, yes, nylon cord, you also share in this great property, and have also spread your dominion over human life in every quarter. Therefore whenever I humbly praise the Lord, I shall also praise thee, oh holy nylon filament!

As soon as their public sentencing had been completed, Glass and two other prisoners were dragged together into a prisoner's van. One of the other two was the conductor of a symphony orchestra who was guilty of the heinous crime of having ripped a precious red book to shreds; to allow such as he to go on living would be to slight the people's indignant wrath. Death by firing squad! The other member of the group was a young woman, a clerk in a food market. She had introduced a suitor to a young woman who was set to be part of the campaign to send educated youth to the countryside, and therefore had directly subverted the Great Strategic Deployment.[5] Death by firing squad!

Four motorcycles with sidecars, each sidecar with a machine gun mounted on it, were in the lead to clear the way. These were followed by three trucks packed with Red Guards armed to the teeth, and the prisoners' vans sandwiched between the trucks. Then there followed bright green jeeps of the garrison police forces, blood red cars from senior cadre headquarters, and raven black hearses from the crematorium. Three white mini-ambulances brought up the rear. The procession of vehicles kept up a steady and shrill wailing of sirens as it made its way majestically through the streets to the execution ground.

The execution site had been jammed with people since much earlier in the day. "When a beheading is to take place, spectators flock to execution square" is the way our proverb recalls an ancient and enduring Chinese tradition. The way in which the neck, suddenly severed from its head, would convulsively pull itself inside the shoulders until, after a very long pause, one was treated to the thrilling sight of that fresh hot blood spurting out; the unforgettable sight of the way that chopped-off head would roll and bounce crazily along the ground, taking a bite out of the earth — all this was almost an indispensable item of spare-time entertainment among all the descendants of our exalted ancestors. After picking apart several succulent crabs and savoring a few mouthfuls of

5. If the young woman were to marry someone assigned to city work, she would not have to go to the countryside.

rice wine, some would feel in the mood to go out to appreciate chrysanthemums, while others preferred to go take in the annual beheadings
that were held each autumn. Both pursuits were wonderfully leisurely,
elegant, refined. But in terms of helping one to sober up, or to improve
one's character, it is clear that witnessing a beheading was far superior.
The way one's heart beat faster, the way one broke out in a sweat, could
drive away all the pain and humiliation of being part of an enslaved race,
and make one realize even more clearly the essential truth that "the
meek are blessed with perpetual joy." Can there be any doubt about it?
When you compare yourself to the poor wretch whose skull is being separated from his shoulders, do you not find that you are indeed far freer,
far happier, far more elegant than he?

Finally, Glass and the other man and the woman were dragged out
of the prisoners' van. The skinny doctor and two other physicians, having scrambled from their respective ambulances, now each followed
close on the heels of his own quarry. The two other doctors kept barking
reminders at the officers in charge of the execution.

"Don't forget, you must hit the head, you mustn't damage the heart!"

"Be careful now, and no kicking! Don't hurt the liver!"

At this, the professor felt compelled to reiterate his own instructions. "Now remember, you're not to shoot him in the head, what I need
are the eyes, *the eyes!*"

Glass heard this last instruction clear as a bell. At that instant, all the
strange and inexplicable things that had transpired in the past several
months became clear to him as if in a flash of lightning. The physical
examination, the smiles, the promises, the comforting words, the milk,
the bread, the cod liver oil, the essence of chrysanthemum [herbal
tonic — Tr.] . . .

He began to struggle, thrashing about like a wounded panther — totally crazed, irrational, hysterical. He was not trying to save his own life;
he was rather exploding, exploding with a hatred of volcanic proportions!

He tried to bite, but his jaw was dislocated. He tried to yell, but his
windpipe was throttled. He tried to hurl himself at the professor, but
the bailiff behind him was superbly trained. The blood vessels in his
neck were distended, and his Adam's apple was struggling upward; but
that nylon cord was inexorably pulling back on him, tighter and tighter,
and now thick frothy blood was oozing forth as the cord cut deeply into
his flesh.

His face turned from white to red, from red to purplish, and from purplish to black, until finally his tongue was forced out of his mouth. Suddenly the condemned man thrust his head fiercely downward and managed to strike his chin against something. Then, gathering all the force at his command, he spat one bloody half of his tongue squarely into that smile the professor had been wearing on his face right from the start. Only then did the professor discern that pair of eyes glaring at him. But what kind of eyes were these? They were not eyes at all but two orbs of fire! A pair of glowing orbs shooting forth fiery flames! They were swelling, they were bulging out! Abruptly, with an insane wrench of the head, the condemned man's two eyeballs bulged forward in their sockets!

Glass continued to thrash about, but no longer was trying to fling himself at the professor. Now he was doing everything he could to claw and squirm his way downward. Even that experienced bailiff seemed to be having difficulty holding his own. Then it dawned on the professor what Glass was up to: he was trying to ruin his eyes!

"Look out! Watch him!" The professor finally lost his composure and barked out his words like a wolfhound: "Shoot him! Shoot him!"

The bullet went right through the young man's heart.

The professor ran and got a pair of surgical scissors and a bottle from the ambulance. Like a hunting dog rushing toward the hare shot by its master, he severed with deft, sure strokes the flesh of the eyelids and then the optic nerves. At last he had the two eyes, those blood-drenched fruits of victory, lying safe and sound on their bed of sterilized gauze at the bottom of his bottle. However the medical professor's long coat, as white and pure as the driven snow, a symbol of knowledge and civilization, had unfortunately been splattered by the fresh blood spurting from the young man's chest.

It was not for nothing that this professor was highly regarded among ophthalmologists; the cornea transplantation went extremely well. There were movie cameras right there in the operating theater, and the entire procedure was captured on film. Plans had already been made to produce it as a documentary in five languages. The central authorities had granted a special exemption to allow use of "Spring River Moonlit Night" as background music.[6]

6. Authorities in the Cultural Revolution banned nearly all traditional Chinese music as "feudalistic" and Western music as "bourgeois." "Chunjianghua yueye," the piece referred to here, is an "ancient tune," or *guqu*, and was one of the first traditional Chinese melodies to be "liberated" as the Cultural Revolution waned.

Mr. Vuillard, president of the International Association of Surgeons, happened to be visiting China at the time. When he saw the
rough cut of the documentary, he praised the chief surgeon's technique,
saying that his movements had been so precise, so deft, so crisp, without
the slightest hesitation or superfluity, that they truly appeared to have
been computerized! He had been especially impressed when he heard
the professor's introductory comments: how the donor had been killed
in an accident and the bereaved mother, without a second thought, had
offered her dead son's eyes to a totally unknown class brother who was
suffering from corneal opacity resulting from advanced years. Mr. Vuillard's eyes filled with tears. "Human kindness! Human kindness!" he
exclaimed. "Now that truly may be called human kindness!"

A week after the operation:
"Director, how are you feeling, sir?" asked the professor, bending
over his patient and speaking softly.
"Just fine, only there seems to be a bright red glow in my eyes."
"Excellent! That indicates that the blood is circulating in normal
fashion."
The eighth day:
"Director, how are you feeling, sir?" asked the professor, bending
over his patient and speaking softly.
"Uhh, not bad, but there does seem to be a warm tingling sensation
in my eyes."
"That's great! It indicates a healthy functioning of the nerves!"
The ninth day:
"Director, how are you feeling, sir?" asked the professor, bending
over his patient and speaking softly.
"Hot! Hot! Open the door, open the windows, all of them!"
"Ahem, Director, sir, your temperature is 98.6° and your blood pres-
sure is also normal. Don't worry, we'll probably be taking off the ban-
dages tomorrow. You may be just a bit overwrought, no?"
On the tenth day, the professor had invited all the department heads
and section chiefs, as well as the important Party members and officials in
the hospital, to attend the "unveiling ceremony." As they all filed toward
the door of the director's room, they could hear his guttural voice roaring,
"I'm so thirsty! I'm dying of thirst! I need to drink some more!"
As they entered the room, they could see the director of the Public

Security Bureau, his face turned toward the ceiling, slurping and gulping water frantically from a large washbasin he was tilting toward his mouth. The excess water was spilling from the corners of his mouth, and water was all over the floor.

"Director, ahh, you..." The professor had just bent over his patient's bed when a heavy hand came sweeping out of nowhere to deliver him a powerful slap.

"You bastard, what the hell are you up to? What the hell have you done to my eyes? Unwrap these bandages, and I do mean unwrap 'em right now!"

"Hurry up, unwrap the bandages!" Holding one hand to his smarting face, the professor issued the order to the nurses.

You could have heard a pin drop in the hospital room as the gauze bandages were unlooped layer by layer; the only sound was the director's panting like an old bull. At last, the final gauze pad was lifted away from the patient's eyes, which were staring straight ahead.

"What a brilliant success!"

"It's a miracle, isn't it?"

"What bright, shining corneas!"

"Flawless as heaven's dome!"

The room fairly exploded with a storm of congratulatory exclamations and applause. And at least this once, the reaction was completely sincere, completely free of hypocritical flattery. For the fact was that the two limpid, perfect corneas of the poor devil who had been gunned down were now sparkling in the director's eyes. Everyone noticed his completely new look. To have encased two crystalline corneas within the wrinkled folds of those thick eyelids was like suddenly equipping a battered-up, old-fashioned bellows camera with a spanking new and gleaming "Contax" lens! Just as everyone was pressing forward to offer their congratulations, the director abruptly let out an hysterical shriek.

"Fire!"

Fire? Where? Craning their necks to look this way and that at the pale green walls, the snow white sheets, and the cream-colored bedstead, everybody was mystified.

"Fire! Look! Fire on the bed! Fire on the walls! Fire on the floor, aaagh, there's fire on all of you!" The patient went on screaming as he picked up a washbasin and hurled its contents at them.

"Water! Bring more water!" The nurse dared not disobey, and ran to bring him another washbasin of water. The director lifted it over his head and with a whoosh doused himself completely.

"Help! Save me! Throw some more water on me!"

The professor proved to have more presence of mind than anyone. He rapped out his instructions to the orderlies who had come to find out what all the ruckus was about: "Hold him down! Bring me some ether!"

A towel soaked in the anaesthetic was applied to the patient's nose and mouth while he twisted and squirmed, legs thrashing, until he finally lost consciousness.

The chief of the Nervous Disorders Department wiped the water from his face and shrugged his shoulders. "He's seeing things, obviously hallucinating!"

The chief of Chinese Herbal Medicine, the same elderly gentleman who had been joyfully proclaiming the operation miraculous just the minute before, now dejectedly fanned himself with an antique fan he had already completely worn to tatters. "Possessed, that's what it is!" he cried. "Possessed by hellfire!"

While sitting through the night with his restless patient, the professor, this noted specialist in ophthalmology, couldn't help dozing off a bit . . .

"We're on fire! The room's on fire! Ohh, no, I'm on fire, too!" Bounding from his bed, the director fled out the door, screaming insanely.

By the time the professor had completely reawoken, the patient was already rushing down the stairway and disappearing out the hospital door. The professor yelled at the top of his voice, ordering all the nurses and orderlies out to search for the patient. But the night being pitch black and the hospital grounds extensive, it took more than half an hour for fifteen or so flashlight beams, stabbing here and flashing there, to bring a shrill scream from one of the nurses.

"There's somebody lying in the pond!"

With everyone lending a hand, they eventually managed to drag the director from the pond. The professor personally knelt down to administer artificial respiration to the patient. One of the nurses pulled back the drowned man's eyelids and shined her flashlight into the pupils of his eyes.

"Look at this, Professor."

The professor fearfully bent over the director's face, so close he was almost touching the dead man's nose. After a long pause, the professor slowly raised his head and stared blankly toward a dark clump of trees. Rivulets of cold sweat slithered steadily down his forehead like slimy serpents, sliding over his cheeks on down to the point of his chin. There they halted, forming big drops that grew, hesitated, recoiled and then finally dropped off listlessly to disappear into the murky darkness.

"That's it, it's over with, it's all . . . over!" The professor slowly settled back, all the strength drained out of him. A chilling terror was coursing through the vertebrae in his spine; his lips were trembling, his teeth chattering, his voice quaking.

"He really did get burned alive . . . burned alive by hellfire!"

# DAI QING

# Anticipation

People are assigned to their employment in China. Especially among intellectuals with specialized skills, it often happens that couples must live hundreds of miles apart for many years to suit the needs of the state. "Anticipation," based on an actual case, depicts this problem boldly, if melodramatically.

When the story was submitted to *Guangming ribao* in fall 1979, the editors could not immediately agree whether to venture publication. When they did proceed, the story elicited a larger number of letters to the editor than any in the newspaper's history. More than 98 percent of the letters were favorable. "Anticipation" also placed among the top five in the national reader preference poll for short stories in 1979. But despite this vote, the story did not receive a prize from the National Short Story Prize Committee, though it announced that it was "basing" its decisions on the same poll. The committee apparently feared, and with good reason, that to give a prize to a story that dramatized a widespread problem and sympathized so completely with its victims would put countless thousands of local officials in an untenable position. Couples everywhere would be able to press their applications to be reunited and have the semi-official sanction of a prize-winning story to back them up.

Translated by Billy Bikales. Originally published in *Guangming ribao* (Beijing), 25 November and 2 December 1979.

Giving the author a prize would do nothing to change the state's economic plans determining job assignments. The only result was likely to be greater disaffection. Readers were naturally indignant that "Anticipation" had been denied a prize, and controversy continued for many weeks.

Dai Qing (real name: Fu Ning) is a college graduate in engineering with several years' experience repairing radio equipment in Beijing. "Anticipation" was her first story and has been her most famous. In 1980 she worked in the Foreign Liaison Section of the National Writers' Association in Beijing; by 1983 she had become a reporter at *Guangming ribao*.

# Anticipation

Like someone just awakened from a nightmare, I was sitting on my bed in the psychiatric ward, gazing through the window at the early spring sunlight. I felt extremely weak, but my mind was clear. The severe shock that had jolted me from my senses had kept me in this place more than half a year. Scene after scene from the past was replaying itself in my mind, in such vivid, perfect detail . . . I am not going to ignore the past by simply calling it "unbearable"; only people who despair of the future feel that way about an unhappy past. I do have a future. I am like someone on a small boat that has been buffeted by fierce winds and finally smashes onto a rock. I may be bruised and broken-boned, but I can feel my two feet landing on solid ground again — before me lie a dense forest and bubbling streams, I can struggle, I can make a life for myself . . .

July 1977 — a hot, sultry afternoon. I was busy correcting my students' papers. This was in my old hometown, Yonghe People's Commune in Shandong Province, where I was teaching in the commune middle school. When I stop to count, I realize it's been nearly fifteen years already . . . Lao Geng, the mailman at our school, walked into my classroom.

"A letter for you, Teacher Xu."

Lao Geng was also in charge of housing and maintenance at the school. After more than ten years of looking after so many of my problems, he understood my worries very well.

"From Chen. It's early this time, only half a month after the last one. Hurry up and see what it's about!"

I snatched the tiny brown envelope. A letter from home! Other people's children could snuggle and frolic in their mother's protective embrace; other wives could get love and encouragement from their husbands if they ran into bad luck; but all the comfort, all the understanding and support I could receive from my family was bound up in those tiny brown envelopes.

Chen and I had been married for fifteen years. Xiao Gang, our thirteen-year-old son and Xiao Hong, our seven-year-old daughter, were both with him now, going to school in Beijing. Around the tenth of each month, I would receive a letter from Chen and the children; this was after he'd received his salary and was ready to submit his carefully calculated "statement" on arrangements for the upcoming month. Things had been this way for so many years already, so why today...?

Dear Xiumei:

I really don't know how to begin this letter. The day we have been waiting for has finally arrived. Last month the academy sent the Central Committee a report about us and all the hundreds of others like us who have been separated for so long. And now, in less than a month, the Center has sent down instructions that the problem should be solved immediately! The institute has already begun checking into the situation. Xiumei, it's too good to be true! Everyone is saying I should be first on the list. You're thirty-seven years old now, Mei, and I'm forty-two. We still have at least twenty years to spend together...

Tears blurred my eyes. There had been many similar letters over the past ten-odd years, but they had only said, "The personnel chief says there may be hope for next year"; or "I ran into the director of the institute and he asked about you. He promised he would try to help"; or "I've heard there's a place in Hubei Province that can take whole families — shall we go there?" But there had never been a letter so excited, or so positive, as this one.

Chen was from Guangxi. Since his graduation in 1959 from the South China Institute of Technology, where he majored in radio technology, he had been a technician in the Computer Research Institute of the Academy of Sciences. Even today I can remember very clearly the first time I saw him...

Summer of 1961. The senior class in our technical school invited several "young scientific workers" to discuss their experiences after graduation. Chen Zhixian was one of them. He was the youngest, the tallest, and the worst speaker. I was a mischievous girl then, and sat in the front row just so I could laugh at his funny southern accent. Whenever Chen Zhixian said something like "Ah main t' sigh" instead of "I mean to say," we would all break down and laugh boldly, continuing until Chen's face turned beet red. I can remember only the general drift of what he actually said. It was something like, "Through our own hard work we have developed our country's first computer, which puts us one step ahead of Japan and other countries in this field . . ." It was Chen Zhixian himself who became fixed in my memory.

Almost as though it had been deliberately arranged, I was assigned to be a trainee in his research section after I graduated. Now we had many chances to see each other. I was always taking part in things: I was a member of the Youth League's propaganda committee; I sang, danced, played sports, and put out reports. I joined everything. Chen, on the other hand, almost never spoke. Except for the time he spent running laps at our track every morning, he was always in the laboratory, even at night. Yet whenever he saw me he would smile shyly, and stand there with a bright look in his eyes fumbling with his two big hands. Many boys were interested in me at that time, and I was always chattering and laughing with them. But, though it's hard to say why, it was only around Chen that I felt somehow emotionally engaged. Who can understand the mysterious ways of love? Gradually I came to despise his stupid awkwardness. You dumb, bashful Guangxi hick! When will you see into a girl's heart, and take a bold stride toward her?

1962, the evening of May Day observances. We were putting on a performance in the city, and afterwards, just after I had changed and packed up to go home, there I saw him. Chen Zhixian was standing at the backstage exit holding a small package.

"You were great," he said. "Would you like something to eat?" Although he spoke with his usual funny accent, this time I didn't laugh. My heart was suddenly engulfed in warmth—at last you've done it, at last you've taken that stride!

We walked along Chang'an Road, that pencil-straight thoroughfare, toward the Computer Institute in the western suburbs. That night I was not the noisy chatterbox I usually was. I remained silent while

Chen's words poured forth like the waters of the Li River of his home province. He talked about the town where he was born; about how he'd lost his parents and was raised in his uncle's house; about how he'd been the first person from his town ever to graduate from university; about how proud all his relatives were when he was assigned to work at such a high-level research institute. And, of course, he talked about the research work he loved so much.

"I feel as though my strength were inexhaustible" he said. "We've already begun testing second-generation crystal tube computers; yesterday I was reading about their circuitry components. We will not let our country fall behind in these new fields!"

The gentle night breezes ruffled his clothing. I felt that within him, within that chest rising and falling with excitement, there beat a heart full of courage and determination, full of a sense of responsibility, and that this was something I could trust, something I could rely on. Impulsively, I moved closer to him. He put his hand on my shoulder and looked at me with deep feeling. "Xiumei — is it okay if I call you by your given name? How would it be if we got together? I've never had a place I could call home, and . . . I really like you a lot . . ." His words were halting and inept, but what a wonderful, intoxicating May night that was!

I was clutching the letter so tightly that it was getting crumpled. Suddenly I noticed that Lao Geng was still gazing at me with concern. I felt like shouting joyfully at the top of my voice, but managed to contain myself. I couldn't lose control. I'd been frustrated so many times, how could I dare expect that this time would be different?

"Oh, it's nothing," I said. "Just something about our daughter's schoolwork."

Lao Geng shook his head as he turned and left. I picked up Chen's letter again. "Academy sent a report . . . instructions have come down . . . already begun checking . . ." Yes, this time it should be for real. I threw my books together and raced home.

To be more accurate, by "home" I mean the deserted little three-room mud house and courtyard left to me by my parents. My father died twelve years ago, and my mother nine years after him. Since then I have been alone. This has been just one more thing that Chen has had to worry about all the time.

Now it looked as though I would finally be moving back to Beijing. But what would I do with our place here? I looked around at the few pieces of battered furniture —all older than I—plus a chipped water jug, a grinding stone, and, standing in the corner, an old bamboo shoulder pole shiny with wear. It was the one that Chen had brought when he first visited our village.

Just as spring winds bring new life to the world, so love had made my own life immeasurably richer. In my time as a trainee, I acted as assistant to Chen and his fellow technicians, and never tired of the work. Each instrument, each chart —everything had a new meaning for me. How beautiful life was, and how easy! Around this time, the leadership was mobilizing staff members to join the big movement to "Return to the Countryside." I signed up without a second thought. On innumerable occasions since then I have regretted this action bitterly, but on the other hand, when I think it over carefully, there really was nothing strange in what I did. It was more an instinctive reaction than any kind of conscious move. My mother was the head of the Old Women's Welfare Association in her area. In wartime she had never said "no" to any matter involving the District Party Committee or the People's Eighth Route Army. When my uncle took me off to school in Beijing shortly before my tenth birthday, my mother's only instructions were "Child, whatever the organization says . . ." And that is exactly how I always acted. As soon as I entered school I encountered the Anti-Rightist Campaign. Thinking back on it, what did we know in those days? One night our headquarters would tell us something, and the next day we would go put up posters and chant slogans, just as the "organization" directed. Next came the steel-refining movement. We went from door to door collecting iron pots and tearing down iron railings. After that it was launching "athletic satellites": day and night I led a group of classmates in running and climbing ropes. During the lean years of 1960–61, a girl like me, brought up under straitened conditions in the countryside, had no difficulty adjusting to algae and gourds for dinner in place of vegetables. Now the organization was saying it needed people to return to the countryside. Of course I would lead the way.

By that time, Chen and I were already discussing marriage. When he heard what I'd done, he fell silent for a long time. I knew there was an impassioned struggle churning within him. In those days, all that we

heard about — or talked about — was our "big communist family," but
Chen still felt a constant, desperate yearning for a small family of hi
own, for the warmth of a family life he had never experienced as a child
No one but me could see this in him.

"Of course it's all right to do this, Xiumei, but we . . ."

"We what?" I replied, "Wasn't it all explained clearly when we were
mobilized? In these difficult times, for the sake of the Party, we must
temporarily assume our share of the nation's burden. I'll be back when
the country has developed. If you don't believe me, then we can go right
now and . . ." I blushed, because I suddenly was thinking how nice i
would be if we could get married right away!

And that's how it happened that we hurriedly and gaily got married
I clutched my bright red marriage certificate along with my certificate fo
returning to the countryside, completely intoxicated in a sea of self-satis
faction. On the one hand I felt a sort of blind contentment with my deci
sion to answer the motherland's call at this crucial time, and on the other
was ecstatic about a perfect marriage. Everyone knew that Chen was no
only handsome and strong, and honest and loyal — he was also one of the
top workers in his field. Chen spent almost his entire savings to buy me a
set of clothes. He really "completely refurnished" me inside and out, with
outfits for all seasons. It was as though he wanted to make up for his no
being able to stay with me after our marriage.

After the wedding, he took me back to my old home. Wherever this
man went, the effects of his two diligent hands were soon evident. After
less than half a month, our courtyard was covered with new earth, our
pigsty had been rebuilt, and there was new thatch on our roof. He even
left behind a bamboo carrying pole he'd brought from Guangxi.

"Your northern poles are much too awkward," he told my parents
"How can Xiumei carry water with them?"

How lively our little courtyard was then! My parents could never get
their fill of their new son-in-law. Both of us calculated that, since we
were still young, separation for a couple of years would be nothing. We
would still just go on working hard at our jobs. Who would have imag
ined, in the midst of that sweet love, that the first signs of family burden
and responsibilities could already be seen? Or that, in the midst of such
self-sacrificing fervor, the road ahead contained pitfalls? We were so
young then, so immature!

Two years passed. Although returning to the countryside and serving the peasants wasn't as romantic and heroic as I'd imagined, still, with my father working for the production team, my mother taking care of the home, and me teaching in the commune middle school, things were all right. The second-generation computer Chen and his co-workers were working on was already being assembled and tested. But working as hard as he did, often late into the night, and going out on assignments all over the country, he contracted stomach troubles. His face, so round and full in his youth, now grew drawn and long—an effect doubly emphasized by his now protruding cheekbones. But his eyes somehow seemed keener and brighter than ever, a sign, it seemed, of his experience and maturity in his work. I worried about him until my heart ached, and when my father died, and Xiao Gang was born, I felt even more strongly that we couldn't go on living apart this way. At the end of 1965, he applied to his work unit to get me transferred to Beijing.

After submitting this application, he was sent to the Northwest to clear up some equipment problems. When I arrived in Beijing several months later for a brief visit, still no word had come about our application. We had not pressed our request—not because we were too busy, but because we felt embarrassed to trouble the organization with a personal matter. We felt that our personal responsibility was to devote ourselves completely to our work. Matters such as deciding how our lives should be organized, or how much salary should be allowed us, were not appropriate things for us to worry about.

Chen's roommate, Xiao Gao, let us have the dormitory room to ourselves, while he camped in his office "like a guerrilla." I took advantage of every moment to clean and sew for Chen, and was determined that he be able to eat all of his three daily meals at "home." I was there for only a month, but could already see a little ruddiness return to his grayed face, could watch him break into a childlike smile of satisfaction when he held up his clean, neat clothes, could watch him rolling in play on the bed with Xiao Gang—and all of this filled my heart to its depths with the joy of being a wife and mother. How wonderful it would be if every day were like this! But I had to get ready to leave. My self-respect would not allow me to stay on as an unemployed "dependent." The last few days, Chen talked even less than usual. At night, after Xiao Gang went to sleep, I lay in silence against his broad chest, listening to his rhythmic heartbeat, smelling the familiar odor that was his alone. The thought of the lonely journey I was about to make brought tears to my eyes. He seemed to hear my unspoken appeal, and brushing away my tears and gazing into my eyes, he said softly, "It's okay, I promise. Don't worry. I'll take care of everything."

The next evening, an old classmate of his came by to see us. This man had been assigned work in the army, and it turned out that he had been urging Chen to go work in his unit, and to have me transferred there to be with him. But Chen had told him that he needed time to think the idea over, and had never even mentioned the whole thing to me.

When I heard about it, I really couldn't restrain myself.

"Why don't you go? Your work is the same wherever you do it."

"Xiumei, don't be too hasty about this. No one is more familiar than I with our current work here in Beijing. To leave right at the critical stage of testing and making adjustments would be wrong . . ."

"No" I cried. "Who knows if we'll ever have such a good chance again? If you won't go and apply, then I will." He didn't try to block my way as I ran to see the director of the institute. Without pausing for breath, I burst into the director's room. He was bent over his desk, his white hair glimmering in the light of his lamp.

"Mr. Director." I stood in the middle of the room with so much to say that I had no idea where to start. He lifted his head, then lowered his old eyeglasses as he peered at me.

"Well, if it isn't Little Lotus Bud!" We used to perform the lotus dance, and the director would always tease us and say that our lotus flowers had blossomed for years without ever bearing seeds, so he started to call all the girls who did the lotus dance "little lotus buds."

"How're things? You won't be getting all weepy and runny-nosed when you say good-bye to Chen this time, will you?"

When I heard this, I lost control and started bawling.

"What? . . . ," The old director realized something was wrong. He got up from his chair and came over to me. He brushed my hair to console me, but now that I'd started I just kept crying harder and harder.

"Mr. Director, Chen wants to take me to work in another unit. You'll let him go, won't you?" The director didn't say anything. He just paced around the room a few times, then poured me a glass of water.

"I know how you feel, but it really would be a shame, you know, if he broke off right in the middle of his work . . ."

"But his health is getting worse and worse."

"I've noticed that too." He stood by the window, watching the snow-flakes floating by outside. "Chen Zhixian is a hardworking and extremely studious comrade. Since he joined us in 1959, he has worked in every aspect of our field, large and small. Some day he's going to be one of our country's most promising computer specialists. From our point of view, it's very hard to let him go. And from the standpoint of his personal development, would you really want to let your personal affections compromise his brilliant future?" The director was watching my reactions carefully as he spoke. "I'll look into your problem and take full responsibility for it, how's that? You can blame it all on me. Look, she's crying again . . . I'll not only take responsibility for it — I promise to solve it. How will that be?"

What could I say? The director took out a cold towel for me to wipe my face, and patted me on the shoulder as though I were a child.

"Little Lotus Bud has been at the blackboard for several years, and now is going to come back to work with technical equipment again. I hope she hasn't forgotten everything she learned in school!"

I laughed through my tears, and left with renewed hope.

Chen later told me that soon after I left the director deputed someone in the personnel office to settle our family problem, and that this comrade immediately began contacting the Office of Labor and Capital and other related offices. Just when everything was ready, and a letter about to be sent transferring me to Beijing, the Cultural Revolution exploded, sending out tremors that shook the entire world. Our tiny family was also caught up in this gigantic swirling whirlpool.

In the beginning, like all ardent and sincere Chinese, we put aside every question of personal advantage and security. We wanted to "concern ourselves with the great affairs of the nation," and to "stop the restoration of capitalism." But within two months both Chen and I had been savagely beaten — I because I was a teacher, and Chen because he put in a few honest words of dissent during the struggle session against the director of the institute. Afterward Chen had no choice but to carry his wounds back to my family home in the countryside and help me convalesce. How many sleepless, terrified nights we spent in that little mud house! But even in circumstances as difficult as this, Chen would stay up

into the middle of the night writing and sketching under the dim glow
of an old electric lamp. My little technician! Is it so impossible for you to
put aside your work?

Almost from the beginning of the Cultural Revolution, Chen was
part of the "above it all" faction. For one thing, he saw through the whole
thing very quickly, for a good honest man like him, what really was there
to "revolt" about? Also, because of the unresolved question of my transfer, he couldn't risk offending any of the innumerable "leaders" who
passed across the scene in quick succession like the horses on a carousel.
In the past, I had still been willing to listen to our mentors when they
told us that "the Revolution should always come first and your personal
problems second"; after considering what they said, I would repress my
own feelings. But now to hear these same words from the mouths of
these new patricians made me as sick as if I'd been presented a dish of
flies to eat. "The tiniest affair of the nation is always a weighty matter,"
they would say, "and the weightiest personal matter is always a trivial
thing." Fair enough, said I, but why did they address these things only to
people like us? "A small matter." How many couples who can see each
other only once a year have ached and suffered and cursed over this
"small matter"? I watched Chen grow colder and more silent by the
day — maybe he still secretly saw a thread of hope, or maybe it was that
the force of the love and hate boiling in his heart was even greater than
in mine.

Life in the village was extremely hard for our family, whose elderly
were very old and whose young very young. In addition to the neighbors
and their mocking banter ("Aren't you the family of a great technician?
Well, why can't you go back to the city then?"), and the flirtatious teasing
those village good-for-nothings directed at me, a simple matter like the
annual allocation of vegetables and firewood was, for our household, a
great problem. In the countryside, a family without a man is doubly
mistreated. Our grain, potatoes, turnips, and other foodstuffs were all
in the fields most distant from our home, and I don't know what we
would have done if it hadn't been for Lao Geng, who was always there to
help us make the long trips back and forth to bring things in. Even poor
little Xiao Gang, only five years old, had to lend his tiny shoulders to
support our sorrowful burden, as he followed behind me with a heavy
sack on his back.

There was no place for us to stay in Beijing. During my visit there
with Xiao Gang over the Spring Festival in 1968, we were all awakened
in the middle of the night by a terrifying pounding at the door. I won't
mince words: my son and I had become "hoodlums," and we were taken,
clutching each other, to the police station. Chen didn't raise even one
word of objection. With his mouth clenched grimly shut, he just got
together all the warm clothing he could find and brought it to us.

In 1969, when I was about to give birth to our second child, no
hospital would take me in, because I was not a registered resident of the
area. Chen put me on a flat board bicycle cart and tirelessly pedalled
from one place to another looking for help. I lay on the back of the cart,
twisting and turning every which way, moaning in pain, while every few
minutes he would turn around and look at me, the tears or perspiration — I couldn't tell which — streaming down his face.

In late autumn of 1972, on a raw, cold, rainy night, the four of us
were huddling inside a small room at the institute's "Eastern Lane of the
Transportation Personnel." This was the very elegant name given to
what had formerly been a large bicycle shed to the east of the institute
office. As more and more institute people got married and needed
housing for their families, the shed was partitioned into small rooms
and some paper was pasted onto the walls. Then, decked out with its
new name, it became a temporary dormitory for staff families.

I knew that in the last few years the institute had transferred in a
large number of new workers, including various aunts and uncles of
staff members. Just the day before, I had heard about another one; a
driver's whole family had been reunited.

"The population of Beijing has grown from four to eight million in
just a few years, Zhixian. Do you mean to say that I alone cannot find a
place here?"

He lowered his head, and didn't look at me.

"True," I continued, "We don't have any special pull we can use to
arrange things for the children of those old bureaucrats.[1] I also realize
we don't have any money to buy fancy presents for their ladyships and
lovely misses. But what we *can* do is give them a hard time. We can skip

---

1. "Old bureaucrats" presumably refers to the leadership of the institute, who could have
arranged Xiumei's transfer back to Beijing.

work, we can go drop in on them every day, borrow money from them, throw our children at them . . ."

Xiumei! This doesn't sound like you!"

"You're right, it doesn't. I've changed. And the reason I've changed is because you, you ineffectual little technician, you . . ." Having finished only half of what I was saying, I could no longer bear to look at Chen's pained expression, his eyes gazing directly into mine . . .

I'd completely lost my head! In all these years, while silently facing untold coldness and rejection, and swallowing untold bitterness, Chen had never uttered a single word in criticism of my having volunteered to return to the countryside. How could I break his heart like this?

"Zhixian, I . . ."

The two of us sat there with our heads in our hands, weeping bitterly. Xiao Hong was startled from her dreams by the commotion and also began to cry. Only Xiao Gang was quiet, staring straight ahead with widened, terrified eyes.

There was no way I could go on living there. Not because of my self-respect or because of the all-pervasive stink that rose from the sewers of the "Eastern Lane of the Transportation Personnel." We no longer possessed the economic means to continue living together. My mother told us in a letter that the production team was threatening to cut off our grain ration, and for a family in Beijing to attempt to live off only Chen's grain ration and his monthly salary of thirty-seven dollars would have led to difficulties anyone can imagine. Every so often, some of Chen's coworkers would offer us a few of their grain coupons, or a piece of their used clothing, but how could we take these? How could we possibly reconcile ourselves to the disgrace of accepting charity from others? Were we supposed to acknowledge that Chen was inferior? That he was incompetent? Lazy? Had committed some crime?

Worn and anxious, we passed another few years. During these years Chen's "fellow sufferers" at the institute scattered themselves like clouds in the wind. Chi Fang, two years his senior and head of his research section, got his wife returned from exile in the Anhui countryside, then took his whole family to live in a mountainous section of Sichuan Province. Back when Chi had joined the institute he was flat broke, and after more then ten years of constant, day-and-night effort at his job, he left the institute still flat broke. When he moved out, his baggage consisted of a cloth sack and one carton of his most precious possessions — his textbooks and work manuals — which he couldn't bear to leave behind.

Xiao Wang, a classmate of Chen's, had already become rather an authority in the field of magnetic data storage. But he left the institute without the slightest regret and returned to his home in Guangdong Province to repair motors in a commune machine shop. No one loved his work more than Xiao Wang, or felt greater pride in the fruit of his years of bitter labor. But when he left, Xiao Wang was disgusted at the institute: "Damned if I'll ever pass through this stinking old gate again!"

One by one, Chen saw these people off. And every time, as the train was pulling out, they would call out to him, "Soon you've got to make up your mind, Chen!" He would nod silently, but never say a word.

As time passed, Chen's position in the institute improved. From project manager, he was promoted to head of the engineering section, and also won a prize for his work on a special research project. Every time a new leader was appointed, he would pat Chen on the shoulder and say "Keep up the good work, Chen. We're sure your family problem will be taken care of quickly." But then the leader would be quickly replaced, or, if he stayed, become far too busy to think about us.

Farewells had become the central theme of our family life. On the eve of each parting, Zhixian would hold me very gently and caress my work-roughened hands.

"Take care of yourself when you get home . . . I'll keep trying to think of a way out . . ."

Later my mother died, and I fell seriously ill myself. It was a long time before I was fully recovered. Chen took the two children to live with him in Beijing. We said it was to give them a better education, but I knew he was only trying to lighten my burden. From that time on, he had to handle an onerous workload by day, and after work go home to care for the two children. At night he would still have to find time for reading and translating. He grew as thin as a skeleton. His face turned gray and ashen, and his eyes were always bloodshot.

In 1976 I happened to be in Beijing when the Gang of Four was smashed. Chen's face betrayed a rare glow of excitement. We celebrated by spending all of sixty-five cents on pork. The children's eyes were wide as saucers at the sight of it. My heart nearly broke as I watched Xiao Hong shout "Eat some, Daddy! Eat some, Daddy!" and at the same time hungrily stuff some into her own little mouth . . . Like everyone else, we were full of hope for the future then; China had been saved, and maybe our own little family could be saved, too!

Sure enough, less than a year after the smashing of the Gang of Four there were important developments in our case. The day I received that letter from Chen, I quietly began to get ready. I waited as the trees turned yellow and then turned green again, and as two new swallow's nests appeared on our roof: almost a year had passed, but there was no further news from Chen.

Although things were progressing slowly, sometimes unbearably slowly, nonetheless my inner mood was freshly joyous. It seemed imminent that Zhixian and I would finally be united and never again have to separate. Day after day I said to myself, "Don't be overanxious, don't be overanxious. After waiting fifteen long years, can't you wait just a few more days?" So I waited. Quietly, nervously, I waited.

I knew that Chen, miles away, was also waiting for that day, although he stayed much more active and involved than I. Some articles they had translated got published, and he received a payment for his contribution. He solemnly took this money and purchased a new sweater for me. It cost over half the whole sum. Over the years, he had always felt so remorseful that he couldn't buy me even one piece of nice new clothing. Now he had been appointed deputy head of the research section, and his formal rank was under reevaluation. He wrote to me excitedly, "It doesn't really matter what title a person has, except as a sign that one's work is highly valued and one's learning well recognized." It seemed that he had only one remaining regret, and that was that I wasn't at his side. But this time he was absolutely certain that our problem would be solved. And once it was, he would be like a locomotive newly primed with coal, racing forward with whistles blowing and hauling a heavy load. He planned meticulously how he would help me get back into my old work at the institute, how he would arrange for Xiao Gang to take the entrance examination for the technical university's junior high school, how Xiao Hong would start studying foreign languages . . .

O my beloved, without your optimism, your fresh vitality, I could never have got through such a trying year.

The day finally arrived.

I had just entered the school gate after the midday nap when Lao Geng, bubbling with laughter, came out to greet me.

"Teacher Xu! People here from Beijing! Two cadres."

People from Beijing? The way I'd always imagined it, I would first receive a job transfer notice, then I would talk with them, say goodbye to the school, and be on my way. At the very best, I had thought, Chen would come in person to get me. But two cadres? Perhaps they had come because Chen couldn't get away from the children and all his work. If this were the case, there really had been some big changes in the treatment of intellectuals.

Half an hour later, the principal called me in. Her manner was warm and kind, but her smile seemed forced, as if something else were on her mind.

"Teacher Xu, these two comrades are from the Cadre Affairs Office of Chen's unit. They've come to take you to Beijing . . ."

"Am I being transferred?"

"You're . . . I'll let the two comrades tell you."

"Teacher Xu, the situation is this. The procedures for your transfer have not yet been completed, we've come to . . . You see, Chen's health is not good, maybe you should first go and take care of him for a while. We'll see to your transfer later."

"What happened?"

"It's nothing serious, but it's always better to have someone who is close to the patient take care of him. We've already bought your train ticket, so if you don't have anything else to do, maybe we should get started?"

As if I might have anything else to do! My husband, my love, the hope and strength of my life, what's happened? What's happened?

All the way to Beijing, they took great pains to keep me comfortable. It makes your heart cold to think of it — I'd been riding trains for over twenty years, and this was the first time I'd ever set foot in a sleeping car. The two cadres avoided my glances, and kept channeling our conversation away from Chen's illness, so I simply decided not to talk at all. As I sat watching the countryside race past, my mind had already flown ahead to Chen's side. Oh, Zhixian, if only this could be the last time I will ever take this train . . .

There was quite a group of people waiting to meet me at the train station, but Xiao Gao was the only one I recognized. In the past he had always laughed and talked happily whenever he saw me, but this time he acted very strangely, as though afraid to see me.

What had happened?

I was surprised that our car didn't follow the familiar old route to the western suburbs, toward the "Eastern Lane of the Transportation Personnel." Instead we drove east. A modern-looking building came into sight. "Tumor Clinic"—no, it can't be cancer!? For a moment, everything seemed to turn dark around me.

"Teacher Xu! Sister Xu!" I heard Xiao Gao shouting in my ear. "Wake up, Chen is waiting for you!" You see what a coward I am... Yes, I want to go see Chen, I want to see my beloved right this minute!

I walked into a ward filled with white bedsheets, and saw my husband quietly lying there, surrounded by all kinds of bottles and tubes.

"Zhixian," I cried, and ran over to him.

His face, so intimate, so familiar to me, was now almost unrecognizable. Always thin and drawn, now it had swollen to almost twice its original size. His skin was dark as a layer of dried tree bark, his lips were cracked, and there were traces of blood at the corners of his mouth.

He opened his eyes and recognized me. He tried to smile, but oh, what sort of smile was that? He grasped my hand and began panting heavily.

"Mei, at last you've come. I... I'm fine, just don't worry about me... Look, our problem still hasn't been... I've let you down, I'm so sorry..."

Muffled sobs could be heard from the others in the room. Later Xiao Gao told me the diagnosis: as a result of the turmoil of the last ten years, and his inadequate diet and constant stomach troubles, Chen had contracted chronic hepatitis. But he had always hidden this from everyone, and always refused to eat well, saving all the good food for the children. A week ago, the leadership of the institute was charged with assisting in the wheat harvest. Since Chen was the leadership of his research section, he felt he should personally lead a group of young people off to the countryside to work. On the third day in the fields, he suddenly collapsed. Not until he'd been taken to the hospital did anyone know he had developed liver cancer, and now was suffering from acute liver failure. Xiao Gao hung his head as he spoke. "God damn me, why didn't I go to work on the harvest instead of Chen?"

I stayed by Chen's bed two full days and nights. At times he was unconscious, at times clear-headed. Whenever he woke, the first thing he did was to grasp my hand.

Although we'd been married sixteen years, the time we'd actually spent together didn't add up to even two. The pressures of life had kept us panting for breath, and we'd hardly had a chance simply to sit down and share our thoughts. Now that talking had become a desperate struggle, he seemed to want to comfort me, and at the same time to use this last chance to tell me about the hopes and dreams he had kept in his heart all these years.

"Mei, we've always wanted to take the kids to see the Great Wall; well, when I get better, let's stop worrying about the cost of the train tickets . . . let's go. The mountains back in Guangxi may be lovely, but they haven't got the majesty of the Wall . . . I went once . . . right when I first came to Beijing, and now that's almost twenty-two years ago . . ."

"Good, we'll go in the fall. Beijing is gorgeous in the fall."

"Xiao Gang and Xiao Hong are such good children. Xiao Hong looks so much like you . . . Mei, I still have some money left over from that article I translated. Why don't you make some new clothes for her?"

"Okay . . . " I knew he was picturing Xiao Hong in her brother's oversized, worn-out hand-me-downs, which she always wears even when she plays with little girls who are dressed up as beautifully as butterflies. I'm sure he was always as unhappy about this as I, but both of us held our feelings in. We never could raise this heartbreaking subject.

"Mei, you've always been a stubborn optimist, haven't you? Promise me that you'll always be that way, okay? Promise . . ."

"I . . . I promise. Now relax and try to get better . . ."

From the day Chen entered the hospital, the institute leadership had begun sending a stream of people over to see him. His co-workers were also taking turns staying by his side. Bit by bit, working in spurts when he was able, Chen handed all of his projects over to them. His colleagues took notes as he talked, all the while brushing away tears from their eyes. The day after I arrived, the top Party leaders in the institute came in person for a visit. By then Chen's condition had worsened considerably. When he saw these senior officials, he lifted his head with great difficulty and motioned for me to go away. I walked only as far as the door.

"You've such a heavy workload . . . and find time to come see me . . . I feel ashamed . . . that I haven't done a better job all these years . . . our computer industry got started when other nations' did . . . and now we're so far behind them . . ." His breath came in great, panting gulps.

"Don't even think about work now, Chen. Just relax and rest."

"I . . . I still have one personal matter I want to go over with you . . . I won't live much longer . . . about my wife, I know she's already on the namelist . . . but now, if I'm not there any longer, can you still take care of her problem, as though I were still alive?

Chen forced his eyes wide open to wait for their reply.

"Zhixian . . ." I ran weeping to his bedside.

"Xiumei, didn't you go out? All I can do now is this tiny bit, you know . . ."

"Zhixian! Zhixian! It'll be all right! It'll be all right!" I was shouting through my tears. He suddenly drew a long breath and coughed violently, spitting up fresh blood. Then he closed his eyes.

The room was filled with the sound of people weeping. Suddenly the door opened and we heard another sound, that of a cane rapping against the cement floor. A tottering old man entered the room. The old director! He had been driven from the institute several years ago, and until now was still "awaiting assignment." His thin and sprightly face was now covered with wrinkles, and his whole body was unnaturally twisted — the result of beatings that had broken three ribs. He headed straight for the head of Chen's bed, as if he had never known any of the other people in the room.

"Zhixian, I've let you down, I'm so sorry . . ." The old man let out a heartrending wail. My heart was in pieces. Not those same words again! Not those words that Zhixian had whispered so many times over the years. He was always saying "sorry" to me. Now the old director was saying "sorry" to him. But how about the old director himself? — An honors graduate in physics from Nankai University in the 1930s, he was one of those fine young people who risked everything to flee to the communist base at Yan'an. He was precisely the kind of revolutionary the Party needed most: one who had technical expertise. But now he had fallen so low, so very low — and who was going to say "sorry" to *him*?

Two entire generations of our finest intellectuals! Their classmates who went abroad to study and settle down have by now, one by one, become world-renowned scholars and scientists. Elegantly dressed and bearing their great reputations with them, they come back to China on visits. Why is it that here in the rich soil of our motherland, the hardy souls who stayed behind have all withered and died? Zhixian, you aren't even forty-five years old, the children aren't grown up yet, you're so immersed in your work, so in love with life, you can't, you can't . . .

I blacked out, and when I came to I was already back on my own bed
in the "East Transportation Lane." My two children were quietly watching over me. I couldn't remember anything that had happened — when
had I come to Beijing? Why wasn't Chen at home? Many people came to
see me every day, but whenever I asked questions they were evasive and
inconclusive. Had he been sent out on assignment again? (One year he
had left us all in Beijing while he went on assignment for over half a
month.) I found myself always waiting for him to come home after work,
waiting for him to throw his books down on the bed and joyfully lift
Xiao Hong into the air...

One afternoon, near the time he got off work, I thought to myself
that I should go meet him. I walked slowly toward the office building as
the setting sun cast a golden hue everywhere. Then I noticed over on the
bulletin board something bright red shining in the sunlight. I went over
to have a look. Oh — it was the latest list of the names of researchers,
associate researchers, and research aides. Chen had graduated in 1959
and had been working so hard ever since — of course his name would be
up there. I ran my eye down the list, one row at a time, looking for
his name:

Research Section #1, Research Section #2... Research Section #15
... how can it not be here? I walked up and rubbed the paper with my
hand. It was red paper with black writing, though by now the ink had
turned green. How stupid they are to use such a bright color, so bright
you can't see clearly! I'd better look again more carefully...

Without my noticing, a big crowd of people had gathered around
me, silently watching. I turned around to a pleasant-looking young
woman:

"What a mess these characters are! Can you help me look for a moment, is Chen... Zhi... xian up there, he's in Research Section #10..."
I watched as she covered her face with her hand and turned away. What
was going on?

"Mom!" Xiao Gang was pushing forward through the crowd, pulling Xiao Hong with him.

"Xiao Gang, come help Mommy find Daddy's name..."

"Mom, let's go home." Xiao Hong was crying.

Several women, some whom I knew and some whom I didn't, led me
slowly home. This was how I was brought to the sedation ward of
the hospital.

I was sitting on the edge of my bed, gazing at the early spring sunlight out the window. Now I remembered everything. This was no dream, this was reality, cold and hard as iron, a reality I had to accept.

One week later, Xiao Gao came to take me from the hospital. He brought me a gift of the first spring flowers of 1979. Could it be April already? He told me that the questions of my residence and work assignment had all been settled appropriately. In theory, since I no longer suffered separation from a spouse, I had lost the right to move back to Beijing. But our comrades were so upset that the leadership at the institute had had to find a way around the problem. Even leaders above the institute level had become involved.

Xiao Gao said that after I rested a while I could go to work. But when I heard this news — news I've awaited eagerly for fifteen years — my only response was a cold, bitter laugh. My companion, my love who was to have shared this joyful news with me, was no longer there. When Xiao Gao told me about Chen's funeral — how he had turned our clothes wardrobe inside out in a futile effort to locate just one article of decent-looking clothing for Chen — I was so wracked with remorse that I nearly tore my hair out. I will never, never forgive myself for being so weak. When it came time for Chen and me finally to part, the time when Chen most needed a good send-off from me, I had lost my mind. If I hadn't, I would have emptied our house and spent every penny to make sure he set off on his new road in a neat, clean set of clothes!

Zhixian, I want to visit you, I want to take the children and visit you . . .

On 5 April, the grave-sweeping festival, I took Xiao Gang and Xiao Hong out to the Babaoshan Cemetery, where we climbed up the seemingly endless steps of the ash storage hall. The spring winds were gusting fiercely, blowing grains of sand hard against our faces. Little tufts of grass, as if able to sense the oncoming spring after hiding from the harsh winter, were reaching their heads up through the cracks in the stones. The children held my hands tightly and walked beside me in silence. We found the urn that contained Chen Zhixian's ashes. He was just like millions of other Beijing people: while alive squeezed into a tiny room of one hundred square feet, and now, dead, curled up among these crowded rows and rows of other urns. The next day, we took that precious little urn and climbed to the highest summit of the Great Wall near Badaling. Zhixian, this is the first time, and the last, that our family has come to the Great Wall together. Amidst the howling mountain winds, Xiao Gang and Xiao Hong cried for their father, and at the end bowed deeply in farewell.

Zhixian, father of these children, my love, you toiled your whole life, you gave up everything for others. You never once entertained a self-indulgent hope; you always just toiled away, silent and devoted. You never wanted more than the most basic things in life, but even these were denied you. I know you always loved the high mountains and great rivers of the North. Open up your arms to them now, unburden your heart to them . . .

The young, tender hands of the children picked up the red satin cloth that held his ashes. Then they waved it in the wind, scattering the ashes toward the jagged mountain peaks below. Zhixian! The recent history of China must never be repeated. All that the intellectuals of our generation have endured must never happen to our children, or to the third or fourth generations after them.

Rest in peace! Rest in the broad embrace of our mother!

# KONG JIESHENG

# On the Other Side
# of the Stream

The great popularity of this story in 1979 can be understood from its treatment of several problems that plagued large numbers of people at the end of the Cultural Revolution: families split and destroyed by politics, youth banished to the countryside, and a spiritual isolation born of disillusionment with public affairs generally. But in addition to these themes, which were not unusual in the stories of 1979–80, "On the Other Side of the Stream" uses coincidence reminiscent of Ming dynasty storytelling to present and then erase the spicy implication of taboo behavior, i.e., incest. In the normally staid press of the People's Republic, this fleeting implication, when combined with the story's other attractions, was enough to make it quickly renowned. Its appearance in March 1979 led to a greatly increased demand for the Guangzhou magazine called *Literary Works* that published it. At the end of the year, it placed third in the 1979 national reader preference poll for short stories. But the National Prize Committee, clearly reluctant to give it a prize, chose to recognize the talent of its young author, and to assuage the expectations of his devoted readers, by giving a prize to another of his stories. That story, called "Because She Was There," tells of a young factory worker who, because of the love and support of his girlfriend, is able to

Translated by Charles W. Hayford. Originally published in *Zuopin* (Guangzhou), 1979, no. 3.

persevere beyond bureaucratic obstacles until his technical innovation is finally accepted for use in production at his factory.

Kong Jiesheng (b. 1952) won a national short story prize in 1978 as well as in 1979, and was selected in 1980 to participate in the annual summer seminar in Beijing for outstanding writers of the younger generation. He writes prolifically, often gracefully, and in 1981 became controversial for his experiments with modernist literary styles. He worked in a lock factory in Guangzhou from 1974 until February 1980, when he became a professional writer with the Guangdong branch of the Writers' Association.

## On the Other Side of the Stream

*Dedicated respectfully to those whose lives are still in darkness. May they soon be set free to enjoy the pure, fresh air of day and the clean, brilliant light of the sun.*

Grim clouds were enveloping the mountain ridge and generating thunderclaps. As the sheet of misty rain gradually disappeared, the streams overflowed with roily water.

On the mainland, there is seldom rain after the Mid-Autumn Festival; but on the island, Hainan Island, the rainy season follows its own whim; it couldn't care less when the Mid-Autumn Festival comes. Just as stubborn, the tropical sun is equally hot in summer, fall, winter, and spring.

Yan Liang, a worker on a state farm, a little over twenty years old, waited for the rushing stream to quiet down a little. Then he put on his old straw hat, picked up his satchel, left his thatched hut, and followed the twisting grassy path that led to the farm headquarters.

One crossed a stream eight times to get to the headquarters, though in fact it was the same stream each time. The stream wound its way back and forth through the hills, obliging people to cross and recross it. Nobody knew the name of the small stream, any more than the names of the innumerable hills and mountains of the Wuzhi range. The Li and Miao tribesmen who had lived here for generations had never thought to name the stream. People didn't even know where the stream came from or where it disappeared to.

When Yan Liang arrived at the headquarters, he scrunched his straw hat down over his eyes, so that he wouldn't be recognized by anyone he knew, and walked into the cramped little farm store. Even though it had then been almost a year since the overthrow of the Gang of Four, this little shop, along with the rest of the state farm, hadn't changed a bit. Outdated political slogans hung everywhere, and the shelves were loaded with books that would never be sold. Out of simple ignorance, they were still selling that Gang of Four poster called "The Moonlight Sentry." The place was just like the legendary Land of Peach Blossoms, so remote from worldly strife that people didn't even know when dynasties changed. Yan Liang finally found something new — an envelope with a picture of the enchanted lady Chang'e flying to the moon.[1] He bought a few cans of food, cigarettes, and some other things. Then, since the illustration of Chang'e had been printed so nicely, he bought a few of those envelopes, too, and carried them home.

Passing back over the stream eight times, he returned to his solitary hut just as the sun was going down in the west. When he took out the envelopes to admire them, he couldn't help a little sad smile. He was all alone in the world, with no family or friends. It seemed everyone else had just forgotten him. To whom could he write a letter?

## One: A Solitary Soul Deep in the Mountains

In the famous words of Tolstoy, "happy families are all alike, unhappy ones are unhappy in their own ways."

Yan Liang had been born into a cadre family, and had originally been known as Gu Yanyan. His father had been a cadre who came south with the People's Liberation Army, and his mother had done underground work in a southern city. At the start of the Cultural Revolution, his father had been the head of a government office and his mother the assistant head of a section in the People's Bank. He also had a sister called Gu Ganggang, to make a family of four. To look at this family from the outside, one would assume it was happy, but in fact this was not so.

From the time he was old enough to understand such things, Yanyan could see that there were problems between his parents. Yanyan

1. In Chinese legend, the beautiful Chang'e, having sneaked a mouthful of an immortality herb her husband has obtained, ascends splendidly to the moon and becomes a marvelous lunar toad.

received a great deal of affection from his parents, but found that his father did not care at all for his sister. From the time she was small, his sister had been left with an aunt in the suburbs, and his father would not let her back into the house. Once when his father was away on business, and Yanyan himself was on summer vacation, he stole away to see his sister. Brother and sister caught crickets in the tall grass, dug clams at the riverbank, and flew a kite by running through the fields. The happiness of their two hearts flew with the kite into the blue heavens. What happy days, but all too short! As soon as their father returned from his trip, he brought Yanyan home in his jeep. Yanyan caught sight of his sister, running along behind the jeep, wiping the tears from her eyes; the tears came rolling down his own face too.

So it was that Yanyan could see his sister hardly once or twice a year. Even then, their meetings had to be secretly arranged by his mother. Every time his sister came, she brought him a little present; sometimes it was a little bird, sometimes a couple of crickets. Yanyan couldn't understand it: such a wonderful sister—why couldn't his father let them all live together?

Yanyan found out that his mother, though she deferred to his father on the subject of his sister, often put up an argument with him on other questions. These were "Party" questions, or questions "of a political nature," and Yanyan didn't understand them very well. Yanyan hadn't had time to sort all this out before the Cultural Revolution was upon them. At that time, he was in the first year of junior high school, and his sister was in the same year in a suburban school. Yanyan threw himself into every kind of "revolutionary activity" of his juvenile comrades in the Red Guards. They broke into many people's houses, burned tons of books, paintings, and calligraphy, and smashed the display windows of department stores that exhibited perfume and cosmetics.

But soon Yanyan's own family was overclouded by the great wings of fate. His mother was found to be a "false Party member" and was thrown into a "cow shed." When this happened, Yanyan's father took his chance to get a divorce as fast as he could. Yanyan was assigned to the custody of his father, while his sister remained "the daughter of a false Party member." All this shocked Yanyan very deeply, but like the true little revolutionary general he was, he accepted it as an unpleasant fact. Besides, how could he defend his mother when his father had so clearly gone along with the accusation that she was a false Party member?

Yanyan was still one of the "five red categories" [see glossary], after all. But when he and his revolutionary comrades were attacking the "cow ghosts and snake spirits," he couldn't help thinking of what had happened to his mother; when he was vilifying the "seven black categories" among his schoolmates, he couldn't help thinking that at another school, his sister was among the "bastards" being accused.

Yanyan began to wonder a little.

His father very quickly got the Party to find him a pretty young nurse as a new wife. He constantly bragged to her that he was the comrade of a certain important cadre's secretary, and was always hinting that he would soon move on to better things. Yanyan wondered who was really the better Party member, his mother or his father.

In the fall of 1968, his father really did become one of the influential people in the military control commission. Yanyan didn't want to be any hindrance to his father's career, so he volunteered to be sent to the countryside, to Hainan Island. He felt no reluctance at leaving his family. But before he left, he did go to visit his aunt and sister in the suburbs. He was shocked to find that, after only two years, the house was an empty shell. His aunt had died, and nobody knew where his sister had gone. "Sister! Where are you?"

Yanyan went to his military production brigade in Hainan, and was assigned to the region of the Wuzhi Mountains: he wrote a letter to his sister's school, but never got a response. The two remained out of touch from that time on, and Yanyan's feelings of nostalgia also gradually faded away. The two of them had not, after all, spent much time together. Yanyan wrote to his father, but after a few letters found he had nothing much to say. He began to realize that, among his family members, it was his mother to whom his thoughts returned, for she, after all, had given him the most love. Should he write to her? But who knew what kind of trouble she was in now?

Yanyan's doubts did not prevent him from reading and rereading Chairman Mao's "Three Classic Articles"[2] in the time left over after chopping wood and clearing land. He learned twenty or thirty "Quotations of Chairman Mao" in song form, and wholeheartedly took part in "Seeking directives in the morning and reporting accomplishments in

2. "Serve the People," "In Memory of Norman Bethune," and "The Foolish Old Man Who Moved the Mountain" were held up for intensive study throughout China in the early 1970s.

the evening."[3] He even paraded along mountain paths holding torches aloft to celebrate the proclamation of the "latest instructions" from the top—even though those instructions were usually unclear and hopelessly ambiguous. After he had been in Hainan for about half a year, Yanyan joined the Communist Youth League. He was put on the local branch committee (at that time, there was no need to be elected to such posts) and conducted the special sessions on "practical application."[4] It never occurred to him that the favorable wind blowing him along the road of life had come from his father, who held important positions on both the provincial and the municipal revolutionary committees, and whose career was rising like a rocket.

Right after Yanyan's application for Party membership had been voted upon, China underwent an enormous change. And Yanyan's fate underwent a similar change. It was just after the Lin Biao affair of 13 September 1971 that the Party branch formally notified Yanyan that the Party committee of the Youth League had rejected his application. From then on, it was also forbidden that he write to his father. The reason was that his father, as a sworn follower of Lin Biao, had played a shameful part in the illegal move by "Lin's family dynasty" to set up an alternative Party central.

The treacherous winds of life had dashed Yanyan's little boat against the fearsome shoals that surrounded him. He was now classified as a "child of the black gang," and from morning to night was shunned on all sides. The stench of his father's bad name carried more weight than his own revolutionary conduct, and he could not forgive his schoolmates for that. At a mere nineteen years of age, Yanyan had already shouldered the black mantle of his father's sins, and could not see when the day of redemption might come.

In the spring of 1973, Yanyan finally managed to get permission to return home for a visit. The first thing he did on this visit was the paperwork to renounce his relation with his father officially. Then he went to ask his mother's whereabouts at the administration department of the bank where she had worked. The answer was so freezing that it made his heart clench.

3. Once every morning and evening, people would stand before a poster of Mao, clench the little red book of Mao's quotations, and attempt or pretend to attempt spiritual communion with the great leader. Sometimes dancing the "loyalty dance" was involved.

4. From an admonition of Lin Biao's to put "living study" of Mao's thought into "living practice."

Mother was dead! They said she had "died from disease." She had
been a little over forty, and had never been sick. What was the real reason she died?

"Lin Biao persecuted a great number of respected cadres. I hope
the Party can reopen my mother's case," said Yanyan.

"First of all, you are no longer her son," replied the political officer.
"Second, she was not only a false Party member, but also an important
undercover agent. We have indisputable proof of this. When she was in
school, she was trained by the [KMT] government in telegraphy. That is
spy training."

Since when had white become black, glory become shame? Yanyan
had often heard his mother talking about that part of her past. The
Party underground, during the war with Japan, had *directed* her to take
those training classes in order to learn telegraphy. But to Yanyan, already familiar with the fate of an outcast, it was clear that nothing useful
could be accomplished by further pleas. And so he quietly walked away.
This meant that the only person in the world he could call his family was
his sister. But where was she? Yanyan no longer was able, or even wanted,
to look for her.

On board the steamer, Yanyan's listless gaze fell upon the mist-
softened form of the great southern city. It occurred to him that he
was bidding eternal farewell to his childhood home. He had spent
the happy years of his youth here, but would never in this life be able
to return.

Back on Hainan Island, he became a completely different person.
No smile crossed his face. He took to smoking cigarettes, and his fingers
turned yellow from the tar. He also took to drinking. At twenty-one, he
was acting like a broken old man. He hated his father and he hated his
own unjust fate. He renounced his father's family name of Gu and took
the name Yan Liang, meaning "Forbidding Cold," to show his lack of
warmth toward people and his disillusionment with the world.

The months and years slipped by. In their militia unit, famous for
being "revolutionary," life was as dull and monotonous as could be. Each
day was only the day before come back again. But one cannot be completely cut off from the world, high as the Wuzhi Mountains might be.
People returning from home leave spoke of the turbulent political
changes on the mainland. These reports only made Yan Liang recall his
buffetings at the hands of fate. He felt cheated, toyed with. At one time,

he had supported the doctrine that children must answer for their parents' crimes; now that very doctrine had become a heavy chain around his own neck. How dirty could politics be? How rotten the world? Were ideals merely dreams?

Yan Liang longed to take leave of this dusty, clamorous world. Just one mile from the company headquarters, there was a nursery for young rubber trees. It was protected from storms by a growth of Taiwan acacia. Someone had to take care of this nursery. This is what led to Yan Liang's putting up his thatched hut not far from the small stream. Except for coming in once or twice a month to draw his pay, grain, rations, fertilizer, and tools, his only contact with the outside world was a transistor radio. Time flowed by like the water in the brook. The radio reported to him the mad stampede of the outside world, but this in no way affected the cold indifference in his mind.

Finally, the air waves carried the news of the fall of the Gang of Four. Yan Liang's first thought was that this was the same old political game as before, but the radio continued to bring novel and refreshing news. It finally seemed his country was moving in the right direction, and that the nightmare that had been haunting him for the past few years might disappear.

His militia unit was reorganized as an agricultural brigade. This caused the brigade members, as always, to produce a new round of cheers and then relapse into silence. Yan Liang soon realized that the disappearance of these devils [the Gang of Four] was glad tidings only to people in the mainstream. Outcasts like himself would always live in a shadow. And sure enough, all the other urban youth, one by one, got transferred back to jobs in the city. Finally Yan Liang was the only one left.

Yan Liang concluded that he would pass the rest of a long life right at this nursery. His life would be like this nameless stream: it would hum along, day and night, murmuring to itself. No one would hear the plaint in its mournful song. It would twist and turn continually, coursing day and night, yet no one would know where it was going.

Truly, little stream, where *are* you going?

## Two: On the Other Side of the Stream

During those years in the agricultural brigade, Yan Liang even forgot what Mid-Autumn moon-cakes tasted like. At Mid-Autumn Festival he just opened a can and heated up his holiday banquet. Then he lit a cigarette, sprawled on his bed, and gave himself over to Cantonese songs coming from the radio—things such as "Rosy Clouds Pursuing the Moon" and "Bright Full Moon"—all of which seemed very familiar, yet at the same time, in this place, quite alien.

The end of the last song, which was called "Enchanted Evening," prompted Yan Liang to go down to the stream to wash up. Stripping to his undershorts, he grabbed a towel and left his hut. He raised his head to admire the moon just as it dodged behind a strip of thin clouds. How radiant and enchanting the moon of his childhood had been, and never crisper or purer than at Mid-Autumn Festival. But here in Hainan, even on the most clear and serene autumn nights, there would always be a few clouds. Was this due to the luxuriant tropical foliage, or to the maritime climate? Yan Liang had forgotten what his school text had said about the formation of clouds. There were, in fact, many things he had forgotten; and there were some things he could not forget if he tried.

Leaning against a betel nut palm, Yan Liang raised his head and waited defiantly for the full Mid-Autumn moon again to show itself from behind the cloud layer. When at last it did, its cool silver rays imparted a glow to the ranks of mountains, and the colors of the night were tender as a dream. As if possessed by a perverse spirit, Yan Liang pointed out to himself that even the bright moon has its perpetually dark side, just as the most just of societies will always have its injustices.[5] His lighthearted mood suddenly turned sour.

Just at that moment, in the midst of a chorus of cicadas, there came and then disappeared the sound of a soft, casual song. Yan Liang turned to see if the radio in his hut were still on, then reproached himself for imagining things. There must be something wrong with his hearing. He went on toward the stream, but the closer he got, the clearer the sound of the song became. Yan Liang stopped and listened carefully. It was the melodious voice of a woman singing a song Yan Liang himself had also once known:

> The bright and clear moon hangs high in the sky,
> Bathes the great earth with its brilliance:
> The silver light everywhere makes me long for home, . . .

---

5. Writers in China are frequently exhorted to focus on society's "bright side," especially the leadership of the Communist Party, rather than to dwell upon the "dark side," meaning actual social problems. In times of extremism, it has been dangerous for writers even to suggest that the dark side exists.

Yan Liang quietly walked to a steep part of the bank. He was suddenly so taken by surprise that he forgot to breathe. There on the other side of the stream was a young woman, washing her clothes in the clear, silver waves. Who was she? Why had she come to this deserted place?

When the moonlight threw his reflection onto the water, the girl sprang to her feet and looked directly toward Yan Liang on the opposite bank. In the moonlight, he could see her eyes flashing this way and that. The clothes she was washing started to drift downstream. Yan Liang suddenly realized he was not properly clothed, and hurriedly turned to leave. In a moment, he heard a loud splashing in the stream, which must, he thought, have been the sound of a terrified girl making a frantic escape. But in another moment, her song again issued from the other side of the stream, for her splashing had only been to retrieve the clothes that had drifted away. It was he who had yet to recover from fright. He knew that another state farm had a tree nursery about ten minutes' walk across the stream in the other direction, and that there was another thatched hut there. But the other state farm had not designated any particular person to look after its nursery, and those people who did come never slept in the hut overnight. Even their daytime visits happened only a few times per month. Occasionally, the banks of the lonely stream would reveal some Li tribesmen, shouldering their muskets and leading their hunting dogs. But where had this girl come from?

Yan Liang went to sleep that mid-autumn night with the sounds of a throng of crickets and of rustling treetops all around him. But all he heard was that comely voice echoing in his ears.

As the sky turned blue, and the first rosy clouds of dawn appeared, Yan Liang stepped across the morning dew down to the river to wash his face. The sound of song floated up again, this time "The Sun Comes Out from Behind the Mountain," and following the joyous song the image of the girl he had spied the night before flashed forth from a grove of wild bananas. She was carrying a towel, plunging through the horsetail ferns, coming down to the stream. Catching sight of Yan Liang, she stopped her song and greeted him with perfect composure: "Good morning."

Somewhat at a loss, Yan Liang looked at the girl and blurted out a "good morning"—a phrase he found strangely unfamiliar because it is so seldom used in the countryside.

She was small and slender, her skin deeply tanned by the sun, her clothes patched, her russet feet bare. She was quite ordinary-looking.

Perhaps Yan Liang could not appreciate the looks of a woman; they all seemed alike to his indifferent eye.

"We're neighbors," the girl said with a beaming smile. "We drink from the same stream." She laughed. "Are you the only one in that hut? What's your name? How long have you been here?"

"My name is Yan Liang, and I've been here alone for four years," Yan Liang replied. Then, noticing her accent, he asked, "Is your family from Haizhou?"

"Why yes, how did you know? Where is yours from?"

"Same as yours."

"Hey, you speak Mandarin very well. What school did you go to? What class were you in?"

"I went to ... High School Eighty-one, class of '68." Mortification overcame Yan Liang as he spoke. His alma mater was a special school for the children of high military officials.

The girl looked him over quizzically. "Senior high or junior high?" she asked.

"Junior high."

"Then you're the same year as me! You certainly don't look it! I thought you were thirty years old. Why don't you get a haircut? Or try shaving? If you go home looking like that your own father'll disown you."

Another stab of pain in Yan Liang's heart. One mention of his "stinking" father and the girl would certainly turn hostile.

Just as she was dipping her washcloth into the water to wash her face, she suddenly cried out, "Oh my, look at that! Look right now!" He followed where she was looking and saw a little bird with bright red feathers skimming and twittering through the morning air. It landed in a bush by the stream, looking like a red flower in full bloom. This exotic tropical bird, which the Li tribes considered to be magical, had never been caught or caged. In fact, it was a rare thing even to see one.

"Oh, how beautiful! This is a wonderful place!"

The comment caused Yan Liang to recall that she had called herself a "neighbor." Could it be that she had moved into the hut across the stream? He wanted to ask, but dared not. When he had washed and was ready to leave, she broke the silence again. "What's your rush, Yan ... uh, what did you say your name was?"

"Yan Liang."

"Look, you haven't even asked me mine! It's Mu Lan — 'Mu' as in Mu

Guiying and 'Lan' as in Hua Mulan.[6] From now on we'll be seeing each other across the stream," she laughed. "I thought I was the only one living here, but when I saw that betel nut palm yesterday, I felt better."

That betel nut palm was one Yan Liang had planted himself after he arrived. It is a strange tree, for it grows only where human beings have settled. In the Wuzhi Mountains, a betel nut palm always signals the presence of a nearby village.

"What are you doing here?" Yan Liang finally asked out of curiosity.

"Oh, you and I are in the same business. Our brigade's tree nursery was almost overgrown with weeds and grass, so they made me come down here to look after it."

Yan Liang couldn't understand why they would send a girl to look after the nursery, but he didn't want to ask any more questions. By this time, the sky was completely light. Yan Liang could feel Mu Lan's intense gaze curiously scrutinizing his every move, and this made him feel somewhat ill at ease. He went up from the bank of the stream.

After that, Mu Lan's song often floated over from the other side of the stream. And Yan Liang encountered her at the bank of the stream a few more times. When this happened, Yan Liang seldom spoke, while Mu Lan chattered away like a little sparrow. Yan Liang learned from her that almost all the urban youths once stationed at her farm had already returned to the city. In her brigade, she was the only one left.

Mu Lan was peppery and forthright, and often used words that normally only boys use. Once she said, "What do they think they're talking about — 'grasp the key link of class struggle and bring great order to the brigade'? Bullshit! The head of our farm, a 'double stand-out' cadre,[7] is a real little bastard. He worked his lousy tail off for the Gang of Four, but the next thing you know he was hot to 'smash the Gang of Four,' too. What a little pile of dogshit! And because this turd was in charge, our whole brigade lost its shirt. And then they talk about modernization!" Yan Liang was about to say that his farm was also on the brink of bankruptcy, but didn't quite dare.

---

6. Mu Guiying is a woman warrior of remarkable valor and intelligence in many popular stories about Song dynasty resistance to Liao invaders; Hua Mulan is another fictitious heroine, a young woman of ancient China said to have disguised herself as her father to lead his troops into battle.

7. A "double stand-out" (*shuang tuchu*) cadre was one who rose quickly during the Cultural Revolution to (1) join the Party and (2) assume a position of power in society. The cadres were usually young "rebels," chosen for their politics rather than their abilities.

At dusk on the eve of the October First National Day, Yan Liang was down by the stream washing his bedsheets when Mu Lan started singing again. She noticed a few lush, ripe papayas on a tree at the stream bank; slipping off her sandals, she pushed aside the spiky leaves of the underbrush and made her way to where she could shake down some papayas. She casually tossed a couple toward Yan Liang, who scrambled over barely in time to catch one of them, while the other fell into the water and bobbed away. This made Mu Lan laugh until she lost her breath, and even Yan Liang couldn't help smiling. Mu Lan shouted, as if she had just discovered something, "Oh ho, your face is always so wrinkled up like a pickle that I didn't think you even knew how to smile! Ha, ha . . ."

Yan Liang smiled again, something of a wry smile, and didn't reply.

Mu Lan went on, "Yan . . . Yan Liang. You know, it really doesn't sound very nice to call yourself a name that means "forbidding and cold." You might as well call yourself Yan Luo, the King of Hell. Ha ha, don't get mad! What's so bad about the King of Hell? I'd really love to be the King of Hell some day. What I'd do is I'd send my deputies—those cow-headed horse-faced messengers like the ones in the pictures in the old Buddhist books—and chase all the goddamn bastards of the world right into hell! Then they'd get a taste of what it's like to shinny up hills of knives and get dunked in boiling oil. But Yan Liang, what I really wanted to ask you was why you never went home to Haizhou."

"I don't have any family there," Yan Liang mumbled evasively.

Mu Lan, keenly observant, quickly withdrew her smile. "I think maybe there's some other reason. C'mon, tell! Look, I don't have a family either. My mother was hounded to death by the Gang of Four and hasn't been exonerated, even though it should happen pretty soon. The reason I can't get transferred back is that I'm a 'counterrevolutionary'!"

"You?" Yan Liang shivered.

"Sure. A few years ago, some people put up a wall poster calling for a more democratic system. Did you hear about it? I wrote a letter supporting it, and—bang!—was stuck as a counterrevolutionary and paraded around to be struggled by all the work teams. Those apes! They beat the hell out of me! It was half a month before I could stand up straight again. But they better think twice if they think they scared *me*!"

Yan Liang looked at her in amazement. He never would have imagined that her delicate body could have undergone such a fascist beating. And how could such a young girl already be a counterrevolutionary? That was something that normally took a lifetime! After a moment of reflection, Yan Liang said, "Your problem will be settled sooner or later. But mine is different. My father was one of Lin Biao's right-hand men, and nobody can live that down. For me there's no way out."

Mu Lan looked at him sympathetically but said nothing. After a moment she said, "It won't be easy for me to remove my counterrevolutionary label, either. They make you a counterrevolutionary in a matter of minutes, but God knows how many years it takes to prove they were wrong. And in my case, the problem is not something the agricultural production brigade can handle — it has to go up to certain big officials. But I couldn't care less who it goes to — I'm not scared!"

After another pause, Mu Lan asked, "Are you going back to your brigade headquarters for National Day on October first?"

"No," Yan Liang answered, without thinking. "Are you?"

"Do you need to ask? Tonight I'll come to your place to pay my respects. May I?"

". . . certainly . . ." Yan Liang didn't quite know what to do.

### Three: An Evening Chat in the Thatched Hut

Yan Liang had just finished tidying up his thatched hut inside and out. In the distance, the peaks of the Wuzhi Mountains reflected the last blood red light of the sunset. He busied himself building the fire for his evening meal. By the time the food was ready, the sky was filled with cloudy moonlight. Outside, Mu Lan's song started up again; this time it was "The Hawthorn Tree":

Song floats lightly on the waters of the golden dusk . . .

"Hey!" called Mu Lan from outside the hut, "Here comes the honorable guest!" In a moment she had followed her laughter into the hut.

"Heavens, why the droopy face? You cooking dinner? Forget it, make it into fried rice in the morning. I've brought you some steamed rolls, and they taste just the way they do back in Haizhou." She laughed.

Mu Lan was not a bad cook, and her steamed rolls stuffed with beanpaste were delicious. Yan Liang sat by the side of the bed, leaving the only bamboo chair for Mu Lan. But Mu Lan kept walking around, humming a tune, inspecting his low-ceilinged kitchen and turning the pages of his few books.

"You sing pretty well," said Yan Liang, searching for something to say.

"Me? Nah! I only sing because of you, because I'm afraid of embar-

rassing you. I bellow it out when I go down to the stream bank, just to
warn you that a woman is around." Having said this, Mu Lan lost herself
in laughter, and the crisp sound of that laughter penetrated into the
night outside. Yan Liang began to realize that Mu Lan, despite her very
open and outgoing manner, took pains to be considerate.

Mu Lan sat down and without the least awkwardness said, "I
don't know how it is, but I keep thinking that I've seen you somewhere before."

Yan Liang found it awkward to meet her gaze, but thought for a
moment and replied, "Back when I used to be so red I was almost purple, I used to go over where you were to hold 'practical application'
sessions. You probably saw me up on the platform making a fool of
myself. My goodness —'practical application' sessions! Now it all sounds
pretty ridiculous."

Mu Lan laughed icily. "No, it couldn't be that," she said. "I never
listened to a word of all that hot air, so that wasn't where I had the honor
of making your acquaintance!"

"So that makes me a hot air artist, a bullshitter?"

"No, we were all victims, but some people woke up earlier than others . . . Oh, now I remember! It was the last time I went to the shop at
your brigade . . . the same day volume five of Chairman Mao's *Selected
Works* came out, that day it was so crowded. I saw a guy with long ratty
hair, sunburnt and skinny. *That* was you. I don't know why, but you made
a special impression on me."

Yan Liang reflected uneasily that, if he had really been so conspicu-
ous in those days, he had been risking considerable trouble. Mulling
over his regret, he started to fish out a cigarette, but then stopped awkwardly with his hand in mid-air. Mu Lan's gaze was fierce. "If you're
going to smoke, give me one too." Clumsily, he lit one for her.

Yan Liang's inhibitions gradually dissipated with the cigarette
smoke. He heaved a sigh. "You were talking just now about how some
people 'woke up' earlier than others," he said. "I saw through their tricks
as early as anybody. But it was like waking up from a nightmare and
finding you're still in the dark."

Mu Lan's glistening black eyes darted up and down Yan Liang once
again, and she laughed. "Did you join the Youth League?"

"I almost joined the Party! But I got kicked out of the Youth League
right when I turned twenty-five."

"Then you believe in communism?"

"To tell the truth I had my doubts. But not any more, of course. Ideals are like the sun in the sky, and reality like the shadows on the ground. When the Gang of Four fell, almost everybody could enjoy the sunshine again. But I've been unlucky enough to stay under a cloud. It's just like the Wuzhi Mountains. Other people can see that there are actually five peaks, but from our vantage point we can see only three. And that's because of the angle we're looking from, that is to say . . ."

"I know what you're talking about," Mu Lan chuckled. "You're something like the decadent poets and the nihilist philosophers."

Yan Liang was startled. He hadn't realized that Mu Lan knew so much. "I guess you don't agree?" he ventured.

"Why not? Everything you said is true." Mu Lan changed her cheerful expression and continued solemnly. "After all, I'm the daughter of one of the 'seven black categories,' I never joined the Youth League, and later I got stuck with political labels. But I never really doubted communism, and still think it's going to come true some day. The communism I believe in is one that can make a person happy. Aren't we always saying that the proletariat can liberate all of humanity? How come not all citizens have the same rights? Why does everybody have to be divided into 'red categories' and 'black categories'? What right do they have to drive people to death so recklessly? What right do they have to call me a counterrevolutionary? Where's the legal distinction between 'revolutionary' and 'counterrevolutionary'? Take you, for example. Why should it make any difference whether your father is 'rotten'? Why should a son have to carry around a father's bad name for the rest of his life?"

Mu Lan's suntanned face had now turned red, and Yan Liang realized from her impassioned talk that she felt even more deeply than he about these things. He sighed helplessly. "Maybe when your kind of communism arrives, we can get out of the fix we're in," he said.

"Why wait? Why should we wait?" Mu Lan's eyes were glowing like the flame of the kerosene lantern. "I didn't bow my head for one minute to those savage bullies! I'll appeal my case level by level to the Ministry of Agriculture, to the courts, to the Provincial Committee, to the procurator-general . . . and if all that doesn't work, I'll write to Uncle Deng himself. I'll denounce them, denounce every one of those damn bastards right into the ground!"

Yan Liang was staggered by Mu Lan's gall and her stubborn cour-

age. But then he reflected that he had not, after all, been publicly la
beled a counterrevolutionary; how could he make a formal appeal to
higher levels?

Mu Lan sighed and her voice became husky. "Our country has gone
through a massive disaster these last ten years, and why did this happen
If it was only because of Lin Biao or the Gang of Four, then tell me how
all those other opportunists got to the top! Did anyone ever ask the peo
ple if they wanted them or not? Okay, so they got kicked out this time –
but if the people can't have democracy, then what's to stop a 'Gang of
Five' or a 'Gang of Six' some year bringing another big mess? So I'm
making my appeal not just for myself. It's also for my martyred mother
and for everyone who's been hounded to death, hoping that we'll never
see a bloody tragedy like this again!"

A long and deep silence. The only sound was the hiss of the kerosene
lantern. Yan Liang had always blamed the outrages of those ten years on
the evil Lin Biao and Gang of Four. He had never considered the flaws in
the social system. Now he sat pondering this question intensely.

Mu Lan fixed Yan Liang with her gaze. "You ought to write to th
People's Daily and tell them just what's happened to you. Why not
Afraid? Afraid of what? The People's Daily is starting to speak for th
people these days. I never used to be very brave, but when I lost every
thing, I lost my fear too. What the hell is there for an 'active counterrev
olutionary' to be afraid of?"

Yan Liang laughed coolly, for he knew that the normal way of han
dling letters from readers was to refer them back to the leaders in one
own work unit, and that only made things worse, much worse.

The night was getting late, and they began to hear the sound of th
autumn dew dripping from the leaves of the trees onto the parche
underbrush. Mu Lan said it was time for her to go. She broke off a switc
of thorny bamboo from the crudely bound broom that stood behind th
door. "Lot of snakes around here," she said, whipping the switch on th
ground a couple of times.

"I'll see you home," said a concerned Yan Liang.

Mu Lan chuckled. "Don't bother. I'm not afraid of snakes. Are ther
wild boars around here? I'm not afraid of them either."

But Yan Liang insisted. When they got to the bank of the stream, M
Lan gave Yan Liang a gentle shove, took a few running steps, an
jumped over the stream. On the other side, she turned back to face him

I don't need you to see me home, but there *is* something I'd like your
elp with. That rickety hut of mine is nice and near to the tree nursery,
ut it's too far from the stream — not very convenient. I think I'll build
nother little nest for myself, and I'll have to use a little cost-benefit
nalysis to choose the location! Ha-ha . . ." Mu Lan didn't wait for Yan
Liang to reply, but ran laughing up the hill.

## Four: Companions in Adversity

The next day, which was National Day, Yan Liang and Mu Lan did a
hole day's work under the steaming sun, finally completing a sturdy
ttle reed hut for her. They built it behind a grove of wild banana trees
n the other side of the stream. Yan Liang scattered sulphur around the
ottage to ward off snakes. When he had finished, Mu Lan said nothing
o thank him; she only grinned and said, "You're pretty handy."

Yan Liang later taught Mu Lan everything he knew about grafting
oung rubber plants. He explained that if she cut her hair and scattered
ome of it around the nursery, the wild boars would be turned away by
he human scent and not trample the plants.

In the evenings, the two of them would get together to read and
hat. Mu Lan was well informed on a wide range of subjects, and they
ilked about everything under the sun. But Mu Lan, ever ready to say or
o anything, showed she was also very solicitous of other people's feel-
1gs. She never asked about Yan Liang's family, just as he never asked
bout hers. Neither wanted to open the other's wounds.

Yan Liang lost his melancholy; Mu Lan's refreshing candor was like
ray of sunshine in his somber life. He felt as if he had known this girl
or years. Perhaps because he had been living alone too long, a cozy
eeling grew in Yan Liang's heart in no time at all.

Once when Yan Liang was squatting at Mu Lan's side, showing her
ow to graft rubber shoots, he found himself shifting his gaze toward
er sweat-lined face.

"What are you doing?" Mu Lan suddenly asked.

". . . What?"

"What are you gaping at? If I did something wrong you wouldn't
ven notice!"

Yan Liang's face turned red, and he lost his composure.

That evening Yan Liang did not go to the other side of the stream.
Ie was sorting through his confused thoughts when Mu Lan appeared,

singing her usual song. As if nothing had happened, she said to Yan Liang, "Say, from now on, don't cook your own food, okay? We're such close neighbors—why cook separately? Besides, you're a terrible cook."

After that they were together even more. Even though Yan Liang did everything he could to repress the thoughts that were coming into his mind, he couldn't help noticing that Mu Lan's eyes often quietly followed him, and that, when she happened to meet his perplexed gaze she calmly blinked her eyelashes without looking away.

They were companions in adversity; fate had been their only matchmaker. Love sprang up in two hearts that were more used to the bitter than the sweet.

Hainan has no autumn. October is the typhoon season. When number thirteen typhoon in 1977 assaulted the Wuzhi Mountains, its center passed directly through Yan Liang's and Mu Lan's area. After the first violent onslaught of the storm, there was actually an interval of clear sky as its eye passed over. Before the stream rose too high, Yan Liang found a wooden staff to help him wade through the rushing water and go see if he could reinforce Mu Lan's hut. He had just patched a few leaks when the wind suddenly blew up again. It savagely drove pellets of rain, like insistent darts, into the groaning forests of the mountain. Mu Lan brewed up some ginger sugarwater to ward off the cold. When the two had finished it and chatted for a while, the sky was already very dark. Wrapping his raincoat around his shoulders, Yan Liang made his way out the door, but hadn't gone more than a few steps when he stopped in amazement. The swollen stream had almost exceeded its banks, and the rushing water made a terrifying roar as it hurtled forward. Through the curtain of rain, he could see on the other bank the betel nut palms snapping back and forth crazily in the violent wind. Crossing over was out of the question.

Mu Lan dashed out and pulled Yan Liang back into the hut. Her eyes sparkled as she wiped the rain from her face. "Don't go," she said evenly, looking straight at Yan Liang. "You can't get across anyway. Stay here."

Yan Liang jumped as if delivered an electric shock.

"Are you some kind of Confucian moralist?" asked Mu Lan. "You believe all the classics of morality?" She was laughing, but it was a brittle laugh that was actually a cover for the inner excitement she also felt.

Yan Liang still couldn't say a thing. Mu Lan began to help him re move his raincoat. "You're shivering, look, you're soaked through!" Yan Liang suddenly grasped Mu Lan's warm hands . . .

Some time later, a gust of wind blew out the guttering flame in the kerosene lantern. They didn't light it again.

This pair of lucky — and yet also unlucky — young people: had they been too hasty? They had known each other only two months! Yet they felt as if they had been fated for one another in some previous existence. In this deserted outpost, on this night of the fierce typhoon, it had been their common fate that had brought them together.

If certain leaders of their state farms had known what they were doing, the consequences would have been terrible. Although most people generally do acknowledge certain moral prohibitions, they do not like to see the enforcement of those prohibitions placed in the hands of cold-hearted bullies. Heaven only knows whether this pair of young lovers, who intended to swear themselves to one another, had done anything wrong. The Lord of Heaven certainly did seem to be enraged, to judge from the roaring fury of the typhoon. Magnificent crashes, from great trees snapping in the wind, continued to sound from time to time. The maddened wind and driving rain shook the little thatched hut angrily. Was Heaven trying to punish someone?

Nonetheless, inside the lovers' hearts, all these noises of heaven and earth seemed far, far away.

## Five: Whose Fault?

The sky lightened. The typhoon had passed. The muddy stream was carrying its burden of splintered branches, blasted leaves, and half-submerged papayas and coconuts down to the sea. Yan Liang took Mu Lan by the hand and led her across the stream to see how his own hut had come through the disaster.

The storm of emotions had also passed. The sweetness of their love seemed to hang in the gentle winds and tear-soft rains as they cuddled together and talked about the future.

"Let's get married tomorrow," said Yan Liang.

"Whatever you want. My gosh, what sorts of paperwork will we have to go through? It'll probably be a pain."

"I have no idea. I guess we'll have to fill out some forms."

"What shall we put on them?" She giggled. "You'll put that your 'family background' is 'anti-Party element,' and I'll put that my 'class' is 'active counterrevolutionary.' Blacker and blacker! Ha ha! . . . But wait, we'll still have to put down our family and residence, and neither of us has any family."

Yan Liang sighed. "Well I do have a sister, actually, but don't know where she is."

"Oh, really? Why not?"

"When we were small, they never let us be together. My father didn't like her. When my parents got divorced, she went with my mother. By the way, my mother's maiden name was also Mu."

Mu Lan turned white and suddenly grabbed Yan Liang's hand. "What was your sister's name?" she blurted out in extreme apprehension.

"Gu Ganggang."

As if struck by lightning, Mu Lan threw aside Yan Liang's hand and leapt to her feet. Two terror-filled eyes stared straight at Yan Liang.

Mu Lan's whitened lips began to tremble. "You . . . you're Yanyan?" she whispered.

Yan Liang's head began to spin. Everything grew foggy.

"Ma . . . no!" Mu Lan let out a jolting scream, covered her face with her hands and ran crazily from the hut. Yan Liang followed her without quite knowing what he was doing, only to see Mu Lan plunging recklessly down the hill. She tripped and fell headlong into the stream, then got up, dripping from head to toe, and rushed on, leaving a trail of shrill cries along the way.

Yan Liang suddenly realized that she . . . she was . . . oh, no! Yan Liang's knees buckled. He stumbled forward a few steps, threw his arms around the trunk of the betel nut palm, and slipped listlessly to the ground. There he sat in the mud, trembling all over, feeling like vomiting.

Somehow he found his way back to his hut and flopped down on his bed. Soon he began to get chills. Yan Liang had once caught malaria, which was common in this tropical area, and he had the usual recurrent bouts of it even after he seemed to have recovered. Now the fever came in waves, causing him to writhe on his cot in pain; it alternated with spells of shaking, which made the cot creak and groan. Hallucinations appeared in his muddled mind. Suddenly he would see himself and his sister flying kites and running gleefully through the fields; then his mother, locked in her "cow shed," would flash before his eyes, calling in despair to her children; next the shameful events that had occurred the night before on the other side of the stream would reappear. How hameful! How evil! But wait—where were these dazzling gold stars oming from? No! It was all dark again. Where are you, Mother? Can't ou save me?

He didn't know how much time had passed. He struggled upright o swallow some quinine, and sat crouched for a while, his head lolling n his knees. Heartless fate had cuffed him once again, destroying ev- rything he had left. Whose fault was this? Whose?

These two late-blooming flowers had borne a bitter fruit. Every- hing was quiet on the other side of the stream. At dusk a few days later, (an Liang was at the bank of the stream and saw . . . his sister. How thin he seemed, how ashen her face. Yan Liang cast his eyes downward un- ertainly, and said nothing. Mu Lan did not lift her eyes either, but fur- ively filled her pail with water and slipped away.

Yan Liang came to realize that, from now on, each time he and his ister met would be a kind of torture for both of them. A chilling hought occurred to him . . .

One day when Yan Liang was propped on his cot with that chilling hought in his mind, his sister slipped quietly into his room. She sat lown woodenly, but Yan Liang jerked upright with a shudder. A glance old him that some deep contemplation lay behind his sister's blood- hot eyes.

After a silence, Mu Lan spoke. "Yanyan, since I'm the elder sister, I ave the responsibility to think things through for both of us. What we lid was not our fault. Forget about what we did. Don't think about it ever gain!" Mu Lan almost broke down, and took a moment to recover. Yanyan, listen. I went to the farm office this morning, and found out hat Mother's unit had sent a letter saying she's been exonerated. They're planning a memorial service and want me to go back for it. The 'arty secretary in our office is such a stinking bastard he didn't want nybody to tell me. The deputy manager of the farm told me in secret. I hink you and I should go back together . . . what's wrong? Don't worry! Mother's spirit would forgive us even if she knew."

Yan Liang silently nodded his head. He was near to choking. His logged throat could not produce a word. Mu Lan stood and put her and gently on his shoulder. Yan Liang quivered.

"Don't be that way, Yanyan. Wipe all that out of your mind . . . You're ny brother; stand up and call me sister." Mu Lan's tone of voice ad changed.

" . . . sister."

"All right. I'll come back this evening." Mu Lan, who also could hardly hold herself together, darted out of the hut.

Yan Liang's heart hurt as if a knife were twisting inside it. He lay his head on the table and sobbed.

### Six: Toward the Light

Yan Liang knew that the farm would never approve a leave for him. But he had already put everything else out of his mind. Luckily, there are many more good-hearted people in the world than evil ones. Even though neither of them had documentation for a trip home, they managed to board a steamer for Haizhou without mishap.

Late that night, the half-moon left a rippling trail of silver on the sea. The hot faces of this brother and sister felt comforted by the salty sea breeze. They leaned over the railing of the ship, peered at the boundless sea, and shared their thoughts.

Yan Liang learned many new things about their past from his sister. After their mother's divorce, she and her daughter had moved to the company quarters of the bank. But within half a month, their mother had been put into the "cow shed," and his sister had been forced to vacate their room. A kind-hearted old man who worked as doorkeeper at the bank had taken her in. One morning, this old man anxiously informed her that her mother had had her collarbone broken and was running a high fever. In her delirium, she had called out for Ganggang and Yanyan. Mother had been so nearby yet so inaccessible. There had been no way to see her. Mu Lan had bought medicine, written a note to go with it, and asked the kindly doorkeeper to find some way of getting these to her mother. She had gone to High School Eighty-one to find her brother and tell him about their mother, but had been surprised to learn that one had to report one's class background in order to get through the school gate. When it had been learned she was a "bitch's daughter," she had been refused entrance. At that point, she had written a letter home to her brother, but had never received a reply. (Yanyan had never even heard of this letter; needless to say, the pettiness of their worthless father had been at work.) This had made her despise her brother completely and feel he was just as much a beast as her father. From then on, she had banished the thought that she had ever had a brother. In 1968 her school had assigned her to go to the countryside, but she had not gone. Within six months, her mother had died in prison without her even having had a chance to see her mother's face. Afterwards, she had joined the old doorkeeper's daughter and this girl's classmates from High School Five in an assignment to work on Hainan Island. She had changed her name, and had said only that she was with High School Five. From then on, she had had no family to turn to, and had floated aimlessly for eleven years until she had come across her equally ill-fated brother. Now it all seemed to belong to another world . . .

At the memorial service, which was held in the cemetery for revolutionary martyrs, the steely Mu Lan melted into tears, while Yan Liang, normally the weaker of the two, stood implacable as a statue. He gazed dumbly at the casket that held his mother's ashes. He could not believe that his mother, who had been a solid, loyal member of the Communist Party, could be packed into such a little box. He began to doubt that it did hold her remains at all.

Who had killed our mother? Who had brought every conceivable suffering upon us, her children?

Yan Liang shook off his timidity. He went along with his sister to the public complaint offices of the departments concerned, and there they stated their case. They also filed an appeal with an Intermediate People's Court, and joined in writing a lengthy wall poster that criticized the leadership of their state farms. They furiously denounced the malevolent toads who took pleasure in persecuting people and the heartless bureaucrats who could only behave like cogs in a machine. Mu Lan's problems were eventually cleared up, thanks to the full support of the Party committee at the People's Bank. The Intermediate People's Court directed Mu Lan's state farm to exonerate her, and the People's Bank deputed someone to accompany the brother and sister back to Hainan so that they would not be prosecuted for having taken leave without authorization. The bank even said that it would bring both of them back the following year and arrange jobs for them.

There was no way to "exonerate" Yan Liang, because he had fallen victim to no law, but merely to the *policy* of denying certain rights to people like him. Yan Liang had come to understand that freedom and democracy were not tasty pastries that others would hand to you on a platter; the more one lived in darkness and adversity, the more one needed to stand up and fight. He and his sister wrote letters to the newspaper demanding that the rule of law be strengthened and that all people be equal before it.

There are still little tyrants around, who feel that "the mountains are high and the emperor is far away," leaving them absolute power to make their own little laws in their own little kingdoms. But their day is coming to an end! The sunlight of the Party will eventually break through the dark clouds and shine into every corner. The Party committee on Mu Lan's state farm had already been reorganized, and a Party work team at Yan Liang's was in the process of reorganizing the leadership there.

Who says the Wuzhi Mountains must swelter all year round? Throw up your arms and shout, for the spring breeze is coming!

### Seven: The Parted Lovers Reunite

The banks of the stream had often echoed with the sounds of song and laughter from brother and sister. What a pity that complete happiness is so elusive. There still remained that one incident, the painful memory of which haunted them both. Each had privately sworn never to marry. Their only wish was to be together, never again having to part.

Oh, if only the leadership everywhere were as benevolent and effective as it was this one time. Yan Liang received a letter from the Party committee at the bank: "Comrade Yan Liang, recently we have come across something your mother left you when she died. Tucked inside the cover of her *Quotations of Chairman Mao*, we found this letter addressed to you. There obviously should be a letter to Comrade Mu Lan as well, but we have been unable to find it. We feel most apologetic, but could you inform Comrade Mu Lan . . ."

Yan Liang hurriedly unfolded this parting letter from his mother. It was written on a very thin piece of paper, with tiny words crowded everywhere. The flimsy paper rustled in his hand. He was shaking as he smoothed it out on his table. The words danced and jumped before his tear-filled eyes:

Yanyan —

I do not have long to live, and I have a few things that I must tell you. Your father is an evil person with a mean soul. You must never follow in his footsteps. When I am dead, you must seek out your sister Ganggang. There is something I have always kept from you both, because you were too young to understand. Toward the end of 1951, I was doing land reform work in the Shiwan Mountains of Eastern Guangdong. At that time, bandits had still not been wiped out in the area, and the mountain districts were extremely poor. Once, in a small hamlet, a destitute woman asked me to hold her baby girl for a moment while she went to the outhouse. She left and never came back. Afterward I found out that her family was so poor that she had been intending to give this female child to somebody. This was your sister Ganggang. I think she's about six months older than you.

Good-bye forever, Yanyan. Don't weep for me. Stand up proud and straight, and live! My last wish is that you and your sister be reunited and stay together always. Look after each other, encourage each other. I'm writing these last letters to you and your sister from a dark prison cell, and I have no way of knowing if they will ever get to you. When I eventually am exonerated by the Party authorities, you and sister must come and report to me in my grave. I know I will hear you.

—Mother

By the time he had finished reading, Yan Liang felt as if arrows were piercing his heart. His tears gushed as if from springs. He sat in a daze, reading and rereading his mother's letter. Suddenly, as if there had been a flash of lightning, he saw the whole world in a different way. Snatching up the letter, he ran out of his straw hut and bounded across the clear little stream . . .

Oh, little stream — people do know your source now. You come from every cloud in the sky, from the dew on every leaf in the forest; you are crystal clear about the human world, its loves and hates, the sweetnesses and the terror.

Oh, little stream — people do know your destination now. Traveling your nine bends and crooks, you witness all manner of human suffering as it is washed before you into the great sea, in just the same way that our road through the world is bumpy, our lives are full of twists and turns, and the brightness of our future disappears and reappears.

Oh, little stream — people do understand you now, as you murmur along night and day. You are telling us: "May the dead achieve eternal life; may the living achieve eternal love. May the sun forever bring light and warmth, may humankind forever enjoy its warmth and solace."

*1 February 1979*

# HUANG QINGYUN

# Annals of a Fossil

During the Cultural Revolution, fables and children's stories were all but completely banned from publication. This undoubtedly was due in part to the double entendre they make possible. As in the use of historical figures to comment on the present, children's stories in China have been used for political commentary that an author would cringe to make directly. The children's story as allegory has, moreover, a special kind of power that may come from its association with the primitive candor of a child; it is, as C. S. Lewis has observed, "the best art form for something you have to say."[1] "Annals of a Fossil" is clearly talking about the Gang of Four (vixen = Jiang Qing, wolf = Wang Hongwen, viper = Zhang Chunqiao, toad = Yao Wenyuan) and, only slightly more subtly, about the Great Fossil Tortoise who is their monument. The story, for which an author could have been shot during 1966–76, provides some telling commentary on the mass psychology of that period.

Huang Qingyun (b. 1920) grew up in Hong Kong and attended Zhongshan University in Guangzhou as well as Teachers' College, Columbia University. An admirer of Charles Dickens, she has written and edited children's literature in China during most of her adult life.

Translated by Graham E. Fuller. Originally published in *Yangcheng wanbao* (Guangzhou), 5 May 1980.

1. "On Three Ways of Writing for Children," a lecture read to the Library Association at Bournemouth, England, and published in its *Proceedings* (London: The Library Association, 1952), p. 23.

## Annals of a Fossil

Once upon a time, when mankind was exploring all creation, people began to approach the ends of the earth. A group of animals who were hiding at the ends of the earth — a vixen, a wolf, a viper, and a toad — began to fear for their lives. If mankind kept on advancing, these animals would soon have no place left to hide. So they decided to convene an emergency meeting.

The vixen, who had seen something of the world, took over as chair and asked everyone to come up with a plan for action.

The viper extended his forked tongue and hissed, "I can stretch my body across their path and stop them."

"I can tear them apart with my claws," snarled the wolf, baring his teeth.

The vixen laughed bitterly, shook her head and said, "That won't work! Mankind has no fear of you! A real man fears no beast. Before you could even move, they would smash you to a pulp!"

The toad, seeing how the two bigger animals' suggestions had already been rejected, didn't dare to venture his own opinion. So he turned to flattering the vixen: "Clever Ms. Vixen, we had best solicit your own valuable opinion." (The toad, as a small creature at a meeting of big animals, knew that the only way he could have a say was to play up to them.)

Sure enough, the vixen drew herself up and said with satisfaction, "I think there is only one thing we can do. We know that mankind has no fear of bird or beast; the only thing they fear is themselves. All we need to do is to get them to tie themselves up in knots and they will destroy themselves!"

The animals asked with one voice, "Do you think such a thing could really be done?"

The vixen answered, "If we all put our heads together, a method can surely be found somewhere." So they crossed the great mountains and traversed the great deserts in their search. But the hands of mankind had already transformed the great mountains into blooming gardens of beauty and the barren deserts into sown fields. After the first day of travel, none of them had been able to come up with a plan.

The next day, they continued to press onward, leaping over stinking ditches and penetrating thickets of weeds. The wolf, who could run the fastest, was the first to come upon a stone tablet that bore many inscriptions. He turned to the vixen and asked, "Learned Ms. Vixen, what is this thing?"

The vixen squinted at the tablet and said, "This is an inscription. Human beings set down in writing those things they believe they ought to do."

"Please read it to us!"

So the vixen read out, "A lifetime's goal lies in the striving; the sweetest fruit is that planted by oneself."

The wolf interrupted, saying, "Don't read any more! All of that has nothing to do with us."

"It does! It does!" cried the toad, who was carefully watching the expression on the face of the vixen. "Suppose the tablet said 'Every day give the toad a piece of the meat it has always longed for—swan flesh.' Such an inscription would certainly have a lot to do with me." The toad's mouth watered at the mere thought of this proverbial, but unattainable, toad's morsel.

The vixen nodded her head in amusement, "Maybe that day will come."

On the third day, they proceeded onward, the wolf again taking the lead. He lost his footing on a slippery slab of rock and fell down with a thud. Cursing, he muttered, "Probably some damn stone tablet again — my nose and head are getting knocked black and blue!" But a voice issued from within the round stone and said, "It is I!"

"Who are you?" the four confederates said with a start.

But the viper recognized this object. He remembered that a long time ago his great-great-grandfathers had known this object and had passed its story down until it had reached himself. So the viper called out respectfully to the stone, "Old Grandpa, what are you doing here?"

Originally, it seems, this had been a great tortoise, who had been overturned, leaving his belly staring up into the sky. The great tortoise sighed and said, "Alas, I've just about turned to stone by now. When mankind began to explore the ends of the earth, they found me and toppled me over; I could not roll back. Fortunately, I was able to pull my head back into my shell so that at least my mouth never actually died. Woe is me!"

When the four confederates heard the fossilized tortoise curse the name of all mankind, they immediately wanted to go and help him turn right-side-up again. But the vixen narrowed her eyes and called out, "Not so fast!" Then she turned to the tortoise fossil and said, "Old Grandpa Fossil, we have all resolved to fight mankind to the bitter end. If you are willing to join us, we will roll you right-side-up. What do you say?"

When the tortoise fossil heard of their resolution to carry their fight with mankind to the bitter end, he hastily pulled his head back into his shell and said, "No, that won't do. I would rather lie here with my feet sticking up into the air forever; that way I can at least keep my head and mouth intact. We cannot beat mankind in a fight. I, at least, have already lived a thousand years; but you, what skills do you have?"

The vixen brandished her tail, saying, "A viper must be poisonous to bring down its prey; a wolf must be cruel to reach the mountain top. A vixen who lacks nine tails [symbol of vicious deceit — Tr.] cannot boast; a toad who lacks ambition can eat no swan flesh. As long as you believe in us, we can do just fine!"

The tortoise fossil still shook its head. "Nothing doing! If by any chance you should lose the fight, then all of you will have scattered to the winds, spraying poison, goring enemies, whatever. Then who but myself will be left holding the bag?"

The vixen said, "Old Grandpa Fossil, all you have to do is join us; if you do, we will not only turn you right-side-up, but, if in the future the four of us should be captured, you at least can be confident of mankind's continuing respect. You have an immortal, imperishable mouth, and a head that became fossilized several thousand years ago. All this is extremely valuable."

The toad eagerly pitched in from one side:

> Please say yes! Say, "Yup, yup, yup!"
> Life is great when you're right-side-up!

While the tortoise fossil still maintained its silence, a group of sewer rats, stinking rats, and blind rats scurried out from beneath him, chattering feverishly. "Come on, Old Grandpa, you can agree to that! If mankind continues to civilize the world, they'll soon chase us out, and we'll have no place to go. If they take over completely, it'll be the end of our kind."

"All right," the tortoise fossil grumbled at long last. "You may turn me over."

Then all the big animals, together with all the little animals, taking their guidance from the vixen, helped the tortoise fossil to turn over. They dragged him along with them for three days and three nights until they brought him to where the stone tablet was. There, with great effort, they placed the stone tablet upon the tortoise's back. It now looked for all the world like the great imperial edict tablets of old.

At that point the vixen, with one jump, leapt onto the back of the tortoise in order to stand over the heads of all the others. She said, "Now hear this! I have come to bestow official position upon each one of you animals. The hated snake, who wears eyeglasses and carries classified documents around with him, shall be my military adjutant. The toad, who has great ambitions and can sing beautifully, shall be my minister of propaganda. The wolf, of powerful appearance, daring and pugnacious, shall be my commander-in-chief. From now on, all of you are my deputies."

But the sewer rats, the stinking rats, and the blind rats chattered: "Why don't you appoint us to anything?"

"Apart from stealing food," the toad said, "you have no talents at all!"

"Who says stealing things doesn't require talent?" the rats retorted. "All a toad can do is dream about eating swan flesh, but can you steal oil? Can you steal an egg? Furthermore, every year on New Year's Eve, we rats marry off our daughters, bore holes, blow horns, and carry sedan chairs.[2] Now *that* is beautiful. Can you do that?"

"All right, all right," the vixen said, "we do need those who can bore tunnels, blow horns, and carry sedan chairs. I hereby consign you to the command of the big gray wolf commander-in-chief. You will be ready for his orders at any time. If we meet with success in the future, we will drive every cat from the face of the earth; then you can run wild to your hearts' content."[3]

The rats were all so happy they raised their tails to the sky and went off chattering. The tortoise fossil was left there, staring at the vixen.

2. All things that, according to legend, rats do late on New Year's Eve in connection with the marrying off of their daughters. But here "blowing horns" and "carrying sedan chairs" are double entendres for contemporary slang referring to unabashed sycophancy.

3. Cats here have a positive connotation not only because they threaten the evil rats but because they suggest Deng Xiaoping and his famous pragmatic aphorism, "Be it black or white, a cat is good that catches rats."

The vixen said, "Don't tell me you're still not satisfied — you who have no ability other than pulling your head back into your shell. We helped you turn over, and for that you still owe us thanks. The only thing you have to do now is to remain eternally loyal to me; but your heart, which has turned to stone, may be incapable of that."

The toad said, "But *my* heart is plenty strong; it aspires even to eat swan's flesh. I can divide my heart and give part to the tortoise."

Commander Wolf said, "What do *you* amount to?! My heart is the great one; when people sing songs, they all praise me as a "wild-hearted wolf" [ person of wicked ambition — Tr.].

Adjutant Viper said, "Without a ruthless heart, one cannot perform great feats. I have a famous viper's heart; let me give the tortoise a piece of my heart too."

The vixen was delighted and said, "You are all so equal-hearted [of one mind — Tr.]! And now, if you will all just wait a little, you will soon be able to witness a miracle."


The dark night was over. Early the next day, the masses all came back again to move stones, clear underbrush, and repair the roads. When they saw the tortoise who bore the tablet on his back, everyone was surprised and asked Uncle Longbeard, the group leader, about it. Uncle Longbeard said, "Everything you see written on that tablet represents the words of very wise men and the precious experience they have had."

A broad-shouldered young man spoke up and said, "Every age has its wise men who say wise things. Every age has its precious experience. But if these sayings are forever repeated down through the ages, they cease to be wise. And if we keep on doing things the same way forever, the experience ceases be precious."

The masses in the rear could not hear clearly what the broad-shouldered young man had said. Their only feeling was that, since the great tortoise had shouldered the tablet and was carrying it aloft, surely they, too, should read it. So each of them kept reading it, reading, reading, and reading some more, and they came to feel that these sayings were all reasonable and, indeed, beyond reproach.

In the evening the people fell sound asleep. But under their beds could be heard chattering voices:

> The magic turtle bears a tablet,
> The tablet bears a sacred scripture;
> If you read it every day,
> Heavy stones can fly away.

When the people woke from their sleep, they were still humming the same song — hum, hum, hum. They went off to see the tablet, humming all the way; they went on humming even after seeing it — even while working and eating they hummed it, feeling that the tablet's inscription was truly something meaningful to them.

Many days passed. One pitch black night, the vixen summoned the viper, the toad, the wolf commander, and his group of rat soldiers, and held a meeting before the tablet. The vixen said with pleasure, "In recent days you have achieved great things; I shall record your names in the book of meritorious service."

The wolf, although pleased, was astonished, saying, "Ms. Vixen, you have asked me to instruct the rat soldiers every day to slip under everyone's beds and sing the songs written by Adjutant Viper—the songs in praise of the tablet. But doesn't mankind also wish to civilize the land? I don't see what point there is to all of this."

Adjutant Viper said, "Commander Wolf, all you know how to do is to bare your teeth and show your claws, you haven't gotten enough politics under your belt; please wait until Ms. Vixen can explain this to you."

The vixen again mounted the back of the tortoise and said, "Yes, indeed, I was just preparing to make a big announcement to you all. To lack sufficient politics under your belt is, of course, not proper; but the greatest impropriety is that all of you lack a tail the likes of mine. Therefore you must all heed my directive. Poor toad, when you were little you did have a tail . . . it's too bad you lost it when you grew up. The little rats are fairly intelligent — they know how to use their tails. But unfortunately they use them to steal oil. They will never accomplish great things. Stupidest of all is the wolf. All he can do with his tail is show happiness or unhappiness. Ridiculous! Why should you broadcast to everyone what you are thinking inside? We foxes would never be that stupid. Indeed, our great skill is in misleading people. When hunters pursue us, we use our tails to whip up dust from the ground to block their sight. When they can't see the way, they make bad decisions, and go off in the wrong directions, while we slink away scot free. These will be our tactics in the present day — is that understood?"

This speech made all the beasts bow down in admiration before the vixen. Then, standing imperiously before them, she began issuing orders and directives, seeking to further her tactics of deception. She told the rats to gnaw open the strong boxes, to break into the storehouses, to steal people's gold and paste it onto the tablet, to steal people's perfume and spray it onto the tablet.

From that day on, people could smell the fragrance of the tablet even when they were far away; and before they even started to read its inscription, they were struck by the glistening of its gold. All were impressed by what they saw. "From ten miles away you can pick up the scent of this monument; its gold lettering flashes from afar. This can't be any ordinary monument: it is surely sacred!" Some people wept with emotion, others bowed down in adoration.

The vixen then called another meeting alongside the monument. But the wolf still didn't understand what it was all about: "What good, Ms. Vixen, is this monument to us?"

The vixen said, "Soon you will know the whole story. This is precisely the moment when we can use your services. Adjutant Viper has hatched a scheme; Minister Toad has put it in verse. Since you, Wolf, have the sharpest teeth, you can use them to carve the verse into the tablet. Then we'll need to paste on a little more gold, and spray on a little more perfume."

Then she turned to the rats and ordered, "You must continue in your diligence; from now on, people must dream of nothing at night but the writing on the tablet."

All of this led to an even stranger event the next day. When the people reported for work, they found the following verse inscribed upon the tablet:

> Hard work is the only thing which
> Allows a hard worker to get rich,
> And then become a son of a bitch.

The people at first naturally found this message rather curious, but since the fragrance of the stone tablet was even more lavish, and the glistening of the gold even more splendid, they again felt that this must be a sacred directive and had no doubts about its authenticity.

In the evening, the people again went to sleep; in their dreams, they heard the chattering of voices under their beds reciting the new verse, which by now had become encapsulated in the following formula: "To be assiduous is to be evil." The consequence was that a great many people stopped going to work. When they stopped working, their stomachs grew hungry. Just when they were wondering what to do next, there appeared on the tablet the glistening strokes of several new pronouncements:

> Seeds planted by oneself will bear sour fruit,
> Fruit plundered from others is tastiest of all;
> He who labors is a fool,
> He who fights and robs is a hero!

All the good-for-nothings said, "Exactly right! These directives from heaven couldn't be more timely!" And they set about seizing everybody else's possessions.

By now the wolf could grasp the power of the vixen's strategy. As the vixen's directives became more numerous, the wolf's engraving of them became all the more zealous. He even wore off two of his claws and several of his teeth. Each day new writings appeared on the face of the tablet, including the following:

> Rats are the angels of the night,
> Cats are consummately vicious.
> Quickly drive the cats away
> And the angels will always be with us.

> The snow white swan is thoroughly ugly;
> The leper toad wears the beauty crown.
> Quickly deliver the swan to the toad,
> And help turn the world upside down.

Now pronouncements were regularly appearing in such quantity that it was all the people could do to keep up with them. Indeed, many people gave up trying to think altogether. A few people did keep on using their brains, however, and these people did not always go along with everything.

Then Commander Wolf sought out the vixen and said, "Ms. Vixen, people are no longer listening so much to your directives. Some people are, in fact, still secretly harboring cats. And some people are still engaged in building public parks."

The vixen said, "I know. This is because certain teachers, and certain parents, are misleading them. But so long as my poems radiate their authority, we still have ways of opposing them."

"The people have ceased to be productive," the rats reported. "We need to steal more gold and perfume, but there is none to be found."

Adjutant Viper said, "I have a special plan to meet this problem. I have often heard people say, 'Gold is no better than dung and dirt.' If people will not produce gold, at least they can produce dung. If we can get the dung and pretend it is gold, our problems are solved."

So a new statement appeared on the face of the tablet:

> Something new! What a thrill!
> The good student beats his teacher, and
> The good child beats his parents, till—
> Those who build parks are shut in dark rooms,
> And those who love you are the ones you kill!

At nightfall the chattering under the beds was noisier than ever; loud voices chanted this verse over and over. Since by that time all cats had been either driven out or hidden by their owners, the rats had full sway. But this time only a few dimwits among the people were chanting along with the rats; the others had turned silent.

When Uncle Longbeard, the girl with pigtails, and the broad-shouldered young man went off to civilize the area, the teachers would no longer go with them. They were fearful that their students might beat them. And people who were parents wouldn't go either, fearing that their children would wreak great havoc. Instead they warned Uncle Longbeard, the girl with pigtails, and the broad-shouldered young man, saying, "You should be careful, you know. Things have now reached the point where rats are preferable to cats, and toads to swans. You'd better watch out! The more you love people, the more likely they will try to kill you!"

The girl with pigtails smoothed down her hair, thought for a moment and then said, "Why should this nice place of ours turn into a home for cruel rats, a place where the lazy are well off and where evil men are in charge? I think all of these problems come about because the people stare at that stone tablet, don't you agree?"

"But the inscriptions on the stone are written in gold!" said old Uncle Longbeard.

The broad-shouldered young man said, "In that case, we must look into the matter of just why these inscriptions should be gleaming so brilliantly." (He was a practical person who put great emphasis on investigating the facts.) He stepped onto the back of the tortoise, examined the writing closely, and then beckoned for everyone to come up close. "Do you think this really is gold? Everyone come take a look!"

The people now saw it with full clarity — it wasn't gold, it was dung with some gold mixed in.

"Why, the gold must have enchanted us!" said the girl with pigtails.

"Everybody sniff!" said the broad-shouldered young man. "Isn't this just as fragrant as can be?"

Everybody sniffed carefully, then retched. As fragrant as can be? It was nothing but rat droppings, snakeshit, wolfshit, and vixen secretions! Everyone was angry. "Those stinking #%⁶&*@s! We've been tricked!"

Uncle Longbeard, still incredulous, said, "But I remember that these were the sayings of the wise men of the past, inscribed by our own hands. How could they be a stinking mess?"

The girl with pigtails was the most observant one there. In a flash she had discovered two wolf toenails and some wolf teeth. "Old Uncle," she said, "all those sayings of wise men have been altered by beasts. Look, here are the broken teeth a wolf has spat out!"

The broad-shouldered young man then told everybody to look around the area, and there they found the fresh tracks of a vixen, a viper, and a toad. "They must still be nearby!" the young man said. "Let's catch them quickly!"

By this time, the vixen had already heard them coming. She ordered Adjutant Viper, Commander Wolf, and Minister Toad to sneak away with her. "Nobody should be afraid," she said. "My nine long tails will save us!"

Then, using her nine tails, she raised such an incredible cloud of dust that no one could see her. But as she raised her eighth tail high into the air, the broad-shouldered young man caught sight of it. And as she raised her ninth tail up, someone seized it. The whole rotten bunch of her henchmen were seized along with her.

The vixen sighed and said, "When you have a lot of tails, you may be able to deceive people, but you can also end up exposing yourself!"

Cats now reemerged. All the sewer rats, stinking rats, and blind rats who could not scurry into their holes in time were captured in one fell swoop.

Then the people took the besmirched and stinking tablet and toppled it over. But the fossilized tortoise hung onto the tablet for dear life and refused to let it go, fearing that if he no longer possessed the tablet, the people would never prostrate themselves before him again. Struggling at the borderline of life and death the tortoise called out: "Every word the tablet has uttered is pure truth. Should the tablet no longer exist, then I, the great tortoise, likewise will no longer exist."

The girl with the pigtails laughed and said, "If you, the great tortoise, were no longer to exist, then . . . you, the great tortoise, would no longer exist! Who cares! But since you can still speak human language, we must not banish you but try to win you over. How about if we send you to a museum? You are, after all, a very rare fossil!"

The tortoise fossil fixed them all with an angry stare, pulled its nose in and said, "I may have turned to stone, but my heart is still alive. Within me there is . . ." He was going to say a viper's heart and a wolf's heart, but caught himself and said, "Within me there is a *loyal* heart, which none of you possesses. I don't want any of your flattery." (He had mistaken the girl's phrase "win you over" for "win your favor." For in his own fossilized mind, "winning favor" was a vital concept, whereas patiently "winning someone over" was unknown.) "I am revolted by all that you do! Ugh!"

The broad-shouldered young man immediately saw to the heart of the issue. "Ah, now I understand. You were the one my great-great-grandfather toppled over. No wonder everything is repulsive to you now — you're used to looking at the world from flat on your back!"

The masses said: "Well, since he is so comfortable looking at everything from flat on his back, then maybe we'd better let him keep on lying on his back just like before, feet sticking up in the air."

So everyone joined together and tipped that fossilized tortoise back over again, pushing him brusquely to one side. Then they exuberantly swept clean the battlefield, and with bold steps set forth to civilize the world and to make beautiful flower gardens.

# LAO HONG

# The Gap

Perhaps nothing bespeaks the continued supreme importance of the family in China quite so clearly as the outcry over the harm done to families during the Cultural Revolution. The required denunciation of "counterrevolutionary" parents by children is the key fact in Lu Xinhua's pathbreaking story "Scar" (August 1978), whose thunderous popular acclaim led to the designation "Scar literature" for hundreds of similar stories that followed. In the present volume, "Anticipation" and "On the Other Side of the Stream" show us families forcibly separated by administrative "necessity" and factional politics respectively. "Nest Egg" and "At Middle Age" sensitively explore the severe strains within families that have managed not to fall apart. According to publishers, these stories brought in record numbers of letters from readers who said their own families had suffered similarly.

The present story treats with elegant brevity the widespread problem of the generation gap. China's younger generation, especially educated youth in the cities, were rebellious, sometimes cynical, and stoutly resistant of attempts to limit their thinking (see Introduction, pp. 34–35). Many of their elders, having spent half their adult lives weathering political storms, tended on the contrary toward caution and prudence

Translated by W. J. F. Jenner, to whom the editor is also grateful for having pointed this story out. Originally published in *Dangdai* (Beijing), 1979, no. 3.

about the costs of political activism. In "The Gap," a man who has borne the "rightist" label for over twenty years seeks out his grown daughter, whom he remembers only as an infant. The author's understated description of their encounter—awkward, fruitless, and diffusely painful—leaves one with the clear sense that their separation is hopelessly permanent. Although the author's manifest concern is with the particular problems between China's "rightists" of 1957 and their offspring, he has written a story whose moral and psychological interest might engage the parents of adolescents anywhere.

# The Gap

One still winter evening Su Zhiyu walked into a small restaurant, ate a light meal of pancakes, and got ready to go to see the daughter with whom he had lost all contact since they had been separated twenty years ago. He had come back to Beijing only a few days previously, and the first thing he had done after settling in was to look up some old friends to find out where his daughter was working and living. Only that morning he had learned that she had a manual job in a bakery in the eastern part of the city, and was living alone in an old-style house at 25 Chunshu Lane in its western part. He had asked the friend who told him this to let his daughter know that he was now completely in the clear. He had been exonerated, restored to Party membership, and assigned in Beijing to a journalism research institute. He would be calling on her about seven that evening. The thought of having to use an intermediary to make contact with his own flesh and blood was painful. But despite that, he had two things to be glad about that day: one was that his former work unit had signed his official exoneration document that afternoon, thereby freeing him at long last from a great burden that had weighed upon his spirit for many years. The other was that he was about to see Susu, as his daughter had been called when a child.

He hurried to the bus stop, then looked at his watch and saw it was only ten minutes to six. If he took the bus, he would be very early—she might not even be back from work. So he changed his mind and decided to take a leisurely stroll to get there. After twenty years away, it would be fascinating to walk along Chang'an Boulevard, from the east to the west of this great capital city, to see how it had changed. He felt relaxed and cheerful as he set out along the bustling sidewalk next to the broad, clean boulevard. He was a slight figure in a short, fur-lined black serge overcoat, with a small satchel in his left hand and his right hand thrust into his pocket.

His lean, weatherbeaten cheeks gave him something of the toughness of a working man. The sharp expression of the eyes behind his glasses suggested intelligence, wisdom, and a slowly matured observation of life. The marked wrinkles on his forehead and beside his mouth, like the graying hair that showed under his blue serge cap at the temples, showed that he was getting on in years and had endured his share of hardship. But his step was still light, and he held himself well: from behind he looked younger than his fifty-eight years. He was deep in thought as he walked. Apart from noticing that there were even more pedestrians and traffic at rush hour than there used to be, he paid no attention to the new buildings or to the ways people were dressed. His gaze was fixed ahead of him, and the time melted away as scene after scene appeared before his eyes.

The months and years seemed to have passed quickly and slowly at the same time. Twenty years ago he had left Beijing, banished to a remote farm on trumped-up political charges. Before he had left, his wife Yuan Wang had withdrawn all their meager savings for him to take with him, and had made sure his bag was filled with things he would need. That evening, they and their two-year-old daughter had hastily swallowed their last meal together before he threw his pack onto his shoulder, picked up his bulging bag, and set out through the door with two comrades who were being sent to work on the same farm. He had staggered down the first few steps, panting, and then had turned with difficulty to look at his wife, who was standing on the dimly lit landing with their wide-eyed, bewildered little daughter. His wife's face had been rigid and white, and after she had gone back inside and shut the door, he had heard the child start to howl.

The first days on the farm really had been hard for one who had always worked with his brain, but as time went on he had gradually adjusted to it. This adjustment finally became an essential part of his life and spirit. Sometimes, for example, he had been told to write an article for a wall newspaper, and had been given a half-day off work to do it.

But the moment he sat down to write, he would feel a nameless emptiness and depression that would leave him confused and wretched. He was well aware that his long term of heavy manual labor had made him a stranger to the life of the mind and had slowly numbed his brain. Only the occasional letters from his wife would set his thoughts racing again, sometimes getting him so excited he could not sleep for nights on end. He read each simple, ordinary family letter over and over again until he almost knew every word and punctuation mark by heart. And yet every letter would make him more deeply aware of what appalling trouble his own political problems had caused for his wife. The child was growing up, and would soon be of an age to start primary school. And what had he done? Toiled here for three years to no avail. Whatever was he going to do? His wife never said anything about the future in her letters, but as a "rightist husband" and "rightist father," he had to think about it. Perhaps it was because he had felt guilty about where he had landed his wife and daughter, and because he had worried about their future, that in the end he decided, with much self-mockery and bitter, confused emotions, to divorce his wife, let the child take her mother's surname, and make a clean and final break with them. He did this not out of hardness of heart, or irresponsibility, but because it was the only solution he could see. He felt that he alone should reap the bitterness he had sown, and that to make them share it would be completely unfair and intolerable. On his repeated insistence, the two of them went through the divorce procedures without ever meeting again. But Yuan Wang did send him a sum of money and a big package of his clothes and other articles. Her last letter had been only one sentence: "Look after yourself, and don't worry about us." From then on, he had lost all contact with both of them.

Over a year after the divorce, when he had done five years on the farm, his case was reconsidered. This, they said, was because he worked well and had come to understand something of his own problem. His rightist label was removed, and he was transferred to another part of the country to be a storekeeper at a vocational school. He had regarded this as a load off his mind. Yet, compared with the farm, where he had worked from dawn till dusk and had fallen asleep the moment he got into bed, his mind as still as a stagnant pond, his placidity was now disturbed by the rocks and stones that life was throwing toward him. Sleep became difficult, and even after he did finally drop off, he would often wake with a start to weep in silent but uncontrollable grief. He had long been separated from the Party that had brought him up, and felt like an orphan who had wandered far into a foreign land. He was homeless, like a little boat adrift on the great ocean. He could not help thinking with anxiety and pain of Yuan Wang and his only daughter, Susu. She must have started primary school. Was she a Young Pioneer yet? Did she still laugh the way she used to when he hugged her? How was her schoolwork going? He could imagine her sitting at the table like a grown-up, textbook in hand, looking up and asking him, "Daddy, is revolution a verb or a noun?" At these thoughts, a tear would fall on his arm, now crisscrossed with blue veins. But what was the point in thinking about all that? He was no longer her father. His "rightist" label had been lifted, but he was still an "ex-rightist," and that was another wrong kind of father to have. He had often wanted to write to them to ask how they were, but when he picked up his pen, he would only lay it down again, or would start a letter and then tear it up. He had not wanted to trouble them, and had hoped that they would forget him completely, as if he were dead, and find themselves a happier life. Late in 1965, after two years of this mental strife, he had asked a co-worker, who was being sent on a job to Beijing, to call on an old friend and ask discreetly how they were. Soon afterwards the colleague had brought back a short letter from this friend. It said:

> Yuan Wang has been very unhappy all these years and has had no news about you whatever. She was very ill last year and almost died. She finally married Chen Zhengping in March. Chen was in the underground with her just before Liberation and was a classmate of hers in the journalism department in college. You once taught him; perhaps you remember him. He now heads the editorial department of a publishing house . . . Your daughter is called Yuan Fang and now is in the fourth grade. She's very bright . . .

The letter had transfixed him with grief. Not knowing what he was doing he had rushed to the edge of town and begun pacing up and down in a small woods. He had wanted to cry his heart out, and tried to concentrate on what to do with the rest of his life. But his thoughts had been far too tangled to make sense of, especially since his future was not his to arrange. It was long after dark when he staggered back to his quarters. He picked up his pen to write something, but collapsed unconscious on his bed. He woke up in the emergency ward of a hospital at one in the morning. No cause of his illness had been diagnosed. He spent over ten days in the hospital, and when he was discharged seemed like a new man. He was no longer miserable and long-faced. Sometimes he would play a game of chess or a couple of hands of cards with his comrades, or go out for a drink in a restaurant. More often, he would stay by himself in his quarters reading the poetry of Qu Yuan, sometimes reciting it aloud, his eyes brimming with tears. He had used private connections to borrow various annotated editions of Qu Yuan's works from a university library. Finding not only contradictions among the commentaries but also foolish mistakes, he decided to prepare a new annotated edition. Once he started using his spare time to pour all his passion into this job, he seemed to have no other care or worry in the world. He even began to put on a little weight, and his face regained some of its color.

But before another year was up the Cultural Revolution had struck like a tidal wave, like a thunderbolt. As an "ex-rightist," he had been dragged out and flung into disgrace with the other "ghosts and monsters." Soon afterwards, he had been sent back to his original home district in Zhejiang province for labor reform, and was not sent back to the vocational school until after the destruction of the Gang of Four. In his eagerness to learn the fate of his old friends, he had sent off a dozen or so letters. Some of the letters disappeared, like stones dropped into the sea, and some were returned unopened. Only a few drew answers. After receiving one of these replies, he had sat stupefied for hours on end in his room, not hearing what the other men who lived there said to him. It had made him forget to eat and forget to go to work. What the letter had told him was unimaginable: his former wife and her new husband of just over a year had drowned themselves together in Kunming Lake one night in August 1966, when the Cultural Revolution was just beginning. Those two comrades, who had done so much for the Party on the eve of Liberation, at the risk of their lives, had been dragged out as traitors while their home was raided. After they had endured as much as they could of beatings and public humiliations, they had finally chosen this way of delivering themselves. But if they had now gone to another world, what was the use of regret and grief?

> Long, long had been my road and far, far was the journey:
> I would go up and down to seek my heart's desire.[1]

He had found himself repeating those two lines of Qu Yuan's over and over again, finding some solace in them. The only other comfort he found was the news that after her mother's death, his daughter had gone to live with her aunt. It had been exciting to imagine himself going to find her after his case had been thoroughly cleared. When he painted himself a joyous picture of the two of them living together, his heart had jumped for joy.

As Su Zhiyu walked along, deep in thought, he did not notice that the street lights had come on. It was unusually warm, and the air was quite still. Feeling a little hot, he undid the top button of his overcoat and loosened his scarf. He congratulated himself on finally being allowed to rejoin the ranks. His feelings took him back forty years to the time he had walked to Yan'an. The promise of a great new age had beckoned him; he had been impelled by the spirit of self-sacrifice. Now he imagined his daughter, who would soon see her father again. Would she recognize him? Would she hold her twenty years of suffering against him? How he had adored her as a child! Had she grown up to look like her mother? Did she have that round and slightly childlike face, the same thick mop of hair, the thoughtful eyes? He wondered how she would react to seeing him. Would she be understanding or angry? Happy or sad? Would they throw their arms round each other and weep? That did not seem necessary. Nor did there seem much point in raking over all that the family had been through these last twenty years. But it hardly seemed the occasion for chatting about his journey and gossiping about friends and relatives. No matter how hard he tried, he could not think what to talk to her about.

It had occurred to him that he had once before been to this street where his daughter lived, but he could not remember how or why. When he finally did trace the street, he easily located the number and found the pine doors of the south-facing entrance to the compound were wide open. He entered a narrow alley that turned east and led to a small Beijing-style courtyard. At this point he realized that he had indeed been here before. It was where his wife's sister had lived, except that the

---

1. David Hawkes, *Ch'u Tz'u: The Songs of the South, an Ancient Chinese Anthology* (Oxford: Clarendon Press, 1959), p. 28.

main entrance had been changed. An old lady was standing under the eaves cutting out coal-dust briquettes with a spade. He went up to her and asked where Yuan Fang lived.

"She lives in that one. She just . . ." Before she could finish, his daughter opened her door and bounded out. "Father!" she said with a smile, then came down the steps and took his bag.

He entered her room, stood still to calm himself, looked around, and sat down awkwardly on a chair that was next to a table with two drawers. The moment he came in, he had felt a gust of cold air, and in the electric light could see particles of dust falling, as if the room had only just been swept.

"Susu," he said, letting her childhood name slip out despite his intention to call her Yuan Fang, "why haven't you lit the stove?" He took off his cap and put it on the table, but undid only the top buttons of his overcoat.

"I'm on the day shift this week," she replied, "and when I get in at night I'm so exhausted I go straight to bed." As she spoke, she went out to ask a neighbor for a thermos of hot water, then bustled around to prepare tea and a warm facecloth for her father.

He gave the room a careful looking-over. There was a narrow bed by the back wall that the plastic bedspread did not quite cover. At the head of the bed was a bedside cabinet on which stood a desk light, a transistor radio, and a big pile of books. Next to the cabinet stood a wooden trunk raised about a foot off the floor on stacked bricks. It, too, was covered by a sheet of plastic, and looked like a little chest of drawers. Scattered on top were a mirror, comb, toothbrush, soap-box, and other things, together with two thermos bottles and a glass. Beside this trunk was a washstand, under which a frying-pan rested on the floor. The cold, unlit stove stood in the corner, its top off and a big pile of ashes at its base. Against the southern wall was a chair next to a small bookcase, to the front of which a white cloth curtain had been attached with thumbtacks. Next to the bookcase was a crockery cupboard, and next to that three flower pots full of dry soil and piled atop one another. In the inner corner was a curtain of patterned cloth.

As he considered all this, he felt that her life must be frugal and busy, though she seemed to have made herself at home in this little room. He looked back at the table. Under the sheet of glass that partly covered it, right in the middle, was a picture of Premier Zhou Enlai;

there were also several photographs of her with some other girls. But what really caught his attention was a square fish-tank standing empty at the back of the table. Nothing else in the room was familiar, but the sight of this fish-tank gave him a jolt like an electric shock. He and Yuan Wang had bought it on a shopping expedition during the first autumn after they were married, and had carried it home as pleased as a couple of children. On another Sunday soon afterwards, they had set out for Beihai Park with a glass jar to buy a pair of goldfish. In the days that followed, they had sat by the tank after their evening meal, talking and watching the two magnificent fish swimming at their ease in the water. When their daughter turned one year old, she had stood in front of it clapping her chubby little hands and gurgling with delight. One winter, perhaps because the room was too cold, one of the fish had died, and they had all been depressed for a day or two. All this had happened twenty-two years ago, but it felt like yesterday. He stood up and leaned forward. With the palm of his hand he wiped the dust from the side of the tank that faced him.

His daughter busied herself shoveling up the ashes from the stove. Then she brought in a flat basket of coal briquettes and kindling to start a fire. When she turned and noticed her father gazing abstractedly at the fish-tank, she was at first mystified, but then made a connection that explained it to her. Her mother had treasured that tank. When many things in their home were being taken or smashed during the Cultural Revolution, her mother had carefully hidden this tank in a pile of rubbish on the back terrace, and it had escaped attention. Whenever, as a child, she had changed the water in the tank, her mother had said, "Mind you don't break the fish-tank, Susu." But she had said nothing else about it. She had just turned eleven when her mother died. Her aunt, when she came to help sort things out, had wept as she retrieved the tank from the rubbish, and had carefully carried it here.

After a moment of heavy silence, Su Zhiyu felt he should show his daughter the final ruling on his case that the organization he worked for had given him. She read it and said nothing. Then he offered her a short explanation. In 1957 he had spoken at a conference on journalism about how press reports could be made more palatable to readers. The present document certified that this had not in fact been an anti-Party or anti-socialist speech. Now he was planning to work on several research projects, including one on this very subject. He intended to write a book that could be many hundred pages long. As his daughter listened, she was impressed by the undying determination that had kept him vital after twenty years of suffering. But she was also worried that any research he might do would turn out to be purely academic — divorced from life and dull. Even if he got it published, what would be the point, except perhaps to let people know that he was still alive and writing? She suddenly had a feeling that the little old man before her was pathetic and ridiculous, his plans merely delusions. But not wishing to hurt him, she gave no sign of what she was thinking.

The kindling in the stove was now burning fiercely. She opened the top to add the coal, the red glow lighting up her face. "After mother and uncle died," she said, as if speaking of strangers from long ago, "my aunt told me about you, but she thought you had probably died already."

"It's all my fault," he replied, controlling himself with great difficulty. "I thought that you and your mother would be all right, and I didn't want to disturb you." He paused to pick up his cup and drink a mouthful of tea before saying with deep regret, "Life is never as easy as one would like. Your mother was a fool to do that for no good reason."

The girl wiped her eyes with her forearm.

"Let's change the subject," he said, gesturing as if to throw something away. "Where is your aunt and her family now?"

It emerged that the aunt's whole family had been transferred to the south two years ago. When they left, two of the three rooms they had occupied were reassigned, leaving the girl this one little room. When her father asked about her present job, she told him she had now been working five years at the grain store to which she had been assigned after finishing high school. She had been sent to the store's bakery a year ago.

"I'm doing quite well," she said with a laugh, speaking in a confident and decisive way. "We workers have nothing to worry about — not like you old revolutionaries and intellectuals, with all your troubles." Realizing she had been too blunt, she worried that she might have hurt him.

"You're still young," he said gently. "There are some things you don't understand yet, and that even I don't entirely understand."

She felt that her father was telling her she was still only a naive child, and was treating her a bit arrogantly. But she couldn't start arguing with him right at their first meeting.

"Susu," he suddenly said, breaking the silence with a different, and deeper, voice, "can you remember me at all?"

She looked up at him with the thoughtful, cautious look that was so like her mother's. She searched her memory, then shook her head.

His whole body shook with a cold shudder, and then he felt uncomfortably hot. He took his overcoat off and laid it on the bed.

"That's hardly surprising," he sighed, then took from his satchel the plastic case that held his employment card. Tucked inside was a slightly yellowed photograph that he now removed. "Look. It's the only picture I have."

She did not immediately take it. She put some more briquettes on the stove, then washed her hands before coming over to pick it up. It showed a stocky, sturdy man in his middle years holding a chubby little girl and standing in front of a statue of a giant panda. The little girl was smiling happily, and had one arm around the man's neck.

"Who is it?" she asked as she stared at the picture. The bespectacled man was a bit like her father, but who was the little girl?

Something seemed to stick in her father's throat. He removed his glasses and polished them with his handkerchief, then rubbed his eyes and barely managed to say, "You were only one year old then, and your mother was away on official business. One Sunday I took you to the zoo . . ."

She handed the photograph back to him, turned around to take a ball of wool from her bedside cupboard, then sat down on the bed and started to knit. Her father was still lost in his memories, talking gently about how she'd loved to play in water as a baby, and once in the bathtub would never come out; how she had been frightened by thunder, and would cling to him if she saw lightning; how she had loved the color red so much that at night she used to sit by the window and gaze for hours at a red light on a chimney far away. To his daughter all this sounded like a children's story told by a stranger. She looked up at him only occasionally, then returned to feverishly clicking her knitting needles. When this happened, her father's heart felt a sharp pain, as if something had bitten it. He suddenly realized that such a long separation could not be as easily shortened or made to disappear as he imagined when he reminisced. It would be even more difficult to rid himself of the deep-seated emotions that had built up in him for so long. He felt pained to look at his daughter's round face, her short thick hair, the straight body in the cotton overalls she was wearing, and especially her thoughtful and bewildered eyes. She looked just like her mother in her youth. Yuan Wang had been his student; later they had married and this daughter, the virtual stranger sitting before him, was their only child. Life's storms had battered them cruelly: separation, death, and now, it seemed, mutual incomprehension.

The fire in the stove was roaring away now and very hot, but the little room was completely still. The lonely stillness was pervasive, unbearable.

"Susu, oh Susu," he thought to himself. "What are you thinking? What ever happened to the love you had for your father when you were little? You used to gurgle with laughter, and how you could pout . . . Has it all gone, vanished without a trace? If time could run backward, if it could let us start our lives again, I'd do it gladly even if it cost a hundred deaths!" The father sat there overwhelmed by his feelings. Several times he stood up only to sit down again.

"What's the matter, father?" she asked, looking at the beads of sweat on his forehead.

"I was thinking," he said, clearly very worked up, but also as if trying to avoid a sensitive subject, "that after I'm transferred back to Beijing and assigned a flat, we could arrange things much better." His daughter did not look up, but frowned.

"You've had a terrible time these last years," he went on with a sigh. "It must've been hard to struggle through it all. But I think you're not taking good enough care of yourself now."

"I'm used to it," she said, smiling at her father. "*You're* the one who needs a family, I'd say."

"What do you mean?" He was rather taken aback, then immediately realized what she was driving at. "What a silly idea, Susu. All these years I've managed by myself. I don't have many days left—what would I do with a family?"

"You should have a family," she insisted. "Don't worry about me. I'm just fine here, and this is the way I want to live for the rest of my life."

He realized that he'd have to change the subject. There seemed to be a barrier between him and his daughter. Did she have a boyfriend? Was she afraid of unpredictable political dangers if she lived with her father? Did she resent his never having looked after her since his divorce from her mother? Perhaps she worried that if he remarried she would not be able to get along with her stepmother. Were all of these insoluble objections in her mind? The thought was acutely painful.

He dropped his gaze surreptitiously to the table top and took a closer look at the books that were piled there. He was astonished to see that apart from a few foreign literary classics, they were mostly Marxist-Leninist works and translated works on the social sciences. History, economics, and politics were all represented. Evidently his daughter had a real thirst for knowledge: she was not as he imagined ordinary young people to be. Next to the piece of glass that covered part of the table lay an open notebook. Just as he was about to pick it up for a look, she noticed what he was doing and tried to snatch it from him.

"You mustn't look at it, father," she said with a smile.

"Is it secret?" He deliberately tightened his grip on it.

"No," she replied straightforwardly. "If you insist, just look at the page it's open to. But on one condition: you have to answer the questions you find there."

A number of questions were written in the notebook:

1. It can be seen from the experience of human society that knowledge continually advances. If the theoretical generalizations that emerge from this advance do not conform with some of the original tenets of Marxism, are they therefore revisionist?

2. Of the various kinds of socialism in the world today, which is the true socialism?

3. Why are we still haunted by the ghost of feudalism? Why have we been unable to rid ourselves of it more than half a century after the May Fourth movement?

4. It is said that people at the top and bottom are keen about the Four Modernizations, but those in the middle are cool. Why is the middle cool?

And so it went on. There were seven or eight questions altogether, and they appalled him. Respecting his daughter's wish he read no further, but put the notebook back on the table. He would never have imagined that his daughter spent her time thinking about these issues rather than matters of daily life. Her questions struck him as a bit too searching, and her mind a bit too audacious. If she went on like this, she could go astray and have a tough time in the future. These were very big questions about the state and the Revolution. They were beyond the understanding of most cadres, let alone a very ordinary young worker like his daughter. Naturally he was glad she was studying, but he worried about the risks she was taking. He would have even preferred that she stop thinking about such things. Suddenly he realized why she did not want to live with him. They were just like strangers: neither could understand the other.

"Why do you have to think about questions like these?" he protested. "The New Long March to achieve the Four Modernizations lies straight and clear before every one of us. If we follow that route, we're bound to succeed. Questions of theory like those should be left for the theoreticians to solve."

"I don't agree." She stopped knitting and looked straight at her father. "We must each understand exactly what our role is in the New Long March. Otherwise, we're sure to trip up."

"It's not as bad as all that." He was now clearly very worked up. "What are you going to achieve with all this hairsplitting? If you ask me, you should be reviewing your schoolwork for the university entrance exams. That's the only proper thing to do."

"Father, if I ask you a question will you promise not to get angry?" she said with a smile. "If you have no answers to these questions, how on earth are you going to write your magnum opus?"

"I'll stay within my area of professional competence, and keep away from theoretical issues," he answered, emphatically but also anxiously.

Never having imagined that her father could be both so childish and so obstinate, she sighed under her breath as she realized there could be no point in carrying on with the argument. A sense of disappointment gradually suffused her. She saw that her father's understanding of some problems was still at the level of twenty years ago, and that he was smug and very pleased with himself. Although he still had his ambitions, in her view they fell far short of what the times required.

"Won't you have a bite to eat, Father?" she said, deliberately changing the subject. "Let me cook you some noodles — made of the very best flour."

"No, thanks." He was barely able to control himself. "You've grown up now, and you have your own outlook on life."

"Oh, it's started snowing," someone shouted in the courtyard.

She opened the door to look, and the cold, damp wind blew several snowflakes into the room before she slammed it shut again.

"I must be going," her father said, looking at his watch and putting on his coat. "I've brought a train ticket to Shenyang for tomorrow. There's some unfinished business there I have to sort out. It'll probably be at least ten days before I'm back in Beijing."

His daughter covered her head with a long gray woolen scarf, then wrapped it around her neck. She left with him and walked him to the bus stop, where they arrived just as a bus did. As it pulled out, he stood by the doorway looking down at his daughter.

The big snowflakes looked as if they were swirling up from the ground instead of falling from the sky; they glistened in the dim street lights.

The farther the bus moved away, the harder it became to make out the image of his daughter. When the bus turned a corner, the conductress called, "There's a seat over there, grandad." Only then did he sit down, half dazed as if just awakening from a dream.

# JIN HE

# Reencounter

In much of the literature of 1979–80, the arrest of the Gang of Four in fall 1976 is treated as a watershed. China's troubles before then are attributed to its high-level leadership — Lin Biao and the Gang — while problems after 1976 are due either to "residual Gang influences" or, at worst, to minor officials only. Although it is indubitable that the arrest of the Gang (or, more fundamentally, the death of Mao Zedong the previous month) was truly a watershed, the present story points out the patent oversimplicity of saying that the removal of four people changed everything. It shows how a powerful Party Secretary, well after the fall of the Gang, cannot face the facts of his own past during the Cultural Revolution, and hence cannot muster nearly the moral courage of the Red Guard "murderer" over whose case he wields total power. The implication that powerholders after 1976 are not entirely pure is neatly complemented by the implication that young Red Guards in the Cultural Revolution were not always evil. The Red Guard in this story had honorable intentions, and was hardly responsible for the chaos that distorted his own and other lives. Yet it is a strength of the story that, although the author's sympathies with the young Red Guard are clear, he also appreciates the complex psychological life of the Party Secretary. This man faces dilemmas that paralyze him and might paralyze most human beings.

Translated by Michael S. Duke. Originally published in *Shanghai wenxue*, 1979, no. 4.

The story was criticized in China's official press for sullying the image of a Party Secretary. This criticism in turn elicited a storm of protest from supportive readers. It is a credit to the 1979 National Short Story Prize Committee that despite the story's pointedness and the controversy it spawned, "Reencounter" was selected as one of the twenty-five best of the year. Jin He (b. 1943) graduated from Inner Mongolia University in 1968. Since 1978 he has been a professional writer at the Liaoning Provincial Writers' Association.

# Reencounter

It happened in the interrogation room of a district police station.

After one criminal had been interrogated and taken away, Chief of Interrogations Li handed another dossier to Zhu Chunxin, deputy secretary of the District Party Committee.

Zhu Chunxin was in his fifties, and of sturdy build, but was getting a bit fat. His hair was cut neatly; his eyebrows were thick and black; his big eyes had a permanent look of deep contemplation; his square chin, though freshly shaven, was still slightly black. He gave the general impression of being serious, experienced, and full of vitality. His responsibilities on the District Standing Committee were for the organization, personnel, and public investigations systems. After the smashing of the Gang of Four, during the campaign to "thoroughly search out thieves, assaulters, and vandals," he went in person to the District Police Station intending to pick out a few of the most reprehensible cases and make examples of them at a public meeting that would be broadcast on loudspeakers throughout the district. This would help to promote the whole campaign. But to pick out such cases and still observe the directive to "seek truth from facts, get hard evidence, and build ironclad cases" was a most difficult undertaking. The preliminary investigation of the first criminal, for example, left much to be desired: the informer's statement, the formal indictment, and the accused's own testimony were widely divergent. Zhu Chunxin's thick black eyebrows came together in a brief frown. He used the interval before the next criminal was brought in to squirm and resettle his slightly overweight body, and to stretch it almost imperceptibly. Then he slouched back in his chair and glanced at the next dossier that Chief Li handed him. His eyes fell upon the summary statement at the top:

> Ye Hui. Male. Twenty-eight. Working class background. Student. Worked in the boiler room of the district power plant before arrest. Criminal activities include following Lin Biao and the Gang of Four during the Cultural Revolution and extensive assault, theft, and vandalism. Most seriously, during a violent confrontation in September 1967, he crippled a worker and killed a student, Shi Zhihong, by impaling him with a long spear. Clearly a prime example of the violent criminal element . . .

Zhu Chunxin's thick eyebrows suddenly twitched as he read the dossier. He looked up as if he had thought of something, but then shook his head slightly and went on reading.

Chief Li pointed at the dossier. "Have you heard of this fellow before, Secretary Zhu?"

"No." Zhu Chunxin shook his head. "I didn't come to this district until 1970. In 1967 I was still in Beining City."

"Ye Hui was one of the urban youths sent to the countryside from Beining," Chief Li explained. "He came here when our district power plant was recruiting workers in 1972."

"Oh . . ." An expression of surprise and anxiety momentarily visited Zhu Chunxin's stern face. Realizing this, he steadied himself, laughed airily, and said, "That was right when I was being denounced. But I didn't know about the violence until later, and never heard anything about this Ye Hui. It was terrible back then—deaths and injuries on both sides!" Zhu Chunxin shook his head sadly and then raised his square chin to ask, "What was Ye Hui doing at the time?"

"He was the leader of a high-school Red Guard organization."

"High-school Red Guards . . . a leader?" Zhu Chunxin's eyes moved back and forth. He seemed to be talking to himself as much as questioning Chief Li.

"That's right," Chief Li affirmed.

"Well . . . violent criminals like this owe a debt of blood and should be punished severely," Zhu Chunxin said coldly. Then he thought of another question: "Does he have any other name?"

"I don't think so . . ." Just as Chief Li was about to say something more, the door to the interrogation room opened and a young worker of twenty-eight or twenty-nine was led in.

"Well, here I am!" He said softly to Zhu Chunxin. The accused was wearing old work clothes. His shirt was spattered with dirty spots of oil, and both elbows were patched. His leather shoes were so worn that it was hard to tell what color they had originally been. This young man obviously did not pamper himself, but neither was he messy. Thick black hair covered half his forehead, and his sharply outlined lips were parted slightly to reveal a row of perfectly even white teeth. He was a handsome young man. Before sitting down on the defendant's stool, he ran his brightly shining eyes over his interrogators and smiled scornfully, looking quite calm and unruffled. When the accused's glance met Zhu Chunxin's, it delivered Zhu a jolt. That look, that smile . . . he seemed to have seen them somewhere before.

"Is it . . . he?" A secret guess flashed through Zhu Chunxin's mind.

"What is your name?" Chief Li began the interrogation.

"Ye Hui," the criminal replied.

"Have you used any other names?"

"No."

Chief Li nodded his head in the direction of Zhu Chunxin to confirm the answer Li had just given to this question. But Zhu Chunxin did not even notice Li's gesture. He was knitting his thick eyebrows and staring intently at the defendant's face. Then he did something very unusual: he left his seat, put his hands behind his back, and paced back and forth briefly before the criminal. Returning to his seat, he tried to assume the expression of pondering a question, but his eyes kept searching the criminal's forehead. He appeared to be looking for something.

"I must explain the Party's policies to you . . ." Chief Li went on to recite the standard speech that preceded the interrogation of all criminals. "Now it's your turn to tell us how you committed your crime," he finished.

The interrogation proceeded in a serious manner, but Zhu Chunxin didn't say a word. He just kept staring at those big characters on the front of the dossier: "Ye Hui. Assault, theft, and vandalism."

"He's the one," Zhu Chunxin was telling himself. "He *has* to be! He's Ye Weige! ["Defend the Revolution" — Tr.] I wish it weren't so, but there's that scar on his forehead! Why won't he admit he used to use the name "Ye Weige"?

"Tell us about your major crimes. Don't try to hide the big ones by giving us the little ones. Remember our Party's policy: confession brings lenience and resistance brings severity."

The sounds of the interrogation grew ever fainter in Zhu Chunxin's ears, while a memory from the past, a memory that he never wanted to recall, unfolded vividly before his mind's eye.

It was September 1967 — a chaotic, painful, and grim autumn.

The mass organizations of Beining City had long since split into two irreconcilable factions, one known as the "East Is Red" General Headquarters and the other called the "Red Union" General Headquarters. When the *People's Daily* issued its call to "step forth and declare your views," the shaken remnants of the municipal Party committee in Beining City, including Zhu Chunxin, all began seriously considering which faction they ought to support. Some of them declined to commit themselves, but Zhu Chunxin, after thinking over the various advantages and disadvantages, decided it would be best to take a position. After weighing all the factors — strength, social influence, and his own personal connections — Zhu Chunxin announced his support of the somewhat stronger East Is Red group. He solemnly declared this group to be a "revolutionary rebel organization," and the other to be only a "mass organization." As a result of his "declaration of views," Zhu Chunxin became a "revolutionary leading cadre" of the East Is Red faction, and, at the same time, naturally became a "three-anti's element" [see glossary] in the eyes of the Red Union faction. Ever more strident cries of "down with . . .!" and ever more ruthless attacks were directed at him from that quarter. In order to avoid confrontation, he was obliged to go into hiding, and to live on the move like a hunted criminal. His home, of course, was unsafe, so he had to live in a factory dormitory, in an agricultural production brigade house, in the darkroom of the New Light Photography Studio, and even in those vital places that no one was allowed to attack — the electric power distribution station and the office of the labor reform brigade. Wherever he went, Zhu Chunxin was constantly assailed by feelings of fear, worry, and humiliation. The incongruity of his status as Assistant Party Secretary of Beining City and all this strange running around and hiding made him perpetually miserable. "What can I do about it?" he thought to himself. "I really don't want to act this way! But if I'm captured by the other side, I'm as good as done for! This is complete chaos. Complete chaos! What sort of a charade is this, anyway?" He was full of unspoken self-pity. The *People's Daily* had once asked satirically, "How can leading revolutionary cadres fear the masses?" Zhu Chunxin didn't say so, but he despised that argument. Not be afraid? That's fine and dandy for you theoreticians to say. Why don't you come down *here* and try it?!

One night in September 1967, during the time when Zhu Chunxin was moving around from place to place, he had quietly moved into an office building where it had been arranged that he stay in a room on the second floor away from the street. Two beds had been temporarily set up in the office, but there were no mosquito nets and the quilts didn't seem to have ever been washed. The white padding looked gray, was greasy and cool to the touch, and exuded the odor of mildew. But as far as the constantly terrified Zhu Chunxin was concerned, this was a fine and rare haven. Fortunately, although the September nights were somewhat cool, it wasn't really too cold. A refreshing autumn breeze was blowing in from the window. The light from inside the room was shining on the rustling leaves of some old poplars outside the window, making them appear to be countless shimmering silver ripples. It seemed that either the broadcasters had grown hoarse or the electronic amplifiers had needed a rest, because the loudspeakers that had been strung along the walls of the tall buildings were no longer dispatching their "solemn statements" or "most strong protests," their "songs of Chairman Mao's sayings," or the song of the "three loyalties." This fact made Zhu Chunxin's new dwelling all the more comfortable and peaceful.

Lin Fengxiang, deputy director of the Municipal Committee Office and Zhu Chunxin's constant companion, closed the window curtain and smiled ironically at Zhu Chunxin. "Tonight we can get one quiet night's sleep," he said.

"Perhaps." Zhu Chunxin was scratching his unshaven square chin with his fingernails. His beard, now full, made a rasping sound. "But if anything goes wrong . . . with us up here on the second floor . . . we could be trapped!"

Lin Fengxiang was under forty. He had been highly appreciated among the Municipal Committee leadership. Not only had he provided the leaders with useful assistance at work; he had also been meticulous about arranging their living conditions. He had done everything quietly and unobtrusively, never going beyond acceptable bounds, always acting with courtesy and refinement, just exactly the right way. Even the most scrupulous and reserved leading cadres had been happy to accept Lin Fengxiang's clever arrangements. Despite his status as a subordinate of Zhu Chunxin's, their common fate in the Cultural Revolution had now made the two men fast friends. Zhu Chunxin's worries about an escape route had also occurred to Lin Fengxiang, but what could he do? Yet he still knew how to console his leadership. "There won't be any trouble," he said, "at least not tonight . . ."

Bang! Bang! Bang! Someone was at the door.

Lin Fengxiang's expression suddenly changed as he swallowed back the rest of what he was going to say. Zhu Chunxin was staring at the doorway, thinking at incredible speed, trying to decide whether someone knocking on the door at this hour were more likely to be an angel or a devil. No one, except a couple of leading cadres and a few reliable workers at headquarters, knew that they were staying here. The leaders had already told them they would not come over tonight, but would pick them up for a meeting tomorrow. So who could be coming tonight? Could the Red Union faction possibly have followed them here? That would be disastrous.

Bang bang! Bang bang! The knocking would not stop.

Zhu Chunxin thought of finding a place to hide, but there was no place in this room to do so. There was no air duct in the ceiling and no room under the beds. He glanced at Lin Fengxiang as if to ask, "Should we answer? Open the door?" Lin Fengxiang had no good ideas, and could only stare blankly ahead. Facing the prospect of meeting his end right here with Secretary Zhu, Lin broke into a cold sweat.

Bang! Bang bang! The knocking was growing louder. Whoever was knocking on the door was losing patience.

From the looks of things, they would have to open the door. Zhu Chunxin helplessly fixed Lin Fengxiang with a meaningful look.

"Okay, okay! . . . We hear you!" Lin Fengxiang was imitating the voice of someone who had just woken up. He went to the door and, his jaw trembling, called "Who is it?"

"Hurry and open the door!" answered a young man outside.

"We're on your side," another said.

"Cowards!" came the voice of a third young man.

"Who're you looking for?" asked Lin Fengxiang.

"We're looking for the people in this room!"

An answer like this could only bring Lin and Zhu even more consternation. Following a signal from Zhu, Lin Fengxiang said, "We've already gone to bed. If you have a problem, we'll talk about it tomorrow!" He leaned against the door, the calves of his legs shaking.

"You sure know how to enjoy yourselves!" another satirical voice called through the door. "Cut the crap! If the dyed-in-the-wools [the "reactionary" opposing faction — Tr.] find you here, this door couldn't stop shit! Hurry and open the door, it's an emergency!"

Zhu Chunxin had to acknowledge the logic of this comment. He exchanged glances with Lin Fengxiang. Lin had already concluded that one person could not block the door in any case, so he finally went to open it.

About a dozen eighteen- to nineteen-year-old youths burst in and stood in the middle of the floor. Some were carrying clubs, and some were shouldering lances. They had daggers and knives of all shapes and sizes tucked under their belts. It was an altogether imposing and murderous sight. As Zhu Chunxin looked in terror at this crowd of uninvited guests, who were not wearing any identifying insignia, he instinctively sprang from his bed. His wildly beating heart had already leaped into his throat.

An unarmed young man stepped forward and addressed him gently and politely. "Are you Secretary Zhu?"

"Uh . . . Er . . . I'm Zhu Chunxin, Zhu Chunxin." Zhu felt angry at himself for his timid and apologetic tone of voice.

"We were dispatched by the East Is Red Command Headquarters to protect you." The weaponless young man smiled calmly. "My name is Ye Weige. Your safety here is the responsibility of the Third Detachment of our army corps."

"Protection? Oh . . ." Zhu Chunxin's eyes immediately lit up with gratitude and excitement. His dark eyebrows kept moving up and down as he scratched at his beard with his fingernails and scrutinized this young man called Ye Weige. Ye's thick black hair was cut very short, and his sharply outlined lips were parted slightly to reveal a row of perfectly even white teeth. His flashing eyes shone with the boldness, passion, clarity and uninhibited arrogance that characterized youth in those times. His olive green Red Guard uniform made him seem even more capable and brave. Zhu Chunxin's wildly beating heart finally began to slow down to normal. "Sit down, please, sit down." He pointed to their beds. "You can sit here, come on, sit down!"

After the Red Guards had seated themselves, Zhu Chunxin, obviously moved, began again. "Our revolutionary rebel comrades at Command Headquarters certainly think of everything! Giving you little generals so much trouble . . . but I guess it makes this place pretty safe after all!"

"No. There is trouble." Ye Weige spoke with an air of seriousness and responsibility. "Command Headquarters believes that the dyed-in-the-wools have already figured out about your moving around from place to place. They're likely to start something."

"Oh?" Zhu Chunxin was startled, and his thick black eyebrows wrinkled tightly. "So soon? What can we do? How can the few of you . . .?" Zhu Chunxin was going to say, "How can the few of you handle them all?" But before the words passed his lips, he switched to, "Your assignment is too difficult!"

Ye Weige smiled, stuck out his chest, and clenched his fist, "Don't worry, Secretary Zhu. There may not be many of us, but as long as the Third Detachment is here, your safety is assured. And if by any chance things here get really dangerous, General Headquarters will send reinforcements." The solemn manner of speech called to mind a fearless warrior swearing allegiance to his superior officer. "When you stand together with us, you are standing on the side of Chairman Mao's revolutionary line. In order to protect Chairman Mao's revolutionary line, the soldiers of the revolutionary rebel faction are willing to spill their blood and even sacrifice their lives!"

As he looked at this fervently militant youth, Zhu Chunxin was so moved that he could not speak for some time. Then he struggled to control his feelings and stepped forward to take Ye Weige's hand. "Thank you, my little general! I . . . I thank you, thank you!"

Ye Weige seemed stupefied as he looked into Zhu Chunxin's face, and slowly pulled his hand away. He had never seen such behavior in a leading cadre. He had not had the slightest thought of winning anyone's gratitude by what he said or did. He was only expressing the sincerity and steadfastness of his great faith, only carrying out his duty, his incomparably noble and sacred duty.

"If something does go wrong," he said, "just don't panic, and don't go near the windows. Block the door solidly . . . the desk ought to do it . . ." Ye Weige mentioned a few more warnings, then turned to leave. "When we come back, the signal will be one knock, a pause, and then three more knocks — knock . . . knock, knock, knock."

Tap, tap, tap . . .

The sound of the gavel rapping brought Zhu Chunxin back from his deep reverie and into the interrogation room once more.

"Why did you get violent? Huh?" Chief Li was staring sternly at the criminal and thumping his hand on his desk top. "The 'Sixteen Points' were clear enough, weren't they? They said 'fight with words, not with weapons.' So what made you resort to violence? You make yourself sound so pure and innocent — what baloney!"

The criminal, sitting on his little square stool, smiled calmly and said, "I'm telling you the truth."

"The truth! The truth! The truth is you're trying to hide something!" Chief Li responded. "Why don't you tell us the name of that leading cadre you were protecting?"

When he heard Chief Li's question, Zhu Chunxin's heart raced and his head buzzed. He resented Chief Li's pressing this unhappy question, and feared that the criminal might crack under the circumstances and call out "Zhu Chunxin!" That would put him in a terribly awkward position.

"I've forgotten," the criminal answered.

"I don't think you've forgotten. I think you're making up a story!" said Chief Li. "No leading cadre would let you get violent! Now go ahead with the rest of the story about your crimes!"

Zhu Chunxin breathed a sigh of relief. He had never imagined he would have a reencounter with Ye Weige under these circumstances. His mood was probably just as depressed as the accused's.

The interrogation continued, but Zhu Chunxin could sit there no longer. A chill ran up his back, and at the same time his face was flushed and hot. His whole body felt stiff and sore. He whispered something to Chief Li, left the interrogation room, and walked around the courtyard outside, hands behind his back. It was September 1977. The autumn air was crisp and clear, but the midday sun was still a bit oppressive. A few old poplars in the courtyard were swaying lightly in the breeze, their lush green leaves producing a soft swishing sound. Zhu Chunxin stood in the shade, looking up at the trees and listening to the rustle of the leaves. Those old poplars seemed to be talking to him in an ironic tone of voice. "Congratulations on your reunion with Ye Weige! But look how ten years have changed your relationship! How dramatic!" Zhu Chunxin started slightly, but then managed to settle himself. "What could I do?" he asked with a wry smile. "I never wanted him to become a criminal!"

The rustling of the leaves gradually grew inaudible and was replaced by the approaching sound of a truck. This aroused his memories again.

It was almost dawn when the sound of truck brakes suddenly came from outside the building. Then came much confused shouting and the noise of iron pipes knocking on the outer door.

"Open up!"

"Hurry and open up!"

The people outside the door were yelling and shouting all at once.

"What are you up to?" asked someone inside the building.

"Catching thieves!"

"You've got the wrong place! No thieves here!"

"Thieves were seen sneaking into this building!"

"You're full of it!"

"Okay, that's it! You gonna open up or not?"

"Forget it! Who knows what kind of riff-raff you are, anyway?"

"Smash it!"

Clink! crash! It was the sound of glass windows breaking.

This all took place in front of the door facing the street, but Zhu Chunxin and Lin Fengxiang could hear everything perfectly clearly from their back room on the second floor. At first they were frightened into immobility by this unexpected event. The people outside, who said they were "catching thieves," were obviously after them.

"Attention soldiers on the second floor!" cried Ye Weige in a low yet forceful voice. "Assemble quickly! The dyed-in-the-wools are here!" Next there came the sound of something being thrown onto a tabletop and cursing from Ye Weige. "Shit! The bastards cut the telephone!"

Following a flurry of footsteps, Ye Weige could be heard expertly assigning his Third Detachment to their various battle stations. "Attack with Words, but Defend with Weapons! The time has come to defend Chairman Mao's revolutionary line with our blood and our lives! Keep the dyed-in-the-wools outside the door at all costs! Comrades in arms, take your positions!"

"They're nothing but a few birds in there! Come on comrades, charge!"

"Charge in and drag out the three-anti's element Zhu Chunxin!"
"Charge!"

Shouts immediately rang out all around the outside of the building; rocks and bricks crashed against the door; the crisp sound of glass windows breaking and the shrill sounds of shouting and cursing melded chaotically together.

Zhu Chunxin and Lin Fengxiang were sitting at the head of a bed in the corner of the room and staring numbly at each other. Zhu Chunxin looked around the room once more, but still could see no place to hide. He made his way carefully to the window and looked out, but could see only a few old poplars, each about seven or eight yards away. There was no escape route in that direction. What could they do? Fear, worry, and desperation assaulted him simultaneously. All he could do was pin his hopes on the courageous fighting of Ye Weige and his troupe of little generals; he even worried whether or not they would have enough weapons.

"Ye Weige! Somebody's broken in on the first floor!" came a voice from within the building.

"How'd they get in?"

"Through the window."

"Switch to Battle Plan Two! Retreat to the second floor and guard the stairway!" Ye Weige was issuing orders with the air of an outstanding command officer who is fearless in the face of danger.

"Zhang Jihong has been injured, Ye Weige!"

"Get him up to the second floor, quick! Then . . ."

The rest of Ye Weige's order was lost in a flood of human voices.

"Charge! Charge up the stairs!"

"Arrest every goddamn bastard in the building!"

Following the latest round of battle cries came another burst of fierce fighting and a hail of bricks. Through it all the pitiful shouts and groans of the wounded could sometimes be heard.

Zhu Chunxin just sat there on his bed, stupefied, his heart thumping away. He had experienced such situations more than once before, and could well imagine the intensity of the hand-to-hand combat. But there was another sort of battle raging inside him — a struggle between two different Zhu Chunxins. One was saying, "As an experienced cadre, it's my duty to tell the two factions to stop their senseless bloodletting, but what can I do? My own blood might have to flow, too." The other Zhu Chunxin opposed the first. "This is a struggle between the two lines! We shouldn't give an inch!" To this the first Zhu Chunxin replied, "That's the height of selfishness!" And the second one countered, "It's revolutionary determination!" The first one came back, "It's a disgrace!" The second one replied, "But what else is there to do? I didn't want things to turn out this way!" A series of groans came from the hallway outside the door. Zhu Chunxin thought he should do something.

"Hey, Lin!" Zhu Chunxin called to Lin Fengxiang.

No one answered. Zhu Chunxin looked all around the room, but there was no trace of Lin Fengxiang. Had he sneaked away?

"No, he probably went to help in the fight!" thought Zhu Chunxin as he gently opened the door and stuck his head out to take a look around. What he saw startled him so much that he nearly cried out. Somehow Ye Weige had already stockpiled the hallway with several wicker baskets full of bricks, a big pile of rocks, and two bundles of assorted wooden clubs. Zhu Chunxin began shivering as he spied the body of a young man lying in the hall only a few yards away. His rich red blood was coursing over the smooth flat floor, shining in the first rays of the morning sun. The East Is Red faction, apparently because they were so greatly outnumbered, had no time to bind up their wounded. He surmised this must be the Zhang Jihong whose name had just been called out.

Zhu Chunxin ran to the young man's side, opened his shirt front, checked the extent of his wound, and began to bind it up for him. Just as he was finishing he heard Ye Weige shouting anxiously. "Hurry! We need that basket of bricks over here!"

Zhu Chunxin looked around blankly.

"What are you staring at? I'm talking to *you!*" The commander's voice was stern and decisive.

Zhu Chunxin finally realized that Ye Weige was giving him a military command. He had become the little generals' "comrade-in-arms" in the true sense. He moved reflexively toward the big basket of bricks and gripped it firmly at the sides. But then his hands seemed to recoil as if burned by a hot iron. He seemed to see the bricks flying up in the air and then falling back into the basket before his eyes. Then it was no longer a basket of bricks, but a mass of human heads, bruised and oozing blood . . .

"Can I do this?" Zhu Chunxin thought to himself. "Isn't it a crime for a person in authority to participate in violence?"

"What are you standing there for?! You want to let that gang of punks get up here?!" another youth, who was guarding the stairway, was shouting angrily as he ran over toward Zhu Chunxin.

Zhu Chunxin had no more time for the luxury of scruples. "What else can I do? I never wanted things to turn out this way." As he grumbled to himself, he exerted all his strength to pick up the basket and carry it over toward the head of the stairway. Fortunately for him, after he had carried it halfway over, the young man who had just come running took it off his hands. This prevented the attackers down below from seeing him in action.

Several assaults by the invaders were turned back thanks to Ye Weige's brilliantly executed counterattacks. Although he and some of his comrades had suffered a few minor injuries, there was no doubt that the invaders had suffered many times more severely. The battle had turned into a stalemate. The attackers began to shout curses at the defenders on the second floor. "You lousy bunch of rioters from the East Is Red General Headquarters are the emperor's running dogs! Zhu Chunxin stirs up the masses! He causes violence and bloodshed! He's going to get everything he deserves!"

The defenders at the top of the stairs were shouting curses back down the stairs while they paused to catch their breath and reorganize their ranks. That was when Zhu Chunxin finally discovered that Lin Fengxiang had not actually gone out on the stairs to join the fight. No one knew where he had disappeared to. It seemed Lin must have feared that the gang below would force their way upstairs and make him a scapegoat along with Zhu Chunxin. He had probably long since found himself a hiding place. But Zhu Chunxin did not mention this in front of the young men. He waited until he had returned to his temporary lodgings before sitting down dispiritedly on the bed and forcing the words from between his teeth: "Despicable hypocrite!" Lin Fengxiang's desertion of duty left Zhu feeling disappointed and empty. At the same time, his feelings of gratitude and affection for the young men were soaring to a new high. "A fine bunch of little generals!" he said to himself. "They really know how to be loyal officers and soldiers in the heat of battle!"

All of a sudden, he heard a strange noise outside his window. Trembling with fear, he went to the window for a look. "My God!" he shouted involuntarily as he burst out the door. "Ye Weige! Ye Weige! They're climbing up!"

"Who's climbing up?" Ye Weige rushed to met him.

"Over . . . over by my window . . ." Zhu Chunxin was shouting in broken sentences. "They're coming up! . . . a long ladder!"

"Don't move! Just wait in the hallway!" Ye Weige, flying into the room like the wind, held a long spear in one hand and two or three bricks in the other. A moment later he emerged from the room with his hand on his forehead and fresh blood leaking between his fingers. Calm and self-assured, he smiled at Zhu Chunxin. "The dog fuckers are gone!"

The blood from the sides of his forehead trickled down to his lips and began to redden his clean white teeth. Zhu Chunxin tore off a piece of his white undershirt to tie up Ye Weige's wound.

A few minutes later, they heard startled shouts from the invaders. "Scatter! Quick, scatter! An East Is Red Brigade is here!"

"Hurry up, hurry!"

Then came another round of confused fighting inside and out. Needless to say, the invaders now suffered very heavy losses. When the battle was all over, Lin Fengxiang came crawling out of the toilet.

"Secretary Zhu!" A police officer was walking toward him.

Zhu Chunxin awoke from his memories to discover that at some point he had begun leaning against an old poplar tree.

"Are you ill or something, Secretary Zhu?" asked the police officer. "Chief Li asked if you have any instructions."

When Zhu Chunxin returned to the interrogation room, the criminal had already been removed. Chief Li was smiling with satisfaction. "Criminal Ye was reasonably good about confessing his crimes," he told Zhu. "He admitted almost the whole story." Chief Li was pointing at the interrogation record. "He admitted that during the violent confrontation one of the attackers, a student by the name of Shi Zhihong, climbed up to the second-floor window with a ladder. When criminal Ye entered the room, Shi Zhihong stood on the windowsill and threw a dagger at him, wounding him on the forehead. Then Ye counterattacked with a long spear, stabbing Shi Zhihong in the shoulder. Shi Zhihong panicked and fell from the windowsill. As more people were trying to climb up the ladder, Ye just kept throwing bricks down without caring whether anyone was injured. He said it was a case of 'Attacking with Words and Defending with Weapons.' 'When the dyed-in-the-wools attacked,' he said, 'they gave us the right to self-defense.'" Chief Li then turned the pages of the dossier and said, "An investigation has shown that the student Shi Zhihong was killed and a worker maimed under that window."

"Oh." Zhu Chunxin nodded his head distractedly.

"Criminal Ye and the deceased Shi Zhihong were not acquainted," Chief Li continued, "so we can eliminate the motive of revenge. But criminal Ye has refused to admit that he was following Lin Biao and the Gang of Four, or that he was undermining and damaging the Great Cultural Revolution. He would not admit a motive for his crimes."

"Oh ..." Zhu Chunxin frowned in distress, and could not find anything suitable to say. He could hardly plead the case of Ye Hui, but neither did he want to go along with Chief Li's conclusions. "It's time to break for lunch," he said. "Let's study the case next time ... maybe tomorrow."

When he went out the front door of the District Police Station, and sat down on the soft seat of the car that was waiting for him, Zhu Chunxin felt as if his head had swollen to the size of a bushel basket. He could not have felt more addlebrained. His mind was like a tangle of hemp, or a whirlpool of muddy water. A jumble of strange abstractions flashed in his mind like neon lights: things like "little general," "benefactor," "criminal," "revolutionary leading cadre," "the law" ... He couldn't even remember clearly how he got out of his car and walked up the stairs into his residence.

"What's wrong, are you sick?" his wife asked. "You're awfully pale. Have you caught cold?"

"Maybe," he said.

"Have something to eat!"

"No, I just want to lie down for a while."

Zhu Chunxin tossed and turned on his bed. All those abstractions that had been flashing before him again and again in the car were still flashing before his mind's eye with the oppressive brilliance of an electric arc. He tried to ponder the implications of his second meeting with Ye Weige ten years later; and he tried to figure out what his own posture should be. But the result was only to pull a hard knot even tighter.

There was a knock at the door. "Someone's here to see you," said his wife, walking to the head of the bed.

This irritated him. "If there's a problem, let him talk to the department in charge. Otherwise come to the office and talk to me tomorrow."

"It's an old woman. She insists that she must see you."

"What about?"

"She didn't say. She says she's Ye Hui's mother."

"Huh? Ye Hui's . . . mother?" Zhu Chunxin rolled off his bed with a start. "Ask her in right away!"

An emaciated old woman worker came in. She seemed already past retirement age. Her simple, kind face was etched all over with the wrinkles of toil and worry. She stood unassumingly in the middle of the floor, her hands held unsteadily in front of her chest as she looked up at the deputy district secretary with eyes that brimmed with distress and supplication.

"I'm Zhu Chunxin." Zhu avoided the old woman's gaze as he pulled a chair over to her. "Please, ma'am, please sit down."

"Oh . . . uh . . . no, thank you . . ." The old woman worker was somewhat overwhelmed by his unexpected politeness. "I've come from Beining City to see you about Ye Hui. My daughter-in-law sent me a telegram. There's just a few things . . . I'll just stand up while I tell you . . . you're not feeling well . . ."

"No, no, no! It's nothing! Please, have a seat," Zhu Chunxin repeated cordially.

"Ye Hui has broken the law . . ." the old woman said, as tears began running down the wrinkles of her face. "I guess there was nothing to do but arrest my son and sentence him. I'm a worker . . . We were very happy when the Gang of Four was smashed! And we were all for the campaign to uncover the thieves, assaulters, and vandals. Only . . . when they uncovered my son . . . what can I say? Why did he have to get mixed up in a killing?

"Yes." Zhu Chunxin nodded his head, but kept his eyes on a teacup that was on his desk. "Your view of this matter is quite correct, ma'am." He continued to address her with great respect.

"But . . ." the old woman continued, "I have some things on my mind . . . I want to tell the leadership. I don't know if I'm correct or not; if I'm mistaken, please criticize me . . ."

"It's all right, there's nothing to worry about. Do speak freely."

"I believe my son's basic nature . . . is not bad." Having mustered her determination to say this, the old woman studied Zhu Chunxin's face apprehensively. Noticing that he had assumed a rather wooden expression, and did not appear ready to scold her, she felt relieved enough to go on. "When the Cultural Revolution began, he was a junior in high school and a branch secretary of the Communist Youth League. When some of the students rose up to attack the principal and denounce their teachers, he was so angry he didn't know what to do. Every time he came home and told me about it, he cried from start to finish — as if they had denounced him! Later I heard that he had become a 'bourgeois monarchist,' and when the time came for the Red Guard pilgrimages to Beijing, they wouldn't let him go! When he came home with this news, he cried and cried . . ." The old woman heaved a long sigh and continued. "Some of his classmates came over to comfort him. I tried to talk to him, too, but he didn't say a thing. He just kept reading all those newspapers and leaflets . . . then he'd just sit there like a fool and stare at the ceiling. I was afraid he was going to go crazy! A few days later he disappeared, and nobody knew where he'd gone off to. His father and I were worried sick — I've only got this one son . . . We searched all the wells, the forests, and the rivers . . . we were afraid he might try to end it all! He came back about ten days later. He was happy as can be! Like a different person! First off he apologized to me . . . said he shouldn't have made everybody worry by leaving home without saying goodbye. Then he took a little package out of his bag and unfolded it layer by layer. Finally he uncovered two fingernail-sized Chairman Mao badges. He carefully pinned one on the front of my shirt. I told him to pin one on too, but he wouldn't do it. He was afraid the badge might get scratched, so he wrapped it up again like a treasure and put it in his shirt pocket. He told me he went to Beijing as a stowaway and had learned an immense amount from the Command Headquarters of the Proletariat. He understood everything now — everything he'd believed in the past was wrong, everything! All that stuff was revisionism! He'd been hoodwinked! A monarchist! 'I was really dumb,' he said. 'How could the son of a worker have been a true and loyal offspring of the bourgeoisie?' He tore up all his 'outstanding student' certificates, saying they were all revisionist crap about 'cultivation.' After that he organized some sort of battle group and was out running around all day without ever coming home. I tried to stop him because I was afraid he was going to get into trouble. But he pleaded with me as hard as he could. 'Mom! The working class should be the powerful backup force of the Red Guard little generals! You should support me! You've suffered most of your life—do you want to sit back and watch our Party and country turn revisionist?' I couldn't out-talk him, whatever I said. I'm still kicking myself for being so stupid. Why didn't I stop him? I didn't know he'd killed somebody until a few days ago . . ." The old woman wiped away her tears. "Just look at me," she apologized. "What am I doing, rambling on like this? I have no education."

"No, you were right to talk . . . quite right!" The muscles of Zhu Chunxin's pallid face had been twitching continuously. This was not from any annoyance at the old woman's long-winded speech; quite the contrary, her tireless narration was like a hammer pounding heavily in his mind, making him feel as if he were the one in the defendant's box, undergoing interrogation. He had not broken the law, but his conscience was putting him on trial!

"Ye Hui's father passed away three years ago. Ye Hui has been married less than a year, and my daughter-in-law is expecting a baby very soon now. She's been crying nonstop these past few days . . ." The old woman was speaking through tears. "She asked me to think of a way out, but what can I do?"

Zhu Chunxin turned his face away, hastily patted his eyes with a handkerchief, then turned back and said, "Are you suggesting that the District Committee should be more lenient in handling Ye Hui's case?"

"No, the judge isn't going to listen to me in such matters. I only wanted to explain a few things to the leadership. I heard that you were in charge of this legal work." The old woman thought for a moment before continuing. "When the Cultural Revolution was still going on, I remember Ye Hui mentioned something to me about you . . . seems like you two worked together on something . . . you probably don't remember . . ."

"Ye Hui mentioned me?" Zhu Chunxin's head was buzzing again, and tiny beads of sweat burst out on his forehead. He was afraid that Ye Hui might have told the entire story about the violent clash in September 1967. "What did he say about me?" he asked.

"It's been ten years . . . I've long since forgotten!" the old woman sighed. "Seems like he said he'd gladly give his life to protect a leader like you . . ." The old woman stood up and nodded apologetically toward Zhu Chunxin. "I've disturbed your rest . . . I'll be going now."

"Why don't you stay a little longer?" asked Zhu Chunxin.

The old woman shook her head. "No, I'll be going back to Beijing tomorrow. At least I've had a chance on this trip to see my poor son for the last time. I've already had five days off, and we're pretty busy at work . . ."

After seeing the old woman off, Zhu Chunxin lay back down on his bed. What she had said and done made him feel even more as if he were lying on a bed of nails. "My son's basic nature is not bad . . ." "What can I do?" "He'd gladly give his life to protect a leader like you . . ." The old woman's words kept ringing in his ears like tearful accusations.

He pulled himself up from the bed, not knowing what else to do, and glanced at his watch. It was already time to go back to work. He rode in his car back down to the District Committee offices.

A huge pile of documents and reports was awaiting his signature. He picked one up at random, read the title, and put it down again. He felt terribly agitated. His second meeting with Ye Hui, and his talk with Ye Hui's mother, had completely ruined the rhythm of his life, his work, and his thinking. He seemed to be realizing for the first time that he was not the only one who had been hurt by the Gang of Four. When he was pulled into the mire, he had dragged an innocent and lovable young man down with him. He felt not only guilt and shame, but the same sort of maddening paranoia that is felt by people who have been paraded through the streets as examples to the masses. He imagined that those punctiliously polite and proper staff workers at the office were in fact greeting him with sardonic smiles; he assumed that two of them who were talking together must be discussing his behavior during the Cultural Revolution. This abnormal state of mind irritated him immensely. He wanted to brush off all these unusual thoughts, but they were like obnoxious houseflies: as soon as he drove one away, a whole swarm returned! He angrily pushed aside his pile of documents.

The clerk of the Party Committee came in to inform him that the final meeting of the conference of model workers "in learning from Dazhai and Daqing on the trade and financial battlefront"[1] would be held that afternoon at 2:30. His presence was requested. There would be an informal reception afterwards. At 4 P.M., the Organization Department wanted him to participate in their discussions of the appointment

1. Dazhai was a model agricultural commune during the Cultural Revolution; the Daqing oilfield was a model for industry.

and dismissal of several cadres. Then there was some sort of delegation that had come from another province to report on progressive experiences; they were leaving that afternoon, and he was expected to put in an appearance. It was also necessary that he see a visiting committee that had come from the provincial government to inspect urban traffic problems. Then there was . . . There were probably a dozen things he "had" to do. Any other time, he could have put his husky body in motion, firmly set his square jaw, and gone on with great vitality to handle every one of these assignments responsibly, confidently, and energetically. But today he declined everything and vented his irritation on the clerk. "Conferences here, delegations there, it's damned tiring! All that noise, protocol, and ceremony! I can't stand all this junk!" Then he had a sudden impulse — to go and talk to Ye Hui.

When his car stopped in front of the District Police Station, Zhu Chunxin began having second thoughts. "What am I doing here?" he asked himself. "Did I come to express sympathy and compassion for a courageous guard who once protected me? No. Did I come to do some placating because I'm afraid that Ye Hui will reveal my own dishonorable actions? No, not that either. Did I come to express repentance to Ye Hui? No again." He could not recall the reasons that had originally moved him. But even as he was thus denying the deliberateness of his actions, his long strides were carrying him through the front door. Maybe all these reasons were part of it. Maybe none were. Probably it was a mixture.

He went first to the station Party committee, explaining that he wanted to talk with a few of the "thieves, assaulters, and vandals" whose cases had been basically decided. He wished to "understand their situations." There was some kind of big meeting going on at the station, and no personnel were available to accompany him. Zhu Chunxin said it would be quite convenient for him to talk with the prisoners alone; he would need only a couple of policemen to deliver them back and forth. He asked for an office in which to do the interviews, summoned one of the "thieves, assaulters, and vandals," and talked with him a few minutes to make things look good; then he asked for Ye Hui.

Ye Hui entered wearing the same clothes he had worn in the morning. His expression was also the same. Neither excited nor surprised, he just stood before Zhu Chunxin smiling faintly.

"Sit down, Ye Hui." Zhu Chunxin had planned only to sit up

straight, but he involuntarily stood all the way up. "Let's talk, all right?"

"I was already interrogated this morning." Ye Hui laughed.

"No, I just want to chat informally, as an old comrade and acquaintance . . . just casually."

"Well, thank you! We met only for one evening. Here we are meeting for the second time, and look!—it's in a police station!" Ye Hui began laughing. "This is hardly the place for old comrades and acquaintances to have a chat!"

"I never saw you after that violent day, but you made a very deep impression on me."

"I nearly died after I was wounded, because I didn't get medical care in time. It took me a few months to recover. By that time the two factions had joined together and set up a revolutionary committee, and I was sent to the countryside. I really never thought we'd meet again."

Zhu Chunxin could think of nothing to reply, so he changed the subject. "Lots of people, myself included, made various kinds of mistakes during the Cultural Revolution. That was because of the disruption and damage caused by Lin Biao and the Gang of Four. We must all learn from that experience, and raise our consciousness. We have to look at it as education . . ."

Ye Hui interrupted with a laugh. "But your mistakes and mine took different forms, and so did our 'educations'! In your case, you can clearly and boldly blame everything on your harassment by Lin Biao and the Gang of Four; but in my case, I must confess to following Lin Biao and the Gang of Four, and to subverting the Cultural Revolution!"

Zhu Chunxin stood up and paced back and forth without speaking. The more one fears that a wound will be poked, the more it will be poked. Every one of Ye Hui's words was hitting him where it hurt.

"Do you mean you think your case has been handled too unjustly?" Zhu Chunxin turned his head sharply and said "I'm willing to . . ."

"No . . ."

"Let me finish," said Zhu waving his hands. "I'm willing to step forward and assume full responsibility for the violence that night in September 1967. That would probably make things a little more favorable for you."

"Take whatever responsibility you like, but for my own crimes, I want to take responsibility myself. I'll be happy to take whatever punishment I get, because I did actually commit a crime. I've never tried to cover up my crime. Shi Zhihong was also a courageous young man, and I was the one who killed him. I don't need anybody's sympathy or pity. My punishment is the price I will pay for an increase in understanding — even though the price does seem a bit too high."

"I know you must hate me."

"No." Ye Hui's strong and healthy chest was heaving violently. He was obviously quite agitated. "I only hate Lin Biao and the Gang of Four. You were one of their victims, too. I have my criticisms of you, but also appreciate certain things about you: you can admit you're not perfect; you're sincere, and you have a conscience. Look at all those cadres who behaved dishonorably during the Cultural Revolution, and only later ran afoul of Lin Biao and the Gang of Four. When they get exonerated and restored to their original positions, all they can talk about is the glory of being harassed. They never mention their own mistakes . . ."

Zhu Chunxin could feel his face turning hot and flushed. He could hardly tell what he was feeling inside. Suddenly he thought of a question. "I remember ten years ago you went by the name 'Ye Weige,' didn't you?"

"That's right," said Ye Hui.

"Then why didn't you admit this morning that you'd used another name?"

"That name has nothing to do with the nature of my crime. Or to put it another way, it has nothing to do with this case." Ye Hui's expression became pained and depressed. "'Ye Weige' was the name I chose for myself after the Cultural Revolution started. It stands for naivety and shame. I want to be rid of it forever . . ."

"How is your chat coming?" Chief Li and two police officers came in and greeted Zhu Chunxin.

"Not too badly," Zhu Chunxin answered dryly. He had originally wanted to say something to Ye Hui about his concern for Ye Hui's family. But now it appeared he could not. He looked into Ye Hui's eyes and muttered irresolutely, "Well I guess our chat is over, okay?"

"Could we invite you to rest a moment in the visitor's lounge, Secretary Zhu?" asked Chief Li, extremely courteously. Then he cast a stern eye toward Ye Hui. "Take the criminal offender back to his cell!" he called through the door.

Zhu Chunxin shuddered violently, and his face turned pale. Two words kept reverberating in his mind: "criminal . . . offender . . ."

ZHANG JIE

# Love Must Not
# Be Forgotten

Essentially banned during all of 1966–76, romantic love burgeoned in
the fiction of the late 1970s perhaps more and faster than any other
theme. Even stories whose main themes were quite different often included love-story subthemes, almost as if this were required by the spirit
of the times. Young readers were especially fond of stories that spoke for
them in protesting the fact that marriage in China, despite years of revolution, was still based on social considerations such as family background, wealth, status (now primarily Party status), and parental desire
to cement alliances. Youth championed "true love," including the notion
in the present story of lifelong, or even eternal, bliss with a partner
specially made for one in heaven, if one "can only find" him or her. The
clash between these romanticized visions of individual liberation and
the iron framework of "feudal" tradition is reminiscent of May Fourth
literature in the 1920s in China.

Yet young people in the late 1970s were themselves hardly free of
practical considerations in choosing marital partners. Popular catch
words expressed the conditions that young women commonly put to
young men before agreeing to marriage: "the three things that turn"
stood for a watch, a bicycle, and a sewing machine, all as widely desired
as they were difficult to procure; "sixty-four legs" specified the amount

Translated by William Crawford. Originally published in *Beijing wenyi*, 1979, no. 11.

f furniture required in the bridal apartment. Most young people, of ourse, wanted both idealism and materialism, true love as well as "sixty-ur legs"; their infatuation with pure ideals was compromised in prac-ce in a great variety of ways.

"Love Must Not Be Forgotten" was hotly debated in leading journals nd newspapers during the spring of 1980. A critic named Xiao Lin rote in *Guangming ribao* (14 May 1980) that idyllic love is an illusion, nd that its pursuit can cause suffering. If the divorced woman in the resent story were to succeed in marrying the senior official she loved, hat would become of the official's wife? Does the fact that the official nd his wife were married for "class love" rather than personal love ean their marriage is inferior? The story represented feeble thinking nd moral laxity, the critic said. Two weeks later, also in *Guangming bao*, Dai Qing (author of "Anticipation," pp. 147–67) rebutted Xiao in. Anyone can see, she argued, that loveless marriages are a wide-pread problem in China today. Why should we tolerate this condition? Vhat is true morality—a marriage based on love or one that maintains cially required appearances?

Youth rallied in support of "Love Must Not Be Forgotten," while any in the older generation remained opposed. Yet thoughtful read-s in both generations, whatever their feelings on the issues, praised he author for daring to raise the question of a person's innermost feel-gs, and to explore them honestly. Zhang Jie (b. 1938), a graduate of eople's University in engineering, wrote nothing before 1978, but has ritten many fine short stories and essays since. Although "Love Must ot Be Forgotten" is certainly not the best of these, the extraordinary ontroversy around it has made it the work she is best known for. In 980 she worked as a scriptwriter at the Beijing Film Studio.

## Love Must Not Be Forgotten

was born in 1949, the year our republic was founded. At thirty a repub-c is still very young, but a woman is in danger of reaching the "unmar-ageable" age.

Don't worry about me; I have a very proper suitor these days. Have ou ever seen "The Discus Thrower," by the great Greek sculptor My-on? My suitor Qiao Lin looks like that sculpture. Even the bulky pad-ed clothing he wears in winter cannot obscure the splendid lines of his physique. He has a swarthy face with a boldly defined nose and mouth. His large eyes rest beneath a broad brow. His face and body build alone would be enough to attract most young women.

Yet I'm the one, strangely enough, who can't decide whether to marry, because I can't figure out just what it is about him that I love and what it is that attracts him to me.

I know that people are gossiping behind my back. "She must think she's pretty great, trying to hold out for something better than that." They see me as inferior stock trying to wangle a good price from some unsuspecting spendthrift. This makes them as indignant as if I had committed bloody murder, or betrayed masses of people.

I can't really blame them, of course. In a society where commercial goods still exist, marriage, like many other things, can hardly escape the labeling process used in commodity exchange.

Qiao Lin and I have been together for almost two years now, yet I still haven't figured out whether his habitual silence is due to an aversion to speech or to a lack of anything to say. Whenever I get the urge to give him a sort of "intelligence test" by making him surrender an opinion on something, all I get are nursery-school responses: "Good!" or "No good!" Everything seems limited to these two categories.

Once I asked him: "Qiao Lin, why do you love me?" He pondered this for a while — an exceptionally long time for him — and from the wrinkles that appeared on his brow I knew the cells inside that beautiful head must have been thinking frantically. I couldn't help feeling sorry, as if I'd done him some great wrong by asking the question.

He finally looked up with those clear, childlike eyes and said, "Because you're good!"

A profound loneliness filled my heart. "Thank you, Qiao Lin!"

I couldn't help wondering whether, when he and I became husband and wife, we would be able to fulfill our obligations to each other. Perhaps we could, because law and morality would have bound us together. But how sad it would be if we were left merely carrying out legal and moral duties! Might there be something finer and more solid than law or morality to bind us together? Whenever I have thoughts like this, I get the strange feeling that I'm not a young woman about to marry but a bookish old sociologist.

Perhaps I shouldn't have bothered thinking about all this. We could lead our lives the way they do in most households, having children and staying with each other, strictly through loyalty as defined by law. Never mind that this is the twentieth century—on this point we might as well follow what people have been doing for several thousand years: treating marriage as a means of perpetuating the family, or as a business transaction in which love and marriage are quite separable. Since so many people have made a go of it that way, who am I to break tradition?

No, I still can't decide. I remember when I was little I would cry all night for no particular reason, robbing myself and robbing others in my family of sleep. My old nursemaid, uncommonly wise despite her lack of education, said an evil draft had leaked into my ears and I would always be that way. It appears her prophesy was more than superstition, because even now I get upset for no particularly good reason, robbing myself and others of peace and quiet. It's hard to change nature, as they say.

I often find myself wondering what my mother would say, if she were still alive, about Qiao Lin's proposal and my own doubts. Would she want me to accept?

I think of her not because she was the sort of domineering mother who would want to run my life from beyond the grave. In fact, she was less like a mother than a friend and confidante. I think about her because I loved her immensely and feel a great loss when I recall that she is gone forever.

She never lectured me. She would only tell me gently, in that deep, almost masculine voice of hers, about the successes and failures in her own life, letting me discover what I needed from her experience. Yet her successes seemed so few, and her life plagued by failures. During her last days, she would follow me around with her fine, sensitive eyes, as if she were sizing up my chances of survival on my own, and also as if she had something important to tell me but couldn't decide whether to say it. She must have been deeply worried about the way I seemed unconcerned! "Shanshan," she once blurted out, "if you can't decide what you want in a man, I think staying single is much better than marrying foolishly."

Others might think it wrong for a mother to speak this way to her daughter, but I feel that what Mother gave me was invaluable advice based on painful experience. I don't believe that she was deprecating me or my knowledge of the world. She just loved me and hoped I could live without suffering.

I said, "Mom, I don't *want* to get married!" I wasn't just being shy or coy. In fact, I didn't know when a girl was supposed to be shy or coy, because Mother had long since told me everything that most people feel should not be told to children. "If you find the right man, you should get married. But I mean the *right* one!"

"The right man probably doesn't exist."

"He exists, all right. But it's not easy. The world is too large, and I'm afraid you won't find him!" She wasn't worried about whether I could get married, only about the kind of marriage I might have.

"Actually, you've gotten along fine without anyone else, haven't you?" I asked.

"Who says I've been fine?"

"Seems that way to me."

"I had no choice —" She fell silent and became lost in her own thoughts. A plain and melancholy expression appeared on her face. That sad, wrinkled face reminded me of the flowers, now withered, that I had pressed between the pages of books as a small girl.

"Why didn't you have any choice?"

"You've got too many 'why's,'" she parried. There was something she wanted to hide from me. I knew it could not be that she was too ashamed to reveal it; she was probably afraid I would miss its true import and misinterpret it. Or perhaps, like everyone else, she had something stored away that was just for herself. The thought made me uneasy, and my uneasiness drove me to ask more rash questions.

"Are you still in love with Daddy?"

"No, I never loved him."

"Did he love you?"

"No, he didn't love me, either."

"Then why did you get married in the first place?"

She paused, groping for words to explain something that would seem unusual and baffling. When she spoke, her voice was full of regret. "When people are young, they don't necessarily know what they want or need in life. They can even get married just because everyone's pushing them to. It's only when you're older and a bit more mature that you really understand what you need. But by that time, you'll have done things you'll regret so much your heart will ache. You'd pay any price for the chance to start over, and the second time around you'd be much the wiser. People say, 'The meek are always happy'; but not me, I'll never enjoy that kind of happiness!" She laughed ironically. "I'll always be a bitter idealist!"

That must have been where my habitual discontent came from. The genes that transmit discontent must have done their job from mother to me with perfect precision and completeness.

"Why didn't you marry again?"

"I was afraid I didn't really know what I wanted," she answered reluctantly. Obviously she was unwilling to tell me the truth.

I don't remember my father. He and Mother were separated when I was very small. All I remember about him is that Mother once shyly admitted that he was a rather handsome, dandyish sort of person. I realized she must have been embarrassed to have chased after someone so shallow and mediocre. "When I couldn't sleep at night," she once told me, "I would often force myself to remember all the foolish mistakes I made when I was young, just to clear my mind. It was all rather unpleasant, of course, and sometimes I'd get so ashamed I'd hide my face under the sheet, as if there were people out there in the dark staring at me. Yet the very unpleasantness let me feel the comfort of atoning for something."

I was really sorry she hadn't remarried. She was a lively person, and, if she had married someone she loved, certainly could have made family life lively and interesting. Though she was not terribly pretty, there was a quiet elegance about her, like the subdued quality of a monochrome landscape painting. She could write beautifully, too. A friend who was also a writer used to tease her by saying, "Somebody could fall in love with you just by reading your works!"

" . . . Then get scared off," Mother would reply, "as soon as he found out his beloved was a wrinkled, white-haired old hag!"

At her age, it was impossible that she still did not know what she wanted. Her self-deprecation was obviously a way of avoiding something. I feel sure of this because certain strange habits of hers had long ago aroused my suspicions.

For example: wherever she traveled on business, she always took one volume of her twenty-seven-volume 1950–55 edition of Chekhov's fiction with her. "Don't touch my set of Chekhov's works," she always warned me. "If you want to read Chekhov, read the other set I bought for you." The warning was obviously superfluous. I had my own set, so why should I touch hers? Besides, why repeat the warning over and over again? Yet she was still afraid of the smallest unforeseen eventuality. That set of books seemed to have an unnatural hold on her.

The reason for two sets of Chekhov in our home might have been to show that fondness for Chekhov was our family hallmark. More importantly, though, it was to give my mother a way to cope with my and other people's fondness for the author. Whenever someone wanted to borrow a volume, Mother would take it from the set in my room. Once, when she wasn't home, a very good friend took a volume from her set. Her reaction when she found this out was as quick as if fire had singed her eyebrows. She immediately took the same volume from my set and ran to exchange it for her own.

From then on, her set has remained in her own bookcase. I could agree with her that the great Chekhov repaid a hundred, no thousands of readings; but did that mean one had to make a point of reading him every single day for over twenty years?

Sometimes, when she was tired from writing, she would sit across from her bookcase with a cup of strong tea, staring dreamily at her set of Chekhov. If I suddenly walked into her room, she would become nervous and upset, and either spill the tea on herself or begin to blush like a young girl on her first date.

"Is she in love with Chekhov?" I imagined. If Chekhov had been alive, such a thing might really have happened.

When her mind grew addled as she lay near death, her last words to me were, "Those books — ". She no longer had the strength to say "That set of Chekhov's selected fiction," but I knew perfectly well what books she meant. "And those notebooks ... that say ... 'Love must not be forgotten' on the front ... cremate them ... with me."

I didn't carry out all of her last requests. I did burn the books, but couldn't part with the notebook that said "Love must not be forgotten." I always thought that if it could be published it would be the most moving piece she had ever written. But of course it could not be published.

At first I had thought that it contained only notes for future writing, because it didn't read like a novel, or like reading notes. Nor did it seem like letters or a diary. Only when I read it through from beginning to end did her cryptic comments join with my own scattered memories to suggest the vague outlines of something. After a great deal of reflection, I finally understood that what I held in my hands was not lifeless, antiseptic writing; it was the searing expression of a heart afflicted with grief and love. And I could see how that heart had had to struggle and suffer under the grief and love it bore. For more than twenty years, a man had occupied all her romantic affections, and yet had remained unattainable. She had used the notebook as his substitute, and had poured into it the thoughts she meant for him. Every hour, every day, every month, every year.

No wonder she had never gotten excited when some very ardent men had proposed to her. No wonder she had dismissed with a laugh all of the idle talk about her, never knowing for sure whether it was well-intended or malicious. Her heart was occupied, that's all; and it couldn't hold any more. I remembered the famous lines the poet Yuan Zhen [A.D. 779–831 — Tr.] wrote after the death of the woman he loved:

Once you've crossed the deepest sea, can other waters vie?
Take away the great Mount Wu and clouds seem less than clouds.

Most people are incapable of love like this, I knew; and when I realized that it was unlikely anyone would ever love me in this way, I felt more discouraged than I can say.

I learned that during the 1930s, when this man was doing underground work in Shanghai, an old factory worker had been killed while protecting him, leaving the worker's wife and daughter destitute. Because he was a moral and responsible person, and felt comradely affection for the worker, he married the worker's daughter without hesitation. Whenever he encountered couples who had married for love and whose "love" made endless trouble for them, he would thank his lucky stars. "I may not have married for love," he would think, "but we have worked together in harmony, like the right hand with the left." For decades they had weathered life's storms together as companions in adversity.

This man must have worked where Mother did. Had I ever seen him? I couldn't identify a trace of him from among our normal house guests. Just who was he, anyway?

I remembered a spring day in 1962 when Mother and I were going to a concert. The concert hall was a long way from our house, and we hadn't taken a bus.

A small, black, chauffeur-driven car pulled quietly up and stopped at the curb beside us. An elderly man with white hair and a black tunic got out. How striking that white hair was! The man gave the impression of uncompromising sternness, refinement, and crystal-like clarity. His eyes, especially, had an incisive brightness as they darted from one object to another, reminding the viewer of a bolt of lightning or the flash of a sword blade. If it were possible for tenderness to fill such cold eyes, it could only come from a truly powerful love for a truly deserving woman.

He strode over and said, "How are you, Comrade Zhong Yu? Haven't seen you for a long time."

"Very well. How are you?" Mother's hand, which I was holding, suddenly turned cold and began to tremble slightly.

They stood facing each other, looking sorrowful, even stern perhaps, but neither was looking at the other. Mother was looking at the bare shrubs at the road's edge. The man was looking at me. "You've grown into quite a young woman. That's great. You look just like your mother."

He didn't shake hands with Mother, but he did with me. His hand was cold and trembling slightly, like Mother's. I felt as if I'd become an electrical conductor, sensing both impulses and resistance. I quickly withdrew my hand from his. "No," I said. "Actually it's not great, not at all!"

"Why not?" he asked in amazement. Perhaps I thought he was just pretending to be shocked, because whenever children blurt out something disarmingly frank, adults make a point of looking amazed.

I looked at my mother's face. Yes, it was true. I did indeed look like her, and that was a bit disappointing. "Because she's not very pretty!" I said.

He began laughing and spoke to me in a jocular voice. "How sad! You mean there really exist girls who think their mothers aren't pretty? Say, can you remember in 1953 when your mother was assigned to Beijing and came to the office to report in? She left you out in the hall, you little rascal, and you ran up and down all the stairs. You peeked into offices, and finally got your fingers caught in my office door. I had to carry you crying to look for your mother."

"No, I don't remember," I said, a bit put off. Why did he have to drag out things that happened when I was still in open-crotched baby pants?

"I guess such things are easier for older people to remember," he mused. Then, turning quickly to Mother, he said, "I've read your latest novel. Frankly, it's not quite right in some places. I think you shouldn't be so hard on the heroine . . . you should remember that loving someone is not wrong in itself, and she didn't really hurt anyone else. The hero might also have been in love, you know, only denied his love in order to preserve another person's happiness . . ."

At this moment a policeman walked over to the car and began to berate the driver for stopping in a no-parking zone. This put the driver in an awkward position. The white-haired man stopped speaking, looked in the direction of the car, and spoke to the policeman.

"Sorry. It's not the driver's fault, it's mine. I . . ."

I watched attentively as the elderly gentleman bent forward, listening to the policeman's lecture. When I finally turned my mischievous smile back toward Mother, she looked miserable, like a little girl in first grade cowering beneath the principal's stern gaze. It was almost as if the policeman's lecture were directed at her!

The car drove away, leaving a light haze of exhaust behind it. Very quickly even the haze was blown away, and it was as if nothing had happened at all. Yet for some reason my memory of the event did not vanish quickly.

Thinking back, it must have been the power of his spirit that had stirred Mother's feelings for him. This power came from his mature, steady political sense, developed in the life-and-death struggles of the Revolution; it came also from his nimble mind, his artistic cultivation, and — though it seems strange to say so — his love of the oboe, which Mother also loved. Yes, she must have worshipped him. She noted at one point that without a sense of adulation, her love couldn't have sustained itself for a day.

I can't guess whether he really loved Mother. But then, if he didn't, why did her notebook contain the following entry?

"This is too large a gift. How did you know I liked Chekhov, anyway?"

"You mentioned it."

"I don't remember."

"I do."

The collected works of Chekhov, then, were from him. To Mother it must have seemed almost a token of love.

Perhaps this man who didn't believe in love had grown white hair before he ever realized there was something inside him that could be called love. How tragic that would have been!

It must have been miserable to love him and to get no affection in return. How she must have strained her mind to figure out just when his car might cross a certain street on his way to and from work, so that she might catch a glimpse of the back of his head through the rear window. Whenever he ascended the platform to make a speech, she would have sat in the audience, with distance, smoke, dim light, and jutting heads between them, looking at his dimly visible face, feeling as if there were a lump in her chest, unable to stop the tears from welling up in her eyes. She would have choked back her tears to hide them from others. When he coughed so much that he had to stop speaking, she would worry why no one kept him from smoking. She would worry that he might get bronchitis. And she would never understand why he was so near and yet so far from her.

And I suppose he must have stared until his eyes were blurry at the stream of bicycles outside the side window of his car. He'd be worried whether her handbrake was functioning properly, and whether she might have an accident. On the rare occasion when he didn't have an evening meeting, he might leave his car and walk over to our neighborhood, just in order to draw near our front gate. No matter how busy he was, he would never forget to scan the magazines and newspapers for things Mother had written. And he would never have understood why life had turned out this way.

When they had the good fortune to meet at work, they must have given each other hasty nods and brushed by as quickly as possible. Even so, this would have been enough to loosen Mother's grip on her senses, to turn the whole world momentarily into a big blank. If she met a co-worker whose name was Wang, she'd be certain to call him Guo and say something that didn't really make sense, even to her.

I knew it had been a desperate struggle for her when I saw entries like the following in her notebook: "We have pledged together to forget each other. But I've cheated on that pledge. I haven't forgotten you, and I somehow feel you haven't forgotten me, either. We've merely deceived each other, while trying to hide our torment. It's not that I've wanted to deceive you. I've tried so hard to forget, I really have. Several times I've left Beijing for this purpose and gone far away. I placed my hopes in the numbing power of time and space, and sometimes felt I really had forgotten. But when my work was done and the return train was drawing nearer and nearer to Beijing, my heart would be pounding so hard that everything became a dizzy blur. I would gaze anxiously toward the platform, as if there were someone waiting for me. And, of course, there was not. Then I would understand that I had not forgotten, that everything was just as it had been before. Year by year, this obsession has become more and more deeply rooted, and to uproot it is beyond my strength.

"At the end of each day, I have a nagging feeling that I've forgotten something important, and at night I awaken with a start from my dreams, wondering if something has happened. No, nothing has ever happened. Then it comes to me with perfect clarity: I don't have *you*, and nothing can make up for that. You and I have already reached our declining years, yet I'm still plagued by a young girl's emotions — why is that? Why must life lead us over such a long, arduous path before the dreams we pursue finally appear before us? And because you and I once closed our eyes to our dreams, not only did we miss our chance at the crossroads of life, we placed ourselves and our dreams on opposite sides of a great chasm."

Yes, that was it. Mother had never let me come to the station to meet her when she returned from her trips out of town. She must have preferred to stand on the platform alone, enjoying the illusion that he was meeting her. My poor white-haired mother, behaving like a love-sick schoolgirl!

She wrote very little about their romance, actually. Most of what she wrote was about the trifles of day-to-day living — why some of her efforts at writing had failed, doubts and misgivings about her own talent, why Shanshan (that was me) was so naughty and whether or not to mete out punishment. Then there was the time she misread some tickets because she wasn't thinking clearly, and missed a perfectly marvelous play. Another time she left her umbrella at home and got soaked to the skin. Her thoughts clearly were on him, day and night, just as if they were really married. In actual fact, if you added up all the time they had ever spent together, it wouldn't total more than twenty-four hours. But those twenty-four hours were probably richer and more profound than the enjoyment some people have in an entire lifetime. Shakespeare's Juliet compared her love to riches when she said: "I cannot sum up half my sum of wealth" [*Romeo and Juliet*, act 2, scene 6 — Tr.]. I suppose Mother couldn't have summed up half her love, either.

It appears that he met an early death during the Cultural Revolution, though her references to this are vague and evasive, very likely because of her own situation at the time. What mystifies me is how

Mother was able to keep writing at all in the midst of vicious attacks. From her veiled references, it seems one can infer that her man had questioned some of the theories of a certain ultra-Red "authority on theory" who was at the height of his power then.[1] "This is nothing but right-wing thought in disguise!" he apparently had said to someone. And I could tell from reading those tear-stained pages that he had been dealt with harshly, but had never given in to his powerful tormentors. Even on the verge of death, the last thing he said was, "If you send me to go see Marx, I'll take my case against you right to him."

This must have happened in the winter of 1969, because that was the winter when Mother's hair suddenly turned completely white, even though she was only approaching fifty. She had pinned a strip of black cloth to her sleeve, and this had caused her trouble. She came under severe criticism for wearing that mourning band, which was considered a backward superstition. Then her attackers insisted on knowing just whom she was wearing it for.

"Who's this for, Mommy?" I once asked her at the time, feeling alarmed.

"A near relation," she replied. Then, worried she might have shocked me, she added, "Someone you're not acquainted with."

"Should I wear one, too?" I had asked. Then she did something she hadn't done for a long time: she patted my cheeks as she had when I was a small child. It had been a long time since this kind of warmth had appeared in her. I often felt that the more years and experience she had behind her, especially after those years when she was persecuted, the more she withdrew from warmth and affection—or perhaps just hid it deeper and deeper—until her apparent lack of emotion made her seem like a man.

Sadly and rather absentmindedly, she laughed. "No, you don't need to wear one," she said.

Her eyes were dry and slightly puffy, as if every last drop of moisture had been cried out of them. I wanted to do something to console her, to make her happy, but she said, "You can go now."

At the time I wasn't sure just why, but I was overtaken by a fear that part of my dear mother had already left me in pursuit of something else.

1. This is a reference to Kang Sheng (1899–1975), a vice-chairman of the Communist Party of China before his death. Though very close to the Gang of Four, he could be denounced only as their "authority on theory" until July 1980, when *People's Daily* began to denounce him by name.

"Mother!" I cried.

Mother must have realized instantly what was going on in my mind. "Don't be afraid," she said, very tenderly. "Just go. Leave Mother by herself awhile."

I was right. Mother had, in fact, written this:

"You have gone, and I feel as though part of my soul has gone with you.

"I don't even know where they've taken you, much less how I might see you one last time, since I count as neither close friend nor relative . . . so we'll simply have to part like this. If only I could have undergone their inhuman tortures in your place, so that you might have lived on! How could I ever believe all those absurd charges against you?[2] You have been murdered, you who were among the best of them all! Would I love you like this if you were not? Yes, I am not afraid to utter those three words now.

"Snow keeps swirling down. Good Heavens! Does even God indulge in pretenses? Trying to cover your blood and the ugliness of your murder with a blanket of pure, clean whiteness!

"I never thought my own existence was very significant, but now I spend every moment wondering whether the things I do and say would bring a frown to that stern brow of yours. I find myself wanting to live right, to lead a good life, like yours, and to do something for this society of ours. Because if won't be like this forever, you know — the sword of Justice is already poised above that pack of dogs!

"I walked alone down that street, the only one we ever walked down together, and listened to my solitary footsteps in the darkness, echoing, echoing . . . In the past, whenever I wandered up and down this street, lingering as long as I could, I never felt the grief that I feel now. I knew then that even though you weren't at my side, you were still living in this world, and for that reason I felt you were with me. But now you are no longer here — I just can't bring myself to believe it!

"I walked to the end of the street and back. Then I turned around and walked it once more.

"I turned around the railing, then faced back as always before. It seemed you were still there, waving goodbye to me. We had once at this spot given each other the plain, blank smiles of mere acquaintances. We were doing our best to mask the deep feelings we shared. That was one

2. Literally, the charges of being a "three-anti's element." See glossary.

evening in early spring, but hardly an inspiring one, since chilling winter winds were still blowing. We had walked along in silence, keeping a good distance between us. You were having difficulty breathing because of your bronchitis. My heart went out to you, and I wanted to slow the pace, but for some reason could not. We nearly flew along, as if some pressing matter demanded that we cover this stretch of road as quickly as possible. How we treasured the only stroll we ever had together, yet we were afraid that one of us would speak those frightening words that had tormented us for years: 'I love you.' I doubt anyone, other than ourselves, could ever believe that we never even shook hands, let alone anything else!"

You are wrong, Mother. *I* believe you. I have seen inside your soul as no one else ever has.

That small street: I would never have known it to be so filled with painful memories. This shows that no small corner of the earth, however plain in appearance, should be written off as insignificant. Who knows how many secret joys and sorrows might be concealed in it?

Sometimes when she had written herself to exhaustion, she would walk back and forth in the small street outside our window. This could happen after she had written until dawn; or it could happen on black and gusty nights, even in the winter, even when the wind was howling like a crazed animal and pelting the window with sand. I always thought it was simply a strange quirk of hers. Little did I know that she was going for spiritual communion with him.

She also liked to stand in front of the window, gazing out at the street. Once she got such a look on her face that I felt sure one of our favorite guests was coming. I hurried to the window for a look. Outside, in the autumn evening, a chill wind was tossing withered brown leaves into the air and blowing them across an empty street.

It was as if he were still alive. Her habit of pouring out her thoughts to him in writing continued as before, right until she, too, was unable to lift a pen. Her parting words to him, on the last page of her notebook, were: "I am a materialist. But now I find myself longing for Heaven. If there really is a Heaven, I know you'll be there waiting for me. I'll go there and see you again. We'll stay there together and never part. We'll never have to deny ourselves for fear of hurting someone else. Darling, wait for me. I'm on my way . . ."

I never would have imagined that Mother, even as she lay dying, could be so taken by love. As she herself had said, it really was an immutable thing. My own feeling was that it was less like love than some kind of tortured yearning, a force somehow stronger than death. If what people call "eternal love" really exists, then this epitomized it. She felt blessed, even to her last moment on earth. She had truly loved, and had no regrets for having done so.

By now their wrinkled skin and white hair have wasted away and turned into other forms of matter. Yet I know that whatever they have turned into, their love for each other endures. There are no legal or moral codes binding them together, and they never even so much as shook hands, but they belong completely to each other. They are inseparable. Through the ages to come, whenever one white cloud pursues another across the sky, or one blade of grass draws close to another, whenever one wave splashes another's foamy crest or light gusts of wind chase each other—they will be there.

I weep every time I see that notebook with "Love must not be forgotten" written across its front. I weep bitterly again and again, as if I were the one who had suffered through that tragic love. The whole thing was either a great tragedy or a massive joke. Beautiful or poignant as it may have been, I have no intention of reenacting it!

The great English novelist Thomas Hardy has pointed out how rare it is that those who call out and those to whom they call are able to come together. I cannot condemn my mother and her beloved for their breach of conventional morality, but will criticize them on one point: why didn't they wait to find the other soul that was calling to them?

If people could wait for each other and keep from drifting into marriage, how many tragedies of this sort would be avoided!

When communism is achieved, will love and marriage still sometimes be treated as separate things? The world is so vast that there may still be times when people whose souls beckon cannot say "yes" to each other; does that mean the problem will still be with us? How very sad. Let us hope we will have found a way to avoid this sadness by that time.

In the meantime, why do I trouble myself with such nettling problems?

In the final analysis, perhaps we ourselves must accept responsibility for all this grief. Who knows? Perhaps the blame lies with the old mind set passed down from earlier times. These days, simply refusing to marry has become a direct challenge to that old style of thinking. Some will say you have psychological problems, or some shameful secret, or perhaps political misdeeds in your past. Or they might say you are too weird and wily, or think you're better than everybody else, have no respect for time-honored customs and are an evil heretic. They will find all sorts of mean, low-minded ways to undercut you until you knuckle under and marry the first person who comes along just to get it over with. Then you're shackled in a marriage without love and, unable to escape, suffer through it for the rest of your days.

I feel like shouting, "Stay out of our lives! Allow us to wait patiently until that right person appears, and even if it never happens, don't make us rush blindly into marriage! Living alone is not such a terrible thing. Perhaps it's just a sign that life in our society is evolving, advancing . . .

# CHEN RONG

# At Middle Age

Although aware that human drama as massive as the Cultural Revolution called for full-length novels, China's writers were understandably excited by the "second blooming" in 1979–80 and primarily rushed to publish short stories. Some felt, moreover, that they were still too near to the mind-boggling upheaval of the Cultural Revolution to view it systematically or with any artistic detachment. The most that was done to achieve greater depth or breadth than short stories could were a few works of "middle-length" fiction, or *zhongpian xiaoshuo*, a term sometimes translated as "novella."

"At Middle Age" was the best-known and generally most highly regarded novella of 1979–80, primarily because of the relatively full and complex view it provides of the burdens of working intellectuals. Dr. Lu Wenting and her friends, having devoted themselves to China's new society in the 1950s, find themselves in the late 1970s to be near exhaustion and nagged by some basic doubts. The author is skillful in weaving disparate aspects of the doctor's life into a narrative whose consistent tone gives it unity. Reader acclaim of the story was remarkably widespread.

Most of the political-literary critics in China also emphasized the story's strengths, yet not all comment was favorable. Some critics objected to the satire of the arrogant Madame Vice-minister, whom the

Translated by Margaret Decker. Originally published in *Shouhuo* (Shanghai), 1980, no. 1.

author calls a "Marxist-Leninist old lady." Others felt it was wrong to sympathize with characters who are fed up and emigrating to Canada. The most ominous criticism used the following logic: "At Middle Age" is a tragic story; all tragedies must be due to villains. But there is no villain here. The various human flaws depicted are insufficient to account for so weighty a tragedy. What could this mean except that the author was faulting China's social system? According to one critic, she was "spreading a dark cloud" over socialist life.[1]

Chen Rong (b. 1935) is from Sichuan Province and, following her home dialect, pronounces the character of her surname as "Shèn."[2] In 1957 she graduated from the Beijing Russian Language Institute, where, majoring in linguistics and Russian literature, she came to admire the great nineteenth-century Russian realists. She has worked as a radio programmer, an editor, and a schoolteacher. In 1979–80 her work unit was the People's Literature Publishing House, where she worked primarily as a writer.

# At Middle Age

## 1

Were those stars glimmering in space? Was she out in a boat, rocking on the water? Lu Wenting wanted to call out, but could make no sound. She wanted to look about her, but could see only countless rings of light before her eyes, shimmering and fading, constantly moving.

It seemed to her that she was floating uncertainly, as if supported by a cloud, her body feeling alternately heavy and light. Was this the confusion of a dream? Or was she perhaps dying or dead?

Now she could remember. She had just gone on duty, just entered the operating room, changed into her surgical gown and gone over to the sink. Yes, and her good friend Jiang Yafen had asked to assist her.

Yafen's application to leave the country had been accepted. Her

1. Xiao Chen, "Buyao gei shenghuo mengshang yiceng yinying: ping xiaoshuo 'Ren dao zhongnian'" (Let's not cover life with a layer of dark clouds: A critique of "At Middle Age"), *Wenhuibao* (Shanghai), 2 July 1980, p. 3.
2. Some sources spell the surname in English as Shen. Here we adhere to the standard Chen for the sake of uniformity. (Many authors, representing various dialects, pronounce their names differently from the official national standard, and to make exceptions in every case would be confusing.)

family was going to Canada, so this was the last time they would operate together.

They stood side by side washing their hands. In the 1950s they had
studied together at medical school; in the early 1960s they had both
been assigned to work at this hospital. After twenty years of friendship
and work partnership, they were about to be separated to opposite sides
of the globe. They felt depressed — not an appropriate mood for surgery. Wenting could also remember trying to say something to clear the
gloom. What was that? Oh yes, she had turned her head to ask, "Have
you bought your plane tickets yet, Yafen?" And what had Yafen answered? It seemed she hadn't answered, though her eyes had grown
bright with tears.

After a long silence, Yafen asked, "You've done two operations already this morning. Are you up to doing a third?"

And what had been her answer? She couldn't remember. It seemed
she hadn't answered, but had only kept rubbing her hands with the
scrub brush, over and over again. It seemed to be a new brush, with stiff,
sharp bristles that pricked her fingertips until they stung. She stared at
the white soap bubbles on her hand, and, watching the time on the wall
clock, allowed three minutes each to scrubbing her hands, her wrists,
and her arms — all as regulations required. When she had done this
three times, using ten minutes, she immersed her hands in a pail that
contained an alcohol solution. That solution, which was 75 percent alcohol, seemed in her memory to be white, but also a bit yellowish. Even
now her hands and arms felt tingling and prickly-hot. Was this an effect
of the alcohol? In twenty years of practice, this was the first time she had
experienced such a feeling while preparing to operate. Her hands and
arms had nearly been soaked white in this same disinfectant, but she
had never before felt this prickling pain. Why did it seem that she
couldn't even lift her two hands?

She could remember that she had already entered the operating
theater, had already given the patient an injection of Novocain near the
eyeball, and was about to begin to operate when Yafen quietly asked her,
"Is your child over her pneumonia yet?"

What was the matter with Yafen that day? She knew well enough
that an eye surgeon in the operating room must clear her mind of all
extraneous thoughts and concentrate completely on the patient's eyes.
Even oneself, one's husband, and one's children must be put entirely out

of mind. How could Yafen have asked about her daughter Jiajia at a time like that? Was she upset because she was leaving for a new country?

"Right now, let's worry about these eyes," Wenting had answered, almost angrily.

With that she bent her head and opened the conjuctiva of the diseased eyeball with a pair of curved scissors. The operation was underway.

One operation after another. How did it happen that three operations had been scheduled that morning? A cataract removal for Viceminister Jiao, surgical correction of Wang Xiaoman's walleye, and a cornea transplant for Zhang Laohan. From 8:00 until 12:30, four and a half hours straight, she had sat on a high operating stool, her body bent under bright light, working with intense concentration. Making an incision, sewing it up; making another incision, sewing it up. When she had made the last suture and bandaged the patient's eye with gauze, she finally stood up. Her legs were numb, her back stiff. She couldn't take a step.

Yafen changed her clothes and was standing by the door calling to her, "Wenting, let's go."

"You go ahead," she said without moving.

"I'll wait for you. Today's my last day at the hospital." Yafen's eyes again grew bright with tears. Looking at her, Wenting wondered whether she was going to cry. Why was she so upset?

"You hurry home and get your things packed and organized. Your husband must be waiting for you."

"He's already taken care of everything." Yafen raised her head, then suddenly exclaimed, "Your—what's wrong with your legs?"

"Sitting too long. They're a little numb. They'll be all right in a minute. I'll come see you tonight."

"Okay, I'll go on ahead, then."

With Yafen gone, Wenting leaned back against the wall, running her hands across the icy cold surface of its white ceramic tiles. She just stood there for a while, then walked slowly toward the changing room.

She could remember changing her clothes and putting on that gray blouse of hers. She could also remember going out the hospital door, and nearly reaching the head of the tiny lane from which her own door would have been visible. But suddenly she had felt exhausted—extremely exhausted in a way she had never experienced before. It was a weariness that shook one from head to foot; it made the road ahead of

er seem dimmer, the little lane suddenly seem longer, and the door of
er home to recede into the distance. She felt she would never reach that
oor.

Her arms and legs went limp; her whole body seemed not her own.
Her eyes grew heavy and incapable of staying open. Her lips turned dry
nd would not move. She felt thirsty, oh so thirsty. Where could she get
ome water?

Now her parched lips trembled slightly.

## 2

"Dr. Sun! Come look! Dr. Lu just said something!" Jiang Yafen,
who had been keeping constant watch at the patient's bedside, was call-
ng softly.

The chief of Ophthalmology, Sun Yimin, was busy reading Lu
Wenting's case record. The two words "myocardial infarction" had
shocked him. His pale face looked grave as he shook his head and
pushed his black-rimmed glasses back up the bridge of his long nose.
He couldn't help reflecting that this was not the first middle-aged doctor in the Ophthalmology Section to have suffered a heart attack. Lu
Wenting was only forty-two, and had never complained of any illness or
affliction. Nothing had ever been said about her having a weak heart. So
why had she had a heart attack? It was disturbingly sudden.

Hearing Jiang Yafen call, Dr. Sun turned his tall, stooped body and
bent over Lu Wenting's pale face. Her eyes were closed, her breathing
weak. Her dry, cracked lips moved, closed, then parted again slightly.

"Dr. Lu!" Sun Yimin called softly.

Lu Wenting fell entirely still again. There was no sign of response
on her withered face, which was swollen in spots with edema.

"Dr. Lu! Wenting!" Jiang Yafen urged gently.

As before, there was no response.

Sun Yimin lifted his head and looked at that ominous oxygen tank
standing in the corner, then stared at the electrocardiograph at the
head of the bed. He relaxed a little when he saw that regular QRS waves
were showing on the fluorescent screen of the oscillometer. He turned
his head to look at the patient again. "Hurry," he said, waving his hand,
"call her husband here!"

An attractive man in his forties, of medium build and slightly balding, came hurrying in. Fu Jiajie had kept watch at his wife's bedside all

night without closing his eyes. He had not left once until Dr. Sun had come and urged him to go and rest on the bench outside the room. Dr. Sun now surrendered his position at the head of the bed, letting Fu Jiajie approach and lean over Lu Wenting's pillow. Fu peered anxiously at that face that was once so familiar, but now, white as paper, seemed to belong to a stranger.

Her lips again moved slightly, seeming to form an inaudible word. Only her husband understood. "Hurry! Bring some water. She's thirsty."

Jiang Yafen quickly handed over the small enamel pot that was on the night table next to the head of the bed. Fu Jiajie took it from her and, carefully maneuvering around the rubber oxygen tube, held the spout of the pot over those lips that looked like two withered leaves. Drop by drop the water fell into her mouth.

"Wenting! Wenting!" her husband called. His hand trembled, and some droplets of water splashed onto her deathly pale face. Again she seemed to move, ever so slightly.

3

Eyes, eyes, eyes . . .

One pair after another, they swam past Lu Wenting's tightly closed eyes as if flowing from a spring. The eyes of men, of women, of the old, of the young; big eyes, little eyes, clear eyes and cloudy — all different, all surrounding her, shining, shining . . .

Here was a pair of eyes suffering from internal hemorrhaging.

Here a pair made milky by cataracts.

Here a pair with a retina detached by an injury.

Here, here, . . . ah! These were Jiajie's eyes! Happiness, worry, frustration, affection, pain, and hope all showed in these eyes. She could see deep into these eyes even without an ophthalmoscope, even without a slit lamp microscope. She could see all the way into his heart. Jiajie's eyes were clear and bright, like the golden sun. His heart was fiery; how much warmth he had given her!

It was his voice, Jiajie's voice! So intimate, so warm, yet so far away. It seemed to come floating from some other world:

> I wish I were a rushing stream,
> And my love a small fish,
> Happily swimming to and fro in the
>     midst of my waves.

Where was this? It was in a silvery world on the surface of a lake that was frozen as solid and clear as a crystal. Red, blue, purple, and white figures were flitting across the ice. The happy laughter seemed it would shatter this transparent palace! Holding hands, she and he were gliding in and out among the flow of people. Laughing face after laughing face passed by, invisible to her; she saw only him. Shoulder to shoulder they glided and turned, laughing and playing — what happy days!

The Five Dragons Pavilion was a sheet of silver in a bed of white, dignified and ancient, lonely and expansive. They leaned against the marble railing on the pavilion terrace. Snowflakes fell on their faces and sprinkled their hair. Their tightly clasped hands mocked the forbidding cold.

She had been so young then!

She had never dreamed of unexpected love or unusual good fortune. As a child, she had been friendless and lonely. Her father had deserted the family, and her mother had raised her. She had no happy childhood memories; all she remembered was a prematurely aged mother in the companionship of a solitary lamp — night after night, year after year, cutting material to sew and to mend.

In medical school, she had lived in the women's dormitory and eaten at the communal dining hall. She would get up before daybreak to memorize foreign vocabulary. When the bell rang, she would put her notebook under her arm and go to classes, where she filled a notebook with small, closely written characters. Next came evening study hall, and after that she would continue to study, well into the night, inside the dissection laboratory. She spent her youth ungrudgingly on class after class, test after test.

It did not seem that love was in her destiny. She shared a room in the dormitory with Jiang Yafen, a classmate. Yafen had eyes that seemed to talk and an enchanting little mouth; she was tall, slender, and always lively. She got letters every week of the kind that could not be shared; every weekend she had secret appointments. Wenting, on the other hand, was often alone, with only her shadow to comfort her. She received no letters, had no dates. It was as though the world had forgotten her.

When she and Yafen were assigned together to work at a famous hundred-year-old hospital, they were informed that medical school graduates assigned there must serve four years of residency and that, during residency, must be at the hospital twenty-four hours a day. They were not allowed to marry.

Yafen felt this was outrageous, and complained behind the officials' backs. "This is no better than a convent!" But Wenting accepted the strict demands with a glad and willing heart. Twenty-four hours at the hospital? That was nothing! She only wished she had forty-eight hours a day to give to the hospital. Not marrying for four years? So what! Weren't there many examples of successful people in medicine who either married late or remained single? The young Dr. Lu put all her energy into her work, conscientiously and industriously seeking to advance medical science.

But things don't always go as one expects. Fu Jiajie suddenly intruded upon her peaceful, mechanical life.

What was this? How had it come about? She never could figure it out, nor did she ever really try to. He had come to the hospital because of a sudden eye problem, and by chance had become her patient. She treated his eyes for him, and it may have been during her conscientious ministrations that feelings of another sort had been aroused in him. These feelings grew, and became ever warmer, until they had altered the lives of both of them.

Winter in the north is so cold! But for her, winter that year was warm. Never before had she realized that love could so enchant a person, so dazzle one. She even felt regretful that she hadn't searched for it sooner. She was already twenty-eight that year—not what you'd consider young. But she was very young at heart. She welcomed her late blooming love with the whole of her pure heart and body.

> I wish I were a wild forest,
> And my love a small bird,
> Building a nest and singing within
>     my dense woods.

It was incomprehensible.

Fu Jiajie studied metallurgy. He specialized in the tensile strength of metals at the Metallurgy Research Institute, and was working on the development of new alloys for building spacecraft. He had a sort of foolish or absentminded air about him. Jiang Yafen called him "The Bookworm." But this bookworm could recite poetry, and extremely well!

"Whose poem is that?" she asked him.

"A Hungarian poet, Sándor Petöfi."

"How funny. A scientist who can find time to read poetry."

"You need imagination to do science well. So in one way it's the very
same as poetry."

Who said Fu Jiajie was foolish?

"What about you? Do you like poetry?" he asked.

"Me? No, I don't understand it and hardly ever read it." She smiled,
deciding to tease him. "We ophthalmologists are surgeons. Every stitch,
very incision must be precise. We don't have room for even a touch
of fancy ..."

"You're wrong," he fervently interrupted. "Your work itself is beautiful poetry. You make hundreds and thousands of people see light
again ..." Smiling, he came close to her, his face near hers, leaning
close, so close. She had never before felt the warm breath of a man
suddenly caressing her face; it confused her, alarmed her. It seemed
something outrageous must happen, and in fact he stretched out two
strong arms and pulled her into his embrace.

It all happened so suddenly. She looked in fright at those two smiling eyes, that pair of parted lips drawing nearer. Her heart raced as she
tilted her head back slightly, unconsciously shying away, closing her eyes
in panic, receiving this inexorable attack of love.

Beihai in the snow seemed especially arranged for her. The thickly falling snow was covering the tall white pagoda, the green of Jade Island, the long terrace facing the quiet lake. And it covered the lovers'
sweet embarrassment.

Thus, much to everyone's surprise, after the four-year term of celi-
bate residency, Lu Wenting was first to have a wedding. This can only be
called the hand of fate. Who could have foreseen that Fu Jiajie would
pop into her life? And if he wanted to get married, how could she
refuse? He had pursued her so stubbornly and longingly, willing to sacrifice everything for her ...

> I wish I were a deserted ruin,
> And my love the tender spring ivy,
> Twining and climbing intimately
> up my desolate brow.

How wonderful life was! How beautiful love! Memories of the past
reappeared at the edges of her mind, and in her critical condition seemed
to give her the will to live. Her eyes opened slightly for a moment.

4

Dr. Lu Wenting remained in a deep sleep after receiving a powerful sedative and painkiller. The chief internist came personally to examine her. He listened carefully to her heart and lungs, examined her electro-cardiograms and her daily log, and instructed the doctor on duty to continue her intravenous infusions, to give her injections of papaverine and morphine, and to watch carefully for any change in her electrocardiograms. There were still dangers of increased cardiac blockage and of complications from other disease.

When he left the patient's room, the chief internist said to Sun Yimin, "Her constitution is just too weak. I remember when she first came to our hospital she was in excellent health!"

"Yes, she was." Sun Yimin shook his head and sighed. "That was eighteen years ago. She was just a girl when she came."

Eighteen years ago Sun Yimin had already built a reputation as an expert ophthalmologist. His superior surgical skills and serious attitude toward his work had gained him the respect of everyone in the field. A robust and vigorous teacher, he took the training of new talent to be his own sacred responsibility. Each time a group of candidates arrived from the medical school, he would interview them himself and personally make the selection. He felt that if this hospital's ophthalmology department were going to produce the best eye surgeons in the country, he would have to begin by selecting the most promising students.

How had Lu Wenting come to be chosen? He could remember clearly. At first the twenty-four-year-old medical school graduate hadn't made much of an impression on him.

That morning, Dr. Sun had already spoken with five new graduates, and was feeling rather disappointed. Although some were well-suited to ophthalmology, they felt the field was beneath them and made it plain that they would not put their hearts into it. On the other hand, those who were willing to do ophthalmology viewed it as a simple field and an easy career. When he picked up the sixth file, labeled "Lu Wenting," he already felt tired, and certainly wasn't expecting anything extraordinary. He was thinking that the medical schools would have to revise their teaching methods in order to instill a more appropriate attitude toward ophthalmology.

At that moment, the door was softly pushed open and a slender young woman walked quietly in. Sun Yimin lifted his head to see a student wearing cotton pants and jacket. The cuffs of her sleeves had been patched with new cloth, and the knees of the pants had already been worn white. Her appearance was plain to the point of seeming unkempt. Sun Yimin looked at the three characters "Lu Wenting" on the folder pocket and again casually raised his head to glance at her. This university student was really nothing but a young girl. She had a small frame, a face shaped like a melon seed, and shiny raven black hair cut just below the ears. She sat in the chair facing him, as quiet as a drop of water.

Chief Sun asked her his standard academic questions. Wenting answered them one by one, restricting herself to the answers and saying nothing more.

"Do you want to be in ophthalmology?" Sun Yimin had almost decided to cut this interview short. His arm rested on the edge of the desk as his fingertips tapped his temple. He had asked the question wearily.

"Yes. In school I was particularly interested in ophthalmology." There was a slight southern accent in her speech.

This answer pleased Sun Yimin. He relaxed the fingers that were pressing at his temple, and his headache even seemed to go away. He immediately changed his mind; he would proceed with this interview. He looked closely at the woman student and asked, "Why were you interested?"

As soon as he said this, he felt it had been a bad question. A person would be hard put to answer. But this student was not flustered. "Our country is too far behind in ophthalmology."

"Good. Go ahead. In what ways are we behind?" Sun Yimin asked.

"I don't know if I can answer you very well, but there do seem to be some operations that other countries have managed and we still have not — using lasers to seal a torn retina, for example. I think we've got to try this, too."

"Yes!" In his own mind Sun Yimin had already given this student a grade of "excellent." "What else?" he asked again. "Any other ideas?"

"Mmm ... use of cryosurgical techniques to remove cataracts should be more widespread. But anyway, lots of problems are worth studying."

"Good, very well said. Can you read foreign languages?"

"Only with a lot of effort and a dictionary. But I like languages."

"Wonderful." For Sun Yimin to offer nothing but praise directly to a new student was practically unheard of. A few days later, Lu Wenting and

Jiang Yafen were the first selected by the ophthalmology department
Yafen had been chosen by Sun Yimin for her cleverness, enthusiasm, an(
activity; Wenting for her sincerity, reflectiveness, and sharpness.

The first year, they did external eye surgery and familiarized them
selves with the general study of ophthalmology. The second year, the
did internal eye surgery, mastered optics, and studied the eye muscles
By the third year, they could perform such relatively complicate(
and fine operations as cataract removal. It was in this year, as a re
sult of a certain incident, that Sun Yimin came to view Wenting wit
new respect.

It was a spring morning — Monday — and Sun Yimin was makin;
the rounds in the ophthalmology ward. A group of doctors in whit(
coats was accompanying him. The patients were waiting anxiously, sit
ting up in their beds and looking expectantly for the professor to exam
ine them personally. They seemed to feel that their illnesses would b(
cured by the mere touch of his hand upon their eyes.

At each bed, Sun took the medical history that was passed to hin
over his shoulder and glanced through it while listening to the patient'
doctor, or another senior doctor, report on diagnosis and treatment
Sometimes he separated the patient's eyelids for a look inside; othe1
times he just patted the patient's arm and urged him to relax when th(
operation came. Then he turned to the next bed.

After the rounds, there was the usual meeting to discuss problem:
and schedule upcoming work. Usually, at this sort of meeting, only Chie
Sun and the physicians in charge would speak. The residents would jus
listen attentively. They dared not speak for fear of making fools o
themselves in front of these prestigious doctors and later becoming th(
laughingstock of the entire department. Events proceeded as usual thi:
time, and when all that had to be said had been said, and all assignment
made, Sun Yimin stood up to go.

"Does anyone have anything else to say?" he asked.

A woman's soft voice issued from the corner of the room. "Coul(
you please take another look at the x-ray of the patient in Room 4
bed 3?"

Everyone turned their heads in the direction of the voice. Sun coul(
see that it was Lu Wenting who had spoken. She wasn't very tall or eye
catching, and Sun Yimin had not noticed her among the retinue tha(
had followed him on his rounds. Later, when he had delivered his talk a

ιe meeting in the office, he had again failed to notice Dr. Lu Wenting.

"Bed 3?" Sun Yimin turned his head and looked to the chief esident.

"Bed 3 is a job injury," the chief resident answered.

"He was x-rayed when he was admitted," Wenting said. "The x-ray chnician's report said there was no evidence of any foreign particle in ιe eye. But after admission, when the wound had been stitched up, the atient still complained of pain. I gave him a nonskeletal x-ray, and I ιink there really is a foreign particle. Please look again, Dr. Sun."

The x-ray was procured and Dr. Sun looked at it. Then the chief ɛsident and the physicians in charge all took turns looking at it.

Yafen stared at her friend with wide eyes, mentally addressing her: Couldn't you wait until after the meeting to tell Dr. Sun? What if you're rong? You'll be the butt of jokes in the whole department! And even if ɔur diagnosis is right, you're implying that the diagnosing doctor asn't careful enough, and *he*, remember, is a physician in charge!"

"You are correct, a foreign particle is present." Sun Yimin took the -ray back and nodded his head. Then he looked at the gathered doc- ɔrs and said, "Dr. Lu hasn't been in ophthalmology long, but she's been iligent in her professional studies, and is serious and conscientious in ɛr work. These are very valuable traits."

When she heard this, Wenting dropped her head, blushing. She adn't expected Chief Sun to praise her in front of everyone. Dr. Sun ɔoked at her expression and smiled faintly. He was well aware that her aring to question the diagnosis of a physician in charge showed that ιis resident not only had a keen sense of responsibility toward patients, ιt also was extremely courageous.

The hierarchy in the hospital was complex and well articulated, ιore so than in other work units. Though it was not explicitly stated, ɛsidents were supposed to listen to physicians in charge; younger doc- ɔrs were supposed to defer to older ones; and the opinions of professors ιd associate professors were beyond dispute. For Wenting, who did not ven have much seniority as a resident, to go ahead and voice her dis- ɡreement with the diagnosis of a physician in charge could not fail to ttract unusual attention from Sun Yimin.

From then on, Dr. Sun's favorite description of Wenting was "a very romising ophthalmologist."

And now it seemed those eighteen intervening years had gone by in

a flash. Lu Wenting, Jiang Yafen, and their classmates had already become the backbone of the ophthalmology department. If they had been
promoted by the customary means of examination, they would long ago
have become head doctors. Yet in fact, not only were they not head
doctors, they weren't even physicians in charge. They had remained
residents for eighteen straight years. The Cultural Revolution had destroyed the ladder of promotion, and the spring rains following the fall
of the Gang of Four had not yet arrived for this group of peren-
nial residents.

"She's like a blade of grass!" Watching the feeble breathing of Wenting, compassion welled up in Dr. Sun. He pulled the chief internist
aside and asked, "What do you think? She couldn't . . ."

The chief internist looked toward the patient's room, then sighed
and shook his head. "I just hope she gets past the critical stage soon."

Deeply worried, Sun Yimin turned and went back into the patient's
room. He walked heavily now, and looked old and stooped. He stopped
at the door when he saw Yafen still leaning close to Wenting's pillow. He
didn't want to disturb the two bosom friends.

It was late autumn, when the days were short and the nights long. At
a little past five, the sky was already dark. The fall wind was rustling
through the leaves of the parasol tree. One, two, three . . . withered yellow leaves floated down in the wind.

Sun Yimin looked out of the window at these drifting, falling yellow
leaves. As he listened to their rasping sound, like weeping, like com-
plaining, he felt listless in a way he had never felt before. Of these two
accomplished ophthalmologists, one had already collapsed, and it was
not clear whether she would ever stand again; the other would soon be
leaving, and it was equally hard to say whether she would ever return.
These were two pillars supporting ophthalmology at this famous hospital. Without them, he felt his department would be like that parasol tree
in the autumn wind, steadily declining day by day.

## 5

Dimly, and murkily, Wenting felt she was going down a long road, a
road that had no beginning or end.

It wasn't a rugged mountain road. A mountain road, though steep
and difficult to climb, still has countless turns that make the climber feel
daring and adventurous. Neither was it a small path through the fields.

For that, though narrow and difficult underfoot, still offers the fragrance of rice blossoms, making a person feel carefree and happy. No, this road was a strip of sand, on which each step left an empty pit behind; this road was a pool of mud that sucked after one's every step; this road was an endless, horizonless wasteland. No trace of civilization as far as the eye could see; only deathly stillness. What a difficult road to follow, what exhausting work!

Take a rest; lie down. The sand is warm; the mud is soft. Let the great earth warm your freezing body; let the spring sun caress your weary muscles and bones. She seemed to hear the spirits of the nether world quietly calling her name: "Rest with us, Dr. Lu!"

Oh! It would be so nice to rest like that, to rest forever. To think of nothing, to know nothing. No worries, no sorrow, no work.

But wait. At the end of that long road, there were patients waiting for her. She seemed to see them—that patient who tossed and turned fitfully because of the pain in his eyes, that patient crying to himself silently because he faced the prospect of losing his sight. She could see them . . . pair after pair of worried, anxious eyes straining toward her, waiting for her, waiting for her to come. And she could hear those patients calling desperately, "Dr. Lu! Dr. Lu!"

This was a sacred call, an order that could not be refused. She lifted her two numb legs and continued to struggle along that long, long road. From her home to the hospital, from the examining room to the wards, from this appointment to that, she did the rounds, every day, every month, every year, walking, walking . . .

"Dr. Lu!"

Who was this? It seemed like the voice of Director Zhao, who headed the hospital. Yes, a phone call from him. She could remember herself putting down the phone at the head nurse's desk, giving her partner Yafen the patients' charts that she hadn't finished reading, and walking toward the office of the hospital director.

To get there, she had to pass through a small flower garden. She strode quickly across its gravel path without even noticing all the delicate white and yellow chrysanthemums blooming in a riot of color. Nor did she notice the burst of exquisite fragrance that came floating from the osmanthus tree. Still less did she notice the butterflies fluttering and playing among the crowds of flowers. She could think only of hurrying to the director's office, getting the errand done, and hurrying back to

her examining room. She had to examine seventeen patients all in on
morning and had only called seven so far. The next morning it was he
turn to be on duty in the ward, and there were still some clinic patien
waiting for their instructions.

She reached the door of the director's office very quickly and, with
out bothering to knock just pushed the door open and walked in. Or s
it seemed in her memory. Immediately, she found herself face to fac
with two visitors, a man and a woman, who were sitting on a couch. Sh
stopped unwittingly just inside the door, thinking she had come at th
wrong time. She turned her gaze on Director Zhao, who was sitting bac
in his leather swivel chair.

"Dr. Lu, please come in!" Director Zhao turned to smile in he
direction.

She entered and sat down in a leather-backed chair near th
window.

How bright that room was! Clean and spacious. And how quiet
was! It didn't have the confusion of footsteps, the babble of voices, th
crying of the young patients in the examining room. Sitting in that sur
shiny room, she had an unusual, and quite unfamiliar, sense of peac
and quiet.

The people sitting in the room were also most decorous and placid
Director Zhao always had the air of a scholar: an erect back, amiabl
face, smiling eyes behind gold wire-rimmed glasses, his hair combe
neatly. He was wearing a snow white shirt and shining black leathe
shoes with matching gray coat and trousers.

The man sitting on the sofa was tall, with graying temples, and wor
a pair of brown-colored dark glasses that prevented one from seeing h
eyes. But Wenting could tell that this person had eye trouble. He wa
leaning back on the couch, unconsciously fingering the cane beside hin
He seemed calm, collected, and self-assured.

The woman seated next to him seemed in her fifties, and was attrac
tive for her age. Her dyed black hair had been given a subtle wave by
hairdresser, was fluffy without being frivolously fashionable — in shor
was in very appropriate taste. She wore ordinary cadre clothes, but
was apparent on close examination that they were well tailored an
quite smart.

Wenting was aware that, from the time she had stood in the dooi
way, this woman's eyes had been fixed upon her, sizing her up. Ther

ere obvious misgivings reflected in the woman's face. She looked un-
sy and disappointed.

"Let me introduce you, Dr. Lu. This is Vice-minister Jiao Chengsi,
nd his wife, Comrade Qin Bo."

Vice-minister Jiao? A vice-minister? But why not? In her years of
rvice, she had treated the eyes of any number of ministers, secretaries,
irectors, and what have you. So she had hardly noticed Comrade Jiao's
tle, but out of habit had concentrated on his eyes. "What's wrong with
ose eyes? Is he losing his sight?"

"Where are you working now, Dr. Lu? In the clinic or the ward?"
irector Zhao was addressing her.

"I'm still in the clinic today, but tomorrow I'll be in the ward."

"Good." Director Zhao was smiling. "Vice-minister Jiao wants to
ave a cataract operation done here at our hospital."

So that was the problem. Director Zhao, with that one sentence, had
ven her an assignment. She began to question the patient. "Is it only
e eye?"

"Yes."

"Which one?"

"The left."

"You can't see at all with it?"

He nodded once.

"Have you had it examined at a hospital before?"

She could remember that he had then mentioned some hospital's
ame, and that she had stood up, preparing to cross over to look at his
e. But it seemed something had happened, and she had not been able
look at it. Why hadn't she been able to look at it? Now she remem-
red. It was Qin Bo, sitting at one side, who had very politely blocked
r way.

"Please be seated, Dr. Lu. Really, please do be seated. There's no
sh. If you wish to examine him, I think you'll want to wait and do it in
a appropriate examining room, anyway. Won't you?" Qin Bo laughed
d turned her head. "You know, Director Zhao, since the time my hus-
nd's eye trouble began, I've become half an ophthalmologist myself."

That's how it had happened that she had failed to diagnose Vice-
inister Jiao on the spot. But she *had* sat in that office for a long time.
hat had she talked about? Oh yes, Qin Bo had asked her a lot of ques-
ns, and very detailed questions they were.

"How many years have you worked at this hospital, Dr. Lu?"

How many years? She couldn't immediately say. She remembered only the year she had graduated, so that's how she answered. "I came in 1961."

"Ah, '61, let's see." Qin Bo was intently counting years on her fingers "That would be eighteen years."

What was she asking this for? Wenting heard Director Zhao say, "Dr Lu has a lot of experience in the operating room. She does marvel ous surgery."

Why was the director praising her like this in front of a patient. Why did he have to do that?

Qin Bo resumed her questioning. "You don't seem to be in very good health, do you, Dr. Lu?"

What did she mean by that? Wenting treated others all day long and very seldom paid any attention to her own health. Their hospital' health clinic didn't even have a file on her, and never before had a high level official asked about the condition of her health. Why was this visitor whom she was meeting for the first time suddenly so interested in he physical health? She remembered hesitating a moment and then saying "My health is good."

Director Zhao again spoke in her behalf. "She's one of the strongest and healthiest doctors we have. I have the impression, Dr. Lu, that you haven't missed a day's work for many years. Isn't that right?"

Wenting did not answer. Missed a day's work or not, healthy or not what did that have to do with this Madame Vice-minister? She could only remember feeling very apprehensive that Yafen would not be able to handle all of their patients by herself.

The lady was staring at her. She laughed again and asked, "Are you thoroughly confident with the cataract removal procedure, Dr. Lu?"

Thoroughly confident? How could one answer that? It was true that in all the countless times she had performed cataract operations, noth ing unexpected had given her trouble. But of course the possibility al ways existed that something could go wrong. If the patient were not to cooperate, or if the anaesthesia were carelessly administered, it was even possible for the fluids of the eye to escape.

She couldn't remember whether she had answered or not; she only remembered that pair of eyes, wrapped in wrinkles — big, probing, un trusting eyes — gazing at her without blinking. She had found it difficul to bear. She had dealt with all kinds of patients, and she felt that the most difficult people were these wives of high officials. After running into them many times, though, she had learned to take them in stride. Now, while she was trying to think of some tactful way to answer, it seemed in her memory that Vice-minister Jiao had shifted impatiently on the couch and turned his head toward Qin Bo. At this, his wife had stopped talking and diverted her eyes from Wenting.

How had this awkward conversation ended? She couldn't recall. Oh yes, Yafen had come running, had stuck her head inside the door and called, "Dr. Lu, that Grandfather Zhang you were scheduled to see has come, and he won't leave until he sees you."

She could remember Qin Bo saying immediately, and very politely, "You are busy, Dr. Lu. Please go ahead. Don't let us keep you."

She stood up and left that bright, spacious office, now feeling that the atmosphere inside was stifling enough to choke a person.

# 6

Director Zhao Tianhui came hurrying to the internal medicine ward just before getting off work.

"Professor Sun! Dr. Lu's health has always been fine ... how could she suddenly fall so seriously ill?" Zhao, with his hands in the pockets of his white medical coat, was talking to Sun Yimin as they walked toward the patient's room. He was eight years younger than Sun, but looked much younger than that. His voice was much deeper.

"It's a warning signal!" Zhao said, shaking his head. "The middle-aged doctors are the mainstay of the hospital. Their work load is the heaviest, and their own family responsibilities are also at a peak. Their health deteriorates year by year, and if things continue like this they're all going to fall ill one by one. You may be the chief of staff and I may be the director, but if that happens we're both useless. How big is Dr. Lu's family? How many rooms do they have to live in?"

He glanced sideways at the depressed, worried-looking Sun Yimin.

"What? Four people and one room? Yes ... yes ... yes ... so that's the situation. What's her salary? *How* much? $37.70 a month? Just look at that! No wonder people say you're better off taking up the barber's razor than the surgeon's scapel. It's true! Hunh? Last year we had a salary adjustment? How come hers wasn't raised?"

"'The gruel is meager and the monks are many.' There wasn't enough to go around," Sun said bitterly.

"This really is a problem. I'd like to ask you, Professor Sun, if you'd talk this over with our Party branch and make an investigation of middle-aged ophthalmologists — their working situations, salaries, home situations, and housing — and put together a report for me."

"Would it do any good? I remember they wanted a report like that when we held the sciences meetings. The report was handed in and nothing happened." Sun was polite, but firm, in his opposition. He stared at the floor, not looking at the man beside him.

"My dear Professor Sun, you don't want to become the top complainer, do you? Come now, it's always better to have it on paper than not to. I can take it to the Municipal Party Committee, or to the Health Department . . . I can bow and scrape before all the little gods . . . beg here, bully there, and one way or another get the complaint heard. The Central Committee has been ordering all over the place that we take special care of our human talent, that we carry out the policy to make amends to intellectuals, that we raise the salaries of scientists and technicians. We can't let this all turn to empty talk once it gets down to the lower levels! The Municipal Committee meeting decided two days ago that we must pay more attention to our middle-aged cadres. So I still think we can get somewhere with this."

Zhao Tianhui did not stop talking until he had stridden into Wenting's room, pulling Sun Yimin by the arm.

Fu Jiajie stood up as Zhao Tianhui, passing by him with a wave of the hand, headed straight to the patient's bedside and bent over her. As he scrutinized her face, he reached for the case record from the attending physician. He shed his hospital director's demeanor as he stepped into the role of doctor.

Zhao Tianhui was a nationally famous thoracic surgeon. At Liberation, he had finished his studies abroad and returned to devote his special skills to the new People's Republic. Politically active, he was regarded in the 1950s as a model who was "both red and expert." He joined the Party, and later was appointed director of the hospital. Having taken on this responsibility, he came to feel the pressures of heavy administrative duties and interminable meetings. These pressures caused him to lose all contact with patients except in important cases involving group consultations. Then came ten years living in the "cow shed" and sweeping the courtyard, which of course gave him no chance to develop his specialty. In the retrenchment of the past three years, he again found himself the director of a hospital, every day sorting through a small mountain of problems. He had no time or energy left for the operating theater.

But now he had come to Dr. Lu's room in person, clearly for the purpose of seeing this patient. The other doctors in the medical ward all gathered around, standing behind him in a circle, quietly observing his bedside manner.

They were somewhat disappointed. He looked at the patient's case record and her electrocardiograms, looked at the fluorescent screen of the heart monitor, and then merely urged that close watch be kept for any changes in the heart scan or any signs of infection. He then turned to Sun and asked, "Has her husband come?" Sun brought Fu Jiajie forward and made introductions, causing Zhao to realize now that this was Dr. Lu's husband. Looking him over, and noticing at once his balding head and wrinkled brow, Zhao wondered why this attractive middle-aged man was already losing hair. If he wasn't taking very good care of his own health, naturally he wouldn't know how to care for his wife.

"You must take great pains to care for her," Zhao Tianhui said as he shook hands with Fu Jiajie. "Dr. Lu needs absolutely quiet bed rest. You mustn't let her move. She'll need someone to help her turn over and to manage the bedpan. She'll need someone to nurse her twenty-four hours a day. Where do you work? You'll have to tell the leaders in your unit that you can't go to work for a while. And, of course, you can't manage this all by yourself. You'll need somebody to relieve you. Is there anybody else in your family who could do it?"

Jiajie shook his head. "We have two children who are both still quite young."

Zhao Tianhui turned toward Sun. "Can the Ophthalmology Department spare someone?"

"For one or two days we could, of course," Sun replied. "But not for an extended period."

"Let's first take care of the situation immediately before us, shall we?"

Zhao Tianhui turned again to gaze at Dr. Lu's pale, thin face. He still couldn't comprehend that this vigorous woman could have fallen ill like this.

A thought suddenly occurred to him. Was it possible that she had been too nervous about doing the surgery on Vice-minister Jiao? No, out of the question! Dr. Lu was no novice, and even with novices how often does the tension of an operation bring on a heart attack? Heart attacks can come unexpectedly — there doesn't have to be any particular precipitating cause.

He tried to rid himself of this idea, but couldn't — not quite. For some reason Vice-minister Jiao's operation and Dr. Lu's illness seemed to be connected. He even felt some regret at having recommended her so forcefully at that first meeting. Vice-minister Jiao's wife had been dead set against her at first.

"May I ask you something, Dr. Zhao? Is Dr. Lu a deputy director?" Qin Bo had asked this question after Lu Wenting had left that day.

"No."

"Well, then, is she a physician in charge?"

"No."

"Party member?"

"No, not that either."

"My dear comrade!" Qin Bo had said, none too politely. "We are all members of the Communist Party. Forgive me for speaking so frankly, but to let an ordinary doctor perform an operation on Vice-minister Jiao! Have you perhaps not given this due consideration?"

She was interrupted when Jiao deliberately thumped his cane on the ground. The vice-minister turned his head toward his wife and said angrily, "What are you talking about, Qin Bo? That's up to the hospital! It doesn't matter who does it!"

Far from giving in, Qin Bo turned and leveled a broadside at Jiao Chengsi. "I don't mind saying I disapprove of your indifferent attitude! You are being irresponsible toward your eyes! You need your health for the Revolution! We must be responsible toward the Revolution, and toward the Party!"

Seeing these two esteemed leaders about to lay into each other, Director Zhao stepped forward to mediate. "Please trust us, Comrade Qin Bo," he said with a smile. "Dr. Lu may have no special titles, but she's a first-rate ophthalmologist. She's fully competent in cataract surgery. You can count on it!"

"I am not upset, Director Zhao, and I'm not merely quibbling in behalf of Vice-minister Jiao." Qin Bo paused to sigh. "When I was at cadre school during the Cultural Revolution, one old comrade there also had cataracts. They wouldn't let him return to Beijing, so he had an operation at a local hospital. You know what happened? His eyeball fell out before the operation was over! My good Director Zhao! Vice-minister Jiao was locked up by the Gang of Four for seven long years. He hasn't been back at work very long. He simply can't lose his eyesight!"

"It won't happen. Our hospital very rarely has such accidents."

Qin Bo pondered this for a moment, then took up the cudgel again: "Would it be possible to ask Chief Surgeon Sun to perform the operation on Vice-minister Jiao personally?"

Zhao Tianhui shook his head and laughed. "Chief Surgeon Sun is almost seventy," he said. "His own eyesight is not very good, and he hasn't performed surgery for many years. His present duties are in academic research and supervision of this group of young and middle-aged doctors. He also teaches occasionally. To have him perform the surgery would, in all honesty, be much riskier than letting Dr. Lu do it."

"Well then, what about asking Dr. Guo to do it?"

"Dr. Guo?" Zhao looked startled. It seemed the Vice-minister's wife had done some homework on his ophthalmologists.

"Guo Ruqing," she prompted.

"Dr. Guo has left the country," Zhao replied with a shrug.

Qin Bo still would not let the matter drop. "When's he coming back?" she asked impatiently.

"He's not coming back."

"Why not?" Qin Bo asked, wide-eyed.

Zhao shook his head and sighed. "Dr. Guo's wife has family overseas. Her father owned a general store in Southeast Asia, and he died not long ago. Two months ago, the Guos applied to leave the country to carry on their family business. The permission was granted, and they left."

"He gave up medicine to be a storekeeper," observed Jiao Chengsi regretfully. "This kind of thing makes no sense."

"It's become a common pattern in the health field, and our hospital's no exception. We have quite a few who've been approved to leave, and more in the process of applying. And they're all experts in their fields."

"These people! What could have gotten into them?" Qin Bo was quite indignant.

Waving his cane in agitation, Jiao Chengsi turned toward Zhao Tianhui. "In the early 1950s, you intellectuals braved hell and high water to come back to China and serve the new society. And *now* look — by the end of the 1970s, our own generation of intellectuals are fleeing to foreign countries. The lesson in this is formidable."

"How can we let this keep happening?" It was Qin Bo again. "As I see it, we have to work harder on people's thought and politics. My dear comrade! Look how the status of intellectuals has improved since the smashing of the Gang of Four! And as the Four Modernizations take hold, living and working conditions will get better and better. Now won't they?"

"Of course, and when our Party committee discussed it, that was our conclusion, too," Zhao said. "Before Dr. Guo left, I went twice on behalf of the Party to speak with him, urging him to stay in every way I knew. But it was useless."

Qin Bo wished to make a further comment, but Jiao Chengsi shook his cane to stop her. "Director Zhao," he said. "I didn't come here bent on finding some famous specialist professor. I have confidence in your hospital . . . or perhaps you might say, I have a special affection for it. A few years ago I had a cataract in my right eye and it was operated on quite successfully here at your hospital."

"Well then! Who did that operation?" Zhao asked.

"I'm sorry to say I don't know her name, and in fact never did," answered Jiao regretfully.

"That's easy enough! One look at your medical record will tell us."

Zhao picked up the telephone. He was thinking that if he could find that doctor, then Jiao's wife would be satisfied.

"Don't bother," said Jiao, waving his hand at Director Zhao. "You won't find anything. That operation had to be done right in the clinic, so no records exist. All I can remember is a woman with a southern accent."

"Hmm. That's not so easy," said Zhao, putting down the phone. "We have a lot of women with southern accents here. Dr. Lu herself is a southerner. Why not let her do it?"

As Qin Bo helped Vice-minister Jiao to his feet, the two finally accepted Director Zhao's recommendation that Dr. Lu Wenting do the operation.

Could it have been this operation that had triggered her heart attack? Zhao Tianhui reflected on this, then shook his head. No, impossible. She had done this operation hundreds of times and could not possibly have been nervous. Besides, he had gone to see her the day o the operation and had watched as she approached the operating table. She had looked calm, unhurried and fully confident. Her spirits had been good.

Zhao Tianhui once again turned his concerned gaze to rest on Lu Wenting's face. He felt that Dr. Lu, as she lay there on the border between life and death, still looked calm, as if she were suffering no pain, but merely sleeping peacefully in the soft warmth of her dreams.

## 7

She had always been calm. Everyone who had worked in the ophthalmology department knew that it was practically impossible to make Dr. Lu angry.

Almost anyone else would have talked back under Qin Bo's nitpicking and condescension. Or, if they hadn't, anger would have shown on their faces, or at least they would have walked away steaming inside. But Lu Wenting? She left that office as calm as a mirror, as if nothing unusual had happened. Whether or not she did an operation always depended on the willingness of the patient: if he was willing, she would do it; if not, she wouldn't. What was all the fuss about?

"I see they want you to do surgery again," Yafen had said when Wenting returned. "Who's the big official this time?"

"It hasn't been decided whether I'll do it."

"Okay, but now you've got to hurry," said Yafen, pulling her along. That old grandfather you've scheduled is really hard to handle. I simply can't get through to him. He's determined not to have the operation."

"That's no good. He's come such a long way, and spent so much on travel expenses. We'd be irresponsible not to cure him if we can."

"Right, so you go and convince him."

As they returned to the clinic, and crossed through the waiting room full of patients, some who recognized them stood up to offer greetings. The two doctors smiled all around, nodding their heads and greeting the patients. Wenting had gone into her own examination room, and was quietly answering a young patient's questions, when suddenly a loud voice called from behind her, "Dr. Lu!"

The bellowing sound attracted the gaze of both the doctor and her patient. What they saw was a tall, sturdy man groping his way toward the examination room. He was wearing a green cotton shirt and pants, and his head was wrapped in a white towel; his shoulders were broad, his girth ample, and his age perhaps something over fifty. His unusual height alone was enough to attract attention, but when added to that voice — people on both sides made way for him. His sight was almost gone, so he was unaware that so many people were looking at him. He merely felt his way, with two outstretched hands, in the direction of Dr. Lu's voice.

Wenting hurriedly turned to meet him, reaching out her hands to assist him. "Please sit down, Grandfather Zhang."

"No, ma'am, you stay there, Dr. Lu … Me, I'm … here to tell you something."

"Then tell, but sit down first." Supporting the old man with her hand, Lu Wenting led him to sit down on the bench.

"Well, Dr. Lu, it's like this. I've been here a good many days now, and I've been thinking. I think I'll be on my way now and come again some other day …"

"You can't do that, Grandfather Zhang. You've come so far to get to Beijing, and spent so much money getting here …"

"Boy, haven't I, though!" Old Zhang interrupted, slapping his knees as he prepared to expand on this topic. "I was thinking I better go back and work the fall, earn myself some more work points. Don't think my eyes can't hack it, ma'am. I can still bumble along. The guy who makes the work assignments in our brigade is nice to me. So I made up my mind to go back, ma'am, but thought I just had to come let you know. These eyes of mind musta given you a darn sight of worry!"

The old man had suffered from an ulcerated cornea for several years and the scar tissue had grown very thick. Everything he had tried for it had failed. Then Wenting, while making the rounds with a mobile clinic in the countryside, had examined him and recommended a cornea transplant. It was for this operation that he had come.

"Grandfather Zhang, your son has spent a lot of money to send you here for treatment. We would feel wrong letting you go back now without treatment."

"Nah! Your heart's good as gold, ma'am!"

Dr. Lu laughed, patted the old peasant's arm and said, "Once your eyes are cured, you won't need anybody to be nice to you in work assignments. With a good body like yours, you can go on working another twenty years."

The old man laughed and answered immediately. "You're darn right! If my lousy eyes'd be good, nothing'd stop me!"

"Then let's go ahead with it," Wenting said with a laugh.

Old Zhang lowered his voice. "Dr. Lu, begging your pardon ma'am, let me give it to you straight. It's the money's got me worried. I'm using all my own here, and can't pay these Beijing hotels any more."

Wenting was momentarily at a loss, but then said, "Don't you worry, Grandfather Zhang. I've already checked the appointment book, and you're next in line. In these next couple of days, as soon as we have the donor cornea, we can get to you right away. All right?"

The old man was persuaded. Dr. Lu saw him out to the hall, but as he returned, her way was blocked by a pretty girl about twelve or thirteen years old.

This child was a real beauty. Round red cheeks, black eyebrows, a straight, high nose, and red lips. Her eyelids were wet with tears that were falling drop by drop down her face. The only problem was that one eye slanted outward. She was wearing white hospital pajamas and calling, timidly, "Dr. Lu! Dr. Lu!"

"Wang Xiaoman! What are you doing here?" Wenting went over to her. She had admitted this young patient only the day before.

"I'm scared. I want to go home." Wang Xiaoman started wiping her tears. "I'm not going to have the operation."

Wenting put her arms around the child's shoulders. "Now, now. Tell your auntie. Why don't you want to have the operation?"

"I'm scared it will hurt."

"Oh, now don't be silly. It's not going to hurt. I'll give you some anesthesia when the time comes. I promise it won't hurt at all." Wenting patted her head, and bent over carefully to look straight into the child's face, as if she were getting a close look at a delicate art object. "Look, it's only this eye," she said with a touch of regret. "Just wait till I've straightened it out for you, just like the other one. It'll make you look nice! Now hurry back to the ward and behave yourself, you hear? The hospital doesn't permit people to run around as they please."

Wang Xiaoman wiped her eyes dry and left, allowing Wenting to return to her examining table and go on calling patients' names.

There had been many patients the last few days, and today was no different. She had to make up for the time she had lost in the director's office. She forgot about Vice-minister Jiao, about Qin Bo, and even about herself, as she saw her patients one by one. Finding out what their problems were, leading them into the examining room, writing prescriptions, setting up new appointments, one patient after the other.

"Your telephone, Dr. Lu," a nurse came running in to say.

"Just a minute, please," Lu Wenting said to her patient as she headed to pick up the receiver.

"Your Jiajia is sick. She had a fever last night." It was the woman from the nursery. "We know you're very busy, so we didn't want to tell you. We took her to the emergency clinic, and they gave her an injection. But the fever still hasn't gone down. She's been moaning and calling for her mother. Can you come?"

"All right, I'll come." She put down the phone.

But she didn't go to the nursery. With so many patients, how could she just pick up and walk away? She lifted the phone again and dialed Fu Jiajie's office number. They told her he was in a meeting. All she could do was hang up.

"Who was that? Something the matter?" Yafen asked.

"No, nothing," she answered. She was thinking that it would probably still be all right if she finished seeing today's patients before going to the nursery. She sat down again at her examining desk and continued with her work. At first the image of Jiajia calling for her stuck in her mind. But this image was later replaced by pair after pair of her patients' eyes. Only when she had seen them all did she finally hurry off to the nursery.

<h1 style="text-align:center">8</h1>

"What took you so long, Dr. Lu?" complained the woman at the nursery.

Wenting hurried into the nursery's infirmary, and there saw little Jiajia, lying alone and cheerless on a small bed. Her cheeks were flushed with fever, her lips parted. Her nostrils fluttered with labored breathing, and her eyes were shut tightly.

"Jiajia, Mommy is here." Wenting bent over the bed.

Jiajia's little head moved on the pillow. She cried out hoarsely, "Mommy — I want to go home."

"Let's go home, then." She quickly took the child in her arms and headed back to the hospital's emergency child care clinic.

"Pneumonia," the pediatrician said sympathetically. "She'll need to be carefully nursed for a few days, Dr. Lu."

Wenting nodded her head, got Jiajia an injection, picked up her medicine, and left the clinic.

It was noontime, and the hospital was quieting down. The clinic patients had left, and the inpatients were sleeping; the doctors, nurses, and staff had all gone home or found somewhere else for a nap.

The big courtyard seemed empty and lonely. Only a few tireless sparrows kept chirping in the parasol tree, enjoying their freedom, flying to and fro. Had these creatures of Mother Nature always been here, gracing humanity with their presence amid the overgrowth of buildings, the air pollution, and the raucous noise of the city? Wenting was surprised to realize that she had been rushing around this hospital every day without ever noticing these birds.

She stood in the middle of the compound holding her child, not knowing where to go. Back to the nursery? She thought of her sick child lying all alone there, and couldn't bear it. Take her home, then? But she had to return to the hospital in the afternoon, and who would watch the child?

She stood blankly for a moment, then, hardening her heart, headed toward the nursery.

Jiajia, who was lying on her shoulder with her head hanging down, immediately began to wail. "I won't go to the nursery. I won't go . . ."

"Jiajia, be good, behave . . ."

"No, no, I want to go home!" Jiajia started kicking wildly.

"All right, all right, we'll go home." Wenting turned in the direction of home.

The route home from the hospital led through a bustling commercial street. There were newly painted billboards advertising fashionable clothes, attractive window displays on both sides of the street, and peasants lined up along the street selling their live chickens, fish, melon seeds, peanuts and other hard-to-get farm products on the free market. But Wenting didn't give any of this a second glance. They had been short on cash ever since the two children had come along, so high-quality goods were of no concern to her. Holding Jiajia in her arms, and worrying about Yuanyuan, she just hurried along.

It was almost one o'clock when she got home. "How come you're so late, Mom?" pouted Yuanyuan.

"Can't you see your little sister is sick?" Wenting snapped. She hurried to take off Jiajia's clothes, put her in bed and pulled the covers over her.

Yuanyuan was standing beside the table. "Hurry and make lunch, Ma," he said anxiously. "Or I'll be late."

Annoyed and distracted, Wenting lost her patience. "Rush, rush, rush! All you can do is rush people!"

Now Yuanyuan felt, in addition to his anxiety over lunch, that he had been wronged. His eyes reddened and tears began to well in them.

Wenting, too busy to give him attention, went out of the room and opened their coal stove. The coal briquette that had been shut inside all morning had already gone completely out; it would take time to get a fire going. She took the cover off a pot, and opened her cupboard. But nothing was there, not even leftovers.

She turned and went back into the room where her son was still standing and looking hurt. She felt guilty. The child was innocent. Why was she venting her anger on him?

Her share of the domestic responsibilities had increased steadily in recent years. During the Cultural Revolution, Fu Jiajie's laboratory had been closed down by the "rebels." His research project had been cancelled. He had become a member of the "eight-to-nine and two-to-three corps," meaning that he went to work at eight A.M. and left at nine, went again at two P.M. and left at three. He had nothing to do all day. All his intelligence, energy, and knowledge went into the household chores. He prepared three meals a day, and even learned to sew trousers and knit sweaters. But at least this freed Wenting from these cares. Now, with the smashing to the Gang of Four and the new policies to push scientific research, Fu Jiajie had become an important person. His research projects were given high priority, and he became frantically busy. Hence the household chores fell in great part upon Wenting's shoulders.

Every day at noon, rain or shine, Wenting rushed between the hospital and her home, exchanging a scalpel for a chopping knife and a white coat for an apron. She had fifty minutes to get the stove going and put a meal on the table. This would allow Yuanyuan to get back to school on time, Jiajie to race back to his lab on his bicycle, and her to get back to the hospital to don her white coat, sit down in the examination room, and greet her first patient.

When something came up, as it had today, the whole family faced the possibility of going hungry. She sighed, took some loose change from a drawer and said, "Here, Yuanyuan. Go buy yourself a sesame seed roll."

Yuanyuan took the money and headed outside, then turned and asked, "What're you going to eat, Ma?"

"I'm not hungry."

"I'll buy you one, too."

Yuanyuan soon returned with a sesame seed roll for her, then headed back to school, eating his own as he walked.

As she chewed the cold, crusty roll, Wenting stared blankly at their 130-square-foot room.

She and her husband had not been fussy about their living conditions. They had lived here ever since they had been married. They had no sofa, no wardrobe, no new table or chairs, not even new bedding. They had just taken their old bedding, put it together, and started their new life.

Their quilts may have been thin, but their bookshelf was packed full. Old Mother Chen in their compound said, "A pair of bookworms! How will they manage?!" But they found their days very pleasant. One room was enough to rest one's body; two sets of clothes were enough to fend off the cold; three meals of plain food was enough to satisfy hunger. It was enough.

What they valued was the time they had together. Every night, two "study areas" were set up inside this humble room. Wenting occupied the single, three-drawered desk, and, with the help of foreign language dictionaries, read through foreign works on ophthalmology, jotting down useful material in her notebooks. Fu Jiajie, spreading his reference books out all over the bed, bent over a pile of boxes and researched the tensile strength of metals. The mischievous children in the compound who came to spy on the newlyweds always found this same evening scene.

They worked deep into the night, turning one working day into two, and without even a notion of overtime pay. On summer nights, their neighbors would relax in the cool of the courtyard, sitting with their fragrant tea, their round rush fans, the gentle evening breeze, the bright stars, the interesting news, the pleasures of idle talk. But none of this could draw the two bookworms from their stuffy room.

Then two new lives, one after the other, came into this small room.

What lovable little things Yuanyuan and Jiajia were! Their arrival brought the small home great joy, but also brought confusion and calamity. A child's cot had to be squeezed into the room, and later changed for a single bed. There was almost no room to turn around in. Drying clothes were fluttering everywhere, while bottles and jars piled up. The crying, laughing, squabbling noise of children shattered the peace and quiet.

Jiajie was very considerate. In an effort to give his wife a retreat from this world of bottles and cans, crying and shouting, so that she could work at night as before, he hung up a piece of green plastic and pulled the three-drawer desk behind it. But it wasn't that easy. When Yuanyuan started primary school, he was given priority in the use of the one valuable desk. Only after his homework was done and the space vacated could Wenting open her notebooks and the medical books she had borrowed from the library. Father Jiajie was last in line.

Wenting was nibbling on her cold sesame roll and looking at the small alarm clock on the window sill — 1:05, 1:10, 1:15. What was she going to do? Did she have to go to work? Tomorrow she had to do the rounds, and there were still many things to be taken care of at the clinic. But who would take care of Jiajia? Should she call Jiajie again? There was no phone nearby. And even if there were, there was no assurance that she would be able to reach him. Besides, he had lost ten years' time. She shouldn't be making demands on his time now. She couldn't expect him to ask for leave again.

Tight furrows appeared on her brow; she was at a loss.

Perhaps the one error of her life had been her marriage. Didn't people always say that marriage was the burial of love? At the time she had been so naive as to think that while this might be true for others, it could never be true for her. If they had thought more carefully about whether they really had the strength to get married, and to shoulder the burden of a family, they might have decided not to take up this heavy cross that would make their passage through life so much more difficult!

The alarm clock went on ticking, unsympathetically. It was already 1:20. There seemed nothing she could do but go and look for Old Mother Chen and ask her help. Mother Chen was an activist in the neighborhood, always willing and eager to help others. Wenting had taken advantage of her many times in the past under similar circumstances. She always insisted on helping for free, in fact would not take compensation in any form. This made Wenting feel guilty, so she did her best not to bother the old lady.

"Just put your mind at ease and go back to work, Dr. Lu!" said Old Mother Chen.

Wenting arranged Jiajia's favorite books and building blocks next to her pillow, instructed Ma Chen in the administration of the medicine, and then hurried off to the hospital.

When she sat down at the examination desk, it was on her mind to ask the head nurse to cut down her afternoon caseload because she had to return home early. But when the patients started arriving, she completely forgot about this.

Director Zhao telephoned her to say that Vice-minister Jiao would be entering the hospital the next day, and that she should make preparations for the operation.

Qin Bo called her twice in a row, inquiring as to what special steps were needed before the operation, what matters the patient and the patient's family needed to cooperate in, and what sort of mental and practical preparation was necessary.

She was hard put to answer all this. She had performed this operation over a hundred times, and almost never had anyone ask her such questions. She could only answer, "There's nothing you particularly need to worry about."

"Mm . . . really? My dear comrade, *everything* requires preparation, doesn't it? And it's always good to get well prepared mentally, isn't it? Wouldn't it be better if I came over so we could sit down together and go over everything carefully?"

Wenting felt obliged to put a stop to this before it went any further. "I have a lot of other patients here," she said.

"Then we'll talk tomorrow at the hospital."

"Fine." Lu Wenting returned to her examination desk and continued working until she had seen her last patient. By this time, dusk had fallen.

She hurried home. As she passed under the window she could hear Ma Chen improvising a song for Jiajia:

> Jiajia's growing
> Year by year.
> She'll soon be
> An engineer!

Jiajia was laughing. Wenting's heart was full of gratitude as she hurried inside and thanked Ma Chen. When she felt the child's brow, and knew the fever had gone down a bit, she finally began to relax.

She gave the child an injection. Then her husband came home, and after him came two guests — Yafen and her husband, Dr. Liu Xueyao.

"I've come to say goodbye," said Yafen.

"Where are you going?" asked Wenting.

"We applied to go to Canada, and our passports have been approved." Yafen had cast her eyes down, and was looking at the floor as she spoke.

Wenting had known that Liu Xueyao's father practiced medicine in Canada. She had also heard that the couple were receiving letters urging them to come to Canada. But, strangely, it had never occurred to her that they really would go.

"How long will you be away? When will you come back?" she asked.

"It's possible we may never come back." Xueyao tried to seem casual as he shrugged his shoulders.

Wenting gazed at her good friend. "Yafen, why didn't you tell me sooner?"

"I was afraid you'd try to persuade me not to go . . . and maybe even more afraid it'd work." Yafen was still avoiding Wenting's gaze, staring at the floor as if she were trying to see through it.

Xueyao pulled package after package of prepared food out of the bag he was carrying, finally producing a bottle of wine. "You haven't made dinner yet, I hope?" he asked in high spirits. "Perfect. I intend to borrow a precious corner of this esteemed household in order to hold a farewell banquet."

## 9

It was a tearful banquet.

Jiajia was sleeping and Yuanyuan had gone to the neighbors' to watch television. Liu Xueyao lifted his glass and, looking at the wine in it, struggled with his strong and complex emotions. "Life . . . life is so unpredictable. My father is a doctor, but he also was well educated in the classics. I loved all kinds of poetry when I was young, and was sure I wanted to be a writer. But I was destined to follow my father in his profession and suddenly it is thirty years later! My father has always been a cautious man. His lifetime motto has been 'excessive talk is bound to bring suffering.' Unfortunately, I've never mastered this piece of wisdom. I love to talk, and to say what I think. I've always managed to put my foot in my mouth, and that's why no political movement has ever passed me by. When I graduated in '57, I only barely escaped the 'rightist' label. With the Cultural Revolution — another layer of skin lost, of course. I'm Chinese, and though I'm no political paragon, I do want with all my heart to see my country grow strong and prosperous. I never thought I'd be leaving my country before I reached fifty."

"Do you have to go?" Wenting asked softly.

"Right. Why indeed do we have to go? I've argued that with myself over and over." Xueyao waved his half-filled glass of deep red wine and said, "I've already lived more than half my life. How much longer will I live? Why do I wish my ashes to be scattered over foreign soil?"

They were all silent as they listened to Xueyao's soliloquy. But he suddenly stopped talking. He stretched his neck and drained his half-full glass of wine at a gulp. "I deserve your scorn," he blurted out. "I'm an unworthy son of the Chinese people."

"Oh, come on! Don't talk like that. We all know what you've been through these past years." Jiajie poured him some more wine and said, "The bad times are behind us, and happy days are on the way. Everything's going to get better."

"That I can believe," Xueyao was nodding. "But when will the good times come to *our* house? When will they come to my daughter? How can I keep waiting?"

"Let's change the subject." Wenting guessed that the reason Xueyao felt he had to leave the country had to do with his only daughter, and that he now felt awkward making the point any clearer. She headed off the conversation by saying, "I never drink, but with you two about to leave, I feel like drinking a toast in your honor!"

"No," Xueyao said, putting his hand over her glass. "I should drink in *your* honor! You're a mainstay of our hospital! You're the new flowering of Chinese medical science!"

"You're drunk!" said Wenting, smiling.

"No, I'm not."

Yafen, who hadn't said anything for a long time, also raised her glass. "I'll drink to you with all my heart! To our twenty-year friendship, and to our ophthalmology expert of the future."

"Heavens! What are you two saying? What's all this nonsense?"

"Nonsense?" Xueyao did indeed seem tipsy, and spoke indignantly. "Someone like you, who lives in such poor housing, who works hard and puts up with complaints, who doesn't seek fame or position, doesn't seek reward, just devotes herself to being a doctor—you are a true servant of the people, a true 'ox for the children.'[3] You eat weeds and give milk. That's what Lu Xun said, isn't it? Isn't it, Fu Jiajie?"

Jiajie, who was silently sipping wine on his own, nodded his head.

"I'm not so unusual," said Wenting, still smiling. "There are people like me everywhere."

"And that's why the Chinese are such a great people!" Xueyao downed another glass of wine.

Yafen looked at Jiajia, who was fast asleep on the bed, and sighed a bit mournfully. "That's right, rather than delay in treating others, you put off treatment of your own child's illness."

Xueyao stood up and poured wine for everyone. "A perfect example of sacrificing oneself for the good of others."

"What *is* this, anyway? Are you two out to get me or something?" Wenting smiled and pointed at Jiajie. "Just ask him. I'm as selfish as they come. I send my husband to the kitchen, I turn my children into street orphans, I bring disaster to the whole family. If the truth were known, I'm an incompetent wife and incompetent mother."

"You're a competent doctor!" Xueyao fairly shouted.

Jiajie drank another mouthful of wine, then put down his glass and said, "On this score, I bear your hospital a little grudge. Doctors have homes, too, and also children. And doctor's children also get sick. Why doesn't anybody ever worry about that?"

"Jiajie," Xueyao interrupted, "if I were Director Zhao, I'd give you a medal . . . and one to Yuanyuan and Jiajia, too. You are the ones who make the sacrifices so that our hospital can have such a great doctor . . ."

"I don't want a medal," Jiajie cut in, "and I don't want any praise. I only wish your hospital would understand how hard it is to be married to a doctor. Even after an ordinary day, she comes home so tired she can

---

3. From the poem "Zichao" (Self satire) written in 1932 by the great modern writer Lu Xun (1881–1936). Two lines from the poem are widely quoted in China, and the official interpretation, originally put forward by Mao Zedong, would translate something like:

> Frowning, I scorn the slings of masters;
> Bowing, I serve as an ox for children.

According to the Maoist interpretation, the lines mean that Lu Xun wishes to oppose the ruling classes and serve the oppressed. Although Lu Xun did have such sympathies, the lines read more naturally, in context, to mean that he enjoys retreating from the fray of the public arena to play with his child at home.

hardly lift a knife to chop vegetables. And when she has to go out with the mobile clinic, or when some emergency call immediately makes her drop everything and run—just think about it! If I don't go to the kitchen, who will? From that point of view, the Cultural Revolution wasn't so bad: it gave me time for so much good training!"

"Yafen always said we should take off your 'bookworm' label," said Xueyao, patting him on the shoulder and laughing. "You not only can do research into the advanced technology of spacecraft, but also can do miracles in the kitchen! You're the mature product of a generation of communism! Who says the Cultural Revolution didn't accomplish great things?"

Jiajie usually didn't drink, and today, when he did take a little, his face turned red. He pulled on Xueyao's sleeve and chuckled. "That's right, the Cultural Revolution was a great revolution to reform all people! Wasn't I reformed into a house-husband? If you don't believe it, just ask Wenting. There's nothing I can't do. What can't I do?"

Their bitter joking pained Wenting, but she couldn't stop them. On this particular occasion, these jokes seemed the only way to ease the sorrow and dispel the gloom. When she saw Jiajie smiling in her direction, she could only force herself to laugh and say, "The only thing he can't do is stitch the soles of cloth shoes. If he could, Yuanyuan wouldn't always be yelling for me to buy him sneakers."

"Now you're asking too much!" said Xueyao with sudden seriousness. "No matter how reformed he gets, he shouldn't have to run around stitching soles like an old woman from the countryside."

"If the Gang of Four hadn't been smashed, who's to say I wouldn't have taken shoes along to stitch at the mass criticism meetings at our institute?" Jiajie said. "Think about it. If things had continued that way—with science, technology, all knowledge destroyed—wouldn't sole stitching be the only thing left?" Jiajie was becoming more and more animated. "Too bad you're leaving, Xueyao. You've got so many good connections." He patted Xueyao on the back. "I hear that housekeepers' salaries are pretty high these days. What if I ask you to keep your ears open for anyone who wants to hire a male housekeeper?"

"You can do that even when I'm gone," said Xueyao, patting Jiajie's hand. "Now they have a paper called *Marketplace News* that carries employment ads. Why don't you give it a try?"

"Great!" said Jiajie, straightening his glasses on his nose. "I can see it now: 'University graduate, good command of two foreign languages, skilled in the culinary arts, sews, washes, can do every sort of chore — light or heavy, men's or women's. Good physical condition, pleasant disposition, industrious and brave, won't shirk or talk back.' And the last item: 'salary negotiable.' Ha-ha!"

Yafen had been sitting silently at one side, not eating or drinking. Seeing everyone laugh, she wanted to laugh with them, but could not. She touched her husband and said, "Okay, that's enough. It's not really funny."

"Funny? This is a widespread social phenomenon!" Xueyao said, waving his hands. "It's the middle-aged, the middle-aged. Everybody nowadays, from the top to the bottom, admits that our middle-aged people are the backbone of the country. Surgery at the hospital depends on middle-aged doctors; the difficult research items get pushed onto our middle-aged scientists. All the hard work in the factories goes to the middle-aged workers. And the difficult courses at school are the burden of the middle-aged teachers . . ."

"Could you shorten your lecture?" Yafen interrupted. "You're a doctor. Such matters are outside your expertise."

Xueyao, now half-drunk, narrowed his eyes. "In the famous words of Lu Fangweng,"[4] he said, "'Even the humble must worry for the nation.' I may be an unknown doctor, but that doesn't mean I ignore national issues. I ask you — everybody says how the middle-aged are the country's backbone, but who knows anything about their joys and sorrows? Outside the home, they carry the main load at work, and inside the home, they carry the load in the family — providing for their aging parents, bringing up their young children. They're the backbone not only in experience and ability, but in suffering and sacrifice, too — and that includes their spouses and children!"

Wenting had been listening in silence. Now she said quietly, "Not very many people realize this, unfortunately."

Jiajie, looking a bit dazed, poured Xueyao some more wine and then laughed. "You shouldn't be a doctor *or* a literary scholar, Xueyao. You're a sociologist!"

Xueyao laughed wryly. "Then I'd be a rightist! Sociologists have to take note of the flaws of society."

---

4. Lu Fangweng, or Lu You (1125–1210), is a famous poet of the Southern Song dynasty.

"How can society advance unless the flaws are discovered and corrected? Finding flaws is leftist, not rightist," Jiajie said.

"Forget it. I don't want to be a leftist or a rightist. But I *am* interested in society. Just take this question of middle age, for instance." Xueyao, with his two elbows resting on the edge of the table, fiddled with his empty glass and again waxed eloquent. "There was a saying in the old society: 'When a man reaches middle age, his retirement years begin.' This shows that in the old society, people were worn out before they got to old age. They considered their lives over at forty; they were no longer of much use. But now we can change the saying to 'When a man reaches middle age, his workhorse years begin.' Right? People of forty and fifty are knowledgeable, experienced, and in the prime of their life — precisely suited to shoulder the major burdens. Middle age is just the time to give full play to one's abilities."

"Brilliant!" Jiajie acclaimed.

"Hold your bravos — I have some even wilder theories." Xueyao gripped Jiajie's arm and continued excitedly. "If you stop there, you might conclude that our generation has reached its golden years. But that's wrong. The truth is, we've had bad luck."

"You've said enough," Yafen again interrupted.

But Jiajie restrained her. "I'm curious about this bad luck."

"The bad luck was that our golden years were squandered in the madness of Lin Biao and the Gang of Four." Xueyao sighed. "Look at you! Practically made a vagrant! But now the same middle-aged people are supposed to shoulder responsibility for the Four Modernizations, and suddenly find they're not up to it. Their knowledge, energy, and health are all inadequate. Having this inordinate load fall to them is another tragedy of their generation."

"You're hard to please, aren't you?" Yafen teased. "If they don't call on you, you whine that your talents are unappreciated, or that you were born in the wrong time. But if they do call on you, you still cry to the heavens that the burden is too heavy and the pay is too low!"

"You have no complaints?" Xueyao countered.

Yafen looked down and said nothing.

After hearing Xueyao's theories, Wenting began to feel that the reason he felt compelled to leave China perhaps went beyond the sake of his daughter. It was for his own sake as well.

Xueyao raised his glass once more. "Come! I propose a toast to middle age!"

## 10

That night, after the guests had gone and the children were in bed, and after Wenting had rinsed the pots and washed the bowls, she returned to the room to see Jiajie sitting slumped at the head of the bed, rubbing his brow and looking blank. This surprised her.

"What are you thinking, Jiajie?" She stood before him looking at his dejected expression.

"Do you still remember that poem by Petöfi?" Jiajie asked, by way of answer.

"Yes, I do."

"'I wish I were a deserted ruin . . .'" Jiajie brought his hand down from his forehead. "And now I really have become one. I already look old, not middle-aged. Look, I'm balding, my hair is white, and look how deep the wrinkles on my forehead are! They're so big even I notice them. Just like a crumbling wall, a total ruin."

It was true. He did look like an old man. Wenting, her heart aching, rushed to his side and caressed his brow. "It's all my fault. I've let the household chores ruin you."

Jiajie took her hand from his brow and held it affectionately in his. "No, it's not your fault."

"I've been too selfish, too involved with my own work." Wenting's eyes were fixed upon his wrinkled brow, and her voice trembled. "I have a family, but my mind isn't on them. No matter what I'm doing here at home, my mind is all tied up with patients' eyes. Wherever I go, it seems hundreds of eyes are following me. It's true! I think only about my patients. I haven't been a competent wife or mother . . ."

"Don't talk nonsense. You've made great sacrifices that only I know about." Trying to hold back the tears that were welling in his eyes, he stopped speaking.

Wenting, disconsolate, leaned on Jiajie's chest. "I . . . I really don't want you to get old . . ."

"It's not important, as long as my love is 'the tender spring ivy, twining and climbing intimately up my desolate brow.'" He softly recited the words of their favorite poem.

The autumn night turned perfectly still. Wenting had fallen asleep on her husband's chest. Teardrops were still clinging to her dark black eyelashes. Jiajie lifted her body and gently settled her properly on the bed. She opened her eyes and asked, "Did I fall asleep?"

"You're exhausted."

"No, I'm not tired at all."

Jiajie reclined on the side of the bed, one hand supporting his head, and said to her, "Even metal can become exhausted. First, microscopic lines of exhaustion develop. Then they gradually grow until a point is reached when the metal finally cracks . . ."

Talk of exhaustion and cracks—the topics of Jiajie's research—had often fallen from his lips and floated past Wenting's ears. But this time the specialized terminology seemed terribly weighty and left a deep impression in her mind.

Ah, what a fearful thing exhaustion is! And cracks! On that quiet night, it seemed to her every corner of the vast world was audibly cracking, cracking, cracking. The beams bearing the towering bridge were cracking, the railroad ties bearing endless rails were cracking, the old bricks in deserted ruins were cracking, and yes, even the green ivy twining and climbing over those ruins was cracking . . .

11

Late night.

The large hanging light in the ward had been turned out, and only the little wall lamps were on, emitting their faint blue light.

Wenting lay in bed, aware only of two bluish dots before her eyes. At times the dots seemed like the flickering fireflies of summer, and at times like will-o'-the-wisp over a marsh. When she focused hard on them, they became the cold eyes of Qin Bo.

Qin Bo's eyes were hard, but on the morning that Vice-minister Jiao was admitted to the hospital, when she had summoned Lu Wenting, her eyes had been warm and intimate.

"Dr. Lu, please, come here and sit down. The vice-minister is having a cardiogram done and will be back in a minute."

Lu Wenting had climbed the stairs of a small, quiet building, and had walked across a dark red carpet to reach the door of the special room for high officials where Vice-minister Jiao was staying. There she had found Qin Bo sitting on a sofa near the door. Qin Bo had immediately stood up and received Dr. Lu with a face full of smiles.

The minister's wife had Wenting sit on the sofa, then sat down herself on the other side of a tea table. But she immediately stood up again and went to get a basket of oranges from the night table at the head of the bed. She brought them to the tea table and said, "Here, have an orange."

Wenting waved a hand in refusal. "No, thank you."

"Come on, try one! These were brought from the South by an old army friend—they're really quite good." Saying this, Qin Bo selected one and passed it to her.

Wenting could not refuse the bright orange. Even though Qin Bo was being cordial today, Wenting felt a chilliness in her spine. Ever since the day they had first met, Qin Bo's eyes had stayed with her like two cold arrows stuck in her back.

"What exactly *are* cataracts, Dr. Lu? I've heard some doctors say something about cataracts sometimes being inoperable." Qin Bo was straining to assume a humble, sometimes even ingratiating, tone of voice.

"A cataract is an opacity in the lens of the eye," Wenting said, looking at the orange in her hand. "We categorize the degrees of opacity as an initial stage, a spreading stage, a mature stage, and a late stage. We usually feel it's best to operate during the mature stage . . ."

"I see." Qin Bo was nodding. "What happens if you don't operate in the mature stage, but put it off?"

"That's not good," Wenting explained. "During the late stage, the lens shrinks, the inner cortex of the lens dissolves, and the ligaments holding it in place become loose and brittle. Operations at this stage are tricky because it's easy for the lens to dislocate."

"I see." Qin Bo was nodding again.

Wenting knew she hadn't really understood, and didn't really even intend to understand. Why did she have to ask all these questions if she couldn't understand and didn't even want to? Just to pass the time? Wenting herself still had so many things awaiting her. She had just arrived at the ward; she had to check on the patients; there was a pile of problems on her mind. She could barely sit still. But she couldn't go. Vice-minister Jiao was a patient, too, and his eyes had to be examined before the operation. Where was he?

"I hear that outside China they have a sort of artificial lens," Qin Bo mused. "After cataract surgery, they put it in the eye, and then you don't have to wear glasses. Is that right?"

Wenting nodded. "Yes, we're also experimenting with that."

Qin Bo quickly asked, "Could you fit Vice-minister Jiao with such a lens?"

Wenting smiled faintly. "As I just said, Comrade Qin Bo, we're still experimenting with that sort of operation. Do you think it would be appropriate to try it on Vice-minister Jiao at this stage?"

"Well, then, forget it." Qin Bo had agreed quickly enough not to experiment on Vice-minister Jiao. But she thought another moment and asked, "What measures do you plan to take with Vice-minister Jiao's operation this time?"

"What measures?" Wenting was baffled.

"I mean, don't you want to work out some sort of surgical plan? Just in case something unexpected happens, you should want to make contingency plans, so that you don't get flustered and botch it when the time comes." Wenting started dumbly back, as if she hadn't understood. Qin Bo added, "I've noticed that when this sort of news appears in the newspaper, they usually hold a small group conference beforehand to discuss the operating procedures."

Wenting, upon hearing this, couldn't help laughing. "There's no need for that; cataract removal is a very common operation."

Feeling miffed, Qin Bo turned her head to one side. But then she turned to face Wenting again, calmly and in good humor. She even managed a smile as she said, "My dear comrade! Let's not underestimate the enemy, shall we? Underestimation of the enemy often results in defeat. There are instances of such things in the history of our Party . . ."

After patiently lecturing Wenting on ideology, Qin Bo once again asked her to consider the circumstances under which a cataract operation might be unsuccessful.

"If a patient has heart disease, or high blood pressure, then one has to reconsider the surgery," Wenting said. "And if the patient has bronchitis, all coughing must be relieved before surgery. Because if the patient coughs after the incision is made, the eye's internal fluids can leak out."

"That's exactly what I'm worried about!" Qin Bo cried out, slapping the sofa. "Vice-minister Jiao's heart hasn't been good for some time, and his blood pressure is high."

"We'll do a thorough examination before surgery," Wenting reassured her.

"He also has bronchitis."

"Has he coughed a lot these past few days?"

"Well, actually these past few days he hasn't but what if he happen to cough on the operating table? Then what? Hmmh?"

Wenting now began to feel how truly difficult this minister's wife could be. What was she thinking? Where was all this worry coming from? Wenting looked at her watch. It was almost time to go off duty She looked at the two perfectly motionless floor-length curtains next to the window, and began to feel impatient. She listened hard for sound: outside the door. A set of footsteps approached, then quietly passed by Another long time passed before she saw the door finally open and Vice-minister Jiao, with a striped blue terry cloth bathrobe draped over his shoulders, come in assisted by a nurse.

"Why were you gone so long?" Qin Bo asked.

Jiao Chengsi shook hands with Wenting, then went to sit down or the sofa. "We have to obey hospital rules," he said, a bit wearily. "Give blood samples, take x-rays, get electrocardiograms. They were nice enough not to make me wait in line, which is already special treatment."

Qin Bo passed him a cup of hot tea. After taking a sip, Jiao said "Actually, they shouldn't go to all this extra trouble just for an eye operation."

Wenting took the patient's file from the nurse, and glanced through it. "Chest x-ray, normal; EKG, normal; blood pressure, a little high."

"How high?" Qin Bo jumped to ask.

"150 over 100. That won't affect the surgery. Have you been cough-ing lately?" Wenting then asked the vice-minister.

"No." Jiao Chengsi answered without the slightest hesitation.

Qin Bo fixed an eye on him. "Can you guarantee that you won't cough once you're on the operating table?" she asked.

"I . . ." Jiao Chengsi appeared to be rattled, and couldn't come up with an answer.

"Don't treat this matter lightly," Qin Bo upbraided her husband "Dr. Lu just told me that if you cough on the operating table your eyebal is going to pop out!"

"Guarantee?" Jiao Chengsi turned toward Dr. Lu. "How can I guarantee not to cough?"

"I didn't say it was as serious as all that," Wenting said, first answer-

ng Qin Bo's comment. "Vice-minister Jiao, do you smoke? It would be
est if you didn't smoke before surgery."

"That's no problem. I can manage that," Jiao Chengsi said.

Qin Bo again fixed him with her eye. "And what if, what if by the
emotest chance you should start coughing? What then?"

Wenting smiled and said, "Comrade Qin Bo, that wouldn't be the
nd of the world, either. If by some chance such a thing should occur, we
an just sew up the incision to avoid any complications. Then when he's
inished coughing, we can reopen it."

"Yes, that's right," Jiao Chengsi said. "When I had my right eye
lone, it was opened and then sewed up and then opened again. But that
vasn't because I had to cough."

"Why was that?" Wenting asked.

Jiao Chengsi put his teacup down on the table, pulled out a pack of
igarettes and, remembering what Dr. Lu had said, put it back again. He
ighed and said, "I had the 'traitor' label then. But I couldn't see out of
ny right eye, so I came to have it operated on. The operation had just
egun when a 'rebel delegation' came bursting in and forced the doctor
o stop the operation, saying a traitor absolutely must not be allowed to
ee light again. I was furious! All the blood in my body rushed to my
ead. It was a good thing the doctor was so stern and cool. She immedi-
tely sewed up the incision, then chased out the 'delegation' and came
ack to finish the operation."

"Ah . . ." This report had startled Wenting. "Your right eye was done
n this hospital?" she asked.

"Yes, right here."

How on earth could there be two such identical incidents? She
eered at Jiao Chengsi, straining to see whether there was something
bout him she could recognize. But there wasn't.

Ten years earlier, she had done cataract surgery on a "traitor" and a
rebel delegation" had come to interfere; the situation had been exactly
s Vice-minister Jiao described. What was that patient's name? Yes, it
vas also Jiao. The same person! It had to be! Later the rebel delegation
ad gone to the big wheels in the rebel leadership, who stuck a poster up
lenouncing Wenting: "The scalpel of Lu Wenting serves the traitor Jiao
Chengsi; this is an out-and-out betrayal of the proletariat!"

How could she not have recognized him? Ten years ago Jiao

Chengsi had been thin, shallow, and listless, and he had come along, with a tattered old jacket over his shoulders, to register at the ordinary clinic. Wenting had recommended surgery and given him an appointment. He had come as scheduled. She had just begun the operation when she heard the nurse outside shouting, "This is an operating room! No one can enter!"

A confusion of shouting had followed. "Operating room be damned! The guy's a big traitor! You operate on traitors, we rebels are gonna rebel! So stand back!"

"We're not letting any stinking intellectual do favors for traitors!"

"Let's force our way in! Charge!"

Jiao Chengsi had been able to hear all this from the operating table. "Forget it," he had said tensely. "If I'm going to go blind, then I'll just be blind. Let's just forget it, doctor."

"Don't move!" Wenting had said as she hurried to stitch up the incision.

Three husky young men had charged into the room, while a few less brave ones stood at the doorway. Wenting had sat perfectly still at the head of the operating table.

What Vice-minister Jiao had just said — that the doctor had "chased out" the rebels — was not true. Wenting had never in her life yelled at a person, and had never thrown anybody out of anywhere. At the time she was wearing her white operating gown, green plastic slippers, and a blue cloth cap. Her face was covered by a large surgical mask. Nothing showed but a pair of eyes and two hands wearing rubber operating gloves. It may have been the first time the rebels had seen such strange attire; or the first time they had felt the peculiar solemnity of an operating room; or the first time they had seen a bloody eyeball appearing through a hole in the snow white linen over an operating table. In any case they had been brought up short. Wenting had remained sitting on her high stool and had uttered only a few words through her mask. "Would you please leave?"

The rebels had looked at each other uneasily, as if realizing that this was perhaps not the place to make revolution. They had turned and left.

As Wenting was removing the stitches in order to continue the operation, Jiao Chengsi had said, "Really, you'd better not do it. Even if you

cure my eye, they'll probably drive me blind anyway. And besides, it
might spread the trouble to you."

"Don't talk!" Wenting practically ordered, while her hands busily
continued the operation. She didn't answer him until she had finished
and was bandaging him with gauze. "I am a doctor, you know."

That same year a "rebel delegation" from Jiao Chengsi's ministry
had stirred up a furor by going to the hospital and putting up posters
denouncing Lu Wenting. But for Wenting, this had been just a new addition to her original list of criminal labels: "reactionary expert," "revisionist sprout," and so on. Now she was also a "protector of traitors." What
did it matter? She had not dwelt upon it, and both the accusation and
the operation itself had gradually faded from her memory. She would
have forgotten the whole thing if Jiao Chengsi had not recalled it
for her.

Qin Bo was now speaking again. "I really admire this kind of doctor,
Dr. Lu. A true enemy of disease and savior of men! It's a real pity no
patient record was kept on that case. We don't even know what her name
was. Yesterday we brought it up with Hospital Director Zhao. If this
doctor came for the operation, then I could feel good about it!"

Wenting looked somewhat embarrassed at this and Qin Bo, noticing, hurried to reassure her. "You musn't take offense, Dr. Lu. Director
Zhao has great confidence in you. And we, of course, also have confidence in you. I hope you won't disappoint the hopes your leaders have
for you. You must follow the example of that doctor who operated on
Vice-minister Jiao last time. Of course we must all follow her example.
Don't you think so?"

Wenting could only nod her lowered head.

"You're still quite young, you know," Qin Bo said encouragingly. "I
hear you're still not a Party member, is that right? You should work
harder to make it, my dear comrade!"

"My family background is bad," Wenting answered with simple
honesty.

"Oh, no! . . . you're looking at it in the wrong way! One can't choose
one's family, but can choose one's path." Qin Bo began to get carried
away with her own oral disquisition. "Our Party has had a policy of paying attention to class background, but not exclusively to class background. The emphasis is on one's behavior. The great door to the Party

is open to anyone who sincerely makes a clean break with his family
closes ranks with the Party structure, and makes contributions to
the people."

Wenting said nothing. Crossing the room and pulling the curtain
she took out her ophthalmoscope and began to examine Jiao Chengsi
"Vice-minister Jiao," she said, "if you have nothing else planned, I'll do
the surgery the day after tomorrow."

"Fine," said Jiao, hurrying to answer before anyone else could. "The
sooner it's done, the sooner I can leave the hospital."

It was past time to go off duty when Wenting bid them farewell and
left the room. Qin Bo came rushing out after her. "Are you going home
Dr. Lu?"

"Yes."

"Let Vice-minister Jiao's car take you."

"No, thank you. That won't be necessary," Dr. Lu said, waving as she
walked away.


12

Near midnight, the patients' ward was quiet and still. The solitary
bluish light on the wall shone dimly on the fluid in the suspended intra
venous bottle as it dripped silently. Drop by drop, unhurriedly, it en
tered the patient's protruding vein. Alone in the deep silence of the
night, it seemed to be the only sign that Dr. Lu was still alive.

Jiajie sat mutely at the head of the bed gazing at his wife. In the
confusion of the past twenty hours, this was the first time he had sa
alone keeping watch by her side. No, it was probably the first time he
had done this in the more than ten years of their life together.

He could remember another time, in their early, passionate days
when he had watched her without moving his eyes for a long time. But
she had turned her head and asked, "Why are you looking at me like
that?" He had had to shift his gaze in embarrassment. This time she
couldn't turn her head, and she couldn't speak. She seemed to have been
divested of her armor, allowing his gaze to rest on her face a long, long
time; she could offer no resistance to it.

He had never noticed before how much she had aged. Her beautiful lacquer black hair had streaks of silver in it. Her smooth muscles had
grown slack; her brow, once satin smooth, was creased with wrinkles

hat little mouth that had turned up charmingly at the corners now
urned downward. Her very life was now like the wick of a lamp burning
s last drop of oil, when only a faint light and warmth remains. He could
ot believe it. His wife—a woman as strong as she!—had overnight
urned as weak as this?

He knew only too well that she was not a weak person. She had a
lender frame, and to look at her one might think the wind could blow her
own. But that appearance was deceptive. Those two thin shoulders had
lways borne the troubles of life—the calamities as well as the routine
ritations—without complaint, without fear, and without depression.

"You're a strong woman," he had often told her.

"Me? No, I'm as weak as they come, not strong at all," she would
lways answer.

On the evening before she fell ill, she had made another of what
iajie called her decisions of strength—to have him go to live at his re-
earch center.

That night, Jiajia had basically recovered from her illness, and
'uanyuan had finished his homework. The two children, one by one,
ad gone to bed. A moment of peace had come to the small room.

It was already autumn, and the wind was carrying its hints of winter
old. The nursery had sent out notices asking families to send over their
hildren's winter clothing. Wenting took out Jiajia's winter coat from the
ear before, took it apart at the seams to let it out, and lengthened the
leeves. She laid it out on top of the three-drawer desk and began to fill it
ith new cotton batting to keep her daughter warm for the winter.

Jiajie took down an article he was working on from the book-
helf, stood beside the table for a moment, and then half reclined on
he bedstead.

"Here, just a minute and I'll be finished with this," Wenting said
ithout looking up, but hurrying her work.

When Wenting had finished stuffing the jacket and had gathered it
p off the table, Jiajie said, "If we only had half a room more here, it'd
e a lot easier. Even another fifty or sixty square feet would be enough,
ist so we could move a desk in."

Wenting was sitting next to the bed, her head lowered, busily sew-
ng. She heard him but didn't answer. A few moments later, she sud-
enly folded up the still unfinished jacket and said, "I have to go to the
ospital for a minute. You can use the desk."

Jiajie turned his head and asked, "You're going to the hospital at this hour?"

"I have two operations tomorrow morning that I'm a little worried about," she replied, putting on her coat. "I have to go and see about them."

Actually, it was not so unusual for Wenting to be running off to the hospital at night. Jiajie had often chided her for it. "Your body's at home, but your spirit's at the hospital."

"Put on something warmer," he said this time. "It's cold out."

"I'll be right back," Wenting answered. Then she laughed and added, somewhat apologetically, "The thing is, these two operations tomorrow are pretty interesting. The old and the young: there's a vice-minister with a wife who's always worrying that I'm going to botch the operation and is making everybody nervous. So I have to go check on him. And then there's a precious little girl who was clinging to me today, saying she always had bad dreams and couldn't sleep."

"All right, my dear doctor!" Jiajie answered with a smile. "But hurry back!"

When she came back, she saw Jiajie still at work under the desk lamp. She didn't disturb him, but went to straighten the quilt over the children. Then she said, "I'll go on ahead to bed."

Jiajie saw her lie down and again buried his head in his manuscript and books. After a while, although he hadn't turned around, he could sense that Wenting had still not fallen asleep. Was the light bothering her? Jiajie bent the light lower and covered it with a sheet of newspaper before continuing with his work.

After another few minutes, he could hear deep rhythmic breathing from her. Now he knew definitely that she was not asleep. She had used this ruse of pretended snoring many times before, wanting him not to feel guilty about her sleep and to concentrate entirely on his writing. Jiajie had seen through this bit of cunning long ago, but had never had the heart to let her know.

Before long, Jiajie stood up, stretched himself and said, "Enough! I'll go to bed, too."

"Don't worry about me," Wenting spoke up quickly. "I'm already half asleep."

With his two elbows resting on the edge of the table, Jiajie looked over his unfinished article again, hesitated a moment, then closed his books one by one and replaced them on the bookshelf. "No, enough," he said with determination.

"What about your article? If you don't use your evenings, when are you going to finish it?"

"No, you can't make up a ten-year loss in one evening anyway."

Now obviously quite awake, Wenting sat up and draped a sweater over her shoulders, then leaned against the head of the bed. "Do you know what I was thinking just now?" she asked very deliberately.

"You shouldn't be thinking about anything! Your eyes should be closed. You have to work on people's eyes tomorrow, you know . . ."

"Don't interrupt. Listen to me. I think you should move to the research center and live there. That way you would have time."

Jiajie stood before her and stared. He could see light in her face, laughter in her eyes. Her idea obviously excited her.

"I'm not joking. I really think you should. You've got to get something done. You're a scientist. The children and I are wearing you out and holding you back."

"No, no! That's not the problem!"

"That *is* the problem!" Wenting interrupted. "I don't mean we should get a divorce or anything. Obviously the children need a father and a scientist deserves a family. But we have to make it easier on you somehow, get you sixteen hours a day to work instead of only eight."

"Two children, all the housework, everything falling on you? Impossible."

"Why's that? The world's not going to stop spinning just because you leave."

He raised all sorts of specific objections, and one by one she answered with ways to handle them. Finally she said, "Aren't you always saying I'm a strong woman? Just don't worry. I can manage. Your son won't starve and your daughter won't be mistreated."

Finally he was persuaded. They decided to try it out beginning the next day.

"Why is it always so hard to do anything in this country?" Jiajie said as he took off his clothes and got into bed. "During the war years, the older generation made great sacrifices for the Revolution. Now our generation is making sacrifices for the Four Modernizations. But who notices?"

Jiajie was talking to himself, for after he had taken off his cloth
and hung them over the chair, he turned to see that Wenting was alread
asleep. This time she was really asleep. There was still a smile on he
face, as if she were continuing to feel satisfaction over her proposal.

Ai! Who would have predicted the experiment would fail on i
first day?

## 13

Her experiment failed, but her operations were successes.

The next morning, when she arrived at the ward ten minutes earl
as usual, Sun Yimin was there to greet her. "I was waiting for you, D
Lu. We have a donor cornea today. Can you use it?"

"Wonderful," Wenting answered happily. "I have a patient who
been waiting impatiently for a transplant."

"You already have two operations scheduled for this morning. Ca
you stand another?"

"Yes." Wenting straightened her posture and laughed as if to prov
there were inexhaustible reserves of strength in her body.

"All right then."

With that Wenting headed for the operating room, arm in arm wit
Yafen. Her spirits were high and her step light, as if she were headed fo
a pleasant rest rather than the stress of the operating room.

In this hospital, surgery occupied a whole floor, and rather grar
diosely at that. The two words "Surgical Ward" were painted in re
against milky white on the ward's glass door. Once a patient had bee
wheeled inside, his family could only pace back and forth outside th
august door, apprehensively peering toward the mysterious, somewh
frightening, interior. It seemed as if the spirit of death lingered ther
and might at any moment reach out its claw to snatch their loved ones.

Actually, the surgical ward was not the palace of death, but a plac
that offered the hope of life. Inside its wide corridor, the high walls wer
painted a pale green, giving the rooms a warm light. On the two sides c
the corridor were operating rooms for general surgery, gynecolog
ophthalmology, and ear, nose, and throat surgery. Everyone wore steri
ized white gowns and tightly fitting caps of sterilized, pale blue clot
with the words "Surgical Ward" printed on them. Beneath their eye
were facemasks, so that only their eyes showed. There was no distinctio
of good and bad looks in this place, or even of male and female. Ther

ere only doctors, assistants, anesthetists, and nurse technicians. This orps in white moved silently here and there, their steps quick and light. here was no noisy laughing and talking. In this vast hospital, into hich nearly a thousand people poured every day, the Surgical Ward as the most quiet and orderly corner.

Jiao Chengsi was brought into the operating room. He lay on a high, hite iron hospital bed, and was covered with white sterilized cloth. His ntire face was covered except for the eye to be operated on, which appeared through an oval hole.

Wenting had already changed her clothes and was sitting on a high und iron stool with her rubber-gloved hands held high. The stool uld be raised or lowered like a bicycle seat, and since Wenting was ort, it always had to be raised when she operated. But today it hadn't eeded adjustment. She turned her head to look at Jiang Yafen, who as seated beside her, and knew that this had been a parting favor from er old classmate.

A nurse pushed a surgical tray into place. The rectangular tray was den with scissors, sutures, various clamps, hemostats, syringes, lens oons — all sorts of delicate surgical tools. Now it was moved into posi-on over Jiao Chengsi's chest, where the doctor could reach for whatever ol she might need. Wenting sat on the stool at the head of the bed with is tray in front of her, appearing rather like a dinner guest, with only at upward-looking eye occupying the space between the guest and the ining table.

"Let's begin. Just relax now. I'll give you some anesthesia. You won't el anything in your eye, and the operation will be over in no time." enting was looking at the eye as she spoke.

Hearing this, Jiao Chengsi suddenly called out, "Wait a minute!"

What was the matter? Wenting and Yafen were both startled. They w Jiao Chengsi tear off the white cloth that was covering his face and rench his neck to get a look at Wenting. He extended his hand to her. *ou* operated on my other eye, didn't you, Dr. Lu?"

Wenting raised her arms high, afraid that the patient might touch er already sterilized hands. Before she could answer, Jiao Chengsi con-nued excitedly. "It *was* you! No doubt about it! Last time you spoke just ke that — exactly! Just the same way!"

"You're right," Wenting admitted.

"Why didn't you tell me before? I must thank you properly!"

"It was no big thing . . ." Wenting could think of nothing more to say. She looked regretfully at the covering that had been torn aside and indicated to a nurse to change it. Then she said, "Let's begin, Vice-minister Jiao, shall we?"

Jiao Chengsi sighed several times, as if he were having difficulty calming down so quickly. Wenting addressed him in a commanding tone. "Don't move and don't speak! We have begun."

So saying, she deftly delivered him a shot of Novocain under the lower eyelid. She then separated the upper and lower lids, impaled them with pins, and fixed them against the sterile white covering. This left the cloudy eye completely exposed under the light of the lamp. By this time, Wenting had completely forgotten who lay before her. All she saw was a diseased eye.

Wenting had done this operation countless times. But each time she approached the operating table to face another eye, she lifted her scalpel with the feeling of a private marching to battle for the first time. This time was no different. As she carefully made an incision in the conjuctiva and then opened the sclera, Yafen at her side was preparing a suture to pass to her. Wenting reached out with two slender fingers and picked up a scissorslike instrument, which she used to grasp the needle and guide it into the incision in the sclera.

Now what? Why wouldn't it go in? She pushed as hard as she could with her fingers, but it still wouldn't enter properly.

"What's wrong?" Yafen gently asked.

Without answering, Wenting held the needle up to the light and examined it. "Is this a new needle?" she asked after a moment.

Yafen didn't know, but turned to ask the nurse who was in charge of the instruments. "Did you change the needle?"

The nurse came over and said quietly, "It's a new one."

Wenting looked again at the point of the needle. "How can I use a needle like this?" she asked, half to herself.

She and the other doctors had complained innumerable times about their substandard surgical equipment. And yet such equipment continued to appear on the equipment tray. What could one do, except pick and choose among what was presented? If she happened upon a good scalpel, scissors, or needle, she would ask a nurse to put it aside for future use.

For some reason, a completely new set of instruments had appeared

...oday, and perverse fortune had brought this blunt needle. Each time his happened, the usually gentle Dr. Lu would become angry and rep- ·imand the nurse severely. The poor nurse could hardly defend herself. A needle was suddenly not a small thing when it poked repeatedly at a patient's sclera and unnecessarily lengthened the time of an operation. Think how much extra suffering this caused!

Wenting knit her brow. There was the patient, lying before her, and this needle was useless. Not wanting to alarm him, she lowered her voice and said to the nurse, "Change this needle!"

Her tone of voice was entirely that of command, and the nurse rushed to bring her the old needle from the sterilizing pan.

The nurses in the operating room respected Dr. Lu highly, but also feared her. They admired her expert surgery, but feared her exacting demands on them. Ophthalmology is surgery, and an ophthalmologist's standing rests completely on the scalpel. A stroke of that knife can bring someone light or plunge him into darkness. For a doctor like Wenting, even though she had no high professional position or repute, that scal- pel in her hand silently bestowed great authority upon her.

The needle was changed. Wenting quickly threaded the prepared suture into the sclera. Now she need only remove the cataract, tie the stitches, and the operation would be completed. Unexpectedly, just as she had completed the incision in the sclera, Jiao Chengsi suddenly moved.

"Don't move!" Wenting said sternly.

Yafen repeated tensely, "Don't move! What's the matter?"

A muffled voice came through the coverings. "I ... I'm ... going to cough!"

My goodness! Just as Qin Bo had said! Why did he have to cough at this very moment? Perhaps it was psychosomatic, a sort of conditioned reflex? "Can you control it?" Wenting asked.

"No ... no, I can't ..." Jiao Chengsi's chest was already heaving as he tried to stifle a cough.

Any ophthalmologist performing this surgery is very tense at the moment when the sclera has been completely opened. The worst thing that can happen then is for the patient to cough.

In a flash, Wenting set about her emergency steps, instructing the patient at the same time. "Hold it just a second. Breathe out. Breathe out, and don't cough." Her hands never stopped as she quickly knotted the sutures. Jiao Chengsi breathed out deep breath after deep breath,

and his chest heaved violently, as if he were about to suffocate. When th
last stitch was in place, Wenting let out her breath slowly and said, "A
right. You may cough now, but gently."

Jiao Chengsi did not cough. His breathing slowly returned t
normal.

"Go ahead and cough. It's all right," Yafen said.

"I'm sorry," the vice-minister apologized. "I don't have to cough nov
Please, go ahead."

Yafen stared in disbelief, almost wanting to say "a grown man lik
you and you still can't control yourself!" Wenting shot Yafen a knowin
glance, and the two women shared a smile. Even this sort of thing was
common experience.

Wenting cut the knotted stitches and began again. This time she wa
able to proceed without a hitch. When she had left the operating tabl
and was seated at the small desk writing a prescription, Jiao Cheng
had already been moved to the rolling bed and the nurse was preparin
to push him back to his room. "Dr. Lu," he called. The soft voice, slightl
trembling, was like that of a small boy who had done something wron

Wenting went to the side of the bandaged Jiao Chengsi and ber
over him. "What's the matter?"

Jiao Chengsi stretched out his two hands and groped in the air unt
he could grasp Dr. Lu's hands, which were still in gloves. He shook he
hands forcefully and said, "Two operations, and both times I gave you
lot of unnecessary trouble. I'm really very sorry . . ."

Wenting was silent a moment, then, looking at that face with it
cross-shaped gauze bandaging, sought to reassure him. "No trouble
Now get your rest. I'll take out your stitches in a few days."

As a nurse wheeled Jiao Chengsi away, Wenting glanced at the wa
clock. A procedure that should have taken forty minutes had taken a
hour. She removed her surgical gown, pulled off her rubber gloves, an
then stretched her wrists into a new gown she had taken from the suppl
stack. "Ready for the next?" Yafen asked as Wenting turned around t
let the nurse tie her new gown in back.

"Yes."

## 14

"I'll do this operation," Yafen said. "You rest a while. Sit this one out
Wenting shook her head and smiled. "No, I'd better do this one. Yo

)n't know this Wang Xiaoman; she's scared to death. But she's gotten to 1ow me a little, so now it's not so bad."

Wang Xiaoman was not wheeled in lying down. A nurse had to half ıll, half drag her into the operating room. She was wrapped in an vkwardly big patient's gown, and was whining that she would not get ıto the operating table. "Auntie Lu! I'm afraid. I've decided not to do it. Go tell my mother!"

Seeing the way the doctors and nurses in the operating room were ·essed only made the girl more apprehensive. Her heart was racing, ıd her calls to Wenting were as if she were pleading for her life. She ·uggled constantly to wrench herself free from the nurse's grasp.

Wenting walked to the head of the bed and greeted her with a smile. ome on, now, Xiaoman, didn't we already talk this over? Be brave! I'll ve you some anesthesia and I promise you won't feel any pain at all."

Wang Xiaoman carefully looked over this new, strangely clad Dr. ı, and finally looked into her eyes. The child seemed to find strength those warm, smiling eyes. Almost in spite of herself, she got up on the )erating table. The nurse covered the little patient with the operation oth. Wenting gestured to the nurse to take the child's two wrists and ·ap them with the belts at the two sides of the table. Just as Xiaoman ıs about to resist, Wenting stopped her. "Be good, Wang Xiaoman! We · everybody's hands down. Don't you move now. It'll be over in a min- e." Wenting was quietly delivering the injection of anesthesia as she lked. "There, I've finished giving you the anesthesia. In just a moment )u won't feel anything."

Wenting was serving not only as surgeon but as protective mother, ·en something like a nursery school auntie. She kept talking to the )ung patient as she took the scissors, clamps, and sutures that Yafen ıssed to her at the appropriate times. When she went to sever the su- erfluous muscle that was causing the child's walleyed condition, she ·uched a nerve, and Wang Xiaoman began to cry and feel nauseous. (ou feel a little sick, don't you?" Wenting comforted. "Don't worry, just )ld on a minute. Ah! What a good girl! Do you still feel sick? Is it a little ·tter now? We're almost finished now. You really are a good child!"

Wang Xiaoman, under the influence of this pleasant lulling voice, :cepted the operation almost as if hypnotized. When she was bandaged p and being wheeled out of the operating room, she remembered her other's promptings. "Thank you, auntie!" she called very sweetly.

The doctors and nurses in the operating room laughed. The long hand of the clock on the wall had made only half a revolution.

Wenting's entire body was covered with sweat. Beads of perspiration had collected on her forehead; her underwear was soaked and sticking to her body. Even the underarms of her operating gown were damp with perspiration. She thought this rather strange. It was not particularly warm that day — why was she perspiring so much? She swung her arms gently. They ached to numbness from having been suspended in the air for so long as she worked.

While she was, for the second time, taking off her gown and stretching her arms out to pull on another, a line of yellow stars suddenly appeared before her eyes. She shut her eyes a moment and shook her head, then slowly stretched her arms into the sleeves of the gown. The nurse who had come over to tie the back of her gown this time suddenly looked at her and said, "Dr. Lu, your lips are white!"

Yafen, who was standing beside her and also changing a gown, turned to look and was startled. "It's true. You look terrible!"

Against her pale face, the dark black circles around Wenting's eyes looked like those of an actress who has applied charcoal eyeshadow before a performance. Her upper and lower eyelids were also swollen. She was the very picture of illness.

Reacting to Yafen's stare, Wenting smiled and said, "What's the matter? I'll be fine in a minute."

She was not merely saying this. She actually believed she could continue. Hadn't she been doing it for many years?

"You want to continue operating?" the nurse asked, without tying her strings.

"Yes, of course." How could she not go on? Cornea transplants cannot be postponed, and patients cannot be kept waiting. Of course she would continue.

Yafen came round in front of her. "Wenting, rest for half an hour first, why don't you?"

Wenting looked up at the clock. It was already past ten. If she delayed half an hour, her colleagues who ate in the cafeteria wouldn't get there on time and would have to eat their food cold. The ones whose spouses worked wouldn't get home in time to make lunch for their families.

"Are we going to continue?" the nurse asked again.

"Yes."

## 15

Certain doctors from this and other hospitals had obtained permission to observe the cornea transplant that day. Now they were standing outside the operating room door talking with Dr. Lu.

Old Grandfather Zhang, laughing and chattering, was being assisted onto the operating table. The table was a bit small for this tall, ungainly fellow. His two feet, clad in cotton socks, were hanging off one end, suspended in air; his two arms also were hanging halfway off each side. Indeed, the sheer energy of his great body seemed to fill every corner of the room. A rubber tree lying there could not have seemed larger or sturdier. His voice was tremendous, and he couldn't keep it silent a moment. "Don't laugh, my girl," he was saying to the nurse. "If that mobile clinic hadn't come to my village, you wouldn't have got me to come for an operation if my life depended on it! Just think about it — it's my flesh and your knife! One slash of that knife and who knows *what* will happen!"

The young nurses laughed through pursed lips and reproved him gently. "Could you keep it down, Grandfather?"

"Oh, I know about that, my girl!" he roared. "You're s'pose to be quiet in a hospital!" Yet his voice was no less loud. He raised an arm to gesture as he spoke. "Oh, you just don't know! When I heard my eyes could get cured when they're already blind, I didn't know whether to laugh or cry! My old man was blind half his life, and ended up goin' to his grave feelin' like a good-for-nothing. So how come when it's my turn get to see the sun again? We've come a long way, hunh?"

Meanwhile the nurses, trying not to laugh, were attempting to cover his excited patient. He kept sitting up. "Now don't move, Grandfather," they kept urging him. "All this has been sterilized, and if you touch it, we have to change it again."

"That's right!" the old man said in all seriousness. "I always follow the local customs! When a body goes somewhere, he's got to listen to the local folks! So in the hospital, I got to follow the hospital rules." But his arms still wanted to pop out here and there.

A nurse standing nearby became concerned. She took hold of the two belts at the sides of the operating table. "Give me your wrist, Grandfather," she said. "I've got to tie it down. This is a hospital regulation."

The old man stared for a moment, then burst out laughing. "You go right ahead and tie them down! To tell the truth, girl, except for these

two eyes givin' me trouble, I move around quite a bit! Back home I st
go twice a day out to the fields. I still jump around like a rabbit! All ov
the place! Can't sit still!"

Again he had the nurses laughing, and this time he chuckled wit
them. But he stopped laughing as soon as Dr. Lu came in. He tilted h
head to listen and called out, "That you, Dr. Lu? I could tell by you
footsteps right away. These old eyes are blind, but the ears are shar
Can't help it, they've got to do the eyes' work!"

Wenting looked at this vigorous patient, and joined those wh
couldn't help laughing at his talk. She sat down and began preparing f
the surgery. From a small glass on the instrument tray, she took out th
precious donor cornea and first sewed it onto an eyeball model made
gauze. At this point Grandfather Zhang spoke up again: "First time
ever heard you could change eyeballs!"

Yafen laughed. "We're not changing your eye," she explained, "just
layer of membrane."

"Bah! So what's the difference?" The old man hadn't looked into th
finer points. He sighed and said, "You really know what you're doin
doctor. Just wait'll I go back home with two new eyes. My neighbors
say I bumped into an immortal. I'll tell 'em I just bumped into Dr. Lu!

Yafen tried to stifle a laugh as she winked at Wenting, who was em
barrassed by what the old man said. "Any doctor would do the same
she said as she continued stitching.

"You think I'm kidding?" Grandfather Zhang answered with gre
seriousness. "A doctor not worth his salt couldn't even get through th
door of this place!"

The preparations completed, Wenting adjusted the brace th:
would hold open the patient's eye, and at the same time said, "We'
about to begin. Don't be nervous."

It was Grandfather Zhang's feeling that if the doctor said som
thing to him and he kept silent, he wasn't being very polite. So Wenting
brief instruction made him open up even more. "I'm not nervous, n
not at all! Just think about it. You cut with a knife and it's going to hurt
little, of course! But don't worry, doc! You just go ahead and cut! I be
lieve in you, doc, and what's more . . ."

"Grandfather!" Yafen interrupted. "Don't you say another word!"

This time the old man kept quiet.

Wenting started working. She picked up a little bore, about th

ameter of a pen, and carefully bored out the defective cornea. Then
e picked up the donor cornea she had sewed to the model eye, and
ing the same bore, bored out a plug the same size, which she fitted
to the patient's eye. Then she took up a needle and carefully began to
ture it in place.

She had to make twelve stitches around this tiny plug. Sewing a slip-
ry, miniscule membrane is different from sewing a nice flat piece of
oth. With each stitch she seemed to focus all her energy and concen-
ation in her fingertips. Her eyes, normally very plain-looking, shone
th a rare sort of wisdom that made them appear quite beautiful.

The operation went extremely smoothly. When the last suture was
it in place, and the final stitch knotted, the donor cornea had been
ecisely fitted into the patient's eye. If it weren't for the black stitches
ound it, one wouldn't be able to tell it had just been transplanted.

"Beautiful surgery!" the doctors who had been watching said qui-
y, in heartfelt admiration.

Wenting let out a quiet breath of relief. Yafen, at her side, did not
eak, but lifted her gaze warmly toward her old classmate. Then she
ok a thick, rectangular piece of gauze and covered the patient's eye.

As Grandfather Zhang was being wheeled out, he seemed like one
t awakening from a dream. But he suddenly became active again, just
he passed through the door. "Gave you a lot of trouble, Dr. Lu!"

The operation was over; Wenting wanted to stand up. But her legs
d turned numb, and she couldn't stand. She paused a moment before
ing again. It was only after several attempts that she finally managed
get up. Suddenly assailed by a pain in her back, she pressed a hand to
r waist. This was a common thing for her. Every time she sat on that
erating stool concentrating for several hours, with every bit of her
nd and energy devoted to her surgery, she was not in the least aware
any physical exhaustion. But as soon as the operation was over, her
tire body seemed to come apart. Even walking became a trial.

## 16

At this moment, Jiajie was riding his bicycle toward home.

He hadn't planned to do this. Early in the morning, in accordance
th Wenting's suggestion of the night before, he had rolled up his bed-
ig, secured it to the back of his bicycle and headed toward the re-
rch center to begin his new life.

But at noon his determination had wavered. Would she be able t(
finish operating in time to get home and make lunch? When he though
of her, overcome with weariness, returning home and having to hurr
to make a meal, he felt quite guilty. This was why he had decided t(
pedal home.

He had just turned into their lane when he saw Wenting leanin;
against the wall as if she couldn't move.

"Wenting! What's the matter?" he called out, jumping from his bik
and rushing to hold her up.

"Nothing. I'm just a little tired." Wenting put her arm over Jiajie
shoulder as he helped her, step by step, walk the rest of the way home.

She had said she was only a little tired, but when he saw her whit
face, covered with perspiration, Jiajie knew differently. "Should I tak(
you to the hospital?"

Wenting closed her eyes as she sat down on the edge of the bed. "N(
need. I'll be better in a minute." She pointed at the bed, as if she hadn'
the energy to say any more and didn't want to move. Jiajie helped he
take off her shoes and jacket. "Well then, you just lie down a while, rest
bit. I'll call you in a little while . . ."

"No need to call me," she said as she was lying down. "I won't fa
asleep anyway. I'll just stretch out and feel better in a minute."

Jiajie turned and left to put a kettle of water on to boil. When h
returned to the room to get some noodles, he heard her say, "I reall
need a rest. Let's take the children to Beihai Park for some fun thi
Sunday. We haven't been to Beihai for more than ten years."

"Okay, sounds great," Jiajie said. But he felt uneasy. It was true the
hadn't gone to Beihai for ten years; she hadn't even mentioned the ide
of going. Why did she suddenly bring it up today?

Jiajie looked at his wife with concern, then went to boil the noodle:
He cut up some green onion and pickled mustard root, and place(
them in bowls. Wenting had fallen asleep by the time he returned wit
the noodles. Seeing her there with her eyes closed, sleeping so peace
fully, he could not bear to wake her. When Yuanyuan came home, th
two of them ate the noodles together.

Then Wenting began to groan on the bed. Jiajie quickly put dow
his bowl and turned toward her. Wenting's face was white as a sheet an(
dripping with sweat. "Something's wrong!" she gasped faintly.

Terrified, Jiajie grabbed her fingers. "Where does it hurt? Where's he trouble?"

She writhed in pain without answering, but pointed to the left side f her chest.

Jiajie raced about the room in confusion. He first pulled open a rawer to look for pain killers. Then, thinking that inappropriate, he vent to look for some tranquilizers.

Wenting was cool-headed even in the midst of her unbearable suffering. She gestured with her hands that he should calm down, then managed to blurt out three words: "To the hospital!"

Now Jiajie realized the seriousness of the situation. Although Wenting went to work at the hospital every day, she had never once suggested going to see a doctor herself. This was obviously nothing minor. Jiajie couldn't allow himself to deliberate any longer; he turned to leave. "I'll go call a taxi," he called back over his shoulder.

There was a public telephone at the entrance to their lane. He ushed to dial the number of the taxi company.

"No cars now," said a cold voice at the other end.

"Wait! Wait! I'm taking a sick person to the hospital!"

Jiajie tried to plead with him, but the person at the other end had hung up.

There was nothing he could do but try to call Wenting's hospital. But the ophthalmology department did not answer. He had the switchboard operator ring the garage. The comrade who answered the phone said, "We can't give you a car without a note from the leadership!"

Where could he get a note from the leadership?

"Hello, hello!" he shouted into the receiver. But there was no sound t the other end.

He called the Political Affairs Office of the hospital. They ought to pay attention to this kind of emergency, no?

The phone rang and rang. Finally a woman answered. After hearing what he had to say, she said very politely, "Please get in touch with the Executive Office about this."

So now he asked the switchboard operator to transfer the call to the Executive Office. The operator recognized his voice. "Why don't you figure out who you want to call, anyway?" he asked. Who *should* he be calling? Jiajie himself didn't know. He could only beg the operator to

connect him with the Executive Office. The connection was placed, an
the phone rang and rang and rang. No answer.

Jiajie was despondent. Abandoning the idea of calling a car, he wer
to find a three-wheeled pedicab. There was a family on their lane wh
ran a "May Seventh" factory that made paper boxes.[5] Pedicabs ofte
came and went to make deliveries there. He ran over to explain the sit
ation, and the old woman in charge was most sympathetic. But unfort
nately both of their two pedicabs were out right then.

What could he do? Jiajie stood in the lane feeling he would go ma
Could he push her there on his bicycle? She didn't look as if she cou
even sit up. How could he push her?

A light gray pickup truck came driving along the road. Almo
without thinking Jiajie ran into the middle of the street and waved h
arms at the driver.

The truck stopped. A big, unshaven face leaned out the window
stare at the man blocking the way. But as soon as he heard that a crit
cally ill person had to be taken to the hospital, he didn't say a word. F
just waved to Jiajie to get into the truck.

They drove up to Jiajie's door and stopped. The driver waited un
Jiajie had carefully assisted Wenting to the side of the truck. Then I
reached out a big hand to help her into the cab and they cautious
drove straight to the emergency room.

## 17

Never had she slept so long, or in such exhaustion. Wenting felt as
she had fallen from a high cloud and crashed to the earth, wracking he
entire body with unbearable pain. She didn't have the least bit
strength. Now she was peacefully reclining, her body still, her moc
quiet as well. She felt blank, utterly empty.

For many years she raced through life without taking the time
stop and realize how rough the road had been. Still less had she ha
time to gauge the problems of the future. Now that she had laid dow
her heavy burden and escaped her various duties, one would think sh
would have had time to look back at her footprints and to peer at tl
path that lay ahead. But her mind was completely empty — no mem
ries, no hopes, nothing.

5. "May Seventh" factories were small operations run by the local residents of neig
borhoods, often women, in response to Chairman Mao's famous directive of 7 May 19
calling for self-reliance and emulation of the People's Liberation Army.

What a fearful void!

Perhaps this was only a dream, a lonely dream. She had had this ream before, and it had always been desolate like this, cold and sorrow-ıl like this.

Once when she was five years old, a north wind had been blowing ıd her mother had gone out, leaving her alone. When night fell, her other still hadn't returned. This was the first time Wenting had felt nely and terrified. She had cried and called out, "Mama . . . Mama!" he scene often haunted her dreams in later years. That howling wind, ıat door that had blown open, that dim light—it was all so vivid! And the end, she could never tell: had reality invaded her dreams, or had ıe taken a dream for reality?

No, this time it wasn't a dream. It was real.

She was lying on a hospital bed, and Jiajie was keeping watch beside ɛr. He looked so tired, slumped against the side of the bed, sound leep. He might catch cold. She should wake him up. But she tried a few mes and couldn't hear her own voice. Her throat seemed blocked by ›mething. It would make no noise. She thought of stretching out her ınd to drape a coat over him, but she couldn't move her hand. It ·emed not to belong to her.

She looked about her and discovered she was lying in a private ›om. This sort of "privileged treatment" was usually reserved for pa-ɛnts who were critically ill. She suddenly felt frightened. I must be . . .

The rustling fall wind rattled the door and windows. The deep ıght overtook the patient's room. She broke out in a cold sweat, but her ɛad was quite clear. She was aware that everything she saw was com-letely real, that this certainly was not a dream. This was the end of life, ıe approach of death.

So this was what death was like—not so fearful, and not painful. It as only the gradual withering of life, the gradual dozing off of con-iousness; it was only a gentle falling, like a leaf floating on the water, ›ing with the waves and finally sinking beneath the surface.

She felt that all was ending, irretrievably. A surge of waves was veeping over her, she was going with the water . . .

"Mama . . . Mama . . ." She could hear Jiajia calling and could see her ıasing along the riverbank. She looked back and opened her arms. iajia, my daughter . . ."

The flowing water engulfed her. Jiajia's face grew indistinct. The :tle girl's hoarse voice became a pitiful sob. "Mama . . . I want my hair braided . . ." Why didn't she go and braid her daughter's hair? The girl had been in this world only six years, and her only aspiration was to have her hair in braids. Every time she saw another little girl with braids in a butterfly barrette, she became excitedly envious. But even this minor demand Wenting had not been able to satisfy. She had had no time. Even a minute was precious to her.

"Mama . . . Mama . . ."

She could hear Yuanyuan calling and could see him running along the riverbank. Again she stretched out her arms, calling, "Yuanyuan . . . Yuanyuan . . ."

A wave pulled her down and she struggled again to the water's surface. But Yuanyuan was nowhere to be seen now. She could only hear his voice from afar. "Mama . . . don't forget . . . white sneakers . . ." All sizes and colors of sneakers whirled before her eyes like the patterns in a kaleidoscope—white, blue, high sides, low sides, white with red trim, white with blue trim. Pick a pair for Yuanyuan; his own are worn out. Let's buy him a white pair; it'll make him happy for a month. But in a flash, all the shoes disappeared, and were replaced before her by price tag after price tag: $2.10, $3.00, $4.20 . . .

Now Jiajie was running after her. The flowing water reflected his madly racing silhouette. He was running so fast that his voice was trembling. "Wenting, you can't leave . . ."

She wanted so to stop and wait for him to catch up, so he could grab her and pull her out. But the water flowed mercilessly, and her body was swept helplessly along in the torrent.

"Dr. Lu! Dr. Lu!"

Many people were calling to her from both banks! Yafen, Yafen's husband Xueyao, Director Zhao, Chief Sun—all in white surgical coats; Jiao Chengsi, Grandfather Zhang, Wang Xiaoman—all in patients' gowns; and so many other patients, some she recognized and some she didn't. All were calling, calling.

I can't leave, I just can't! There are so many things I haven't finished in this world, so many responsibilities I haven't fulfilled. I can't let Yuanyuan and Jiajia become motherless children. I can't leave Jiajie alone at middle age. I can't leave my hospital, my patients. I can't leave. I can't give up this life despite the way it mistreats a person.

I can't drown in this water of death. I must struggle, resist, and stay in the world. But how is it I'm so tired? I have no strength to resist, no strength to struggle. I'm sinking, sinking . . .

Ah! Goodbye forever, Yuanyuan! Goodbye forever, Jiajia! Will you remember your mother? In her last moment of life, your mother is taking with her a deep love for you. I will miss you so much. Let me hug you tight. Listen to me, children! Forgive me for not loving you enough; forgive me for retreating so many times from your outstretched arms, drawing back from your smiling faces, forcing you to do without your mother's embrace.

Goodbye forever, Jiajie! You gave everything for me. Without you, each step in life would have been difficult. Without you, my life in this world would have been dull and empty. You sacrificed so much for me. If you would allow me to, I would kneel before you and ask you to forgive me. Forgive me for not being able to repay your wholehearted care and gentleness, for having taken so little care of you, for giving you so little. How many times have I told myself that as soon as I get a little free time, I'll be a better housewife, I'll leave work on time and come home to have your dinner waiting for you? I'll give the three-drawer desk to you, and make it possible for you to finish your writing. But now it's too late. I have no more time left.

Goodbye, patients! Goodbye forever! For eighteen years, the most important part of my life has belonged to you. You occupied my mind wherever I went. Your eyes were ever with me. You have no idea what great comfort and happiness you gave me every time I was able to cure one of your eyes! How sad that I won't have this kind of happiness again! Goodbye forever, my dear family. Goodbye forever, hospital. Goodbye forever, my patients! I hate leaving you . . . I . . .

## 18

"Heartbeat abnormal!" the doctor monitoring the fluorescent screen called.

"Wenting, Wenting!" Jiajie called in a tight voice to his wife, who lay struggling to breathe.

The doctor on duty and some nurses came running in.

"Give her an intravenous injection of lidocaine!" the doctor ordered.

A nurse hurried to insert a needle into the patient's arm. But when they had injected only half of the lidocaine, the patient's hands had already formed fists, her lips had turned gray, and her eyes had turned up. Then her heart stopped beating.

Emergency measures were put into effect. Several doctors in turn administered external heart massage. A respirator was clamped over the patient's mouth and began its gurgling noise. Finally, an electric pacemaker was applied to her chest, and after a jolt from this special instrument, her heart started to beat again.

"Prepare an ice compress!" the doctor on duty called, his face dripping perspiration.

Wenting's head was covered with a rubber ice compress.

## 19

Outside the window the sky was suffused with a blue-gray light. Dawn had finally come. Dr. Lu Wenting had survived the night and entered a new day.

The dayshift nurse came in and quietly pulled open the blinds that had been tightly closed all night. Immediately, fresh air accompanied by the happy singing of birds flowed into the room, dispersing the thick odor of medicine and the oppressive atmosphere inside. Dawn was bringing hope to a life at the brink of death.

The nurse who came to take her temperature, the orderly who brought her breakfast, and the doctor on dayshift arrived one after another in a steady stream. The patient had survived the night and seemed to have regained her will to live. A new vitality permeated the sick room.

Little Wang Xiaoman, her eye in a bandage wrapped diagonally across her face, was pleading with the nurses in the medical ward for all she was worth. "Let me go see Dr. Lu! Just let me have a look at her!"

"No. Dr. Lu was in critical condition last night. No one can go in."

"Auntie! You don't understand! She got sick when she operated on me! Let me see her. I won't say a word . . ."

"No!" The nurse grew stern.

"I can't even just look at her?" Wang Xiaoman was about to cry. Just at this moment, she turned to see Grandfather Zhang coming toward them, supported by his grandson. She ran toward him. "Grandfather Zhang, hurry up and come talk to her! She won't let anybody in!"

Wang Xiaoman pulled the old man, whose head was also wrapped in bandages, to face the nurse. When he came to a stop, he said, "Comrade, let us go in and see her a bit!"

When the nurse saw that now an old man had joined the child, she began to raise her voice in annoyance. "How come all the ophthalmology patients are running all over the place causing trouble?"

"Bah!" said Grandfather Zhang. "Listen to this! What're you talking out?" His voice was much softer than before, however. "You don't now the whole story here. Why did Dr. Lu get sick? Because she orked on us! Aghh! Matter of fact I can't *see* her right now anyway. was just thinkin' I could stand by her bed and pay my respects for minute."

The nurse began to soften when she saw how sincere the old fellow as. She could only try patiently to deter him with words. "It's not I that on't let you in. Dr. Lu has had a heart attack and she must not be exted. Don't you wish the best for her? If you go in and startle her, that ouldn't be good for her at all."

"Oh, so that's the problem!" The old man let out a long sigh. He ent to slump down on a bench in the corridor. Then he slapped his nees and began to blame himself. "It's all my fault, old geezer me. ushy, pushy, always pushy. Begging her to do it sooner. Gosh! Who ouldda thought . . . If anything happens to Dr. Lu, that'd be awful!" His head was tilted in dejection as he spoke.

Sun Yimin was also on his way to see Wenting before going on duty. s he came hurrying along, he was surprised to find himself pulled to a alt by Wang Xiaoman. "Are you going to see Dr. Lu?" she asked.

Sun Yimin nodded.

"Take me in to see her too, okay?"

"In a few days I will. You can't go in now."

Hearing the voices, Grandfather Zhang also stood up and groped is way to find Sun Yimin's sleeve, which he grasped firmly. "We'll listen you, Chief Sun. We won't go in. But I got somethin' to tell you today. I on't care how busy you are, you got to hear me out on this one."

Sun Yimin used his free hand to pat Grandfather Zhang's arm. "All ght. Go ahead."

"Chief Sun! Dr. Lu's a really good doctor! You leaders gotta spend oney to make her well! You save her, and she'll save lotsa other people! in't there some special medicine? You get it for her and don't you be ingy, hear? I asked around and I know you gotta buy them expensive edicines out of your own pocket. Dr. Lu's got a home 'n' family. How's e gonna pay if she gets sick? Can't a big hospital like this squeeze some it for her?"

When Grandfather Zhang was finished he was still holding on to Sun imin with both hands, bending his ear toward the chief for an answer.

Sun Yimin was not a demonstrative person. He never showed anger or pleasure on his face, but on this occasion, he felt so moved that he grasped the old man's hands. "We'll certainly do everything we can for her!"

The old man seemed to relax at this. He called his grandson over and groped for the cloth schoolbag the boy was carrying. "Here, here're some eggs. Since you can go in, you got to give 'em to her."

"Uh . . . no need for this," Sun said reflexively.

This angered the old man. "If you don't take 'em I'm gonna wait here all day!" he said loudly, pulling at Sun Yimin's sleeve.

Sun had to accept the bag of eggs, telling himself that after a while he could get a nurse to return them and explain. But Grandfather Zhang had foreseen this possibility. "Chief Sun! If you get somebody to bring 'em back to me, it won't work, you know!"

There was nothing Sun could do, so he accepted the eggs and escorted the old man and the young girl downstairs.

Next to arrive at the ward were Zhao Tianhui and Qin Bo. "I was too bureaucratic, Director Zhao," Qin Bo was saying as they walked along. "I didn't understand the situation. But why didn't *you* know what was going on?" She was very agitated. "If the vice-minister hadn't recognized her we'd still be in the dark about the whole thing."

"I was out doing labor reform when the first operation occurred," Zhao Tianhui answered helplessly.

Sun Yimin joined them as they entered the patient's room. The doctor reported on the crisis and emergency measures of the night before. Zhao Tianhui looked at the patient's record and started nodding. "Continue keeping her under close observation."

Jiajie, upon seeing so many people come in, hurried to stand up. Qin Bo didn't even notice him. She possessed herself of the small round stool he had been sitting on, sat down and said, "Are we better today, Dr. Lu?"

Lu Wenting opened her eyes slightly but didn't answer.

"Vice-minister Jiao told me all about it," Qin Bo sighed. "He's very grateful to you. At first he wanted to come in person to see you, but I wouldn't let him. I came for him. If there's anything you'd like to eat, if you need anything or have any problem, whatever it is, be sure to tell me. We'll help you out with everything. Don't hold back. We're all comrades of the Revolution!"

Lu Wenting closed her eyes.

"You're still young. Be more optimistic! You're sick, yes, but since
hat's the way it is, you must accept . . ."

Qin Bo would have gone on, but Zhao Tianhui interrupted her.
"Comrade Qin Bo, let the patient rest, will you? She's just recovering."
"Yes, yes, of course. You rest well, now," Qin Bo said as she stood up.
"I'll come and see you again in a couple of days."

Qin Bo was frowning as she left the room. "I'd like to give you my
opinion on something, Director Zhao. How is it that greater care isn't
aken of doctors of Dr. Lu's ability? How can she be allowed to fall ill like
his? Our middle-aged people are the backbone of our country. My dear
omrade, we must treasure such talent!"

"Yes," Zhao Tianhui answered.

"Who is she?" Jiajie whispered to Sun Yimin as he watched Qin Bo
disappear from the room.

Sun Yimin, looking over the top of his glasses, frowned and said, "A
Marxist-Leninist old lady."

## 20

Lu Wenting's condition took a turn for the better that day. She
could, without too much effort, open her eyes. She drank a few spoon-
fuls of milk and some orange juice. But she lay on her back, staring
straight ahead, with a dull, expressionless look in her eyes. She seemed
indifferent to everything around her. She seemed indifferent even to her
own serious illness and the misfortune it was bringing to her family. Her
dull apathy was in fact an indifference toward life.

Jiajie had never seen her this way. It frightened him terribly. He
called and called to her, but she would only move her palm, ever so
slightly, as if she wished not to be disturbed, as if she had found semi-
paralysis, which so frightens others, to be comfortable, and had decided
to keep herself confined in that state from now on.

Time passed slowly as Jiajie sat anxiously at Wenting's bedside. He
had already gone without sleep for two nights. He felt that he, too, had
reached the limits of exhaustion and was about to crack. During this
two-day vigil, he had seen another case in which a middle-aged woman,
a wife and mother, had not recovered. He had heard the terrified
screams of her children. This had made him rest his head next to Wen-
ing's and whisper a helpless entreaty. "You have to live, you have to, you
must have to!"

His heavy breathing startled Wenting from her half-sleep. She opened her eyes and looked toward him, but didn't seem to see him. He dull gaze caused Jiajie's whole body to tremble. "Wenting!" he calle in despair.

Her gaze again rested on his face, but was still that cold, indifferen extremely distressing look. It made him feel that her spirit had alread fled her body and was roaming somewhere in space.

Jiajie didn't know what he could say or do to coax her back to desire for life. This was his wife, the dearest person to him on earth From that winter day when they had wandered through Beihai Park when he had read poetry to her, how many days and nights had passed All along, she had been the dearest person to him. He couldn't be with out her. He had to keep her!

Poetry! Recite poetry to her! Just as he had back then! More thar ten years ago, it had been that love poetry that had opened her heart to him. Today, he could use the same poetry to recall pleasant memories to her, and to recall in her the courage and desire to live.

Jiajie knelt by her bed with tears in his eyes, reciting:

> I wish I were a rushing stream,
> And my love a small fish,
> Happily swimming to and fro in the
>     midst of my waves.

The lines seemed to stir her. She turned her face to look long and hard a her husband. When her mouth trembled slightly, Jiajie leaned close to hear the indistinct words she was uttering. "I can't . . . swim any more . . ."

Restraining his tears, Jiajie continued:

> I wish I were a wild forest,
> And my love a small bird,
> Building a nest and singing within
>     my dense woods.

Wenting again barely managed a few words. "I can't . . . fly any more . . ."

Jiajie felt thoroughly miserable, but again restrained his tears and went on:

> I wish I were a deserted ruin,
> And my love the tender spring ivy,
> Twining and climbing intimately
>     up my desolate brow.

With this, two tears rolled from Wenting's eyes and fell on her snow white pillow. She again forced out a few words. "I can't . . . climb up ny more . . ."

Jiajie lay his head on her breast and cried like a child. "I haven't iken good care of you . . ."

He suddenly opened his tear-filled eyes and fell mute. He could see Venting's eyes again staring off into space, senseless and still, as if she adn't heard his crying, hadn't heard him calling out, and were once gain entirely insensible to her surroundings.

The ward doctor had heard Jiajie's voice and came hurrying in. Vhen he saw what was happening, he said to Jiajie, "Dr. Lu is very weak. ou . . . don't want to talk with her too much."

So Jiajie kept watch silently for the afternoon.

## 21

Two days later Jiajie received a letter that had been mailed from the eijing airport. He opened it and read:

Dear Wenting,

Who knows if you will ever be able to read this letter? It may become a permanently undeliverable letter. How I hope that won't be so! It just can't be so! I know you are seriously ill, but I'm sure you will recover. There is still much you can do; you've just reached your prime; you can't leave us so soon!

Last night, when we went to say goodbye to you, you were still unconscious. Originally we wanted to go to see you again today, but there were too many last-minute things to do. We just couldn't find the time. I shudder to think that last night's farewell might be the last time we see each other. After more than twenty years of sharing our professional and personal lives, no one knows me as well as you, nor you as well as I. I never thought we would end up parting like this.

I am writing to you from the waiting room in the Beijing airport. Can you guess where I am standing? I'm just beside that souvenir counter on the second floor. No one else is here — only that display behind the glass counter. Remember? The first time we flew on a plane we stopped here, at this very counter, and admired the handicrafts for a long time. There was that pot of narcissus that was so beautifully realistic — it even had a drop of dew on one of its slender leaves. You said you liked it best. But when we bent down to look at the price tag we both ran away in horror! Now I'm standing by that counter alone. Another pot of narcissus is here, but this pot is a different shade of brown. Someone must have bought that other pot. As I look at this pot of narcissus, I don't know why, but I just want to cry. I suddenly feel that a whole part of my life is over with.

I remember when Fu Jiajie first started coming to see you, there was that time he came to our dorm room and recited a line of poetry from Pushkin: "All that is past will become dear memory to us." I was contemptuous then; I said poetry like that was imprecise. "Even the misfortunes of the past will become dear memory?" I challenged him. He laughed and refused to debate with me. I'm sure he thought that I just couldn't appreciate poetry. But now I do. Now I feel that line could hardly be more precise. It mirrors my feelings perfectly at this moment, as if it were written for me alone! I really do feel that everything in the past is dear to me.

I hear a roar—another plane has taken off. I wonder where it's going? In just an hour I, too, will climb the boarding stairs and leave this country where I was born and raised. It makes me want to cry when I think that I have only sixty minutes more to stand on the soil of my native land. My tears have got this stationery wet. But I don't have another sheet, Wenting, so I'll just have to continue using this.

I don't know why I feel so sad. I suddenly feel as if I've made a mistake. I shouldn't leave. I hate to part with everything, I really do! I hate to leave our hospital, our operating room, that small desk of mine in the examining room! I always used to call Chief Sun an ogre behind his back, because he can't stand anybody making the slightest mistake. But now I long to hear his scolding once again. He is such a demanding teacher. Without his strict demands, I wouldn't have the skill I have today.

The loudspeaker is wishing all the passengers a pleasant journey. Can it be pleasant? When I think that I have to get on that plane soon, I feel empty and lonely. I feel like a balloon floating aimlessly in the air. What kind of a place will I land in? What will await me there? I feel uneasy, even afraid. Yes, afraid. We're going to a strange country, a society entirely different from our own. Can we fit in? How can I not be afraid?

Xueyao is sitting on a couch here, staring blankly ahead. All the time he was busy packing and arranging details, he had no time to reflect, and seemed not to waver in his determination to leave. But last night when he put the last piece of clothing in his suitcase, he suddenly said, "Now we're going to be lonely guests on the other side of the world." Since then he's been silent. He hasn't said another word. I know he has strongly conflicting feelings, too.

Yaya has been the most enthusiastic about going. She's been so excited she can hardly wait. There were a few times I could hardly keep from smacking her. But now she's standing in front of the large window in the airport waiting room, looking at the busy airfield. She seems not so eager to leave either.

"Do you have to go?" I remember that night at your home you asked me this.

I can't give you a simple answer. Why do we have to go? These last months, almost every day, Xueyao and I have fretted and debated about whether or not we should go. There were lots of reasons that finally made us decide to do it — for Yaya, for Xueyao, and for me too. But none of the reasons could reduce the pain we felt. Really, we shouldn't leave. Our country is just beginning a new era, and we really shouldn't run away from the task that history (and our race, too, I should say) has presented to us. The "rebels" in the Cultural Revolution were right when they said, "We have been raised by the blood and sweat of our workers and peasants. We must not betray them!"

Compared to you, I am weak. I haven't suffered nearly as much as you have in these last ten years, but I haven't been able to take it as well as you. I was always exploding at the malicious slander and vile gossip that went on constantly. This doesn't show that I was stronger than you, but just the opposite — that I am more easily upset. There were times I actually thought it would be better to die than to live with such insults. Only because of Yaya was I able to rid myself of this idea. I barely managed to get through the years when Xueyao was imprisoned as a "suspected spy" and I could hardly believe it when I saw the smashing of the Gang of Four.

Of course these are all past sorrows. Fu Jiajie was right when he said "the bad times are behind us, and happy days are on the way." Unfortunately, the traitor Lin Biao and the Gang of Four have created prejudices in a whole generation that can't be changed in a short time. For the policies of the Central Committee to reach the grass roots, they will have to "cross a thousand mountains and tens of thousands of rivers," as the saying goes. Deep resentment is not easy to get rid of, and people's tongues are fearful things. The nightmares of the past still terrify me. I lack your kind of courage!

Remember when the "pebbles" [see glossary] who had put themselves in charge of the "health and medicine front" cited your name and mine at a mass criticism session against "bourgeois specialists"? When we were leaving together, just outside the hospital gate I said, "I don't get it. We just make a little progress in some specialized fields, and right away they want to knock it down. Next time they have a meeting like this, I'm not going! I'll protest!" But you said, "Why bother to protest? I'll go as often as they want. When it comes to doing the operations, they still have to look to us! And when I go home, I can do my research as usual." I asked you, "Don't you feel their criticisms of you are unfair?" You just laughed and said, "I'm so busy every day I don't know which way is up. No time to think about it!" I really admired that spirit! Then when we were about to part that day, you said something slightly different. "Don't tell Fu Jiajie about all this. He's got enough troubles of his own." We walked on a bit in silence. I looked at your face and saw that it was calm, and that your gaze bore confidence. You seemed unshakable in your beliefs. To me it was obvious how great the willpower was that made you forge onward in the face of that barrage of stones. If I had half your courage and willpower, I wouldn't have come to the final decision I am making today.

Forgive me, please. That's all I can say to you. I am going. I am leaving my heart with you, and with my beloved country. Wherever life may take me, I shall never forget my loving homeland. Believe me! That's all I can say to you. Believe that we will return. Whether in a few years or in ten or more, after Yaya has grown up a little, after we've accomplished something in medicine, we'll certainly return.

Finally, I wish from the bottom of my heart that you will recover your health quickly. You must learn a lesson from this illness and take better care of yourself. I'm not urging you to be selfish. It's

your selflessness that I have always admired. I only wish you a
healthy body, so that the new flowering of China's medicine
may be even sweeter than before!

Goodbye! My dear friend!

Yafen<br>
*Written hurriedly at the airport*

## 22

A month and a half later, Lu Wenting was well enough to leave the
hospital. That she had been able to recover at all had been a great surprise to the internists who had treated her.

Fu Jiajie, with a grateful heart, was busily attending to his wife. He
helped her put on her woolen underwear and cotton padded jacket,
and then helped her into a warm overcoat. Finally he wound a camel-
colored scarf about her neck.

"How are things at home?" she asked.

"Fine. Yesterday your Party branch sent some people over to help
straighten the place up."

She immediately began to think of that small room, that bookshelf
covered with a white cloth, the small alarm clock on the window sill, the
three-drawer desk . . .

She had lain so ill for so long that she now felt very light, despite the
layers of clothing she wore. When she stood up, her legs shook under the
weight of her body. She was leaning almost entirely on her husband.
With one hand gripping his sleeve and the other pressed against the
wall for support, she was able to take a step forward. Continuing, step by
step, she slowly walked out of the ward.

Director Zhao Tianhui, Chief Sun Yimin, and colleagues from ophthalmology and medicine followed along behind her, watching her go
one step at a time along the long corridor, to the door and outside.

It had been raining for several days in a row, and a cold wind was
whistling through the bare branches of the trees. The sun was especially
radiant after the rain, and its rays illuminated the long verandah in
front of the hospital. The cold wind blowing in their faces made Jiajie
hold his wife even more carefully as the two walked together into the
sunlight and cold wind.

A black sedan was waiting at the bottom of the stone steps. Director Zhao had personally telephoned the administration office to get it there.

Dr. Lu Wenting, with great difficulty, leaning on her husband's arm and going one step at a time, went out the door.

*Beijing*
*November 1979*

# GLOSSARY AND
# NAME LIST

*Anti-Rightist Campaign.*     A major campaign in 1957 in which work units were required to identify the "rightists" among them who had been criticizing the Party. See Introduction pp. 11–14 for details.

*Beijing.*     Peking.

*Cadre.*     A term often used in the singular in writing about contemporary China to refer to any of a variety of administrators such as government bureaucrats, factory managers, and school principals. A cadre is not necessarily a Party member.

*Categories.*     See "Five red categories."

*Cow ghosts and snake spirits.*     A term used for intellectuals during the Cultural Revolution. See "Sweep Away Everything."

*Cow shed.*     A popular term for the confinement areas established for errant cadres and intellectuals ("cow ghosts and snake spirits") during the Cultural Revolution. Generally, each work unit fashioned its own cow shed in a makeshift manner.

*Cultural Revolution.*     Formally called the Great Proletarian Cultural Revolution and now officially dated from 1966 to 1972, this strident campaign, the largest in human history, was conceived by Mao Zedong as a final attempt to create unending revolution in China. The result was incalculable dislocation and suffering.

*Deng Xiaoping (b. 1904).*    Vice-premier of the People's Republic and China's most powerful leader in the late 1970s and early 1980s.

*Five black categories.*    See "Five red categories."

*Five red categories.*    During the Cultural Revolution, much of the populace was divided into good ("red") and bad ("black") categories. There was never an authoritative definition of these categories, and popular usage was not uniform. Generally, the "five red categories" were industrial workers, poor peasants, lower middle peasants, revolutionary cadres (those who had joined a communist organization by 1947), and revolutionary soldiers. The situation with the "black categories" was more confusing. The "four black categories" usually referred to former landlords, rich peasants, counterrevolutionaries (including spies, former KMT people, and "rightists") and "bad elements," meaning common criminals. The term "five black categories" referred to the same people, but counted counterrevolutionaries and rightists as two groups. "Seven black categories" added two more: capitalists and "capitalist-roaders." Since one's category was inherited, the children of red families were purely red, and those of black categories unalterably black.

*Four black categories.*    See "Five red categories."

*Four Modernizations.*    A plan to achieve the modernization of China's industry, agriculture, national defense, and science and technology by the year 2000. First enunciated by Zhou Enlai at the Fourth People's Congress (13–17 January 1975), the plan became a dominant policy of the Deng Xiaoping regime in the late 1970s. Also referred to as "the

New Long March" in an attempt to revive the spirit of the Party's epic Long March from Jiangxi Province to Shaanxi Province in 1934–35.

*Gang of Four.*  In October 1976 four high-ranking radicals were ousted and made the major scapegoats for the catastrophes of the preceding ten years. The four were: Jiang Qing, widow of Mao Zedong and a member of the Central Politburo during the Cultural Revolution; Zhang Chunqiao, a vice-premier of the People's Republic and leading Marxist theoretician; Yao Wenyuan, also a vice-premier and a powerful political critic of literature; and Wang Hongwen, a former Shanghai worker who rose quickly in the Cultural Revolution to become a vice-chairman of the Communist Party.

*Great Leap Forward.*  A major campaign in 1958–59, born of Maoist idealism, to produce everything "more, faster, better, and more economically." The result was terrible economic dislocation and widespread suffering. See also Introduction, pp. 14–15.

*Guangming ribao (Enlightenment Daily).*  China's national newspaper for intellectuals, published in Beijing.

*Guangzhou.*  Canton.

*Hua Guofeng (b. 1921).*  Mao Zedong's chosen successor and the most important transitional figure between the regimes of Mao and Deng Xiaoping. Chairman of the Communist Party from 24 October 1976 until 29 June 1981.

*Jiang Qing (b. 1914).*  Also Chiang Ch'ing. See "Gang of Four."

*KMT.*  The Kuomintang, or Nationalist Party, which ruled China before the Communist revolution in 1949.

*Lin Biao (1907–71).*  Also Lin Piao. A vice-chairman of the Communist Party and Mao Zedong's "closest comrade in arms" before he died in an apparent coup attempt against Mao. In the late 1970s, a political *bête noire* to rank with the Gang of Four.

*Mao Zedong (1893–1976).* Mao Tse-tung. Chairman of the Communist Party of China, 1943–76.

*May Fourth Movement.* This term is used in two senses. Narrowly it refers to a student demonstration that was held in Beijing on 4 May 1919 to protest the Chinese government's docility in accepting Japan's special rights in Shangtung after World War I. More broadly, it refers to intellectual ferment both before and after 1919, including experimentation with a modern vernacular writing style, exploration of Western literature and culture, and radical critiques of Chinese society. See Tse-tsung Chow, *The May Fourth Movement: Intellectual Revolution in Modern China* (Stanford, Calif.: Stanford University Press, 1967).

*New Long March.* See "Four Modernizations."

*Pebble.* During the Cultural Revolution, workers and soldiers were ordered into China's universities, hospitals, and other intellectual and professional institutions to bring "common sense" into "stultified" intellectual life. Mao Zedong's metaphor for this was pebbles (the workers and soldiers) being mixed into thick sludge so that air might penetrate.

*Rebels.* Also "revolutionary rebels." Extreme-left activists in the Cultural Revolution.

*Red Guards.* Young people in the Cultural Revolution who spearheaded the attacks on cadres and intellectuals, and eventually on one another. Generally, they sought idealistically to uphold Mao Zedong and his revolution, but they were often the pawns in power struggles and ended up doing great damage. Also called "little generals."

*Renmin ribao (People's Daily).* China's central daily newspaper, published in Beijing.

*Seven black categories.* See "Five red categories."

*Sixteen Points.* Issued in August 1966, this was the first document from the Central Committee of the Chinese Communist Party on the topic of the Cultural Revolution.

*"Sweep Away Everything."* The major slogan used to attack intellectuals during the Cultural Revolution in the late 1960s was "Sweep Away All Cow Ghosts and Snake Spirits." After the Cultural Revolution, intellectuals themselves adopted the phrase ironically, shortening it to "Sweep Away Everything" and applying it to the whole 1966–76 period.

*Three-anti's element.* In 1952 there was a major "Three-Anti's Campaign" against "waste, corruption, and bureaucratic attitudes." People charged with these faults, at that time and in subsequent years, have been called "three-anti's elements."

*Zhou Enlai (1898–1976).* Chou En-lai. Premier of the People's Republic, 1949–76.

# TRANSLATORS

JOHN BERNINGHAUSEN is associate professor of Chinese at Middlebury College in Vermont, where he is also chairman of Foreign Languages and chairman of East Asian Studies. His Ph.D. is in Chinese from Stanford University, and he is currently working on the fiction of Mao Dun.

BILLY BIKALES began to be interested in China as an undergraduate at Princeton University, and has also studied at Middlebury College and National Taiwan University. He is currently head of the China Department at Lindblad Travel in New York.

WILLIAM CRAWFORD is assistant professor of Chinese at the University of Pittsburgh. During 1979–80 he was visiting associate professor of English at Beijing Normal University. He is co-author of *Liu Tsung-yüan* (Boston: Twayne, 1973).

MARGARET DECKER graduated from Princeton University in East Asian Studies in 1975, and is currently working toward a Ph.D. in modern Chinese literature at Stanford University. From 1979 until 1982, she taught English at Nankai University in Tianjin.

MICHAEL S. DUKE is assistant professor of Chinese at the University of British Columbia, and has taught at George Washington University, the University of Vermont, and National Taiwan University. He is author of *Lu You* (Boston: Twayne, 1977) and has published on both the Song period and twentieth-century China.

GRAHAM E. FULLER has a B.A. and an M.A. in Russian language and Soviet studies from Harvard University. He has served as a United States Foreign Service Officer for many years in the Middle East and East Asia.

DONALD A. GIBBS is associate professor of Chinese at the University of California, Davis. He is a pioneer in Western study of China's classic work on literary theory, the *Wenxin diaolong*. In the modern field, he is co-compiler of *A Bibliography of Studies and Translations of Modern Chinese Literature, 1918–1949* (Cambridge, Mass.: Harvard University Press, 1974) and *Index to Chinese Literature Monthly* (New Haven: Yale University Press, 1978).

HOWARD GOLDBLATT is associate professor of Chinese at San Francisco State University and author of *Hsiao Hung* (Boston: Twayne, 1976) and several articles on modern Chinese literature. His many translations include *The Execution of Mayor Yin and Other Stories* by Ch'en Jo-hsi (Bloomington: Indiana University Press, 1978), *The Field of Life and Death and Tales of Hulan River* by Hsiao Hung (Bloomington: Indiana University Press, 1979), and *The Drowning of An Old Cat and Other Stories* by Hwang Chun-ming (Bloomington: Indiana University Press, 1980).

CHARLES W. HAYFORD has a Ph.D. in History from Harvard University (1973) and has taught at Harvard and at Oberlin College. He has also served in Hong Kong as the representative of the Yale Association. Author of *Y. C. James Yen and the Ting Hsien Experiment in Mass Education* (forthcoming), and several articles on modern Chinese social history and Sino-American cultural relations, he is now living and writing in Evanston, Illinois.

W. J. F. JENNER teaches Chinese literature and cultural history at the University of Leeds in England. From 1963 to 1965, he worked at the Foreign Languages Press in Beijing, where he translated the autobiography of Pu Yi. His other books include *Modern Chinese Stories* (with Gladys Yang) (Oxford: Oxford University Press, 1970); *Memories of Loyang: Yang Hsüan-chih and the Lost Capital, 493–534* (Oxford: Oxford University Press, 1981); and forthcoming translations of Lu Xun's *Selected Poems* and the *Xiyouji.*

PERRY LINK is associate professor of Oriental Languages at UCLA, where he specializes in modern Chinese literature. He has taught Chinese language at Princeton University and Middlebury College. During 1979–80 he was in China doing research on contemporary literature. He is interested in popular thought and is the author of *Mandarin Ducks and Butterflies: Popular Fiction in Early Twentieth-Century Chinese Cities* (Berkeley and Los Angeles: University of California Press, 1981).

| | |
|---|---|
| Designer: | Laurie Anderson |
| Compositor: | Innovative Media |
| Printer: | Vail-Ballou Press |
| Binder: | Vail-Ballou Press |
| Text: | 10/13 Baskerville |
| Display: | Friz Quadrata |